CIVIL PROCEDURE

Seventh Edition

By

Jack H. Friedenthal
Edward F. Howrey Professor of Law
The George Washington University Law School

Arthur R. Miller
University Professor
New York University
Formerly Bruce Bromley Professor of Law
Harvard University

THOMSON

™

WEST

Mat #40734987

Sum & Substance Quick Review of Civil Procedure is a publication of West

© West, a Thomson business, 2000, 2005
© 2008 Thomson/West
      610 Opperman Drive
      St. Paul, MN 55123
      1–800–313–9378
Printed in the United States of America

ISBN: 978–0–314–19117–5

 *TEXT IS PRINTED ON 10% POST CONSUMER RECYCLED PAPER*

Preface

This book is designed to help you understand the basic concepts and principles of civil procedure. It often is difficult to understand a textual discussion of a procedure problem in the abstract; consequently, we have illustrated numerous principles with hypothetical examples to insure that the operation of each aspect of the litigation process is seen against a concrete factual background. **This new edition brings the book up to date by including important new concepts and case decisions that have arisen.**

This is an unusual "treatise." Its *exclusive* purpose is to help students learn and understand the materials encompassed in civil procedure courses. There are no footnotes. **The work may be used with any of the casebooks used in law schools.** Case citations are kept to a minimum to preserve a comprehensible flow and to avoid interminable scholastic qualifications. Of course, in order to facilitate a succinct treatment of the basic issue of civil procedure it has been necessary to generalize to a great degree. Although we have sought to limit out generalizations to well accepted controlling principles, the reader should recognize that this work is not designed for the daily practice of law in which exceptions to generalizations and exceptions to the exceptions frequently dominate a practical problem. Our ultimate goal has not been to cover American civil litigation and trial practice in all their intricacy, but to prepare a basic student text on a complex topic whose application is subject to many refined levels of sophistication.

The text is structured to assist your classroom study and supplement the standard casebooks in this area. We have allowed ample space for comments and annotations from your class sessions and other readings. We wish to emphasize that this book is neither a series of "canned briefs" nor a skeletal course outline. It is **designed as a full service teaching tool to allow you to maximize your comprehension of civil procedure.**

These materials place some emphasis on practice in the federal courts, particularly the Federal Rules of Civil Procedure. This is because these Rules have served as a model for procedural reform in a large majority of the states and provide the background for most civil procedure courses. State practice is not slighted, however, and comparisons between different approaches are drawn throughout this work.

The authors are anxious to develop and improve the new text format in future editions and we solicit your comments, criticisms, and advice. Please send your remarks to Thomson/West, Attn: West Education Group, 610 Opperman Drive, Eagan, MN 55123.

JACK H. FRIEDENTHAL
HOWREY PROFESSOR OF TRIAL ADVOCACY,
    LITIGATION AND PROFESSIONAL
    RESPONSIBILITY
THE GEORGE WASHINGTON UNIVERSITY
    SCHOOL OF LAW

ARTHUR R. MILLER
UNIVERSITY PROFESSOR
NEW YORK UNIVERSITY
FORMERLY BRUCE BROMLEY PROFESSOR
    OF LAW
HARVARD UNIVERSITY

*

About the Authors

Jack H. Friedenthal is the former Dean and now the Howrey Professor of Law at The George Washington University Law School where he has taught since 1988. Dean Friedenthal received his A.B. (Great Distinction; Phi Beta Kappa) from Stanford University and his J.D. (Magna Cum Laude) from Harvard Law School. He is the author or co-author of numerous widely recognized books and articles, including *Civil Procedure* [casebook] with Miller, Sexton & Hershkoff (West) and *Civil Procedure* [hornbook] with Kane & Miller (West). Professor Friedenthal has served as a Special Master for cases between the National Football League Management Council and the NFL Players Association regarding disputes as to their collective bargaining agreement and as a member of the Infractions Committee of the National Collegiate Athletic Association. Professor Friedenthal has also taught law at Stanford University, Harvard Law School, and the University of Michigan, where his courses have included Civil Procedure, Evidence, Conflict of Laws, Trial Advocacy, Domestic Relations, Legal Writing, Law & Poverty, and Law for Undergraduates.

Arthur R. Miller is now a University Professor at New York University after being the Bruce Bromley Professor of Law at Harvard Law School, where he taught for 34 years. He earned his A.B. from the University of Rochester and his LL.B. from Harvard Law School. He has frequently appeared on television, as legal editor for ABC's *Good Morning America*, as moderator for Court TV's *Millers Law*, on the Discovery Channel's *Justice Files*, and as moderator of Socratic dialogues broadcast on PBS. Professor Miller is author or co-author of over forty books, including *Federal Practice and Procedure* [multi-volume treatise] (West), *Civil Procedure* [casebook] with Friedenthal, Sexton & Hershkoff (West), and *Civil Procedure* [hornbook] with Friedenthal & Kane (West). He also carries on an active law practice, particularly in the federal appellate courts. His dynamic lectures and exam-taking advice are eagerly sought by law students and bar examination candidates nationwide. Professor Miller has also taught at the University of Minnesota and the University of Michigan. His courses in recent years have included Civil Procedure, Advanced Civil Procedure, Complex Litigation, Copyrights, and Computers & the Law.

*

TABLE OF CONTENTS

TABLE OF CONTENTS

TABLE OF CONTENTS

TABLE OF CONTENTS

TABLE OF CONTENTS

TABLE OF CONTENTS

TABLE OF CONTENTS

TABLE OF CONTENTS

TABLE OF CONTENTS

TABLE OF CONTENTS

TABLE OF CONTENTS

TABLE OF CONTENTS

TABLE OF CONTENTS

TABLE OF CONTENTS

TABLE OF CONTENTS

TABLE OF CONTENTS

TABLE OF CONTENTS

UNIT ONE

JURISDICTION AND GOVERNING LAW

*

CHAPTER I

INTRODUCTION AND HISTORICAL BACKGROUND

A. SCOPE OF CIVIL PROCEDURE. [§1.0000]

Civil procedure courses generally encompass the process, in civil as opposed to criminal cases, of selecting a proper court in which a case can be heard, identifying the nature of the grievances and the defenses thereto, determining the proper parties, preparing for trial, deciding the case with or without trial (and, in the event of trial, with or without a jury), challenging the decision on appeal, enforcing a final determination, and giving appropriate effect to a judgment in subsequent litigation. This book will deal with all of these subjects in the same chronological order in which they occur in litigation.

1. Sources of Procedural Law. [§1.1000]

In any jurisdiction the ultimate source of procedural regulation is the local constitution. Although constitutions typically provide some specific direction with respect to the nature of a jurisdiction's courts and their powers [see, e.g., United States Constitution, Article III], and the right to trial by jury [see, e.g., United States Constitution, Seventh Amendment], very little else is set out in detail. Usually the legislature, operating under a general power to establish a judicial system, enacts a Civil Procedure Code. In 1934 Congress delegated much of its procedure-making power to the United States Supreme Court, and many state legislatures have since granted similar powers to their highest courts. In general, these delegations have been very successful. Judges seem able to make important procedural changes when legislators, who are directly subject to political pressures from interest groups and often have little political incentive to deal with the subject, cannot do so.

a. Importance of the Federal Rules of Civil Procedure. [§1.1100]

Pursuant to its rulemaking powers [28 USC 2072], the United States Supreme Court in 1938 promulgated a comprehensive set of Federal Rules of Civil Procedure for use in the Federal Courts, encompassing many reforms of prior practice. These rules have provided a model for the states, a number of which have adopted the rules in total, others in large part. The rules are referred to throughout this book as "Federal Rules."

B. HISTORICAL ANTECEDENTS OF MODERN PROCEDURE. [§1.2000]

Much of the language, form, and even the substance of modern procedure was developed as part of English common law over a period of nearly 1,000 years. From the power of the king to deal with grievances when they affected not only the parties but the peace of the realm, there developed a king's court or King's Bench (or Queen's Bench, as the case may be) with wide-ranging jurisdiction over many cases. Together with the Court of the Exchequer and the Court of Common Pleas, both of which developed out of the king's ministerial offices, they provided a system of monetary redress for deserving litigants. However, as these courts, known as the "law courts," developed, their procedures became rigid and the types of cases they entertained became static despite changing social conditions.

1. The Writ System. [§1.2100]

To take a grievance to a law court, a complainant would first purchase a "writ," which essentially was an order. Once served by the sheriff, the writ required the defendant to appear in court to respond to the complainant's allegations. There were a number of different types of writs, each covering a specific type of case. To prevail, a party first had to be certain that the writ being employed covered the facts to be proved. If the wrong writ was chosen, the defendant would win. Under the writ system, procedure and substance were intertwined. Each writ had its own set of rules for stating the case, making defenses, and many other aspects of procedure. To be a top notch lawyer, one had to know all the nuances of the practice under each and every writ.

2. Development of Law Within the Writ System. [§1.2200]

Some writs proved more flexible than others. Broad statements of fact were permitted, for example, under the so-called writ of trespass on the case. As a result, much of the common law of torts and contracts developed within the scope of that writ and many causes that originally developed in "case" ultimately generated new writs of their own. As time went on, however, the writs became more and more rigid, so that new situations calling for legal relief could not be covered. Moreover, since the existing courts could give only monetary relief, any cause requiring some other remedy, for example, to enjoin someone from an improper act, could not be accommodated.

3. **The System of Equity. [§1.2300]**

To redress those grievances that did not fall within the jurisdiction of the law courts, people turned once again to the king or, more specifically, to the chancellor who was delegated by the king to hear these new matters and, when appropriate, provide relief. The chancellor's power to grant relief ultimately resulted in the development of an entirely different set of "courts of equity." These courts not only handled different matters and gave different relief, they also had entirely different procedures from those of the law courts.

4. **Scope of Equity. [§1.2400]**

In the main, equity operated only when relief in the law courts was unavailable. Equity decrees were wide-ranging; for example, the chancellor (or the chancery court, which developed to handle this business) could order an individual not to begin or continue certain conduct (injunction), or to carry out a contract obligation (specific performance), or to change an erroneously drafted legal document to reflect the true intent of its makers (reformation), or to carry out a fiduciary obligation (control of trustees and guardians), or to render an accounting, or to disclose information needed by one side in a pending law court trial.

5. **Procedural Differences Between Law and Equity. [§1.2500]**

In the law courts the pleadings were rigid and often included various fictional allegations required by the writs; in equity the parties stated the facts in long narratives. In the law courts witnesses gave oral testimony and the facts were determined by a jury; in equity all testimony was by written statement under oath, and the chancellor decided all matters of fact and law. If a defendant lost at "law" and failed to pay the judgment, the sheriff seized and sold the defendant's property and applied the proceeds to the judgment; a defendant who did not obey an equity decree could be held in contempt and fined or sent to prison until he complied.

6. **Merger of Law and Equity Courts in the United States. [§1.2600]**

The dual law-equity system was imported into the United States, but with some major differences. For example, in many, but not all, states and in the federal courts, the same judges exercised both equitable and legal powers. However, cases were designated as being in law or in equity and were dealt with differently according to that designation. Many of the differences in treatment were eliminated beginning in 1848 when a number of states, led by New York, developed comprehensive new codes of procedure, which provided a uniform procedure for all civil cases. At the present time there are very few states that still have procedural distinctions depending upon whether the case seeks legal or equitable relief. Nevertheless, to the extent that differences between law courts and equity courts are locked into a federal or state constitution, it still is important to know and recognize the character of the different actions. The most notable context in which the distinction is still vital is in determining when there is a right to jury trial; the United States Constitution, as well as many state constitutions, provides a right to jury trial in law but not in equity cases [see Chapter Thirteen].

CHAPTER II

SELECTING A PROPER COURT

A. INTRODUCTORY ANALYSIS. [§2.0000]

One of the most important decisions a trial lawyer must make is choosing a proper court in which to litigate. The decision is a two-step process. First, the lawyer must determine what court or courts will hear the dispute and what must be done to lodge the case there. This requires consideration of the following factors, discussion of which provides the student with an excellent analytical framework for grappling with problems involving the material covered in Chapters Two and Three of this work. (a) Does the court have subject matter jurisdiction [see **§2.1000–§2.5520**]? (b) Does the court have jurisdiction over the person or the property of the defendant? [see **§3.0000–§3.4800**]? (c) Has the defendant been given notice of the institution of the lawsuit and an opportunity to be heard? [see **§3.5000–§3.5620**]? (d) Has service of process been carried out in the manner prescribed by the procedural rules of the particular court? [see **§3.6000–§3.6620**]? (e) Does the court have venue in the action [see **§2.7000–§2.7720**]? (f) If the action has been instituted in a state court, can it be removed to a federal court? [see **§2.6000–§2.6810**]? Second, the lawyer must decide which of the courts that are open and available for litigating his client's claim provides the most advantageous forum. This question can only be answered in tactical terms, taking account of economics, geography, procedural rules, timing, and a variety of other factors that are partially instinctive and partially a product of experience.

B. FEDERAL SUBJECT MATTER JURISDICTION. [§2.1000]

The remaining material in this chapter will focus on the subject matter jurisdiction and venue principles governing the United States district courts. The reason for this is that the federal scheme, which, given the character of the federal courts, is a national scheme, provides a useful and particularly relevant model for exploring problems of subject matter jurisdiction, venue, and federalism. Not surprisingly, therefore, many first year teachers of civil procedure and many procedure casebooks focus on the federal scene in developing this material. It should be understood, however, that the analysis that follows is designed for procedure courses, not for more advanced courses in federal courts or federal jurisdiction.

1. Sources of Federal Judicial Power. [§2.1100]

The power of the federal courts derives from Article III, Section 2 of the Constitution, which describes the types of cases over which the federal courts can be given jurisdiction by Congress. The most important of these are: (a) cases arising under the Constitution, laws, and treaties of the United States; (b) cases between citizens of different states; (c) cases involving the United States; (d) cases involving admiralty and maritime jurisdiction; and (e) cases between a state and citizens of another state.

a. Suits Involving a State. [§2.1110]

The Eleventh Amendment prohibits one of the states or a foreign country from being sued in the federal courts without its consent, except when the plaintiff is the United States. Disputes between states may be heard in the Supreme Court of the United States under that tribunal's original jurisdiction.

b. Congressional Exercise of Constitutional Power. [§2.1120]

Congress has never given the federal courts jurisdiction over all of the cases described in Article III of the Constitution. For example, the requirement that a case involve more than a certain amount in controversy [see **§2.4000–§2.4510**] prevents many of the cases described in the Constitution (particularly diversity of citizenship cases) from being heard in the federal courts. Congress also may limit the jurisdiction of the lower federal courts by directing that certain types of disputes be heard in particular federal courts, or by depriving the federal courts of power to grant particular remedies, or by imposing other limitations on the exercise of judicial power.

2. Narrow Interpretation of Federal Subject Matter Jurisdiction. [§2.1200]

Although the federal judicial system is national in character, the federal district courts only have jurisdiction to hear those disputes described in Article III of the United States Constitution and only to the extent that Congress, by statute, has expressly granted them authority over those cases. Not only are the federal courts tribunals of limited subject matter jurisdiction, but the tradition has been to interpret that jurisdiction in a restrictive fashion. This has been thought necessary in order to make certain that the federal courts encroach as little as possible on the judicial power of the states, thereby carrying out one of the basic principles of American federalism.

a. **Plaintiff Must Plead and Prove Federal Jurisdiction. [§2.1210]**

Because of the philosophy described in the preceding section, the existence of federal subject matter jurisdiction must appear on the face of the complaint [see **§5.4100**], and the party invoking federal judicial power usually has the burden of proof when its existence is challenged. The parties may not consent or agree to confer subject matter jurisdiction on the court.

b. **Subject Matter Jurisdiction Defect May Be Raised at Any Time. [§2.1220]**

Because important constitutional principles are involved, a subject matter jurisdiction defect is never waived and may be raised at any time, including on appeal. Moreover, the federal court has an independent duty to inquire into its own subject matter jurisdiction, and therefore may raise the issue on its own initiative. If jurisdiction is absent, the case must be dismissed.

3. **Concurrent and Exclusive Jurisdiction. [§2.1300]**

In many contexts Congress provides that both state and federal courts have subject matter jurisdiction over a particular dispute. Jurisdiction over these cases is said to be concurrent. For example, litigation arising out of a tort between citizens of different states in which the amount in controversy exceeds $75,000 may be brought in either a state or a federal court. Similarly, an action under the Federal Employers' Liability Act, although it involves a federally created right, may be heard in a state or federal court. On the other hand, Congress often provides that certain disputes can be adjudicated only in the federal courts, typically because of the importance of the federal policies at issue and the need for uniform application of a federal statute. In these situations federal jurisdiction is said to be exclusive. For example, actions arising under the federal bankruptcy, copyright, or patent acts must be brought in the federal courts.

C. FEDERAL QUESTION JURISDICTION. [§2.2000]

Article III of the United States Constitution permits Congress to give the federal district courts subject matter jurisdiction over "all Cases, in Law and Equity, arising under this Constitution, the Laws of the United States, and Treaties made, or which shall be made, under their Authority." A case falling within this jurisdictional grant is said to involve a federal question.

1. **Rationale of Jurisdictional Grant. [§2.2100]**

The policy considerations underlying this grant of subject matter jurisdiction are the belief that federal courts are more likely than state courts (a)

CHAPTER II

to have the necessary expertise to deal with federal issues properly, and (b) to afford a hospitable environment for federal interests and policies. Giving the district courts this federal question jurisdiction also furthers the development of a uniform body of federal law.

2. Statutory Basis. [§2.2200]

Congress did not enact a statute giving the lower federal courts general original jurisdiction over federal question cases until 1875. The language of that provision, which is virtually identical to the constitutional provision, has remained substantially the same despite the enactment of a series of successor statutes. The current statute [28 USC 1331] provides that the federal district courts shall have original jurisdiction over all civil actions in which the matter in controversy *"arise[s] under* the Constitution, laws, or treaties of the United States" [italics added].

3. Meaning of "Arises Under." [§2.2300]

In determining whether federal question jurisdiction exists, the crucial issue is: Does the matter in controversy arise under the Constitution, laws, or treaties of the United States? Unfortunately, the federal courts have never articulated an easily applied definition of this concept. It is clear, however, that a right or immunity created or protected by federal law must be an essential element of the plaintiff's cause of action. One formulation frequently repeated by the courts is that federal question jurisdiction exists only if the plaintiff's right or immunity will be supported by one construction of federal law and defeated if given another construction.

Illustration 1. [§2.2310] P brings an action against FBI officers seeking damages for illegal arrest, false imprisonment, and unlawful search and seizure. Federal question jurisdiction will be sustained because the plaintiff's claim rests on the Fourth and Fifth Amendments to the United States Constitution.

Illustration 2. [§2.2320] P brings an action alleging patent infringement. The case is within a federal court's federal question jurisdiction because the rights involved arise under the United States Patent Act.

> **Illustration 3. [§2.2330]** In a suit concerning the ownership of real property held under a federal land grant, federal question jurisdiction will be sustained when the plaintiff's cause of action requires an interpretation of a clause in the land grant.

> **Illustration 4. [§2.2340]** P brings an action against a drug manufacturer, seeking damages for injuries caused by ingestion of one of the defendant's drugs. Although P alleges violation of the Federal Food, Drug and Cosmetic Act (FDCA) as an element of its state law claim, there is no federal question jurisdiction because Congress has determined that there would be no private federal cause of action for FDCA violations [*Merrell Dow Pharmaceuticals Inc v. Thompson* (1986)].

> **Illustration 5. [§2.2350]** P brings an action to quiet title to land, claiming that the title was invalid because the Internal Revenue Service (IRS) failed to provide notice of the seizure as required by 26 USC §6335(a). Federal question jurisdiction over this state-law claim is proper because the interpretation of the federal statute is necessary to determine whether notice was given by the IRS. The absence of a private federal cause of action is not always dispositive. [*Grable & Sons Metal Products, Inc. v. Darue Engineering & Manufacturing* (2005)].

4. **Plaintiff's Pleading Determines Existence of Federal Question Jurisdiction. [§2.2400]**

An important limitation on federal question jurisdiction is the rule that the federal question must appear on the face of a well pleaded complaint. The issue of federal law must be substantial, not pleaded merely as an afterthought or in an attempt to acquire federal jurisdiction. Nor is it enough that the case ultimately will turn on a question of federal law because the defendant probably will, or in fact does, raise a defense based on federal law. Finally, the plaintiff will not secure federal question jurisdiction by anticipating federal defenses in his or her complaint, since these are not part of the cause of action.

Illustration 1. [§2.2410] In settlement of a dispute, X railroad agreed to give Y a free, lifetime pass on all of its lines. Congress later enacts a statute prohibiting such passes and therefore the pass to Y is not renewed by the railroad. Y brings suit in a federal district court for specific performance of the settlement agreement, alleging that the federal statute does not apply to him and, alternatively, if it were construed to apply to him, it would violate the Fifth Amendment of the United States Constitution. The case must be dismissed for lack of subject matter jurisdiction because the plaintiff's cause of action is based on a claimed breach of contract, which is a purely state-created right. The references in the complaint to the federal statute simply anticipate a potential defense under federal law. Even if the railroad actually raises a defense under the federal statute, it will not be part of the plaintiff's claim and the federal question will not be part of a well pleaded complaint [*Louisville & Nashville RR v. Mottley* (1908)].

Illustration 2. [§2.2420] P institutes a suit for breach of contract, alleging that D owes him $11,000 under a patent licensing agreement. D's only defense is the patent's invalidity. Even though D's entire defense arises under the federal patent statute, inasmuch as P's complaint alleges only breach of the state-created contract right, the action will have to be adjudicated in a state court.

a. Criticism of the Rule. [§2.2430]

The "arising under" requirement excludes many controversies involving a federal question defense from the original jurisdiction of the federal district courts. Arguably, this is undesirable because the federal courts are better able to decide issues of federal law than are state courts. Furthermore, in practice, the rule may involve a substantial waste of judicial resources because of the need to dismiss the federal action and bring a new state action. For example, after the Supreme Court dismissed the *Mottley* case [see **§2.2410**], it was recommended in a Kentucky state court and ultimately wound up before the United States Supreme Court again on appeal from the highest court in Kentucky under the Supreme Court's appellate jurisdiction. The plaintiffs lost on the merits of the very same federal defense that the Supreme Court refused to consider in its first decision.

b. Defense of the Rule. [§2.2440]

The "arising under" requirement can be justified in terms of its relative ease and certainty of application. It also is consistent with the principle that a court should be able to determine the existence of subject matter jurisdiction at the outset of the litigation. Finally, the *Mottley* practice honors the philosophy that the federal courts are courts of limited jurisdiction and that this jurisdiction should be restrictively applied in order to honor the autonomy of the state courts [see **§2.1200**]. The fact that occasionally there will be a case like *Mottley* is simply an inevitable byproduct of federalism.

c. Declaratory Judgments. [§2.2450]

The effect of the "arising under" requirement in declaratory judgment actions is not clear. There are two possible approaches. First, the jurisdictional sufficiency of a declaratory judgment action might be tested in terms of the actual contents of the plaintiff's complaint. Second, the court might examine the affirmative action that might have been brought had the dispute that is the subject matter of the declaratory judgment request been allowed to mature into litigation to see whether it would have arisen under federal law. The second, more restrictive, test seems consistent with the Supreme Court's rejection of attempts to create federal court jurisdiction by pleading material that purports to be part of a federal claim that in reality is a defense to a threatened cause of action.

Illustration. [§2.2451] In connection with the *Mottley* illustration [see **§2.2410**], suppose that the X railroad institutes an action requesting a declaration of non-liability to Y because of the federal statute prohibiting free passes. Under the first and broader test noted above, the railroad's complaint does present a federal basis for immunity from liability. However, under the second test, the issue of federal law would arise only as a defense, as it did in the *Mottley* case itself, and jurisdiction would not be sustained.

---

5. Meaning of "Federal Laws." [§2.2500]

The reference to "federal laws" in both the Constitution and Section 1331 includes the Constitution, treaties, federal statutes, federal common law, and federal administrative regulations.

a. Federal Statutes. [§2.2510]

Numerous federal statutes create substantive rights that are enforceable in the federal courts on the basis of federal question jurisdiction.

13

Some of the better known enactments are: the patent, copyright, antitrust, securities, civil rights, and various interstate commerce acts.

b. Federal Common Law. [§2.2520]

In some instances, federal courts are free to create substantive common law principles, either as an original matter or by borrowing state law. There basically are three contexts in which a federal court may develop federal common law. The first is when the issue bears directly on a matter of concern to the national government (as, for example, the rights and duties of the United States on the commercial paper it issues) and a uniform federal principle must be developed. The second is when there is significant conflict between a federal policy or interest and the use of state law. The third occurs when Congress has enacted a statute and, because of the inherent limitations on legislative drafting and the inability to foresee every problem that may arise, it is necessary for the federal courts to fill in substantive or procedural gaps in the text of the enactment, either by fashioning federal interpretive law or by the simple expedient of absorbing state law. [Federal common law is discussed in greater detail in **§4.6000–§4.6600.**]

Illustration. [§2.2521] The state of Illinois institutes a suit against citizens of Michigan alleging that the latter have created a public nuisance by polluting an interstate navigable waterway. The plaintiff argues that its claim is governed by the federal common law of nuisance being developed in the environmental protection field and, therefore, arises under the laws of the United States for the purposes of federal question jurisdiction. The argument should succeed unless Congress has provided otherwise.

---

6. No Amount in Controversy Required. [§2.2600]

At one time the general federal question statute, Section 1331, required that the matter in controversy in a federal question case exceed $10,000 exclusive of interest and costs. But this general requirement had nearly been emasculated by statutes providing special exceptions. Then in 1981 Congress amended Section 1331 to abolish the general amount in controversy requirement, leaving it intact only in specified, rare situations. [The amount in controversy requirement is discussed generally in **§2.4000–§2.4510.**]

7. Actions Involving the United States. [§2.2700]

The United States Constitution provides that the judicial power of the federal courts shall extend to "controversies to which the United States shall be a Party." Given the varied and extensive character of the activities of the federal government, it is not surprising that the United States is a party to approximately one-third of the actions in the federal courts.

a. United States as Plaintiff. [§2.2710]

Section 1345 of the Judicial Code grants jurisdiction to the federal district courts over civil actions instituted by the United States pursuant to any congressional authorization. The United States also may bring suit when there is no specific statutory authorization to do so if the case involves a matter of sufficient importance to a legitimate activity of the federal government to give it standing to sue. This interest need not be proprietary or pecuniary; an action involving the "general welfare" often will permit the United States to sue. However, the government may not lend its name to a suit that only affects one individual.

Illustration. [§2.2711] A naval officer, B, was assigned to sea duty and left his personal property in Virginia, where he had been stationed. Under a federal statute, the personal property of service personnel can be taxed only by their "home" state, which in B's case was New Jersey. The United States institutes an action to enjoin Virginia from collecting personal property taxes from B. Even though there is no federal statute expressly authorizing suit by the government, the district court has jurisdiction because of the United States' interest in the proper implementation of its policies and programs involving national defense and service personnel.

---

(1) False Claims Act. [§2.2712]

The government frequently is involved in actions brought pursuant to the False Claims Act, which allows private citizens to sue on behalf of the government in order to impose liability on individuals who have presented false claims for payment to the United States. These "qui tam" actions reward the individual who brings the suit with a percentage of the government's recovery, which in some cases has given the relator millions of dollars.

15

b. United States as Defendant. [§2.2720]

More complex problems are presented when suit is brought against the United States because the doctrine of sovereign immunity prevents the United States from being sued without its consent.

(1) Resurgence of Sovereign Immunity Doctrine. [§2.2721]

For a number of years the defense of sovereign immunity was regarded by a number of courts and commentators with disfavor and courts were more willing to conclude that a particular government or governmental entity had consented to suit. In more recent times, the pendulum has swung back in favor of enforcing sovereign immunity. The Supreme Court has reaffirmed the strong presumption in favor of sovereign immunity and stated that unless a statute expressly and unequivocally waives sovereign immunity in its text, the United States has not given its consent for bringing an action against the federal government. The most important congressional waivers of sovereign immunity by the federal government are discussed in the next two sections.

c. Non–Tort Claims. [§2.2730]

The Federal Court of Claims is a specialized court that was established over a century ago to adjudicate money claims against the United States. Its current jurisdiction includes actions involving a claim based on (a) the United States Constitution; (b) a federal statute; (c) a regulation of an executive department; (d) a contract, express or implied, to which the government is a party; or (e) any other damage claim not sounding in tort. The federal district courts have concurrent jurisdiction with the Federal Court of Claims over these matters if the claim does not exceed $10,000 [see 28 USC 1346(a)(2)]. Recently, Congress gave the Court of Federal Claims exclusive jurisdiction to hear post-award bid protest actions.

d. Federal Tort Claims Act. [§2.2740]

With certain exceptions, the Federal Tort Claims Act [28 USC 1346(b)] gives the district courts exclusive jurisdiction over claims against the United States for money damages based upon the negligence of government employees when a private person would be liable under the same circumstances acting within their scope of employment.

D. DIVERSITY OF CITIZENSHIP JURISDICTION. [§2.3000]

Article III of the United States Constitution gives Congress the power to confer jurisdiction on the federal courts over controversies between citizens of different states; between a state and a citizen of another state or between a citizen of a state and a foreign nation or a subject thereof. The present statutory implementation of the constitutional provision is 28 USC 1332(a), which provides for both "diversity" and "alienage" jurisdiction.

1. **Rationale of Jurisdictional Grant. [§2.3100]**

Although the original purpose of the constitutional provision for diversity cases is somewhat uncertain, it generally is assumed that federal court jurisdiction was thought desirable to protect out-of-state litigants against possible prejudice in state courts. Alienage jurisdiction also appears to have a similar foundation—the protection of foreign states and their citizens against local biases and influences that might embarrass the relations between the United States and other governments.

a. **Debate Over Continued Justification for Diversity Jurisdiction. [§2.3110]**

The desirability of preserving diversity jurisdiction has been a matter of considerable controversy for many years. It has been argued that the expanding responsibilities of the federal courts to decide cases involving important national policies make it unjustifiable to expend the federal judiciary's limited resources to adjudicate disputes arising under state law. In addition, it is argued that the local prejudices that troubled the Founding Fathers no longer exist to any appreciable degree. The supporters of diversity jurisdiction argue that local prejudices still exist, that the federal courts are superior tribunals and provide a model for the improvement of the state courts, and that the availability of a national forum for out-of-state litigants, both individuals and business organizations, provides a stable environment for the resolution of interstate disputes.

(1) **Legislative Proposals. [§2.3111]**

Although Congress has given serious consideration to proposals to abolish diversity jurisdiction, it has opted instead to narrow the scope of that jurisdiction through various legislative means. Most notably, in 1988 Congress passed the Judicial Improvement and Access to Justice Act, thereby increasing the amount in controversy minimum to a sum exceeding $50,000 [This requirement is discussed in detail in **§2.4000–§2.4510.**] and limiting the exercise of alienage jurisdiction in suits involving permanent resident aliens [see **§2.3421**]. The minimum was raised again in 1996, this time to more than $75,000 exclusive of interests and costs. Additional proposals have been introduced to limit diversity jurisdiction by prohibiting the use of such

17

jurisdiction by a plaintiff who files suit in his home state. In 1995, the House of Representatives sought to limit diversity jurisdiction by encouraging the settlement of lawsuits through a "loser pays" provision that makes an offeree of a settlement offer liable for costs and attorney's fees if the offeree rejects the offer and then fails to obtain either a judgment, or a judgment of equal or greater value than the amount of the settlement offer. The proposal was not enacted.

b.   Amount in Controversy. [§2.3120]

All diversity cases are subject to the requirement that the matter in controversy exceed $75,000, exclusive of interest and costs. [This requirement is discussed in detail in **§2.4000–§2.4510.**]

c.   Probate and Domestic Relations Cases. [§2.3130]

The federal courts have refrained from exercising diversity jurisdiction, even though it would be technically appropriate to do so, over a variety of controversies involving probate and domestic relations matters. The reason is that these subjects are particularly local in character and are best left to the state courts, which are in a better position to apply the forum state's policies in these fields. However, this judicial restraint is limited to disputes that lie at the center of probate and domestic relations law. For example, although a federal court will not issue a divorce decree or probate a will, it will enforce certain court orders or personal obligations that arise out of marital or decedent estate disputes. Nevertheless, in *Elk Grove Unified School District v. Newdow* (2004), the Supreme Court reaffirmed the federal courts' traditional practice of abstention. Writing for the majority, Justice Stevens held that "while rare instances arise in which it is necessary to answer a substantial federal question that transcends or exists apart from the family law issue, * * * in general it is appropriate for the federal courts to leave delicate issues of domestic relations to the state courts."

2.   Requirement of Complete Diversity. [§2.3200]

The general diversity statute has been construed consistently to require complete diversity between the parties on each side of the controversy—each plaintiff must be from a state that is different than the state each defendant comes from. [*Strawbridge v. Curtiss* (1806)]. The Supreme Court has held that the complete diversity requirement is not mandated by the Constitution itself; accordingly, Congress could eliminate it, although this is not likely because the effect would be to increase the number of diversity cases in the federal courts.

Illustration. [§2.3210] If a citizen of New York and a citizen of New Jersey sue citizens of Connecticut and Rhode Island, complete diversity exists and the federal court has subject matter jurisdiction. However, if a citizen of New York and a citizen of New Jersey sue citizens of Connecticut, Rhode Island, Massachusetts, and New York, no diversity jurisdiction exists because there are citizens of New York on both sides of the action.

a.   Exception: Statutory Interpleader Cases. [§2.3220]

The Federal Interpleader Act [28 USC 1335] permits someone who is holding property claimed by two or more persons to deposit the property with the court and let the claimants litigate among themselves. The statute has a jurisdictional provision based on diversity of citizenship. Because of the special characteristics of interpleader, the Supreme Court has construed the statute as only requiring minimal diversity. Thus, all that is necessary for jurisdiction under the statute is that any two of the claimants to the fund or property that is the subject of the interpleader be of diverse citizenship. [Interpleader is discussed in **§8.4000–§8.4900.**]

Illustration. [§2.3221] A bank, incorporated in Delaware and having its principal place of business in New York, brings a statutory interpleader action against five claimants to a bank deposit. Four of the claimants are from New Jersey and one is from Connecticut. Under the Supreme Court's interpretation of the Interpleader Act, diversity exists because the state citizenship of at least one of the claimants is different from the state citizenship of the other claimants.

b.   Rule Interpleader. [§2.3230]

The above described exception to the complete diversity requirement has no bearing on Rule 22 interpleader [see **§8.4710**], in which complete diversity must exist between the stakeholder and all of the claimants. In contrast to statutory interpleader, diversity of citizenship among the claimants is not relevant to the analysis in a rule interpleader case, except insofar as one of the claimants may be a citizen of the same state as the stakeholder.

Illustration. [§2.3231] A bank, incorporated in Delaware and having its principal place of business in New York, seeks to bring an interpleader action against five claimants to a bank deposit. If the five claimants are from New York, the action could not be brought as a statutory interpleader action because there is no diversity among the claimants. Similarly, the action could not be brought under Rule 22 because there is not complete diversity between the stakeholder and the claimants. On the other hand, if the five claimants are from New Jersey, the same result obtains for statutory interpleader (no diversity among the claimants), but a rule interpleader action would be permitted (the five New Jersey claimants are completely diverse from the Delaware/New York stakeholder).

c. **Exception: Multiparty, Multiforum Trial Jurisdiction Act of 2002. [§2.3240]**

The Multiparty, Multiforum Trial Jurisdiction Act of 2002 [28 USC §1369] establishes federal subject matter jurisdiction based on minimal diversity in cases arising from disasters in which at least 75 natural persons have died in an accident at a discrete location. Minimal diversity exists when any party is a citizen of one state and any adverse party is a citizen of another state, a citizen or subject of a foreign state, or a foreign state.

If there is minimal diversity between adverse parties in a case arising from such a disaster, a federal district court may hear the case if (1) any defendant resides in a state other than the one where a substantial part of the accident took place, (2) any two defendants reside in different states, or (3) substantial parts of the accident took place in different states. However, if "the substantial majority of all plaintiffs" and "the primary defendants" are citizens of the same state, and the claims asserted are governed primarily by the laws of that state, a federal district court must abstain from hearing the case. The Act does not provide definitions of either "substantial majority" or "primary defendants."

d. **Exception: Class Action Fairness Act of 2005. [§2.3250]**

The Class Action Fairness Act of 2005 (CAFA) [28 USC §1332(d)] effectively establishes a form of minimal diversity jurisdiction over large, multi-state class actions. The statute provides that the federal district courts shall have jurisdiction over class actions involving more than 100 class members when at least one plaintiff class member is diverse in citizenship with regard to the defendant, and when the sum or value of all of the class members' claims exceeds $5,000,000. Thus, for qualifying class actions, CAFA abrogates both the requirement of complete diversity and the requirement that at least one class member claims more than $75,000 independently of the others. [CAFA and the exceptions to its broad jurisdictional grant are discussed in **§8.1810–§8.1824.**]

3. **Parties Considered. [§2.3300]**

The citizenship of all proper parties to the action is considered in determining whether diversity of citizenship exists. Purely nominal or formal parties who have no interest in the action are ignored, however. If the presence of a particular party would destroy jurisdiction, but that party is not "indispensable" to the continuation of the action [see **§6.6000**], it may be possible to dismiss the action as to that party in order to preserve the court's subject matter jurisdiction.

a. **Realignment. [§2.3310]**

A federal court has the power to realign a party in accordance with that litigant's real interest in the controversy; the effect may be either to create or to destroy jurisdiction. The court is not bound by the way the plaintiff captions the action or describes the parties.

b. **Derivative Suits. [§2.3320]**

In shareholder derivative suits the corporation on whose behalf the action is brought, although theoretically a beneficiary of the action, almost always is antagonistic toward the shareholder-plaintiff. As a result, the corporation usually is treated as a defendant. The stockholder-plaintiff's allegation in this regard is accepted at face value.

4. **Determining the Citizenship of Natural Persons. [§2.3400]**

The citizenship of a natural person for diversity purposes is her domicile. The test for domicile is that an individual must physically reside in a place and have an intention of remaining there for the indefinite future. The determination is a factual one. There is a presumption that, once a domicile is acquired, it continues. However, that presumption may be rebutted with a showing that the party in question changed her domicile by again satisfying the twin requirements of physical presence and an indefinite intent to remain [see **§2.3710**].

a. **American Citizens. [§2.3410]**

For diversity purposes, an individual must be both a citizen of the United States and a citizen of a particular state. Thus, an American domiciled abroad can neither sue nor be sued in the federal courts on the basis of diversity jurisdiction.

> **Illustration. [§2.3411]** A, a native born American, works in New York City but maintains a residence in Connecticut, where he lives with his wife and two children, is registered to vote, and has a driver's license. The family also has a home in Florida and spends three months and a number of long weekends there each year. A, who is 61, intends to retire to Florida in a few years. If A becomes involved in a dispute with B, a citizen of California, A can sue or be sued in a diversity action. A is a citizen of the United States and of Connecticut for diversity purposes since that is his domicile now and will be for the indefinite future.

b. Aliens. [§2.3420]

To qualify for alienage jurisdiction, a natural person must be a citizen or a subject of a foreign state. Someone who is neither a citizen of the United States nor a national of another country—a person without a country—cannot sue or be sued in the federal courts on the basis of alienage jurisdiction. Only the American citizenship of someone with dual citizenship is considered for diversity purposes; therefore, dual citizens may not invoke diversity jurisdiction, although a few courts have recognized a narrow "dominant nationality" exception. In addition, alienage jurisdiction does not extend to suits between citizens of foreign countries; a citizen of the United States must be part of the litigation.

(1) Aliens Admitted to the United States for Permanent Residence. [§2.3421]

Congress amended Section 1332(a) in 1988 in order to establish the rule that, for purposes of Sections 1332, 1335 [statutory interpleader, see **§8.4000–§8.4900**], and 1441 [removal, see **§2.6000–§2.6810**], an alien admitted to the United States for permanent residence shall be deemed a citizen of the state in which the alien is domiciled. The effect of the amendment is that an alien permanently residing in the United States may not bring suit against a party domiciled in the same state as the alien; the amendment removes the permanent residing alien from an alienage jurisdiction analysis and places him in the diversity category, which does not permit suits between citizens of the same state.

Illustration. [§2.3422] X, a citizen of Germany, is a permanent resident of the state of Maine. Since X is treated as a citizen of the state of Maine for diversity purposes, X cannot bring suit against a fellow Maine citizen under the diversity statute. Although X could pursue such a claim under the court's alienage jurisdiction if he were not a permanent resident of Maine, the amendment instructs a court to treat X as a state citizen for diversity purposes, despite X's foreign citizenship.

(2) Interpretation of the Amendment. [§2.3423]

As the above illustration demonstrates, the amendment serves principally to limit diversity jurisdiction by preventing suits between permanent residents and citizens who are domiciliaries of the same state. However, the treatment of a permanent resident alien as a state citizen opens up the possibility of a suit between two foreign citizens falling within the subject matter jurisdiction of the federal courts. Although the plain language of the amendment permits such a suit, this interpretation presents troubling constitutional questions since suits between aliens are not provided for in Article III of the Constitution, and Congress is thought to lack the power to expand federal subject matter jurisdiction beyond the extent provided for in Article III. Accordingly, some courts construe the statutory amendment as a limitation on alienage jurisdiction, but decline to read it as creating jurisdiction between aliens not previously available in the federal courts.

c. Suits by Representatives. [§2.3430]

According to the traditional practice, when an action is brought by a representative—such as a trustee, guardian, executor, or administrator—it is the citizenship of the representative rather than the citizenship of the beneficiary that controls. This rule has been criticized as encouraging the appointment of an out-of-state representative solely to invoke diversity jurisdiction, with the result that the federal courts are required to decide disputes that in reality are between co-citizens [see §2.3800–§2.3830]. The representative practice probably can be justified only in terms of its consistency with the rules dealing with capacity to sue [see §6.3000].

(1) Representatives of Estates, Infants, and Incompetents. [§2.3431]

Congress drastically limited the ability of parties to create diversity through the appointment of representatives in the 1988

23

amendment of Section 1332(c)(2), which provides that the legal representative of an estate and the guardian of an infant or incompetent will be deemed to share the citizenship of the party represented. The representative's citizenship is thus ignored for diversity purposes in these instances, obviating the time and expense of a judicial inquiry into the bona fides of a particular appointment.

d. Class Actions. [§2.3440]

In line with the basic rule on representative parties [see **§2.3430**], diversity of citizenship in many class actions traditionally has been determined in terms of the citizenship of the class representatives. Accordingly, jurisdiction existed even if some members of the class were citizens of the same state as the parties opposing the class. Under this rule, the class could create or destroy diversity by carefully selecting representatives for purposes of filing suit [see **§2.3820**]. However, the Class Action Fairness Act of 2005 (CAFA) made it impossible for the plaintiff to destroy diversity in most class actions involving more than 100 class members and more than $5,000,000 in aggregate claims. Under CAFA, the federal district courts have jurisdiction over qualifying class actions on the basis of minimal diversity—that is, when at least one plaintiff class member is diverse in citizenship with regard to the defendant. [CAFA and the exceptions to its broad jurisdictional grant are discussed in **§8.1810–§8.1824**.]

e. Special Cases. [§2.3450]

The following rules for determining citizenship in special cases are generalities at best. A minor is deemed to have the same domicile as her parents until emancipated. Traditionally, a married woman's domicile has been treated as the same as her husband's, although this rule is tending to break down when the spouses are living apart. Members of the armed forces and prisoners maintain the same domicile they had before entering the military or being incarcerated. An out-of-state student retains her pre-school domicile, typically the family domicile.

5. Citizenship of Corporation. [§2.3500]

Ever since 1958, a corporation has been treated, for diversity purposes, as a citizen of both its state of incorporation and the state in which it maintains its principal place of business. The corporation therefore is viewed as having dual citizenship and there is no jurisdiction if the opposing party is a citizen of either of these two states. The actual citizenship of the corporation's shareholders is not considered.

a. Principal Place of Business. [§2.3510]

A corporation has only one principal place of business for diversity purposes; this is true regardless of the number of states in which it may be doing business. Three tests have been developed by the lower federal courts for determining a corporation's principal place of business. The first, which seems to be the more popular, is the so-called "nerve center" test; it focuses on the location of the executive and administration functions of the corporation. The second is the so-called "muscle" test; it looks to the place where the corporation's manufacturing or service activities are centered. In many cases the first and second tests will produce the same result. Some courts, recognizing that the first and second tests differ in semantics more than in substance, have adopted a hybrid approach known as the "total activities" test; it considers the totality of the relevant circumstances surrounding a corporation's business activities in order to locate the principal place of business for diversity purposes.

Illustration. [§2.3511] A, a citizen of New York, sues a corporation that is incorporated in Delaware and has its principal place of business in New York. Since New York is represented on both sides of the litigation, diversity jurisdiction does not exist. However, if A of New York sues a corporation that is incorporated in Delaware and has its corporate headquarters in Pennsylvania and the bulk of its manufacturing facilities in New Jersey, there is diversity jurisdiction under all the tests described in the preceding section even if the company is doing extensive business in a number of states, including New York.

b. Direct Actions Against Liability Insurers. [§2.3520]

As a result of a 1965 amendment to the diversity statute, when suit (typically one involving an automobile accident) is brought against a liability insurer under a state direct action statute, rather than against the insured, the company is deemed to be a citizen of the same state as the insured, as well as a citizen of its state of incorporation and the state where it has its principal place of business. The amendment was designed to eliminate cases from the federal courts involving purely local disputes when an out-of-state insurer is a defendant.

6. Unincorporated Associations. [§2.3600]

In sharp contrast to the rule for determining corporate citizenship for diversity purposes [see **§2.3500**], the citizenship of an unincorporated association, such as a partnership or labor union, must take account of the citizenship of each and every member of the association. In 1990, the Supreme Court ended a dispute among the courts of appeal and explicitly extended the rule of unincorporated associations to cover limited partnerships [*Carden v. Arkoma Associates* (1990)]. Therefore, the place of an unincorporated association's or a limited partnership's activities is not relevant. This rule obviously tends to limit the availability of diversity jurisdiction in actions involving these entities. As a result, members of large associations often attempt to use the class action procedure, which looks only to the citizenship of the representative [see **§2.3440**] for purposes of acquiring diversity jurisdiction.

a.　Exception: Class Actions. [§2.3610]

For most class actions involving more than 100 class members and more than $5,000,000 in aggregate claims, the Class Action Fairness Act of 2005 (CAFA) [28 USC §1332(d)] abrogates the traditional rule that an unincorporated association shares the citizenship of each of its members for diversity purposes. CAFA provides that for purposes of original and removal jurisdiction, an unincorporated association shall be deemed to be a citizen of the state where it has its principal place of business and the state under whose laws it is organized. [CAFA is discussed in **§8.1810–§8.1824.**]

7.　Time for Determining Citizenship for Diversity Purposes. [§2.3700]

Diversity of citizenship is determined by examining the citizenship of the parties on the date the action is commenced. Subsequent changes in the domicile of one or more of the original parties is irrelevant. Although using the date of commencement appears to be arbitrary, other possible tests, such as the date on which the cause of action arose, are just as arbitrary and often are significantly more difficult to determine.

a.　Change of Citizenship. [§2.3710]

An individual may change his or her state citizenship simply by changing domicile. This may be accomplished by physically moving to a new residence and manifesting an intention to remain there for the indefinite future. No minimum period of residence in the new jurisdiction is necessary. [See **§2.3800–§2.3830** for a discussion of devices to create or destroy diversity.]

> **Illustration. [§2.3711]** A, a lifelong resident of New York, moves with her family to Arizona on the advice of a doctor. A is a domiciliary of Arizona for diversity purposes from the time of her arrival in Arizona as long as she intends to make her home there for the indefinite future and has no fixed plans to return to New York or move elsewhere.

8. Devices to Create Diversity Jurisdiction. [§2.3800]

A federal statute [28 USC 1359] provides that there is no jurisdiction when a party has been "improperly or collusively made or joined" for the purpose of creating federal subject matter jurisdiction. Until recently, this statute was given a relatively narrow interpretation and the federal courts upheld any lawful transaction that created jurisdiction, regardless of its motivation. The result was to encourage assignments of claims and the appointment of out-of-state representatives for the sole purpose of establishing diversity of citizenship.

a. Assignment of Claims. [§2.3810]

The United States Supreme Court has held that the assignment of a claim to someone whose citizenship differs from that of the debtor will not create diversity jurisdiction when the assignee is solely a collection agent and has no bona fide stake in the claim other than a fee. However, if the assignee has a substantial interest in the claim, or if the assignment was made for a legitimate business purpose, diversity will be upheld.

b. Appointment of Representative. [§2.3820]

In recent years, a number of federal courts have carefully scrutinized the appointment of certain out-of-state representatives to determine whether there was a legitimate purpose for the appointment or whether it was undertaken solely to fabricate diversity of citizenship between the representative and an in-state defendant. These courts have concluded that absent an independent justification for appointing someone other than the plaintiff's "natural" representative, diversity jurisdiction should be denied. However, since the amended Section 1332(c) provides that the legal representative's citizenship is to be ignored in cases involving a decedent's estate, an incompetent, or an infant [see **§2.3431**], the possibility of manufacturing diversity by appointing a non-resident representative has been effectively eliminated in a large number of cases.

> **Illustration. [§2.3821]** A two-car collision occurs between X and Y, both citizens of Arizona. X is killed and is survived by his wife, also a citizen of Arizona. Z, who is the surviving wife's brother and a citizen of California, is appointed the administrator of X's estate and he brings a diversity action against Y in an Arizona federal court. When subject matter jurisdiction is challenged, the only reason advanced for the appointment of an out-of-state representative is that X's wife is not experienced with financial matters. Prior to 1988, many federal courts would have dismissed the action upon an examination of the purpose of the appointment and the motives of the parties involved. Updated Section 1332(c) spares the court from such an inquiry and allows immediate dismissal of the case.

c. **Devices to Destroy Diversity Jurisdiction. [§2.3830]**

The typical scenario in which a party seeks to destroy diversity jurisdiction occurs when a plaintiff attempts to block a defendant's removal of the case [see **§2.6000–§2.6810**] to federal court by appointing a representative of the same state as the defendant, assigning the claim to a party of the same state as the defendant, or joining parties as defendants who are citizens of the same state as the plaintiff. The federal anti-collusion statute [see **§2.3800**] only applies to the improper creation of federal jurisdiction. However, in recent years a number of federal courts have invoked their "inherent" power to strike down assignments and appointments designed to destroy diversity jurisdiction. In the case of a joinder of defendants intended to defeat a removal petition, many courts will ignore the citizenship of the joined party if the removing party (the defendant) can demonstrate either that the plaintiff made fraudulent representations in his pleadings or that there is no possibility that the plaintiff could establish a cause of action against the in-state defendant. If the removing party fails to make such a showing, the case will be remanded to the state court.

E. AMOUNT IN CONTROVERSY REQUIREMENT. [§2.4000]

The purpose of a requirement that the matter in controversy involve more than a certain threshold dollar amount is to avoid burdening courts with claims that are thought to be too insubstantial. In some states an amount in controversy requirement is used to divide subject matter jurisdiction between two or more courts of first instance—an inferior court, often a small claims or city court having jurisdiction only over claims for less than a certain amount, and a court of general jurisdiction having power to hear any case involving more than that amount.

1. **Diversity Cases in Federal Courts. [§2.4100]**

   The diversity of citizenship statute [28 USC 1332] currently requires that the matter in dispute exceed $75,000 exclusive of interest and costs.

   a. **Federal Question Cases in Federal Courts. [§2.4110]**

      Since 1981, there has been no general requirement of an amount in controversy in federal question cases under 28 USC 1331. In a few rare circumstances, Congress has continued to impose an amount in controversy requirement by including a specific provision in a federal statute.

2. **Plaintiff's Complaint Determines Amount in Controversy. [§2.4200]**

   The plaintiff's complaint controls the question whether the required jurisdictional amount is in controversy. If the plaintiff interposes a good-faith allegation that he is entitled to more than $75,000 exclusive of interest and costs, a motion to dismiss for failure to meet the statutory requirement normally will be denied. It is only when it appears to a legal certainty that the plaintiff cannot recover more than the jurisdictional minimum that a motion to dismiss will succeed.

Illustration. [§2.4210] Plaintiff claims $30,000 actual damages and $75,000 punitive damages. However, under the applicable substantive law, punitive damages are not recoverable for the injury sustained by the plaintiff and the decisions so holding are so recent that no valid argument can be made that the federal court could conceivably ignore them. Since there is a legal certainty that the plaintiff cannot recover the minimum jurisdictional amount, the action will be dismissed for lack of the required amount in controversy.

---

   a. **Measuring The Amount In Controversy When Damages Not Sought. [§2.4220]**

      When a plaintiff seeks a remedy other than damages (for example, an injunction or the specific performance of a contract) the court will determine whether the jurisdictional amount requirement is satisfied by appraising the value of the right that the plaintiff seeks to vindicate or establish.

Illustration. [§2.4221] Plaintiff files a diversity of citizenship action to enjoin city officials from enforcing a business regulation ordinance that is invalid under state law. Whether the jurisdictional amount is met is determined by looking at the loss that plaintiff will suffer if the ordinance continues to be enforced. The entire net worth of plaintiff's business is not relevant unless the ordinance prevents plaintiff from engaging in any transactions and as a result renders the business worthless.

---

3. **Aggregation of Separate Claims. [§2.4300]**

The rules relating to when it is permissible to aggregate the value of separate claims in order to satisfy the federal jurisdictional amount are erratic. The basic rules are in the following two illustrations.

Illustration 1. Single Plaintiff Single Defendant. [§2.4310] If a single plaintiff has two claims against a single defendant, each in the amount of $40,000, she may sue in federal court since they aggregate to more than $75,000. It does not matter whether the claims are related or unrelated.

Illustration 2. Multiple Parties. [§2.4320] If two or more plaintiffs each have a $40,000 claim against a single defendant, they may not aggregate their claims if the rights of action are considered separate and distinct. The same is true if one plaintiff has separate claims for $40,000 against two or more defendants. Since the jurisdictional amount requirement is not satisfied, the action must be dismissed.

---

a. **Exception. [§2.4330]**

If two parties have a common, undivided interest in the subject matter of the action and a single title or right is involved, the interests of the co-parties may be aggregated in determining the amount in controversy. For example, a partnership may sue for a $76,000 debt, even though the partnership is owned by two equal partners, each technically having only an interest of $38,000 in the claim.

b.   Exception: Class Actions. [§2.4340]

The Class Action Fairness Act of 2005 (CAFA) abolishes the rule against "multiple party" aggregation and the requirement of complete diversity, providing for federal subject matter jurisdiction over most class actions in which more than 100 class members are involved and the amount in controversy exceeds $5,000,000, exclusive of interest and costs. Thus, even when there is only minimal diversity and no single plaintiff claims more than $75,000, the federal courts may have jurisdiction over a class action worth more than $5,000,000 as a whole. For example, a federal district court could exercise original or removal jurisdiction over a $6,000,000 class action brought against an Indiana pharmaceutical company by a 500–member class made up largely of Californians, even if each class member claimed only $12,000 and some class members were citizens of Indiana.

c.   Supplemental Jurisdiction. [§2.4350]

In *Exxon Mobil Corporation v. Allapattah Services, Inc.* (2005), the Supreme Court held that the plain language of the supplemental jurisdiction statute [28 USC §1367] permits federal subject matter jurisdiction over claims arising out of the same case or controversy by additional plaintiffs. *Allapattah* overrules the Court's prior decision in *Zahn v. International Paper Co.* (1973) that additional plaintiffs with jurisdictionally insufficient claims could not join in the federal court suit of another plaintiff who did meet the jurisdictional amount requirement [see **§2.5330**]. Following *Allapattah*, claims by parties that fail to meet the amount in controversy requirement may be brought when combined with claims by other plaintiffs that do satisfy that requirement. Analytically, the mechanism for allowing these claims is not aggregation of insufficient claims, but rather the inclusion of the jurisdictionally insufficient claims within the court's supplemental jurisdiction. Thus, the Court's conclusion that Section 1367 overrules and supercedes *Zahn* does not abolish the traditional doctrine that the independent claims of two or more plaintiffs may not be aggregated to reach the required jurisdictional amount in controversy. [Section 1367 is discussed in **§2.5423.**]

Illustration [§2.4351] If one diverse plaintiff has a claim for $76,000 and one or more additional diverse plaintiffs have claims arising out of the same case or controversy against the defendant but only for $25,000 each, the rule is that the additional plaintiffs can join in the first plaintiff's federal court suit [*Exxon Mobil Corporation v. Allapattah Services, Inc.* (2005)].

4. Effect of Counterclaims. [§2.4400]

As noted above [see **§2.4200**], the plaintiff's complaint determines whether the jurisdictional amount requirement has been satisfied. The amount of a counterclaim, whether compulsory or permissive, cannot be aggregated with the claim to meet the jurisdictional amount. This is true either when an insufficient counterclaim is aggregated with an insufficient claim to meet the jurisdictional amount requirement, or when the counterclaim itself exceeds the jurisdictional amount but the original claim is for less than $75,000. [See **§7.1400** for a discussion of permissive and compulsory counterclaims.]

a. The Horton Case. [§2.4410]

The Supreme Court decision in *Horton v. Liberty Mutual Ins. Co.* (1961), indicates a slight modification in the rule described in the preceding section. In that case, an insurer brought a federal court action seeking to set aside a Texas Industrial Accident Board award of $1,050. The company asserted that the defendant would claim $14,035, as he had in the original workmen's compensation proceeding before the Board. The defendant, who in fact subsequently brought suit in a state court for $14,035, moved to dismiss the federal action for lack of the jurisdictional amount. He also asserted a conditional compulsory counterclaim for $14,035 to cover the possible denial of his challenge to the federal court's subject matter jurisdiction. The Supreme Court held that the amount in controversy was $14,035, which at that time satisfied the $10,000 amount in controversy requirement.

b. Discussion of Horton. [§2.4420]

Some commentators have urged that *Horton* should be restricted to its facts because of the peculiarities of Texas workmen's compensation law, and lower federal courts have not given it wide application. If it were to be read more broadly, however, the case would stand against the generally accepted view that the federal courts are courts of limited jurisdiction [see **§2.1200**], and that a plaintiff may not create federal jurisdiction by anticipating defenses [see **§2.2400**]. Arguably, the plaintiff's own claim in *Horton* was nothing more than a request to set aside the Board's award of $1,050, which is substantially less than the statutory amount. On the other hand, there is something to the notion that both plaintiff and defendant in *Horton* were asserting the opposite sides of a single claim, which was for $14,035. Certainly the claimant's state court action and conditional counterclaim support that conclusion.

5. Removal Jurisdiction. [§2.4500]

The amount in controversy requirement and the principles discussed above are fully applicable to a case that is removed to a federal court from a state court. [Removal is discussed in **§2.6000–§2.6810**.]

Illustration. [§2.4510] A New Yorker sues a Michigander in a New York state court for $1,500. Defendant asserts a compulsory counterclaim for $100,000. Removal is unavailable. Note that because defendant cannot remove, plaintiff has imposed a state forum on a defendant who otherwise would have the right to litigate in a federal forum.

F. SUPPLEMENTAL JURISDICTION. [§2.5000]

Although the federal courts are empowered to adjudicate only those cases described in Article III of the Constitution over which Congress has given them subject matter jurisdiction [see **§2.1200**], the doctrine of supplemental jurisdiction, now codified in a federal statute [see **§2.5400**], enables federal courts to hear some matters that are asserted in connection with cases that do not themselves satisfy either the Constitution or any federal jurisdiction statute. This doctrine is premised on the notion that a federal court acquires jurisdiction over a case or controversy in its entirety. Once jurisdiction has been conferred, claims or issues related to the primary controversy may be adjudicated by the court even though they would not fall within the court's original subject matter jurisdiction if they were sued upon separately.

1. Rationale of Supplemental Jurisdiction. [§2.5100]

The doctrine of supplemental jurisdiction derives from the equitable notion that a court empowered to adjudicate a controversy should consider all related issues in order to do complete justice among the parties and avoid further litigation. Fairness, convenience to the litigants, and judicial efficiency are the policies that the doctrine seeks to effectuate. More specifically, use of supplemental jurisdiction enables a court to avoid dividing the litigation of related claims between state and federal courts. Without the availability of supplemental jurisdiction, piecemeal litigation would result because of the limited subject matter jurisdiction of the federal courts [see **§2.1200**]. If the alternatives are one state court action or lawsuits in both state and federal courts, litigants might decide not to exercise the option to use a federal forum for the jurisdictionally sufficient claim but rather simply bring a single action in a state court. Parties should not be faced with a choice of this type, and the right to use a federal court should not be impaired by the presence of jurisdictionally insufficient supplemental matters.

Illustration. [§2.5110] P Files suit against his employer, an inter-state railroad, under the Federal Employers' Liability Act. Federal question jurisdiction exists. The defendant railroad files a third-party claim against t to secure indemnity for any sum the railroad may have to pay to P. No diversity of citizenship exists between the railroad and T and the third-party claim does not arise under a federal statute because both the original and the third-party claims arise out of the same injury and it would be desirable to try them together. The court has supplemental jurisdiction over the railroad's claim against T.

---

2. **Negative Aspects of Supplemental Jurisdiction. [§2.5200]**

There are certain aspects of supplemental jurisdiction that suggest caution in its invocation. First, it represents an expansion of federal court jurisdiction at the expense of the state courts and therefore raises a serious issue concerning the distribution of judicial power between the federal and state courts. Second, the inclusion of supplemental claims may produce a very complex lawsuit that raises intricate or unsettled matters of state law. The result might confuse a jury or create procedural unfairness to one or more of the parties. Third, a single trial, even when more efficient, might well result in more prolonged and more costly litigation than contemplated by the original parties.

3. **Origins and Expansion of Supplemental Jurisdiction. [§2.5300]**

Prior to the adoption of 28 USC 1367 in 1990, supplemental jurisdiction existed as a judicially created doctrine under the headings of ancillary jurisdiction, pendent jurisdiction, and pendent-party jurisdiction. Although these categories never were sharply defined in the common law doctrine, an appreciation of their essential differences is necessary, both for understanding the pre–1990 cases decided without the aid of Section 1367, and for understanding Section 1367 itself, which essentially codified these separate doctrines under the single statutory rubric of supplemental jurisdiction.

a. Ancillary Jurisdiction. [§2.5310]

In its formative years, ancillary jurisdiction was used primarily to protect a federal court's jurisdiction over property against any interference by a state court. In addition, there were instances in which ancillary jurisdiction was invoked to permit the court to adjudicate any questions of title, possession, or control of the res that might be raised by claimants who were barred from the federal court because they could not meet its subject matter jurisdiction requirements. In 1926, the Supreme Court markedly expanded the scope of ancillary jurisdiction to include compulsory counterclaims that lacked an independent jurisdictional basis. The Court established the test that a secondary claim arising from the same "transaction" or "series of occurrences" that is the subject matter of the original controversy falls within the federal court's ancillary jurisdiction [*Moore v. New York Cotton Exchange* (1926)]. A much greater expansion of ancillary jurisdiction came in 1938 with the adoption of the Federal Rules of Civil Procedure. As discussed below [see **§2.5500**], the use of the transaction-and-occurrence standard in certain Rules governing joinder of claims and parties created a fertile field for the increased application of ancillary jurisdiction, since the court in *Moore* had used a transaction test for defining the scope of the ancillary jurisdiction doctrine. Thus, ancillary jurisdiction enabled federal courts to resolve claims for which no independent basis of subject matter jurisdiction existed. This generally occurred in diversity of citizenship cases in which a claim was jurisdictionally deficient because it failed to satisfy the requirements of complete diversity or amount in controversy.

b. Pendent Jurisdiction. [§2.5320]

Pendent jurisdiction was invoked when the original plaintiff sought to join a state law claim lacking an independent subject matter jurisdiction base with a jurisdictionally sufficient claim in federal court (most commonly a federal question claim). The two claims had to be closely enough related so that they "derive[d] from a common nucleus of operative fact." The rationale of the pendency doctrine was exactly the same as for other forms of ancillary jurisdiction— judicial economy, convenience, and fairness to the parties [see

§2.5100]. Further, since pendent jurisdiction allowed a plaintiff to avoid the choice between a federal forum and piecemeal litigation, pendent jurisdiction often safeguarded the plaintiff's ability to invoke a federal right in a federal court, a rationale for the doctrine usually not present in the ancillary jurisdiction context.

(1) Scope of Pendent Jurisdiction. [§2.5321]

The leading case of *United Mine Workers v. Gibbs* (1966) held that a federal court may exercise pendent jurisdiction whenever the jurisdictionally sufficient claim and the jurisdictionally insufficient claim are derived from a "common nucleus of operative fact" and the claims are such that the plaintiff ordinarily would try them together in one proceeding. The *Gibbs* opinion also requires that (a) the pendent claim be so related to the main claim that there is a single constitutional "case" and that (b) the main claim be "substantial." *Gibbs* also directed the trial court to consider a number of discretionary factors designed to indicate whether the federal court ought to exercise jurisdiction, despite a finding that the court had the power under the Constitution to do so. The *Gibbs* discretionary factors were codified in Section 1367(c). [For a discussion of this statute, see **§2.5430.**]

c. Pendent–Party Jurisdiction. [§2.5330]

Throughout most of its history, pendent jurisdiction was confined to the addition of jurisdictionally insufficient claims brought by one plaintiff against the same defendant. In later years, a number of lower federal courts sought to expand its scope to permit the addition of parties with respect to whom federal subject matter jurisdiction otherwise would not have existed; however, the Supreme Court acted to set strict limits to so-called pendent-party jurisdiction. In *Zahn v. International Paper Co.* (1973), the Supreme Court forbade federal courts from exercising subject matter jurisdiction over cases in which a diverse plaintiff with a state-law claim for less than the required amount in controversy sought to join its claim with a related, jurisdictionally sufficient claim by another diverse party. In *Finley v. United States* (1989), the Supreme Court held that a plaintiff with a federal question claim against one defendant could not bring a closely related state-law claim against another defendant, unless the second claim independently met the complete diversity and amount in controversy requirements. And, in *Owen Equipment & Erection Co. v. Kroger* (1978), the Supreme Court ruled that a court's pendent-party jurisdiction could not be used to avoid the requirements of complete diversity of citizenship, even though the plaintiff's pendent claim arose out of the same transaction as the main action and the main action satisfied all diversity requirements.

In 1990, Congress enacted Section 1367 as a direct response to *Finley*'s invitation to provide explicit authorization for pendent-party jurisdiction. Section 1367(a) authorizes the federal courts to exercise supplemental jurisdiction over "claims that involve the joinder or intervention of additional parties." In *Exxon Mobil Corporation v. Allapattah Services, Inc.* (2005) [see **§2.4330**], the Supreme Court resolved a long-standing split among the federal courts, holding that Section 1367 overruled *Zahn*, because it authorized supplemental jurisdiction over all claims by diverse parties arising out of the same "case or controversy," even if some plaintiffs' claims do not meet the amount in controversy requirement. However, in *Allapattah*, the Supreme Court acknowledged that Section 1367(b) codified *Kroger*'s limitation of supplemental jurisdiction in the diversity context to cases in which the adverse parties are completely diverse [see **§2.5420**]. Although "the presence of a claim that falls short of the minimum amount in controversy does nothing to reduce the importance of the claims that do meet this requirement," the presence of a single nondiverse party may "contaminate" every other claim in an action, eliminating the fear of bias against out-of-state parties.

Illustration 1. [§2.5331] P, a New York domiciliary, brings a breach of contract action against D, a New Jersey domiciliary, for $80,000. Q, also a New York domiciliary, wishes to join P's action against D and bring, as a co-plaintiff, a $30,000 breach of contract claim. *Zahn v. International Paper Co.* (1973) [see **§2.5330**] previously eliminated the possibility that Q's claim could be heard in a federal court. However, *Exxon Mobil Corporation v. Allapattah Services, Inc.* (2005) [see **§2.4330**], held that Section 1367 overrules *Zahn* and permits the federal courts to exercise supplemental jurisdiction over all claims by diverse parties arising out of the same "case or controversy," even if some co-plaintiffs' claims do not meet the amount in controversy requirement. Thus, Q may join P's action against D if Q's breach of contract claim arises from the same "case or controversy" as P's claim against D.

Illustration 2. [§2.5332] A plaintiff brings a federal question claim arising under a federal statute that does not explicitly authorize pendent-party jurisdiction and seeks to join to that claim a closely related state claim against a second defendant. Immediately following *Finley*, even if the federal statute in question had conferred exclusive jurisdiction on the federal courts, the second claim could not have been brought as part of the same action. However, under Section 1367(a), that claim now falls directly within a court's supplemental jurisdiction [see **§2.5400**].

Illustration 3. [§2.5333] A, a citizen of Delaware, brings a $1 million personal injury claim against a corporation organized under the laws of California and having its principal place of business in New York. The corporation institutes a third-party indemnity action against its supplier, a corporation organized under the laws of Delaware with its principal place of business in Texas. Although the claim by the defendant corporation against the third-party defendant supplier has an independent basis of subject matter jurisdiction (suit between citizens of different states for an amount exceeding $75,000), the plaintiff cannot amend her complaint to name the supplier as a defendant. Under *Kroger*, and under Section 1367(b), the requirements of complete diversity prevent the court from exercising its supplemental jurisdiction over a state law claim between two Delaware citizens.

---

4. Supplemental Jurisdiction Statute. [§2.5400]

In 1990, Congress enacted Section 1367 and essentially codified the common law doctrines of ancillary and pendent jurisdiction under the collective name "supplemental jurisdiction." Section 1367(a) provides federal courts with the power to exercise supplemental jurisdiction "over all claims that are so related to claims in the action within such original jurisdiction that they form part of the same case or controversy under Article III of the United States Constitution." By including the discrete doctrines of ancillary, pendent, and pendent-party jurisdiction under one uniform standard, the supplemental jurisdiction statute simultaneously embraces these prior doctrines and eliminates the definitional and procedural distinctions between and among them. Although the statute is silent as to what comprises the constitutional limits on the power of the federal courts, it commonly is understood that Section 1367(a) incorporates the constitutional analysis of *United Mine Workers v. Gibbs* (1966) [see

§**2.5321**]. The rationale for codifying the constitutional language in Section 1367, rather than using *Gibbs'* more precise formulation of a "common nucleus of operative fact" is that the statute will embrace whatever scope the Supreme Court gives to a constitutional "case," a scope that may well change over time.

a.   **Pendent–Party Jurisdiction Revisited. [§2.5410]**

Section 1367(a) explicitly states that "supplemental jurisdiction shall include claims that involve the joinder or intervention of additional parties." Thus, the statute provides a general authorization of supplemental jurisdiction in a way that satisfies *Finley's* requirement of an explicit congressional mandate [see **§2.5330**] for pendent-party jurisdiction. However, Section 1367(b)'s limitation on supplemental jurisdiction over joinder of parties in diversity actions [see **§2.5420**] presents a significant qualification to Section 1367(a)'s rather broad endorsement of the pendent-party doctrine.

b.   **Cases Founded Solely on Diversity. [§2.5420]**

In accord with other legislative initiatives that limit the scope of diversity jurisdiction [see **§2.3111**], Section 1367(b) forbids district courts that have original jurisdiction based solely on diversity from exercising supplemental jurisdiction over claims by plaintiffs against persons made parties by impleader [Rule 14], joinder of indispensable parties [Rule 19], permissive joinder of parties [Rule 20], or intervention [Rule 24], and also bars supplemental jurisdiction over claims by persons proposed to be joined as plaintiffs under Rule 19, or who seek to intervene as plaintiffs under Rule 24, whenever "exercising supplemental jurisdiction over such claims would be inconsistent with the jurisdictional requirements of section 1332." [See **§2.3000–§2.3800** for a discussion of diversity jurisdiction requirements.]. Although Section 1367(b) properly is said to be a codification of *Kroger's* refusal to allow supplemental jurisdiction to undermine the requirements of complete diversity [see **§2.5330**], Section 1367(b)'s limitations extend much beyond *Kroger*, as that case dealt only with the joinder of parties by Rule 14 impleader. However, it is important to note that in cases in which the court's original jurisdiction is based on a federal question, Section 1367(b)'s limitations are inapplicable.

Illustration 1. [§2.5421] A citizen of New York seeks to bring a claim for $250,000 worth of property damage against two truckers who collided on the avenue in front of his house, thereby setting fire to his new sports car. One trucker is a citizen of New Jersey and the other is a citizen of New York; the plaintiff seeks $250,000 from each defendant. Because party joinder would occur under Rule 20, the plaintiff cannot bring his claim against the New York trucker in federal court. There is no independent basis for jurisdiction, as complete diversity is lacking, and Section 1367(b) specifically disallows supplemental jurisdiction over claims by plaintiffs against Rule 20 defendants when the court's original jurisdiction is founded solely on diversity, as the claim against the first driver is in this case. The exercise of supplemental jurisdiction would violate diversity requirements (because the claim is between two New Yorkers).

Illustration 2. [§2.5422] A citizen of New York brings a common law tort claim against a corporation that, for diversity purposes, is a citizen of New Jersey and Pennsylvania. The defendant corporation brings a Rule 14(a) indemnity action against a second corporation that, for diversity purposes, is a citizen of New York and Illinois. As discussed earlier [see **§2.5333**], the plaintiff could not amend his complaint to bring a claim against the third-party defendant, nor could he make a claim pursuant to Rule 14 against the third-party defendant, since diversity is lacking and Section 1367(b) blocks any claims by plaintiffs against Rule 14 parties when the court's jurisdiction is founded solely on diversity and the exercise of supplemental jurisdiction would violate diversity requirements. However, the third-party defendant, pursuant to Rule 14, can bring a Rule 14 claim against the plaintiff that would be covered by the court's supplemental jurisdiction, since Rule 14 claims generally are considered to satisfy the requirements of Section 1367(a), and the language of Section 1367(b) does not expressly limit claims by defendants. This presents the anomaly that the plaintiff may have a compulsory counterclaim to the third-party defendant's Rule 14 claim against the plaintiff that the plaintiff is unable to bring since Section 1367(b) excludes such claims from the court's supplemental jurisdiction. Nevertheless,

> the Supreme Court affirmed this reading of Section 1367(b) in *Exxon Mobil Corporation v. Allapattah Services, Inc.* (2005).

(1) Co–Plaintiff's Jurisdictionally Insufficient Claims. [§2.5423]

Although the Section 1367(b) exclusions cover claims by parties proposed to be joined as plaintiffs under Rules 19 and 24, there is no provision for limiting claims by parties proposed to be joined as plaintiffs under Rules 20 (permissive joinder) or 23 (class action). The omission of these two categories of plaintiffs means that a Rule 20 co-plaintiff or a class action member's claim that is jurisdictionally insufficient may be brought within the court's supplemental jurisdiction, even when the court's jurisdiction is based solely on diversity, assuming another plaintiff independently meets the diversity requirements. In *Exxon Mobil Corporation v. Allapattah Services, Inc.* (2005), the Supreme Court held that Section 1367(b) "by its plain text" overruled its decision in *Zahn v. International Paper Co.* (1973) [see **§2.5330**] that every plaintiff must satisfy the amount in controversy requirement, notwithstanding the statute's legislative history, which seems to indicate Congress' express intention not to overrule *Zahn* or to lessen the diversity requirements through enactment of the supplemental jurisdiction statute. The Court concluded that if Congress truly intended to preserve *Zahn*, it should have enacted a statute containing the necessary exclusions.

c. Discretionary Nature of Supplemental Jurisdiction. [§2.5430]

Section 1367(c) codifies the second prong of the Supreme Court's decision in *United Mine Workers v. Gibbs* (1966) and establishes four factors by which a court may exercise its discretion and decline to exercise supplemental jurisdiction over a claim. The four factors are: 1) if the claim raises a novel or complex issue of state law, 2) if the supplemental state law claim substantially predominates over the claim(s) over which the court has original jurisdiction, 3) if the district court has dismissed all the claims over which it has original jurisdiction, or 4) if there are exceptional circumstances presenting compelling reasons for declining jurisdiction.

Illustration. [§2.5431] In an action that is brought under a federal labor statute, the plaintiff union joins an additional claim seeking to recover attorney's fees under a recently enacted state statute. Independent subject matter jurisdiction does not exist over the state claim. The federal court may refuse to take jurisdiction over the state claim if the state statute had not yet been interpreted by the state courts and its application is uncertain.

5. **The Federal Rules and Supplemental Jurisdiction. [§2.5500]**

In the same way that the adoption of the Federal Rules created the possibility of a great expansion of the ancillary jurisdiction doctrine [see **§2.5310**], the Rules dealing with joinder of claims and joinder of parties substantially enlarge the scope of application for supplemental jurisdiction under Section 1367. Even though Rule 82 provides that the Federal Rules can neither extend nor limit the jurisdiction of the federal courts, a number of the Rules, particularly Rules 13, 14, and 24, use a transaction-and-occurrence standard and therefore offer natural opportunities for the federal courts to invoke supplemental jurisdiction. Moreover, the liberal policy of the Rules toward joinder would be impeded were the supplemental jurisdiction statute unavailable. Yet a commitment to liberal joinder does not, of itself, aid in determining which joinder rules should be contained within the supplemental jurisdiction statute and which should not. The unarticulated assumption underlying the notion that a joinder rule using a transaction-and-occurrence test is contained within the supplemental jurisdiction statute is that claims arising out of the same transaction and occurrence also contain a "common nucleus of operative fact," the definition of a constitutional case offered by the *Gibbs* Court and believed by many to have been implicitly adopted by Section 1367 [see **§2.5400**]. However, if the transaction-and-occurrence test is in truth broader or narrower than the "common nucleus" test, the application of Section 1367 to the joinder rules would not be as straightforward as is sometimes assumed. The two sections that follow provide a thumbnail sketch of the current law and cross-references to other chapters in this work that treat this matter in somewhat more detail.

a. **Supplemental Jurisdiction and Joinder of Claims. [§2.5510]**

Supplemental jurisdiction permits courts to hear compulsory counterclaims under Rule 13(a) [see **§7.2100**]; however, permissive counterclaims require independent jurisdiction [see **§7.2200**]. Cross-claims under Rule 13(g) fall within a court's supplemental jurisdiction [see **§7.3300**]. Furthermore, supplemental jurisdiction extends to any new parties added to a compulsory counterclaim or a cross-claim [see §7.4200]. On the other hand, supplemental jurisdiction over claims joined under Rule 18 applies only to claims that have a sufficiently close relation and satisfy the requirements of a constitutional case; since claims joined under Rule 18 may be completely unrelated, the availability of supplemental jurisdiction must be decided on a case by case basis.

b. Supplemental Jurisdiction and Joinder of Parties. [§2.5520]

In cases in which jurisdiction is founded solely on diversity of citizenship, Section 1367(b) provides that supplemental jurisdiction will not apply to claims brought by or against indispensable parties joined under Rule 19 [see **§6.7200** and **§8.3530**] or against permissively joined parties under Rule 20 [see **§6.7200**]; however, claims brought by parties joined as plaintiffs under Rule 20 may well fall within a court's supplemental jurisdiction [see **§2.5423**]. None of the above exclusions applies in cases founded on federal question jurisdiction. A claim by or against an intervening party, whether that party is a Rule 24(a) intervenor of right or a Rule 24(b) permissible intervenor, is not contained within the court's supplemental jurisdiction in cases founded solely on diversity jurisdiction. In federal question jurisdiction cases, however, supplemental jurisdiction probably applies to claims by or against Rule 24(a) parties [see **§8.3520**], but not to claims by or against Rule 24(b) parties [see **§8.3510**], since only the former rule contains a transaction-and-occurrence test. Supplemental jurisdiction generally is available for third-party impleader claims under Rule 14(a) [see **§7.5710**]; however the restrictions imposed by Section 1367(b) on claims by plaintiffs against Rule 14(a) parties presents an important limitation [see **§2.5420**]. Finally, supplemental jurisdiction is available for interpleader claims under Rule 22 [see **§8.4710**].

c. Venue, Process, and Personal Jurisdiction. [§2.5530]

When a federal court has supplemental jurisdiction, the venue statutes need not be satisfied. [See **§2.7000–§2.7710** for a discussion of venue]. By way of contrast, the party to be brought in must be served with process in accordance with Rule 4. [Service of process is discussed in **§3.6000–§3.6620**]. However, it has not been definitively decided when and to what extent an independent basis for personal jurisdiction must exist regarding any claim or party added to a case under the supplemental jurisdiction statute. [Personal jurisdiction is discussed in **§3.3000–§3.4800**]. Nonetheless, the clear conceptual distinction between personal and subject matter jurisdiction argues strongly against the notion that even a broadly defined supplemental jurisdiction scope, allowing the court to hear multiple, related claims in one action, can confer on the court a power over individuals.

G. REMOVAL JURISDICTION. [§2.6000]

The removal jurisdiction of the federal courts permits defendants in certain state court actions to substitute a federal forum for the state tribunal originally selected by the plaintiff. Although the right to remove a case from a state to a federal court is strictly statutory [28 USC 1441], there being no provision for it in the Constitution, the validity of the practice is now undisputed.

1. Purpose of Removal. [§2.6100]

The basic purpose of removal jurisdiction is to provide the defendant some opportunity to bring a state case that falls within the federal courts' subject matter jurisdiction to a federal tribunal for adjudication. Removal jurisdiction is designed to extend the policies underlying the grant of original federal court subject matter jurisdiction and the benefits of a federal forum to defendants. In a case involving parties of diverse citizenship, removal protects a non-resident defendant from any local bias that might be encountered in a state forum because of the defendant's "foreign" citizenship. In a case involving a claim raising an issue of federal law, removal equalizes the power of both parties to litigate a federal question in its natural forum.

a. Removal Operates Only from State to Federal Court. [§2.6110]

Cases may be removed only from a state to a federal court. There is no procedure for sending a case instituted in a federal court to a state court or from a court in one state to a court in another.

2. Requirements for Removal. [§2.6200]

There are a number of conditions on the removability of the typical case. These conditions are somewhat different for certain types of cases, including those brought under Section 1369 of Title 28 and those to which the Class Action Fairness Act of 2005 applies. [See **§2.6620–§2.6630** for a discussion of the removal of these cases].

a. Basis for Subject Matter Jurisdiction Must Exist. [§2.6210]

Section 1441(a) states that only a civil action that could have been brought in a federal court originally may be removed. Thus, removal is proper only if the state court action arises under a federal statute, or if the citizenship of the parties involved and the amount in controversy would enable a court to exercise diversity of citizenship or alienage jurisdiction. Therefore, the basic subject matter jurisdiction principles discussed in earlier sections regarding federal question jurisdiction [see **§2.2000–§2.2740**], and diversity of citizenship jurisdiction [see **§2.3000–§2.3830**], and the amount in controversy requirement [see **§2.4000–§2.4510**] are fully applicable to removal jurisdiction.

b. Only Defendant May Remove. [§2.6220]

According to Section 1441(a), only a defendant may remove a case from a state to a federal court. Section 1441(b) provides that when removal jurisdiction is predicated on the existence of a federal question, any defendant may remove, even a citizen of the forum state. However, a case can be removed on the basis of diversity of citizenship only if none of the parties properly joined and served as a defendant is a citizen of the state in which the action was commenced.

Illustration. [§2.6221] P, a citizen of Illinois, sues D, a citizen of Michigan, in a Michigan state court. The defendant may not remove if diversity of citizenship is the only possible basis for federal jurisdiction. However, if the original suit had been brought in an Illinois state court, the defendant, being a non-resident, could remove on the basis of diversity of citizenship. If the suit involves a federal question, it is removable either from a Michigan or an Illinois state court.

---

c. Plaintiff's Claim Controls. [§2.6230]

Under the so-called well-pleaded complaint rule, the basis for removal must appear as part of the plaintiff's claim; it cannot be brought in by way of defense or counterclaim. This is the same rule that applies in determining the existence of subject matter jurisdiction in an action originally commenced in a federal court [see **§2.1210–§2.2400**].

Illustration. [§2.6231] P, a citizen of New York, sues D, also a citizen of New York, in a New York state court alleging non-payment of royalties under a patent licensing agreement. Defendant

---

asserts that the federal patent that is the subject matter of the agreement is invalid. Although D has raised a federal question in her answer, the case may not be removed to a federal court because there is no jurisdictional basis in P's complaint; state contract law governs the merits of the non-payment claim.

(1) Time for Determining Removability. [§2.6232]

In general, the right of removal is determined from the time the notice of removal is filed. If the right of removal becomes apparent at a time after the initial pleadings are filed [see **§2.6710**], the right of removal is ascertained from the point at which the defendant actually files the removal notice. The exception to this rule is for diversity cases, in which the removal right is determined at the time of the filing of the original action. Thus, a change of domicile by the defendant after institution of the action cannot create a removable case. On the other hand, if the plaintiff removes a non-diverse defendant from the complaint after commencement of the action, removability will be determined on the basis of the citizenship of the parties remaining in the litigation.

d. Plaintiff Can Limit Defendant's Ability to Remove. [§2.6240]

In many situations, the plaintiff has considerable ability to prevent the defendant from removing because he or she has the option of not asserting a federal claim or of joining a non-diverse party. When this occurs, the defendant has no choice and must continue to litigate in the state court, unless the plaintiff has concealed a legitimate ground for removal by fraud, mistake, inadvertence, or artful pleading. On the other hand, once a case is properly removed, the plaintiff may not defeat federal jurisdiction by reducing the claim to less than the requisite jurisdictional amount or by joining a non-diverse party.

3. Separate and Independent Claim or Cause of Action. [§2.6300]

Section 1441(c) provides that if the plaintiff has alleged a separate and independent federal question claim or cause of action that would be removable if sued on alone, the entire case still may be removed even though the plaintiff joins it with one or more otherwise non-removable claims. This provision prevents a plaintiff from destroying the defendant's statutory right of removal by joining unrelated or marginal parties or claims whose presence would defeat removability. However, Section 1441(c) is only applicable in cases in which the separate and independent claim or cause of action is based on federal question jurisdiction; the elimination of removal under this provision in diversity cases represents yet another example of Congress' intention of limiting the scope of diversity jurisdiction [see **§2.3111**].

a. Court's Discretion to Remand Portion of Case. [§2.6310]

Section 1441(c) provides for the removal of the entire case when a separate and independent claim exists. The statute gives the court discretion either to decide all the issues in the action or to remand all matters in which state law predominates.

b. Rationale of Section 1441(c). [§2.6320]

There are two policy justifications underlying the discretion given the court by Section 1441(c). The first is to enable the federal court to promote judicial economy by retaining otherwise non-removable claims that have a substantial factual or evidentiary overlap with the removable claim; this avoids wasteful parallel state litigation. The second consideration is that if the federal court could not retain the entire action but had to remand the non-removable elements of the case, a defendant would be forced to defend two separate actions. The practical effect would be that defendants might be deterred from exercising their removal right and the federal interest in providing an opportunity to litigate in a federal forum would be thwarted.

(1) Supplemental Jurisdiction. [§2.6321]

The usefulness of Section 1441(c) is questionable in that the supplemental jurisdiction statute [see **§2.5000–§2.5530**] presumably would permit a federal court to hear the **entire case** that Section 1441(c) makes removable. One meaningful difference is that, while the supplemental jurisdiction statute requires "closely related" claims forming a constitutional case [see **§2.5400**], Section 1441(c) provides for removal of a "separate and independent" claim. However, if "separate and independent" is taken to permit removal of entirely unrelated claims under Section 1441(c), there are clear constitutional difficulties, as the limited nature of federal subject matter jurisdiction mandated by the Constitution cannot be overridden by legislative enactment.

4. State Court Need Not Have Jurisdiction. [§2.6400]

Until recently, removal jurisdiction was considered to be derivative. Consequently, a federal court could acquire jurisdiction by way of removal only if the state court had original subject matter jurisdiction over the action. This requirement led to the peculiar result that when a case fell within the exclusive jurisdiction of the federal courts and therefore was not within the judicial power of the state court in which it was brought, a federal court could not acquire jurisdiction by removal but had to dismiss the action. Section 1441 was amended in 1986 to provide that a federal court is not barred from acquiring jurisdiction by way of removal merely because the state court did not have jurisdiction over the claim.

Illustration. [§2.6410] P brings suit in a state court alleging patent infringement. Although the state court does not have original subject matter jurisdiction over the claim because the claim falls within the exclusive jurisdiction of the federal courts, D may remove the case to a federal court [Section 1441(f)].

---

5. Venue in Removed Actions. [§2.6500]

Section 1441(a) of Title 28 provides that the venue of a removed case is the federal district or division embracing the place where the state action is pending. Therefore, it is irrelevant that the federal court to which the action is removed would not have been a place of proper venue under the venue statute had the action been brought there originally. [See the discussion of venue in **§2.7000–§2.7710.**]

6. Special Statutory Removal Provisions. [§2.6600]

In addition to the general removal statute, there are other federal statutes authorizing removal in particular circumstances. For example, removal is available when a federal officer is sued or prosecuted in a state court for acts done under color of federal office, or a federal employee is sued for injuries allegedly caused by his or her operation of a motor vehicle within the scope of employment. Furthermore, removal is permitted by a defendant who is denied or cannot enforce in a state court a right under any law guaranteeing equal civil rights.

a. Non–Removable Claims. [§2.6610]

In some circumstances Congress has made the determination that the plaintiff should have an unimpeded choice of forum and has enacted statutes prohibiting removal. Most notable are cases under the Federal Employers' Liability Act and actions under state worker's compensation laws.

> **Illustration. [§2.6611]** P, a citizen of Wisconsin, brings a tort action in a Wisconsin state court under the Federal Employers' Liability Act against his employer, a railroad, which is incorporated in Illinois and has its principal place of business in that state. Although the case would be removable under Section 1441, a defendant cannot remove an FELA suit because of the specific statutory prohibition.

b.   **Multiparty, Multiforum, "Single Accident" Actions. [§2.6620]**

Section 1441(e), enacted in 2002, provides special removal rules for multiparty "single accident" actions, arising from an accident in which at least 75 individuals die, that could have been brought in a federal district court under the minimal-diversity jurisdiction of 28 USC 1369 [see **§2.3240**]. This section also provides removal jurisdiction for state court actions in which the defendant is also a party to an action that could have been brought, in whole or in part, under Section 1369, if the claims in both actions arise from the same accident. Actions removed under Section 1441(e) are subject to different requirements than other actions.

(1)   **Consent of All Defendants Not Necessary. [§2.6621]**

An action can be removed under Section 1441(e) regardless of whether all defendants consent to the removal.

(2)   **Timing of Filing of Notice of Removal. [§2.6622]**

Under Section 1441(e), a notice of removal may be filed before trial of the action in state court within thirty days of the date on which the defendant first becomes a party to an action under Section 1369, arising from the same accident as the state court action, in a federal district court.

c.   **Class Actions. [§2.6630]**

Section 1453 of Title 28, enacted as part of the Class Action Fairness Act of 2005, provides for the removal of certain class actions, as defined by Section 1332(d) [see **§8.1810–§8.1824**], to a federal district court. Class actions removed under Section 1453 must meet the minimal diversity and the five million dollar amount in controversy requirements of Section 1332(d)(2). Section 1453(d) lists certain types of class actions that are not removable under this statute. Actions removed under Section 1453 are subject to different requirements than other actions.

CHAPTER II

(1) Consent of All Defendants Not Necessary. [§2.6631]

A class action may be removed under Section 1453(b) without the consent of all the defendants.

(2) No Restriction Based on Citizenship of Defendants. [§2.6332]

Section 1453(b) provides that a class action may be removed to federal court even if a defendant is a citizen of the state in which the action was filed.

(3) One–Year Limitation Does Not Apply. [§2.6333]

The one-year limitation on removal of actions for which federal subject matter jurisdiction is based on Section 1332 does not apply to class actions removed under Section 1453.

7. Procedure for Seeking Removal. [§2.6700]

28 USC 1446 sets forth the procedure for removal. Essentially, the defendant has thirty days from receipt of plaintiff's complaint to file a petition in the appropriate federal court indicating the grounds for removal. A requirement that the defendant post a bond to cover the plaintiff's costs in fighting an improper removal was abolished in 1988. The defendant then must notify the plaintiff and the state court that the removal has taken place. Once this is accomplished, the state court is prohibited from proceeding with the case.

a. Delayed Removal. [§2.6710]

If a case that is originally not removable according to the initial pleadings becomes removable, as when the plaintiff amends his complaint, the defendant has thirty days from the date he received the document on which it first appeared that the case was removable to file a notice of removal. However, if the case is to be removed on the basis of diversity jurisdiction, it must be removed within one year of the commencement of the action.

8. Remand. [§2.6800]

If removal is challenged, the federal court will determine whether it can proceed with the action or must remand it to the state court. 28 USC 1447 provides that if any time prior to final judgment it appears that the federal court lacked subject matter jurisdiction at the time of removal, the court must remand. However, remand for a procedural defect must be sought within thirty days from the time of removal. Appellate review of orders remanding removed actions to state courts, as well as of denials of motions to remand generally is not available.

a. **Who May Seek Remand. [§2.6810]**

The right to a remand because of a lack of subject matter jurisdiction is not waivable, since litigants cannot confer subject matter jurisdiction on the federal courts [see **§2.1220**]. Consequently, either party or the court may secure remand prior to the entry of final judgment. However, after a final judgment is rendered, a party may seek remand only if it appears that at no time could the federal court have exercised original jurisdiction.

Although the courts are in conflict, the trend is to hold that both the parties and the court lose the power to remand a case for a procedural defect once the thirty day time period has passed.

H. VENUE. [§2.7000]

Venue refers to the system of rules governing the allocation of cases to particular courts within a judicial system.

1. **Purpose of Venue Rules. [§2.7100]**

The usual purpose of venue requirements is to try to insure that an action is brought in a court located in a place that has some relationship either to the litigants or the subject matter of the dispute. Venue principles also afford a means by which a court system can distribute judicial business rationally and evenly among the courts that comprise it.

a. **Venue Distinguished from Jurisdiction. [§2.7110]**

It is important to differentiate jurisdiction and venue. Jurisdiction questions involve a court's power to adjudicate; thus, both subject matter and personal jurisdiction are matters of constitutional dimension. Venue rules deal with identifying the appropriate place or the particular court in which judicial power may be exercised, and essentially are based on notions of convenience. Therefore, venue is something of much lesser significance than jurisdiction. A practical consequence of this distinction is that although a party cannot confer subject matter jurisdiction on a court by consent, he or she can agree to litigate in a court that does not have venue. In the federal system, when a court lacks subject matter or personal jurisdiction, the action must be dismissed; but if venue is improper, the court may be able to transfer the action rather than dismiss it if the interests of justice would be served thereby [see **§2.7500** and **§2.7630**].

b.   Waiver of Venue. [§2.7120]

Because of the non-constitutional character of venue and the fact that it essentially is designed to serve the convenience of the litigants, the defense of lack of venue usually will be deemed waived unless it is raised very early in the action. In the federal courts the defense must be asserted by pre-answer motion or in the answer itself. It also may be waived if the defendant takes procedural steps, such as initiating discovery, that indicate an ability or willingness to litigate in the forum chosen by the plaintiff.

2.   Determining Venue. [§2.7200]

An examination of the venue provisions of various states and the federal courts reveals numerous factors that courts and legislatures have felt are relevant to determining a proper venue.

a.   Factors Considered. [§2.7210]

The following list is illustrative, but not exhaustive, of the factors that are considered appropriate in determining venue. In some jurisdictions a single factor will be the exclusive basis for venue. In others, it is sufficient if any one of several of them is satisfied. (a) Where the defendant resides (this is the most commonly used venue factor). (b) Where the cause of action arose. (c) Where the defendant is doing business. (d) Where the defendant has an office or representative. (e) Where the plaintiff resides. (f) Wherever the defendant may be found, served, or summoned (this provision is based on the common law notion that the right of action follows the person; note, however, that it does not serve any of the usual objectives of a venue requirement—convenience of the parties or witnesses or the rational distribution of the court's workload—except when the defendant resides out of the jurisdiction). (g) Where the seat of government is located (this test usually is reserved to actions by or against the government or a governmental unit).

b.   Forum Selection Clauses. [§2.7220]

Contractual forum selection clauses that enable the parties to agree on a venue for litigating any future disputes arising out of the contract have gained widespread acceptance in both federal and state courts. Subject to various statutory restrictions, these clauses usually are enforced, particularly when the parties to the contract were both represented by competent counsel and possessed equal bargaining power. A party wishing to bring suit in a venue outside the limits set by the forum selection clause has a heavy burden to show that the clause is unreasonable in the circumstances of the case, or that the clause was obtained unfairly. Often, the clause's enforcement will be considered in the context of a motion to transfer venue or of a motion to dismiss for improper venue.

3. **Local Actions. [§2.7300]**

One of the oldest and most confusing venue limitations is the somewhat elusive concept of a local action. A local action, as distinguished from a transitory action, must be brought in a court where the res is located. Although the types of cases constituting a local action vary widely among the states, generally they include actions concerning real property—such as suits to gain possession of land, to foreclose a lien, or to quiet title. The decisions are divided as to the proper classification of certain other actions affecting realty such as trespass, breach of a contract to convey, or for the establishment of a trust.

a. **Local Action Concept Analyzed. [§2.7310]**

The famous case of *Livingston v. Jefferson* (1811) held that an action for trespass to land in Louisiana, which had been brought against Virginia citizen Thomas Jefferson in a Virginia federal court, was a local action and therefore could be maintained only in Louisiana. The concept is premised on notions of honoring the sovereignty of a state over matters relating to land within its borders and the reality that the state in which land is located is in the best position to interpret and apply the governing property law. The potential harshness of the local action rule is amply illustrated by the *Livingston* case because a Louisiana court could not have acquired personal jurisdiction over Jefferson, unless he chose to come into the state. Thus, the plaintiff was left with a legal right but no available remedy. Of course, this situation is significantly ameliorated today because of the development of expanded notions of personal jurisdiction [see **§3.3000–§3.3600**], which would allow the situs court to assert jurisdiction based on the out-of-state defendant's involvement with local land [see **§3.3340**].

4. **Venue in Federal Courts. [§2.7400]**

The general federal venue scheme is set forth in 28 USC 1391.

a. **Diversity of Citizenship Cases. [§2.7410]**

Section 1391(a) provides that when the case is based solely on diversity of citizenship jurisdiction, venue is proper only in (1) a judicial district where any defendant resides, if all defendants reside in the same state, (2) a judicial district in which a substantial part of the events or omissions giving rise to the claim occurred, or a substantial part of property that is the subject of the action is situated, or (3) a judicial district in which any defendant is subject to personal jurisdiction at the time the action is commenced, if there is no district in which the action otherwise may be brought.

> **Illustration. [§2.7411]** A, a resident of California, sues B, a resident of New York, and C, a resident of New Jersey, for injuries sustained as a result of an automobile accident in New York. Section 1391(a)(1) is inapplicable since all of the defendants do not reside in the same state. Section 1391(a)(2) **is** applicable since the accident took place in New York, and thus New York is a venue in which a substantial part of the events giving rise to the claim occurred. Finally, venue cannot be located under Section 1391(a)(3), since that provision is only applicable in cases in which there is no district in which the action otherwise may be brought, and under Section 1391(a)(2), venue is proper in New York.

b. Federal Question Cases. [§2.7420]

Section 1391(b) provides that in an action not based solely on diversity of citizenship—federal question cases—venue is proper only in (1) a judicial district where any defendant resides, if all defendants reside in the same State, (2) a judicial district in which a substantial part of the events or omissions giving rise to the claim occurred, or a substantial part of the property that is the subject of the action is situated, or (3) a judicial district in which any defendant may be found, if there is no district in which the action otherwise may be brought.

> **Illustration. [§2.7421]** The illustration in **§2.7411** would be analyzed in precisely the same manner if the claim arose under a federal statute. That is, New York is the only proper venue.

c. Similarities and Differences Between Diversity and Federal Question Cases. [§2.7430]

Both sections of the venue statute explicitly indicate that venue otherwise may be provided for by law. This provision enables Congress to include venue provisions in federal statutes, often allowing for a broader choice of venue then is provided for in Section 1391. For example, the federal interpleader statute [see **§8.4000–§8.4900**] allows a suit to be brought "in the judicial district in which one or more of the claimants reside." It also should be noted that the venue determination is focused on judicial districts and not on states. Thus, in states with more than one judicial district, venue in one district does not necessarily permit the action to be brought in another, even closely situated, district. However, since venue is primarily a matter of judicial administration, a transfer of venue from one district to another within a state may be appropriate [see **§2.7630**].

(1) **Sections 1391(a)(1) and 1391(b)(1). [§2.7431]**

Both sections use the defendants' residence as the basis for the venue determination. This should be contrasted to the diversity of citizenship statute, which makes subject matter jurisdiction turn on the citizenship, not residence, of the parties. [See the discussion of citizenship in **§2.3400–§2.3450**.] The cases are divided as to whether "residence" should be read as meaning "citizenship" or whether it means a lesser association with the forum than does "citizenship." In addition, it should be noted that, prior to 1990, Section 1391(a)(1) contained an additional clause providing for venue based on the residence of the plaintiff. This clause was removed from the venue statute since there was no justification for permitting a greater number of possible venues in diversity cases as compared to federal question cases. However, the residence of the plaintiff is still used as a basis for determining venue in some state courts [see **§2.7210**]. Finally, both provisions are applicable only in cases in which all the defendants reside in the same state. However, once this condition is satisfied, any of the judicial districts in which a defendant resides is a proper venue for the action.

(2) **Sections 1391(a)(2) and 1391(b)(2). [§2.7432]**

Both of these provisions use the location of an event or some property in dispute, rather than residence, as the basis for determining venue. However, in contrast to the old venue statute, which limited venue to the district in which the claim arose, the current statute permits venue in any district in which a substantial part of the events or omissions giving rise to the claim occurred. The revised statute is at once broader and more efficient, in that it relieves the court from the burden of determining **the** district in which the cause of action arose and permits a more flexible inquiry intended to ensure that the proposed venue has some substantial relation to the events or property in question.

(3)   Sections 1391(a)(3) and 1391(b)(3). [§2.7433]

Both of these provisions are applicable only in cases in which venue otherwise cannot be satisfied by Section 1391. Thus, Sections 1391(a)(3) and 1391(b)(3) are not alternatives to the other sections of the venue statute, but rather are safeguard or fallback provisions designed to locate a venue when venue cannot be brought in any other district according to the rules discussed above. The two provisions differ in language but it is not clear that the difference has any practical significance. Section 1391(a)(3)—the diversity provision—permits venue in a district in which **any defendant is are subject to personal jurisdiction** at the time the action is commenced. By contrast, Section 1391(b)(3)—the federal question provision—permits venue in a district in which **any defendant may be found.** Before a 1995 amendment, the diversity provision permitted venue only in a district in which **all** the defendants were subject to personal jurisdiction, but the federal question provision permitted venue in a district in which **any** defendant may be found. This made the federal question provision broader, because only one defendant needed to satisfy its terms. One explanation given for this was that it comported with the more general contemporary practice of limiting the scope of diversity jurisdiction [see **§2.3111**]. However, this distinction was abolished in 1995 and both provisions now can be satisfied by "any defendant." On the other hand, the curious verbal distinction between where a defendant may be found and where a defendant is subject to personal jurisdiction still exists. If "found" were taken to mean physically present, then the federal question provision would be narrower than the diversity provision, because one could be subject to personal jurisdiction in a district (Section 1391(a)(3)) without being physically "found" there (Section 1391(b)(3)). It is not at all clear why Congress would want the federal question provision to be narrower. The better view, adopted by most courts, is that a defendant "may be found," by definition, wherever the defendant is subject to personal jurisdiction, rendering the two passages equivalent in meaning.

d.   Corporations. [§2.7440]

Section 1391(c) provides that, for venue purposes, a defendant that is a corporation shall be deemed to reside in any judicial district in which it is subject to personal jurisdiction at the time the action is commenced. Section 1391(c) is thus a special residence provision for corporations; once residence is determined, venue is proper in that district if the requirements of Section 1391(a)(1) or Section 1391(b)(1) are satisfied. In a state that has more than one judicial district and in which a corporate defendant is subject to personal jurisdiction, the corporation will be deemed to reside in any district in that state within which its contacts would be sufficient to subject it to personal jurisdiction if that district were a separate state. If no such district exists, residence is determined by the district in which the corporation has the most significant contacts.

Illustration. [§2.7441] A, a resident of Buffalo, New York, purchases a vacuum cleaner from Dustball, Inc., a corporation organized under the laws of Delaware with its principal place of business in New Jersey, and its only activities in New York taking place in Manhattan. A purchased the vacuum from Dustball, Inc.'s only store, located in Manhattan. When the vacuum cleaner exploded in Buffalo, A brought suit against Dustball in a Federal District Court in the Western District of New York. Dustball, Inc. has no contacts at all with the Western District of the state, as its business activities in the state are exclusively centered in Manhattan, which is in the Southern District of New York. Since Dustball would not be subject to personal jurisdiction if the Western District of New York were a separate state, Dustball is not a resident of the Western District under Section 1391(c); to use Dustball's residence as a basis for venue, A would have to bring suit in the Southern District, where Dustball would be subject to personal jurisdiction if that district were its own state. The anomaly is that although personal jurisdiction operates throughout an entire state, the personal jurisdiction standard in the corporate-residence venue provision is limited to judicial districts. It should be noted that although Section 1391(a)(1) does not allow venue to be located in the Western District (Dustball resides, under Section 1391(c), in the Southern District), A could lay venue in the Western District under Section 1391(a)(2), since a substantial part of the events (the exploding vacuum cleaner) took place in that district.

---

(1) Scope of Section 1391(c). [§2.7442]

Section 1391(c) is a significant limitation on the old venue statute, which treated a corporation as a resident of all the districts of a state if the corporation did business anywhere in the state. The new statute also settles an uncertainty as to whether the provision applies to corporate plaintiffs as well as corporate defendants, as Section 1391(c) clearly indicates that it pertains only to a "defendant that is a corporation." As to unincorporated associations, such as labor unions and partnerships, the Supreme Court has held that they are to be considered corporations for venue purposes. However, corporate residence for venue purposes should be distinguished from corporate citizenship for diversity purposes [see **§2.3500–§2.3520**]. Since the statute is given effect "for the purposes of venue under this chapter," its definition of corporate residence should be held to apply, at the least, to every venue statute the appears in Chapter 87 of Title 28, which includes Section 1391 through Section 1413.

e.   **Aliens. [§2.7450]**

Section 1391(d) provides that an alien may be sued in any district.

f.   **United States as a Defendant. [§2.7460]**

Section 1391(e) provides that an action against only the United States or one of its employees may be brought (1) where a defendant resides, or (2) where a substantial part of the events or omissions giving rise to the claim occurred, or a substantial part of the property that is the subject of the action is situated, or (3) where the plaintiff resides, if no real property is involved.

g.   **Defendants in Different Districts. [§2.7470]**

When, in non-local actions, defendants reside in different judicial districts in the same state, venue is proper in any of those districts [28 USC 1391(a)(1) and 28 USC 1391(b)(2); see **§2.7430**].

h.   **Local Actions. [§2.7480]**

The common law rule regarding local actions [see **§2.7300**] continues to be applicable to actions in the federal courts. When a local action involves property located in more than one district in the same state, venue is proper in any of those districts [28 USC 1392].

i.   **Special Venue Provisions. [§2.7490]**

There are a great many special federal venue provisions. Some tend to expand the choice of venue otherwise available under Section 1391; for example, in statutory interpleader cases [see **§2.3220**], venue is proper where **any** of the claimants reside. Others restrict the venue choice; for example, in patent infringement cases, a non-corporate defendant may be sued only where he or she resides or has a regular and established place of business. Each of these special provisions reflects the convenience factors peculiar to the types of actions covered by the statute.

5. Remedies When Venue Is Improper. [§2.7500]

When venue in the chosen forum is improper and is challenged by the defendant, the general rule calls for the case to be transferred to a court within the same judicial system where venue is proper. When, as is often the case, several courts have proper venue, the forum court will transfer the case to the court most convenient to the parties and witnesses.

a. Federal Courts. [§2.7510]

The problem of transfer when venue is improper in a federal court is somewhat more difficult since the transfer often will have to be made to an entirely different state. In such a situation, Section 1406(a) authorizes a federal court to make an interstate venue transfer, rather than dismiss the case, to a court where the action "might have been brought" by plaintiff. [For a discussion of the meaning of "might have been brought," see **§2.7632**.] By avoiding a dismissal, the plaintiff can be protected against the possibility that the statute of limitations has run since the commencement of the action. The Supreme Court has even permitted a court to transfer under Section 1406(a) when it lacked personal jurisdiction over the defendant [*Goldlawr, Inc. v. Heiman* (1962)].

6. Change of Venue for Convenience. [§2.7600]

Even when venue is proper, the forum court typically is given considerable discretion to authorize a change of venue in order to have the case decided in a court that has a more significant affiliation with the litigation.

a. Within a State. [§2.7610]

Since transfers from one court of a state to another may be accomplished easily, they are freely granted. Typically, all that is necessary is that the moving party show that the new forum is more appropriate in terms of the convenience of the parties and witnesses as well as the location of the tangible evidence.

b. Outside the State: Forum Non Conveniens. [§2.7620]

The judicially created doctrine of forum non conveniens authorizes a state court to dismiss a case, even though it has personal and subject matter jurisdiction and the court's venue technically is proper, when there is another forum that is significantly more convenient for the parties. The effect of this doctrine is that the plaintiff's forum choice is superseded. Some of the factors a court will consider on a forum non conveniens motion are the location of the evidence, the cost of producing witnesses, the source of the governing law, the availability of procedures to compel the appearance of unwilling witnesses, and the original court's desire not to overburden taxpayers, jurors, or the judicial system with cases that are only tangentially related to the forum. State courts are reluctant to resort to forum non conveniens if there are any contacts between the parties and the initially chosen forum. Thus, if the plaintiff is a citizen of the forum, a forum non conveniens motion rarely will be granted regardless of where the cause occurred or the witnesses are located. [Forum non conveniens in the federal courts is discussed in **§2.7633**].

Illustration. [§2.7621] P, a homeowner in West Virginia, sues a Delaware trucking company for the destruction of his West Virginia home by one of D's trucks, which ran off the road and into the house. The action is brought in a Maryland state court. All of the witnesses and physical evidence are in West Virginia and the law of West Virginia will control. Defendant only maintains a small office in Maryland; its corporate records are at its home office in Delaware. A motion by defendant to dismiss for forum non conveniens probably will succeed since all of the convenience factors suggest that litigation in Maryland is inappropriate and that West Virginia is a substantially more logical forum.

---

(1) Availability of an Alternative Forum. [§2.7622]

There is some dispute as to how certain the initial forum must be that there is another court that will be able to assert jurisdiction over the dispute. The better rule is that a dismissal for forum non conveniens should be granted only if it is clear that an alternative forum is available. This often may mean that the court will not dismiss but will hold the action in abeyance until the new action is brought and the defendant complies with any conditions imposed by the original court, such as waiving a statute of limitations defense that otherwise might be raised in the more convenient forum or consenting to the new court's personal jurisdiction even though the defendant otherwise would not be amenable to process.

c. Within the Federal System. [§2.7630]

Section 1404(a) of the Judicial Code provides that for the convenience of the parties and witnesses and in the interest of justice, a federal court may transfer an action to any district or division where that action "might have been brought" originally.

(1) Factors Considered. [§2.7631]

The statute spells out three factors that a judge may consider on a motion to transfer: (a) the convenience of the parties, (b) the convenience of witnesses, and (c) the interest of justice. Because this is a very general standard, the decision whether to transfer largely is left to the discretion of the trial judge who usually will undertake an evaluation similar to that on a motion to dismiss for forum non conveniens [see **§2.7620**].

(2) Where the Action Might Have Been Brought. [§2.7632]

The Supreme Court, in *Hoffman v. Blaski* (1960), construed the qualification in Section 1404(a)—"where it might have been brought"—to restrict transfer to those courts in which the plaintiff could have instituted the action as an original matter. Therefore, transfer is permitted only to a district in which the requirements of personal jurisdiction and venue would have been satisfied without reference to the possibility that defendant might have waived them. The same considerations are applicable to the construction of Section 1406(a) when an action is transferred from a place of improper venue [see **§2.7510**].

Illustration. [§2.7632–1] D, a citizen of New York, moves under Section 1404(a) to transfer a case from a federal court in New York to a federal court in California. However, D could not be served with process in an original action in a federal court in that state. Therefore, even though D is willing to submit to the jurisdiction of the California federal court, the transfer motion will be denied.

---

(3) Forum Non Conveniens. [§2.7633]

Although the doctrine of forum non conveniens continues to exist in the federal courts, its utility has been almost entirely superseded by Section 1404(a). The only instances in which a federal court will dismiss on the basis of forum non conveniens is when the appropriate alternative forum is a state court or a court in another country. There has been a growth in the number of cases involving the latter situation in recent years.

(a) Transfer and Forum Non Conveniens Standards Compared. [§2.7633–1]

The Supreme Court has held that a transfer under the statute may be made on a lesser showing of inconvenience than normally is necessary under the forum non conveniens doctrine. However, so much depends upon a particular judge's handling of the facts of the case that generalization about these two procedures is not helpful.

7. Multidistrict Litigation. [§2.7700]

Section 1407 permits the temporary transfer of multiple civil actions involving common questions of fact to a single district for consolidated pretrial proceedings. The statute authorizes the Judicial Panel on Multidistrict Litigation to order transfers on its own initiative or on a party's motion. The Panel usually holds a hearing and any party involved in any of the actions may introduce evidence relevant to the merits of a temporary transfer. The statute directs the panel to consider the convenience of the parties and witnesses as well as other factors relating to the just and efficient conduct of the actions.

a. Statute Applied. [§2.7710]

Consolidation of multidistrict litigation typically occurs when the number of instituted actions is significant or, although few in number, when the pending cases are extremely large or complex. Most of the cases to date involve mass air disasters, antitrust claims, patent infringement actions, and securities litigation.

b. Retention of Case By Transferee Court. [§2.7720]

Although Section 1407 clearly provides that any transferred action "shall be remanded" to the original district from which it had been transferred at or before the conclusion of pretrial proceedings "unless it shall be otherwise terminated," the usual practice under the statute for many years was for the transferee court to retain the coordinated cases for purposes of a consolidated trial after pretrial proceedings have been completed. Federal courts would achieve this result either by securing the consent of the parties or by invoking Section 1404(a). However, in *Lexecon, Inc. v. Milberg Weiss Bershad Hynes & Lerach* (1998) the Supreme Court invalidated this practice. The Court held that under the plain statutory language, the Judicial Panel on

Multidistrict Litigation was required to remand cases to their original districts, and that transferee courts could not preempt this statutory obligation by transferring the cases to themselves. Given the Court's characterization of the statutory remand requirement as absolute, a likely conclusion is that the Panel would be required to remand even if all parties consented to trying the case in the transferee district. However, one court of appeals has declined to read *Lexecon* to require that result. Moreover, in *Lexecon* the Court suggested that upon remand the original districts would be empowered to transfer the individual cases back to the pretrial-transferee district for trial, provided the cases satisfied the usual Section 1404(a) requirements.

*

CHAPTER III

JURISDICTION OVER PERSONS AND PROPERTY

A. JURISDICTION: SCOPE NOTE. [§3.0000]

Among other meanings, the word "jurisdiction" refers to the authority of a court to hear and decide a particular case. This chapter deals with the relationship the court must have to the defendant (or to property that is subject to its control) before it properly can exercise its power to adjudicate a dispute involving the defendant's rights (or affecting the ownership of property). [See also the discussion of subject matter jurisdiction in Chapter Two.]

B. SOURCES OF JURISDICTIONAL POWER. [§3.1000]

Courts generally are authorized to exercise jurisdiction over persons and property by statutes or rules, subject, of course, to constitutional limitations. Accordingly, the process of determining whether the court may proceed requires an examination of the governing jurisdiction statute or rule to determine whether it is applicable, and then an inquiry as to the constitutional validity of that application.

1. Overview: Traditional Bases of Jurisdiction. [§3.1100]

Initially, it was thought that a judgment would be enforceable only if the law enforcement officers of the state in which the court was sitting could take the defendant or the defendant's goods into custody. Thus, during the nineteenth century, the basis of jurisdiction most commonly provided for by statute and court rule was the presence of the person or property involved in the action within the **territorial** boundaries of the tribunal, which rendered them subject to the court's authority [*Pennoyer v. Neff* (1877)]. In addition, the defendant, whether he or she could be found within or without the forum state, was permitted to **consent** to a court's jurisdiction over the person. Three different categories of jurisdiction were formulated to correspond to three forms of this territorial power.

a. In Personam Jurisdiction. [§3.1110]

In personam jurisdiction exists when the defendant is personally served with process—the court's formal order to appear before it (also called a summons)—while physically within the court's **territorial** province or while **domiciled** within the state. The defendant can also **consent** to in personam jurisdiction.

b. In Rem Jurisdiction. [§3.1120]

A court may assert in rem jurisdiction to determine rights in property within the state. The same concept gives the court power to determine a status, such as a marriage or custody of a child, that can be said to be within the territorial power of the court.

c. Quasi In Rem Jurisdiction. [§3.1130]

Quasi in rem jurisdiction may be exercised when property owned by the defendant is found within the state and attached—legally seized by the court. This procedure gives the court power to adjudicate a dispute unrelated to the property, although recovery will be limited to the value of the property and the judgment will have no further effect [see **§3.4600–§3.4610**]. The decision in *Shaffer v. Heitner* (1977) [see **§3.4220**] has sharply limited the independent utility of quasi in rem jurisdiction.

2. Overview: Fairness, Affiliation With the Forum, and Notice. [§3.1200]

As the United States has become more unified and its population more mobile, the conceptualistic framework relating to jurisdiction over persons and property has shifted away from the relatively straightforward principle of the territorial power of the forum state and toward a consideration of whether it is fair to require the defendant to defend in the particular state, whether that state has a reasonable nexus with the dispute, and whether the defendant has been given adequate notice of the action and an opportunity to defend it. The categories of in personam, in rem, and quasi in rem are still utilized by many courts but they are augmented by these new concepts. Thus, the student must understand the traditional rules as well as the more recent modification of jurisdiction doctrine.

3. Effect of Lack of Jurisdiction. [§3.1300]

When judgment is rendered by a court that lacks jurisdiction over the person or property of the defendant, and the defendant has made no appearance whatsoever, upon subsequent challenge by the defendant, the judgment will be declared a nullity as being in violation of the applicable jurisdiction statute or the Due Process Clause of the state or federal Constitution. The defendant need not appeal the judgment to establish its invalidity; instead, the judgment may be attacked collaterally whenever and wherever the plaintiff attempts to enforce it. The Full Faith and Credit

Clause of the United States Constitution, which normally requires one state to enforce judgments rendered in another state, does not require enforcement of a jurisdictionally defective judgment. Thus, the judgment cannot be enforced anywhere. [See **§3.7000** for a complete discussion of challenging the court's jurisdiction.]

C. IN PERSONAM JURISDICTION. [§3.2000]

When a court has general in personam or personal jurisdiction over the defendant, it is empowered to adjudicate any of the plaintiff's legal or equitable claims against the defendant and render a judgment for damages in any amount or order that the defendant do or not do any act. That judgment will be enforceable against any property of the defendant, whether located inside or outside the forum state. Once personal jurisdiction is obtained it persists until the end of the litigation regardless of intervening events, such as the defendant's departure from the jurisdiction. In a case involving multiple defendants, a court may adjudicate claims against only those defendants over whom it has personal jurisdiction.

1. Jurisdiction Over Individuals: Traditional Bases. [§3.2100]

Traditionally, personal jurisdiction over a natural person has been valid, both from a statutory and constitutional point of view, (a) when the individual or an appropriate agent is **personally served** with process within the state, (b) when the defendant is **domiciled** in the forum state, (c) when the person **consents** to jurisdiction, whether that consent is express or implied, or (d) when the defendant waives the defense of lack of jurisdiction. The traditional limitations on the territorial reach of process had their roots in the notion that a state's sovereignty could not be asserted beyond its borders, which meant that a court's power could not extend to people or things in another jurisdiction absent domicile or consent. However, a number of special rules expanded the application of these principles even before the modern trend of emphasizing considerations of fairness and the defendant's relationship with the forum. [Service of process is discussed in **§3.6000–§3.6720.**]

a. Application to Transient Persons. [§3.2110]

Personal service within the forum state traditionally has been fully effective to confer personal jurisdiction even when the defendant is a transient and has no connection with the forum other than physical presence within it at the time of service of process.

67

> **Illustration. [§3.2111]** D, a passenger on a regularly scheduled airline flight, was served while the plane was flying over the forum state; the plane did not land in that state. At least one court has held that the service nonetheless would be effective to give the forum state personal jurisdiction [*Grace v. MacArthur* (1959)]. The result in this situation and in many analogous to it can be criticized because it permits the assertion of jurisdiction on the basis of highly fortuitous events and leads to the wooden application of the territoriality doctrine.

(1) Effect of Shaffer v. Heitner. [§3.2112]

The Supreme Court's decision in *Shaffer v. Heitner* (1977) [see **§3.4220**] seemed to cast considerable doubt as to whether in personam jurisdiction constitutionally could be acquired over an individual simply by serving process on her within the territory of the forum state without the defendant having other affiliations with that state amounting to "minimum contacts." [See **§3.3100** for a discussion of the minimum contacts doctrine.] That doubt was shortlived, however [see **§3.2113**].

(2) Transient Jurisdiction Upheld. [§3.2113]

In *Burnham v. Superior Court of California, County of Marin* (1990), the Supreme Court addressed the continued viability of transient jurisdiction. Burnham, a resident of New Jersey, was served with process while temporarily in California to conduct business and visit his children. The subject of the suit did not arise out of or relate to his activities in California, and Burnham challenged the court's exercise of jurisdiction over him, alleging that he did not have sufficient "minimum contacts" with California. The Supreme Court unanimously held that personal jurisdiction could be constitutionally asserted over Burnham by the California court, but the justices differed in their analytical approaches to the case. Justice Scalia, joined by three other justices, wrote that the traditional theory of transient jurisdiction remains a viable basis for the assertion of in personam jurisdiction. Justice Brennan, joined by three other justices, argued that personal service usually is sufficient to establish personal jurisdiction but that all assertions of state-court jurisdiction must undergo a "minimum contacts" analysis [see **§3.3100**].

b. Domicile. [§3.2120]

Domicile refers to the place where a person maintains his or her permanent home, which, once established in a particular jurisdiction, persists until a new permanent home is established elsewhere [see **§2.3400**]. A state may assert personal jurisdiction over any domiciliary of that state—even though that person is not physically present there at the time jurisdiction is to be established. As will be discussed later [see **§3.6300–§3.6420**], there invariably is a method of service of process designed to notify absent domiciliaries of the commencement of the action.

(1) Residence Distinguished. [§3.2121]

Domicile should be distinguished from residence, which is the place where a person happens to be living at a given time, whether or not he or she intends to make it a permanent home. Of course, domicile and residence usually will coincide since most people live at their permanent homes, but this is not always the case. When the defendant maintains more than one residence (for example, a summer and a winter home) the question of which one is the domicile depends on such factors as where the particular individual works, votes, registers his or her automobiles, educates his or her children, pays taxes, and which one the person believes is his or her permanent abode. Unlike domicile, residence by itself does not confer personal jurisdiction in the forum, although an individual is subject to suit in the state in which he or she is currently residing if personal service of process is effected there.

c. Consent. [§3.2130]

Unlike subject matter jurisdiction [see **§2.1210**], the defendant may consent to the personal jurisdiction of a court. Consent may be given either before or after the action is begun and may be express (by agreement or stipulation) or implied (by conduct). Consent given after an action has been initiated usually takes the form of a waiver of the jurisdictional issue.

(1) Agent to Receive Process. [§3.2131]

The defendant may appoint (or in some circumstances be required by law to appoint) an agent who is empowered to accept process for him or her with regard to either a specific transaction or on any cause of action. Service on the appointed agent is effective to give the court personal jurisdiction over the defendant.

> **Illustration. [§3.2131–1]** As one of the terms of a standard printed lease agreement covering farm equipment being rented from a New York company, L, a resident of Michigan, appointed a New York resident with whom he was not acquainted (and who actually was affiliated with the company) as his agent for the receipt of process in that state for any legal dispute that might arise under the lease. Alleging that L had defaulted in payment, the company served process on the designated agent, who then forwarded a copy to L. Absent any proof that L had not actually received notice, the New York court has personal jurisdiction over L [*National Equipment Rental, Ltd. v. Szukhent* (1964)].

d. Judgment By Confession. [§3.2140]

A cognovit note is a type of contractual promise to pay money in which the debtor confesses judgment in the event of a default in payment and typically also consents to be subject to personal jurisdiction in a particular court. A number of states still give effect to these clauses under certain circumstances; most, however, have prohibited them because they often are oppressive. Judgments by confession have come under increasing attack in recent years, especially in the consumer context, but the United States Supreme Court has declined to strike the practice down as unconstitutional [see **§3.5620**].

e. Implied Consent By Filing Suit. [§3.2150]

By initiating a civil action in a court, the plaintiff consents to that court's in personam jurisdiction for the purpose of a counterclaim by the defendant.

f. Implied Consent: Defendant's Appearance. [§3.2160]

If the defendant responds to the plaintiff's complaint and defends on the merits without making a timely challenge to the court's lack of personal jurisdiction, the defendant is said to have made an appearance in the action and to have implicitly consented to the court's jurisdiction and to have waived the right to object to it. [See the discussion in **§3.7000–§3.7400** on challenging the court's jurisdiction.]

g. Implied Consent: Non–Resident Motorists. [§3.2170]

Virtually every jurisdiction has a statute providing that a non-resident who drives a motor vehicle on the public highways of a state implicitly appoints the registrar of motor vehicles (or some other similar official) as an agent for accepting process in lawsuits that arise out of the use of the forum's roads by the non-resident.

(1) Constitutional Validity of Non–Resident Motorist Statutes. [§3.2171]

The theory upon which the implied consent of a non-resident motorist is based is that the state's constitutional police powers give it the right to regulate the use of its highway and to protect its citizens by providing them with a local forum for the redress of any grievances against non-resident motorists for accidents occurring within the state. The United States Supreme Court upheld the constitutionality of these statutes in the famous case of *Hess v. Pawloski* (1927). In part, of course, that decision reflected the particular apprehension created by the automobile—a dangerous instrumentality—and the right of the state to respond to the threat it posed to local citizens.

(2) Theory Criticized. [§3.2172]

This form of implied consent is a legal fiction; drivers are unaware of the "consent" to be sued that they supposedly are giving by entering a state. Moreover, the United States Constitution would not permit a state to "regulate its highways" so as to exclude non-resident motorists. From the hindsight of contemporary notions of personal jurisdiction we know that the reasons these statutes have been upheld probably are (a) that there is considerable logic to having an automobile accident case tried in the state where the event occurred, and (b) that the defendant's alleged voluntary presence in the state and involvement in an accident there is sufficient to make it fair to oblige the non-resident to defend a suit growing out of that accident in that state [see **§3.3000–§3.3640**].

(3) Effect of Driver's Death. [§3.2173]

The fictional character of jurisdiction by consent in non-resident motorist cases is further illustrated by the situation in which the defendant driver dies. The law generally provides that an agency appointment is revoked by the death of the principal. Application of this principle to non-resident motorist statutes obviously makes little sense and would impair their effectiveness significantly. Some states recognize the fictional nature of the statutory consent and simply do not apply the normal agency rules regarding revocation at death; others avoid the problem by providing that the motor vehicle registrar is the agent of the estate in the event of the motorist's death.

h. Implied Consent: Other Areas of State Application. [§3.2180]

After the constitutionality of the non-resident motorist statute had been upheld, state legislators extended its philosophy and enacted similar statutes to cover such matters as the operation of watercraft, aircraft, and other "dangerous instrumentalities" within the state. Statutes also were enacted to give state courts jurisdiction over claims arising out of local sales of such commodities as securities and insurance by foreign individuals and companies. In these contexts the jurisdictional provisions tended to be part of a larger regulatory scheme.

2. Corporations: Traditional Bases. [§3.2200]

A corporation always has been subject to suit in its **state of incorporation.** This is logical since the place of incorporation is the location most analogous to an individual's domicile and permitting that state to assert jurisdiction seems consistent with the traditional territoriality principle. Indeed, inasmuch as a corporation is viewed solely as a creature of the law of the state of incorporation, it initially was thought that it could never be sued outside that state. However, even before the advent of the contemporary notions of jurisdiction, this restrictive principle had been significantly eroded.

a. Express Consent. [§3.2210]

A corporation always can consent to personal jurisdiction in any state in the same ways as can an individual litigant [see **§3.2130–§3.2180**]. In addition, a number of states provide by statute that a foreign corporation cannot do business within the state unless it registers and expressly appoints an agent within the state for the purpose of receiving service of process in actions arising out of local activities.

b. Implied Consent. [§3.2220]

At a relatively early date, a number of states enacted statutes analogous to non-resident motorist statutes, providing that, by **doing business** in a state, a corporation implicitly appointed the secretary of state (or a similar officer) as its agent for accepting process in disputes arising from the corporation's activities in the state. This theory allowed a corporation to be sued on its activities within the state even if it ceased "doing business" after the cause of action accrued but before the action was instituted. However, these statutes did not make a corporation generally amenable to suit on causes of action arising from activities outside the forum state.

(1) Meaning of Doing Business. [§3.2221]

Over the years the crucial question of what constituted "doing business" within the meaning of an implied consent statute was subjected to numerous judicially developed definitions and distinctions that often were difficult to administer. This often led to the use of a checklist of factors that resulted in a somewhat wooden application of the law.

c. Presence. [§3.2230]

Another basis for the assertion of personal jurisdiction over a foreign corporation was a finding that the corporation transacted a sufficient quantity of business in a state to be deemed present there. Many courts held that the presence concept subjected a corporation to personal jurisdiction on any cause of action, whether it arose from its activities within or without the state. However, by ceasing to act within the state the corporation could terminate its presence there and it would no longer be amenable to jurisdiction on that basis, even with regard to its dealings while it was active within the state.

D. CONTEMPORARY NOTIONS OF JURISDICTION. [§3.3000]

As stated earlier, during the past 60 years there has been a trend away from the requirement of territorial power that was established in *Pennoyer v. Neff* and toward allowing a court to assert personal jurisdiction whenever the circumstances make it fair to require the defendant to defend in a particular forum because of the contacts that individual or company has had with the forum, especially those activities that relate to the subject matter of the litigation. The ground was first laid for this development when state legislators enacted and courts upheld statutes based on a fictional implied consent. However, truly dramatic doctrinal change followed the United States Supreme Court's recognition of expanded state power in this area under the Due Process Clause of the Fourteenth Amendment. As will be discussed subsequently [see **§3.3200–§3.3360**], the states have exercised this power by enacting greatly expanded jurisdiction statutes.

1. Minimum Contacts Doctrine. [§3.3100]

The decision in *International Shoe Co. v. Washington* (1945) provided a new judicial attitude toward jurisdictional power and eliminated any need to resort to such fictions as "consent" or "presence." As the Supreme Court said: "[D]ue process requires only that in order to subject a defendant to a judgment in personam, if he be not present within the territory of the forum, he have certain **minimum contacts** with it such that the maintenance of the suit does not offend **traditional notions of fair play and substantial justice.**"

a. **Rationale of International Shoe. [§3.3110]**

The *International Shoe* formulation that "minimum contacts" equals "fair play and substantial justice" resulted from a number of factors: first, an awareness of the complexity and mobility of twentieth century America, which made interstate business and torts so common that the territoriality principle simply was inadequate; second, changes in notions of state sovereignty and state powers; third, recognition that a theory of jurisdiction based on implied consent was a fiction designed to avoid the rigors of the territoriality principle that failed to address itself to the policy considerations underlying the need to expand the personal jurisdiction of state courts; and fourth, dissatisfaction with the mechanical way the corporate "presence" and "doing business" standards were being applied.

b. **The Criteria for Jurisdiction Recognized By International Shoe. [§3.3120]**

The *International Shoe* decision recognized two separate criteria for a court's assumption of jurisdiction over an out-of-state party. First, if the cause of action arose out of that party's activities within the state, jurisdiction would be proper. This basis previously had been approved with regard to non-resident motorist statutes. Second, even if the cause of action arose from some conduct outside the forum state, jurisdiction within that state nevertheless would be proper if the out-of-state party engaged in continuous and systematic business within the state. This basis previously had been upheld under the "presence" theory as related to corporate activity.

Illustration 1. [§3.3121] P purchased a photocopy machine from D in state X. Later P moved the company to state Y and took the machine with him. The machine has broken down and P wants to sue D in state Y. If D has continuous and systematic activities in Y in the form of salesmen soliciting orders, the assertion of jurisdiction by a court in state Y would not be constitutionally invalid. On

---

the other hand, if D's only contact with state Y has been the sale of a few machines through a non-exclusive arrangement with a retail office supply company, D probably could not be subjected to jurisdiction there on P's claim.

Illustration 2. [§3.3122] An airline maintains a permanent office in California to purchase equipment and to conduct other aspects of its business. Suit is brought against it there by a Californian on a cause of action involving an airplane crash in another state. Jurisdiction may be asserted over the airline. The fact that the cause of action did not arise from the defendant's activities within the forum is relevant, but not controlling.

c. Continuous and Systematic Contact Narrowly Defined. [§3.3130]

Continuous and systematic contact as a basis for jurisdiction by a state over a non-resident defendant when the cause of action is unrelated to the defendant's activities in the forum state has been somewhat circumscribed. The Supreme Court has held that **purchases and related trips alone are not a sufficient basis** for a state court to assert jurisdiction over a non-resident defendant in a cause of action unrelated to the purchases. Even purchases at regular intervals may be an insufficient contact. The Court suggests that minimal contacts even if systematic and continuous do not meet the "minimum contacts" test [*Helicopteros Nacionales de Colombia v. Hall* (1984)].

Illustration. [§3.3131] D owned an air charter service that operated out of state X. D contracted with P, from state Y, to fly P around within state X. D occasionally sent pilots to be trained in state Y. D also bought some spare parts for planes there. After an accident in State X, P sues D in State Y. D's contacts with state Y are probably too minimal for D to be subject to the jurisdiction of state Y.

d. Scope of Application: Individuals and Corporations. [§3.3140]

Although the *International Shoe* case involved jurisdiction over a foreign corporation, the minimum contacts analysis theoretically equally applies to individual defendants as well as to corporations.

75

However, corporations often have greater resources and more varied interstate activities, making them better able to defend in a foreign state. These considerations undoubtedly influence the decision in particular cases and even may affect the application of constitutional principles to the minimum contacts analysis. As a practical matter, it is much easier for a court to find that a foreign corporation has the required minimum contacts with the forum than it is when the defendant is an individual.

(1) Presence of Subsidiary Corporation in the Forum. [§3.3141]

When a corporation's only contact with a state is that its subsidiary is doing business there, the parent corporation is subject to personal jurisdiction in that state only if the subsidiary is so closely controlled by the parent as to be considered its agent. When the subsidiary and the parent are independent entities, they will be treated as such for jurisdiction purposes.

e. Scope of Application: Traditional Jurisdictional Categories. [§3.3150]

In *Shaffer v. Heitner* (1977), the Supreme Court applied the *International Shoe* doctrine to quasi in rem jurisdiction and suggested that all assertions of jurisdiction were subject to minimum contacts analysis. The *Shaffer* decision thus cast considerable doubt as to whether in personam jurisdiction constitutionally could be acquired over an individual simply by serving process on her within the territory of the forum state without the defendant having other affiliations with the state amounting to minimum contacts. But in *Burnham v. Superior Court of California, County of Marin* (1990) four justices refused to apply the *International Shoe* analysis to in-state service; its applicability to in rem jurisdiction also remains unclear [see §3.2112–§3.2113].

2. Long–Arm Statutes: In General. [§3.3200]

Prior to *International Shoe*, most states had restrictive jurisdictional statutes geared to the earlier notion of territoriality and the fictions developed under it. Since that decision, most states have seized upon the Supreme Court's recognition of their broad constitutional power under the Fourteenth Amendment and have enacted so-called long-arm or single-act statutes that vastly broaden the authority of their courts to assert jurisdiction in specified cases over defendants who are not subject to the territorial power of the state. The proper invocation of jurisdiction under one of these statutes requires the confluence of the following factors: (a) the particular facts of the case must fall within the language of the state's long-arm statute; (b) the defendant must have the required minimum contacts with the forum to satisfy constitutional principles of due process; and (c) the defendant must be given reasonable notice of the institution of the suit and an opportunity to defend it.

a. Content of Long–Arm Statutes. [§3.3210]

Nothing requires a state to exercise all of its constitutionally permissible jurisdiction. In fact, many long-arm statutes have a more limited scope. Often they particularize the categories of contacts with the state that will give rise to personal jurisdiction. On the other hand, statutes in a few states (for example, California and Rhode Island) simply provide that their courts can assert jurisdiction over any action unless that assertion of jurisdiction would violate a provision of either the state or federal constitution. Statutes that take this form are easy to draft and automatically adjust to changes in due process principles. They may be criticized, however, because they offer no guidance to the bench and the bar, they represent a legislative abdication of the difficult task of defining jurisdictional policies for the state, and they convert every jurisdictional question into an issue of constitutional dimensions.

3. Long–Arm Statutes: Jurisdiction Based on Single Contact. [§3.3300]

Under the long-arm statutes found in numerous states, a single contact by the defendant with the forum state is a sufficient basis for the assertion of personal jurisdiction over a cause of action that arose directly out of that contact. The existing United States Supreme Court precedents suggest that this is within the constitutional power of the states. However, a single contact is not adequate to assert jurisdiction over a claim unrelated to the contact.

a. Tort Claims. [§3.3310]

Although the Supreme Court has not spoken authoritatively on the point, a defendant probably has sufficient contact with a forum to permit jurisdiction whenever (a) the defendant or an agent commits a tortious act within the forum that gives rise to the cause of action sued upon, or (b) the defendant's conduct outside the forum brings about foreseeable injurious consequences within the forum. Some long-arm statutes require that the defendant regularly do or solicit business in the forum to justify jurisdiction in the second situation.

(1) Determining Where the Tort Occurred. [§3.3311]

Because some long-arm statutes require that a tort or tortious conduct occur in the forum, it becomes necessary to identify the situs of the tort. The cases are not consistent on the question of where a tort occurs. What appears to be a majority of the existing decisions favors the place where the injury resulting from the negligent conduct occurs; the others look to the place of the negligent conduct itself.

Illustration. [§3.3311–1] A New York bottler of soft drinks, whose products are distributed nationally, is sued in an Illinois state court in an action for personal injuries brought by a consumer who was injured in Illinois when one of the defendant's bottles (which the plaintiff purchased in Illinois) exploded. The Illinois jurisdiction statute permits service on out-of-state defendants who commit tortious acts in that state. Given the national character of the defendant's business, which suggests that its soft drinks have entered Illinois on other occasions, it would not violate the United States Constitution for the court to accept jurisdiction. Nevertheless, jurisdiction will be held proper only if the statutory words "tortious act" in the Illinois statute are read to include the place of injury.

---

(2) Effect on Implied Consent Statutes. [§3.3312]

The enactment of an omnibus long-arm statute generally renders superfluous the various statutes based on implied consent discussed earlier, the most common of which were the non-resident motorist statutes [see **§3.2170–§3.2180**]. In those states that have not adopted the long-arm principle, however, the wording and scope of application of these earlier statutes continue to be quite crucial.

b. Products Liability Cases. [§3.3320]

Products liability cases frequently involve the defendant's out-of-state manufacture of a defective product that allegedly has caused injury in the forum. Whether the court constitutionally can assert jurisdiction under a long-arm statute in this context will depend on whether the defendant purposefully availed itself of the market in the forum state, not merely by injecting its product into the stream of commerce, but by some action purposefully directed toward the forum state [see **§3.3400–§3.3420**].

Illustration. [§3.3321] Widget, Inc. manufactures altimeters in Massachusetts for private and commercial airplanes. It sells its product to airplane manufacturers in Washington, Florida, and Illinois who install them in their aircraft. P, a citizen of California, brings suit against Widget in California alleging that her son was killed in an airplane crash in California as a result of a malfunction in one of the defendant's altimeters. Widget moves to dismiss for lack of jurisdiction. The motion should be granted. Although defendant could foresee that its altimeters would be installed in aircraft that might land or take off in California, defendant took no action purposefully directed toward that state. Defendant sold its product in three other states and had no control over where it would ultimately be used. The product entered the forum state only through the activities of third parties. Since minimum contacts have not been established, due process bars the application of the California long-arm statute.

---

c.   **Contract Actions. [§3.3330]**

Most long-arm statutes provide that the execution of a contract within a state or a promise to furnish goods or services within that state is a sufficient contact with the state to permit it to assert personal jurisdiction over all the parties to the contract in any action arising out of the contract. The constitutional limits on a court's power to assert jurisdiction under a long-arm statute's contract provision on the basis that some aspects of the negotiation, performance, or breach of a contract touched the forum have not yet been fully developed by the courts. However, in *Burger King Corp. v. Rudzewicz* (1985), the Supreme Court upheld the constitutionality of a Florida federal court's assertion of jurisdiction over a Michigan franchisee in an action under a contract providing that the franchise relationship was established in Miami and was governed by Florida law. Although the Court stated that a contract with an out-of-state party cannot alone automatically establish sufficient minimum contacts in the other party's forum, jurisdiction in the particular case could be upheld because there was a substantial and continuous relationship between the Michigan franchisee and the Miami head of the franchisor. The Michigan defendant had received fair notice from the contract and the dealings that he might be subject to suit in Florida, and he was a sophisticated and experienced businessman who did not act out of duress or disadvantage.

79

Illustration 1. [§3.3331] D, a Kansas insurance company, solicited and sold an insurance policy to a citizen of Louisiana. Premiums were paid by the insured for several years. After the insured's death, her heirs, who also were citizens of Louisiana, sought to recover the proceeds of the policy. In an action in a Louisiana court, jurisdiction over the Kansas company will be upheld under a long-arm statute despite a constitutional challenge under the Fourteenth Amendment. This would be true even if the defendant sold only one policy in Louisiana [*McGee v. International Life Ins. Co.* (1957)]. It should be noted that one vital consideration in this situation is the forum state's interest in protecting its citizens against insurance companies, a policy typically manifested by the enactment of extensive regulatory legislation [compare **§3.2180**].

Illustration 2. [§3.3332] P brings suit against D, a securities dealer, on a contract made in another state. Personal jurisdiction is asserted solely on the basis that D has registered as a securities dealer in the forum state. A motion to dismiss should be granted because the cause of action does not arise from a contract that has any relationship to the state and no other basis for jurisdiction under the long-arm statute appears to exist.

Illustration 3. [§3.3333] P, of New Jersey, agrees to buy 10,000 men's suits from D, of North Carolina, every year for the next five years. The contract is negotiated and signed in North Carolina, but the suits are to be delivered in New Jersey. D fails to deliver and P sues. Jurisdiction in a New Jersey court under a long-arm statute will be upheld despite a constitutionally based challenge, since jurisdiction can validly extend to contracts for the delivery of goods in that state. The long-arm statute could not apply, however, if the suits were to have been delivered outside of New Jersey.

Illustration 4. [§3.3334] A Utah resident negotiates by mail to purchase horses located in Illinois. His agent inspected them in Illinois and tried to take delivery of the animals in that state, where

the breach occurs. It is unclear whether Illinois may exercise jurisdiction over the Utah buyer as a constitutional matter even though the failure of the contract in Illinois can be brought under the language of that state's long-arm statute. The situation is rather special. Permitting an Illinois court to take jurisdiction would create a situation that would be unduly burdensome on most mail order buyers in view of their minimal contact with the mail order seller's home jurisdiction and their limited resources, at least when compared with those of the mail order house.

d. Actions Involving Local Property. [§3.3340]

Many long-arm statutes provide for in personam jurisdiction when the cause of action arises out of property within the forum state owned by the defendant or in which he or she has some lesser interest. State statutes vary, however, with regard to the types of property covered. Some include defendant's interest in any form of property—real, personal, or intangible; other statutes are limited to actions related to real property.

Illustration. [§3.3341] D, a New Yorker, owns a summer home in Vermont. P brings suit in Vermont alleging that because of D's failure to maintain his drainage ditch in good condition water has backed up and damaged P's adjacent property. Jurisdiction would be proper under a statutory provision covering causes arising out of the ownership of property within the state and its application to these facts would be constitutional.

e. Actions Involving the Internet. [§3.3350]

The development of the Internet has raised interesting questions of personal jurisdiction; the issue has been tackled by several courts, but not as yet by the Supreme Court. The Internet increases the potential for both affordable communication and the exercise of long-arm jurisdiction. The first cases to consider the issue came to differing conclusions: one court held that a passive website was enough to satisfy the state's long-arm statute; another court held that a passive website was not enough for jurisdiction under the state's long-arm statute; and a third court took a sliding-scale approach and looked at the interactivity and commercial nature of the website. In recent years, numerous courts have chosen to follow the sliding-scale approach. Others have focused on whether the website intentionally sought to attract the attention of people in the forum. The application of state long-arm statutes and the constitutional meaning of minimum contacts and fair play with respect to the Internet has been heavily litigated in the last few years.

f. Other Bases of Jurisdiction. [§3.3360]

Several long-arm statutes provide for jurisdiction based on other types of contacts between the forum and the defendant. These include, but are by no means limited to, actions against directors or officers of a domestic corporation; actions involving the collection, assessment, or levy of a tax by the forum state's taxing authority; actions against a personal representative of a decedent over whom the forum court could have asserted jurisdiction had the decedent not died; actions involving certain matrimonial disputes; and actions to recover a deficiency judgment on domestic commercial obligations. Although the constitutionality of these provisions has never been dealt with explicitly by the United States Supreme Court, they seem valid because they involve significant contacts between the defendant and the forum.

4. Constitutional Limits: Necessity of Purposeful Affiliation With Forum. [§3.3400]

In *Hanson v. Denckla* (1958), the Supreme Court emphasized that "it is essential in each case that there be some act by which the **defendant purposely avails itself of the privilege of conducting activities within the forum state, thus invoking the benefits and protections of its laws.**" The Court held that Florida had not satisfied this test in attempting to assert jurisdiction over a Delaware trustee in a dispute over the validity of a trust that had been established by a Pennsylvania domiciliary who subsequently moved to Florida where she later died. The trustee had remitted trust income and corresponded with the settlor of the trust after she had moved to Florida and she had exercised a power of appointment there. The Court concluded that the trustee had not invoked the protection of the forum state's laws to a degree that was sufficient to give rise to personal jurisdiction in Florida. Four justices dissented, arguing, among other things, that they believed that Florida's interest in adjudicating questions relating to one of its resident's estate, its contacts with the trust, and the fact that many of the claimants under the will were residents of Florida, made it a fair and convenient forum.

a. Satisfying the Affiliation Requirement. [§3.3410]

As the five to four division indicates, the result in *Hanson* was close, one that many commentators argued was wrong. In general, state and lower federal courts refused to take literally the passage quoted in the preceding section, emphasizing the relation between the defendant and the forum rather than the subject matter of the dispute and the forum. These courts held that the requirement that the defendant has "purposely" availed itself of the "privilege of conducting activities" in the forum could be satisfied by implication, for example, when the defendant did no more than enter its product in the "stream of commerce" under circumstances in which it should have reasonably foreseen that some units would reach the forum. This trend was arrested, at least in part, by the Supreme Court's six to three decision in *World-Wide Volkswagen Corp. v. Woodson* (1980). The plaintiffs in that case sued in an Oklahoma court for injuries received in Oklahoma while driving through that state on a trip from New York to Arizona. The plaintiffs alleged that their vehicle, which they had purchased in New York while they were New York citizens, was defective. Two of the defendants, the New York retailer who had sold the car to the plaintiffs and the New York area distributor, claimed that Oklahoma could not constitutionally assert jurisdiction over them. The Court agreed, stating:

> The forseeability that is critical to due process analysis is not the mere likelihood that a product will find its way into the forum State. Rather, it is that the defendant's conduct and connection with the forum State are such that he should **reasonably anticipate being haled into court there**. . . . It is foreseeable that purchasers of automobiles sold by [defendants] . . . may take them to Oklahoma. But the mere "unilateral activity" of those who claim some relationship with a non-resident defendant cannot satisfy the requirement of contact with the forum State.

(1) Actions Purposefully Directed Toward the Forum State. [§3.3411]

In *Asahi Metal Indus. Co. v. Superior Court* (1987), the Supreme Court further limited the exercise of long-arm jurisdiction. Although *Woodson* barred jurisdiction when the defendant's product entered the forum through the unilateral activity of a consumer, it left open the possibility of jurisdiction when the defendant had a clear-cut, advance knowledge or intention that the product would reach the forum through the distribution chain. In *Asahi*, a Japanese manufacturer engaged in regular and extensive sales of tire valves to a Taiwanese manufacturer. The Japanese company knew that some of the valves, incorporated into tire tubes in Taiwan, would be sold by the Taiwanese company in California. Nonetheless, when the Taiwanese company

83

sought indemnification from the Japanese company in a products liability action in California, the latter claimed lack of jurisdiction. Justice O'Connor, in her opinion for four members of the Court, understood the teaching of *Woodson* to be that a manufacturer's contacts must be "more purposefully directed at the forum State than the mere act of placing a product in the stream of commerce." The Japanese manufacturer's mere awareness that the valves it sold to the Taiwanese manufacturer eventually would end up in California was not sufficiently purposeful, in her opinion, to establish minimum contacts. The defendant must indicate an intent to serve the market in a forum state, as by designing the product specifically or advertising there. Justice Brennan, in his opinion for four members of the Court, found no requirement in *Woodson* for any "additional conduct" beyond the placement of a product into "the regular and anticipated flow of products from manufacture to distribution to retail sale." Thus, the question of what is the appropriate standard to be used to determine whether a manufacturer has established sufficient "minimum contacts" with a forum state has not been fully settled. But eight justices agreed that, even assuming that minimum contacts existed, the California state court's exercise of jurisdiction over the Japanese manufacturer was unreasonable and would offend notions of fair play and substantial justice, considering the minimal interests of California in litigating the lawsuit between two foreign companies, the insignificant interest of the plaintiff in litigating in California, the international context of the dispute, and the high burden of California litigation on the defendant. [See the discussion of these factors in **§3.3500.**]

b.   **Satisfying the Benefits and Protections Requirement. [§3.3420]**

Initially the requirement of *Hanson v. Denckla* that the defendant must have invoked the "benefits and protections" of the forum's laws was generally held to have been satisfied merely when the defendant's products, property, or activities might have received the benefit and protection of various services (police, fire, and judicial) provided by every state. However, *Kulko v. Superior Court* (1978) reinforced the *Hanson* decision and made it clear that the required "benefits and protections" of the forum state must be direct. *Kulko* held that the act of a divorced father of sending a child from New York to California to live with her mother was "not a commercial act and connotes no intent to obtain nor expectancy of receiving a corresponding benefit" from California "that would make fair the assertion of that State's judicial jurisdiction."

84

c. Actions Not Arising Directly from Contacts With the Forum State. [§3.3430]

In an extension of the minimum contacts doctrine, the California Supreme Court decided in *Vons Companies v. Seabest Foods, Inc.* (1996) that at least in the context of franchise relationships, personal jurisdiction is proper when litigation results from alleged injuries that merely have a substantial connection to the defendant's other activities in the forum state. In the *Vons* case, the defendant meat supplier cross-complained against two out-of-state restaurants who were not originally parties to the litigation, seeking damages for economic interference and indemnification against the plaintiffs' claims resulting from food poisoning incidents at the restaurants. The restaurants had extensive business contacts with their California-based franchisor, the defendant, and their franchise agreements specified that all contract disputes would be litigated in California under California law. Although the alleged tortious activities did not arise directly out of the restaurants' contractual or business contacts with the forum state, the court found that jurisdiction was proper. Like the franchisees in *Burger King*, the out-of-state restaurants purposefully availed themselves of an ongoing contractual relationship with a business in the forum state [see **§3.3400**]. The court ruled that in these circumstances a claim need not arise directly from a defendant's contacts with the forum to warrant the exercise of specific jurisdiction. As long as the claim bears a **substantial connection** to the nonresident's forum contacts, the exercise of specific jurisdiction is appropriate. The California Supreme Court found support for its conclusions in decisions of the Sixth and Seventh Circuits, and the decision may be indicative of a growing trend. The Supreme Court has yet to address the issue of the constitutional status of this "connected to" jusrisdiction.

5. Other Factors Affecting the Assertion of Jurisdiction. [§3.3500]

International Shoe began a trend away from territorial power and toward reasonableness—from "is it there?" to "is it fair?" A variety of factors other than the defendant's contacts with the state determine whether asserting personal jurisdiction over a particular defendant would be "fair play and substantial justice" under the *International Shoe* test. When the defendant has continuous and systematic contacts with the forum state, the Supreme Court has not directly addressed the requirement of "fair play and substantial justice," but several lower courts have looked to the same factors that would be considered in a case arising out of the defendant's specific activities in the state.

a. **Interests of the Plaintiff and Forum State. [§3.3510]**

When determining whether the exercise of personal jurisdiction over a non-resident defendant is fair and reasonable, courts consider the **interest of the plaintiff** in litigating in the forum and the **interest of the state** in providing a forum for the litigation at issue. **Efficient resolution** of the controversy is also an important factor.

b. **Convenience of Forum. [§3.3520]**

The convenience of litigating in the particular forum is important in determining the overall fairness of allowing a court to assert personal jurisdiction over a non-resident defendant. The most commonly mentioned elements of convenience are the availability of evidence, presence of witnesses, applicability of the forum state's laws, and proximity to the home states of both the plaintiff and the defendant.

(1) **Forum Non Conveniens. [§3.3521]**

Many long-arm statutes contain express provisions authorizing the court to dismiss or stay an action over which it has jurisdiction if it believes that, in the interests of justice, the action should be heard in another forum. Sensible application of the forum non conveniens doctrine [see §2.7500–§2.7510] is of great significance to the rational administration of modern long-arm statutes.

c. **Jurisdiction By Necessity. [§3.3530]**

When the circumstances of a particular case are such that there is only one jurisdiction in which the controversy may be litigated and that jurisdiction has a strong connection with the subject matter of the suit, there is some indication in a few cases that a court in that state may be allowed to assert jurisdiction over the parties "by necessity" even though the usual jurisdictional standards are not fully met. Since the absence of an alternative forum is not expressly referred to in many decisions, the dimensions and constitutional validity of the jurisdiction by necessity concept are not clear.

(1) **Doctrine Applied. [§3.3531]**

The Supreme Court has held that the state in which a common trust fund had been established pursuant to a local regulatory scheme has a compelling interest in entertaining periodic suits to settle the trustee's accounts and determining its liability for malfeasance and its right to fees. This result was reached even though some potentially interested beneficiaries of the trust whose rights against the trustee would be foreclosed could not be identified or located; some were holders of contingent interests and many did not live in the forum state and were beyond the territorial power of the court under traditional jurisdiction principles [*Mullane v. Central Hanover Bank & Trust Co.* (1950)]. In a subsequent case, however, the Supreme Court expressly declined to decide whether the jurisdiction by necessity doctrine existed.

d. Substantive Limitations. [§3.3540]

Various substantive policies, such as considerations of not encumbering interstate commerce and maintaining free speech, should not impose limitations on a court's power or willingness to assert jurisdiction in situations in which it otherwise would have the statutory and constitutional authority to do so. The Supreme Court explicitly has stated that First Amendment concerns do not enter into the jurisdictional analysis. It is a "needless complication." Any possible chill on freedom of the press is protected by constitutional limits in the substantive law [*Calder v. Jones* (1984)].

e. Threat of Multiple Liability. [§3.3550]

Whenever it is possible that courts in several states may assert jurisdiction over the same party or property regarding competing claims by different plaintiffs, the possibility of inconsistent judgments arises. In the situation in which several states are attempting to escheat the same property (typically debts), the Supreme Court has held that a state may not exercise jurisdiction unless it can guarantee the debtor that it will not be subjected to multiple liability. When the claimants are states, they may sue one another and invoke the original jurisdiction of the Supreme Court to resolve the conflict, but it is unclear what should be done when there is a threat to a private litigant of multiple liability because two or more suits may be brought in different jurisdictions on essentially the same claim [*Western Union Telegraph Co. v. Pennsylvania* (1961)].

Illustration. [§3.3560] D has systematic and continuous contacts with Vermont. P sues D in Vermont for shoddy work done on a building in Florida. No activity related to the lawsuit took place in Vermont, neither P nor D has its principal place of business in

---

Vermont, and no evidence or witnesses are located in Vermont. Asserting jurisdiction probably would be unreasonable.

6. Personal Jurisdiction in the Federal Courts. [§3.3600]

In general, the federal courts have the same jurisdictional reach that is available to the local courts in the same state. However, under certain circumstances the federal courts have additional jurisdictional power.

a. Nationwide Service Statutes. [§3.3610]

Various federal statutes—the Interpleader, Copyright, and Patent Acts, for example—contain provisions authorizing nationwide service of process in actions arising under them. Federal Rule 4(k)(1)(C) indicates that service under these statutes is effective to establish personal jurisdiction over the defendant. The Supreme Court never has ruled on the issue of reconciling the minimum contacts doctrine with nationwide service of process authorized by federal statute, but all of the lower federal courts that have addressed the issue have applied a national contacts standard (requiring minimum contacts with the United States as a whole) when process is served under an applicable federal provision. This standard recognizes that the underlying nature of the claims (the subject that the federal statute addresses) involves nationwide activities and that the Fifth Amendment Due Process Clause, rather than the Fourteenth Amendment, measures the legitimacy of the federal government's assertion of jurisdiction.

b. Supplemental Personal Jurisdiction. [§3.3620]

When a plaintiff brings federal and state law claims against a defendant who has no contacts with the state but is subject to nationwide service for purposes of the federal claim, there is some question whether a federal court may exercise personal jurisdiction over the defendant for the state claim by employing a form of supplemental jurisdiction. [See also the discussion of supplemental jurisdiction in Chapter Two.] Neither the plain meaning nor the legislative history of the statute creating federal supplemental subject matter jurisdiction supports the conclusion that Congress intended that statute to expand personal jurisdiction. Furthermore, the exercise of supplemental personal jurisdiction seems to violate a defendant's Fourteenth Amendment rights embodied in the minimum contacts test. The Supreme Court has not yet addressed the validity of the practice but several lower courts have upheld the doctrine.

c. **Other Federal Question Cases. [§3.3630]**

In *Omni Capital International v. Rudolf Wolff & Co.* (1987), the Supreme Court held that in a federal question case in which the statute sued upon did not provide for nationwide service of process, the federal court had to adhere to the forum state's law regarding the exercise of jurisdiction over non-resident defendants. Federal Rule 4(k)(2), as amended in December, 1993, addresses the *Omni Capital* situation, authorizing the exercise in federal question cases of extraterritorial jurisdiction over the person of any defendant against whom a claim is made arising under any federal law if that person is subject to personal jurisdiction in no state. This exercise of jurisdiction is still subject to Fifth Amendment limitations with respect to the defendant's affiliating contacts and the due process requirements of fair play and substantial justice.

d. **100–Mile Bulge Rule. [§3.3640]**

In federal court actions, a defendant joined under Rule 14 or Rule 19 may be served in a judicial district outside of the state in which the action is brought if service is made within 100 miles of the place from which service issues [Federal Rule 4(k)(1)(B)]. It is not clear how the minimum contacts analysis applies to such a defendant; many courts have held that the defendant need only have sufficient contacts with the state in which he is served, not the forum state.

E. JURISDICTION OVER PROPERTY. [§3.4000]

When property is located within a state, the traditional concept of territorial power gives the courts of that state the right to adjudicate its status or ownership regardless of the whereabouts of those claiming an interest in it. Jurisdiction over the property is obtained by attachment (if it is tangible) or by garnishment (if it is an intangible, such as a debt). These acts have the effect of bringing the property under the court's custody.

1. **In Rem Jurisdiction. [§3.4100]**

In rem jurisdiction is asserted over property located within a state in order to adjudicate conflicting interests in or claims to it. Examples are quiet title actions, actions to determine the ownership of corporate shares, various admiralty proceedings, forfeitures of contraband, abandoned property proceedings (escheat), and probate actions. The property itself, rather than its owner, is conceived of as being the defendant in actions of this type. In some contexts, the status of a person domiciled in a state, such as the status of a married person, also is considered a "res" over which the state in which the person (or the status) is located has in rem jurisdiction.

2. Quasi In Rem Jurisdiction. [§3.4200]

Quasi in rem jurisdiction refers to situations in which the court assumes jurisdiction technically on the basis of the court's power over property within the forum in order to litigate a personal dispute that may or may not relate to the property. In contrast to in rem jurisdiction, the plaintiff in a quasi in rem action does not claim that he or she owns or has an interest in the attached property. However, the plaintiff does claim that it, or its proceeds at a judicial sale, should be transferred to the plaintiff in full or partial satisfaction of a personal claim. The policy justification supporting this type of jurisdiction lies in (a) a state's desire to provide a forum for one of its citizens who sues a non-resident who happens to have an interest in property within the state, (b) the fiction that someone who has a property interest within the state can be said to be "present" there, and (c) the notion that the claimant or owner of local property receives the benefit of the forum's protection and therefore it is not unfair to extract the quid pro quo of requiring him or her to defend any claims by someone who has attached the property. [The effect of a quasi in rem judgment is discussed in **§3.4600.**]

a. Quasi In Rem Jurisdiction in the Federal Courts. [§3.4210]

Prior to 1963, the federal courts did not have any original quasi in rem jurisdiction. An amendment to Federal Rule 4(e) in that year permitted the assertion of this type of jurisdiction, correcting what had been nothing more than an historical anachronism. Subsequent to the December, 1993, Rule 4 amendments, Rule 4(n) authorizes quasi in rem jurisdiction.

b. Shaffer v. Heitner. [§3.4220]

In *Shaffer v. Heitner* (1977), the Supreme Court rejected quasi in rem jurisdiction in a case involving the Delaware sequestration of shares of stock of a corporation incorporated in Delaware but having its headquarters in Arizona. The defendants, corporate directors and officers, were not from Delaware, and the cause of action was unrelated to the stock and arose in Oregon. The Court, in a broadly worded opinion, held that the minimum contacts-voluntary affiliation test of *International Shoe* and *Hanson v. Denckla* [see **§3.3100** and **§3.3400**] was to be applied in quasi in rem actions. The precise application of this decision is unclear in several respects, especially since two justices wrote concurring opinions suggesting that when real property was attached, the *Shoe-Denckla* test might be met. There is no question, however, that *Shaffer* significantly limits the availability of quasi in rem jurisdiction. In states that have very embracive long-arm statutes, quasi in rem jurisdiction no longer may have any independent significance.

3. Nature of Property Interest. [§3.4300]

In rem and quasi in rem jurisdiction may be based on the presence within the forum of any form of property right—real, personal, or intangible.

a. Debts. [§3.4310]

In *Harris v. Balk* (1905), it was decided that the situs of a debt is wherever the debtor is located. Thus, a party's interest in a debt is attachable, and quasi in rem jurisdiction may be asserted wherever a person who owes the defendant money can be found. If a defendant's interest is garnished by attaching his or her debtor, the debtor is obliged to give notice of the action to the defendant so as to insure the latter of the right and the opportunity to defend the claim against the debt by the garnishing plaintiff; if notice is not given, the defendant's debtor will not be exonerated of the obligation to pay the debt to the defendant. The rule of *Harris v. Balk* has been criticized because it leaves the creditor at the mercy of the debtor's fortuitous wandering, which may subject the creditor to jurisdiction in a state that has no relationship with the claim being asserted or with either of the parties. The decision in *Shaffer v. Heitner* [see **§3.4220**] seriously undermines *Harris v. Balk* by limiting the ability to establish jurisdiction by attaching a debt by requiring the forum to be one that satisfies the principles of *International Shoe* and *Hanson v. Denckla.*

Illustration. [§3.4311] P is a citizen of Connecticut. D lives and works in Rhode Island but maintains a bank account in Connecticut. He is owed $1,000 by X, a Californian who is spending the summer in Connecticut. Under *Harris v. Balk,* P could commence a quasi in rem action in a Connecticut state court by attaching the bank account and/or the debt owed to D by X. The result is uncertain today after *Shaffer v. Heitner* and would depend on an evaluation of all of D's contacts with Connecticut.

---

(1) Improper Extension of the Principle. [§3.4312]

In *Seider v. Roth* (1966), a Canadian citizen insured by a New York company was involved in an auto accident in Vermont with New York residents. The New York residents were allowed to sue in New York on the basis of quasi in rem jurisdiction by attaching the insurance company's contractual obligation to defend and indemnify the Canadian insured. The *Seider* decision was a substantial departure from prior quasi in rem cases because the very existence of the debt that was attached depended on the outcome of the case. If fully extended, the *Seider* principle would have allowed quasi in rem jurisdiction in any case in which the substance of the action involves a dispute over title to the attached property. This "boot strap" jurisdiction was rejected by a number of courts in other states even before the decision in *Shaffer v. Heitner.* The logic of the latter case [see **§3.4220**] seemed to undermine the constitutionality of *Seider.* Nevertheless, some New York state and federal courts continued to uphold *Seider* on the ground that the "true defendant" was the insurance company and the attachment procedure was merely a means of asserting jurisdiction over the company wherever it was doing business.

(2) Elimination of the Improper Extension. [§3.4313]

In *Rush v. Savchuk* (1980), the Supreme Court ended any suspense as to the continuing validity of the *Seider* principle by holding it unconstitutional under the reasoning of *Shaffer v. Heitner.* States are free to enact statutes making insurance companies directly liable to injured plaintiffs, but they cannot achieve that result through an artificial application of quasi in rem jurisdiction.

b. Domestic Relations. [§3.4320]

The traditional theory of divorce jurisdiction was that a marriage creates a res, which gives the state in which it is located, historically the state where the marriage was entered, the power to adjudicate any action relating to it. Today, however, a court in the state of either spouse's domicile may determine the status of the marriage. Although this newer approach is more consistent with the minimum contacts philosophy than is the older fiction of the marriage being a res that can be territorially located, courts continue to adhere to the in rem analysis in addition to using the newer approach.

(1) Limitation on Divorce Jurisdiction. [§3.4321]

Although a court has jurisdiction to enter a divorce decree based on the domicile of one of the spouses or the presence of the marital res, there must be personal jurisdiction over an absent spouse to permit the court to determine his or her duty to pay alimony or support or to divide the property between the parties.

4. Attachment as a Prerequisite to Jurisdiction. [§3.4400]

Although older Supreme Court decisions have indicated that in rem or quasi in rem jurisdiction cannot constitutionally be asserted until the property has been brought under the control of the court through attachment, the matter is not clear, and a number of states do not require attachment. The argument in favor of attachment is essentially a practical one. If the court does not obtain control over the property, the defendant may sell or otherwise dispose of it or transport it to another state, thus robbing the court of jurisdiction. Any proceedings that have already taken place would be wasted, since there is no property to be bound by the judgment. On the other hand, modern notions of due process prohibit prejudgment attachment, at least until the defendant is notified and given an opportunity to be heard [see **§3.5600**]. Moreover, if jurisdiction based on the presence of property can be obtained without attachment, the case may proceed to judgment without an often unnecessary hearing on the attachment application, and, assuming the property is not sold or destroyed by the defendant, it can then be taken to satisfy the judgment. Under this scheme, it is the plaintiff who suffers primarily if the property is no longer available; and it is the plaintiff who can choose to attach or not to attach as the special facts of each case seem to dictate.

5. Determining the Situs of Property. [§3.4500]

Since the situs of real and tangible personal property is not difficult to identify, these forms of property create few problems regarding whether they are within the court's territorial power for purposes of in rem or quasi in rem jurisdiction. The major difficulties arise in attempting to ascertain the situs of intangibles.

a. Intangible Property. [§3.4510]

In the case of intangible property—such as notes, bonds, and debts—plausible claims may be made that it is "located" in any number of states with which the property right or the defendant has some relationship, such as the state of the debtor's or creditor's residence. When the property is represented by a written instrument, courts often permit jurisdiction wherever the paper is found and attached.

b. Stocks and Bonds. [§3.4520]

The location of stocks and bonds pose a difficult problem. It may be argued that these assets are located where the issuer of the security, often a corporation, is incorporated or located, or at the domicile of the stockholder, or where the certificates themselves are kept. Chapter 13 of the Uniform Stock Transfer Act, which has been enacted by a number of jurisdictions, requires the seizure of the instrument itself or an injunction against its transfer.

6.   **Effect of Judgment. [§3.4600]**

Persons claiming an interest in property affected by an in rem or quasi in rem judgment are bound only if they have been given reasonable notice of the action [see §3.5100–§3.5510]. In some cases an in rem judgment will be limited by its own terms to the rights of the parties who appeared in the action in the res that is the subject matter of the action; in others, such as the settlement of decedents' estates, it may purport to determine ownership of the property as against the entire world. A quasi in rem judgment binds only the attached property and if the claim exceeds the value of the property the excess cannot be collected under the judgment.

a.   **Application of Former Adjudication Principles. [§3.4610]**

Even when proper notice is given, the decision in a quasi in rem action has no res judicata or collateral estoppel effect unless the defendant appears and converts the proceeding into a personal action [see §3.7400]. In some jurisdictions there may be collateral estoppel effect given to issues actually litigated when the defendant makes a limited appearance. [See §3.7400 for a discussion of the limited appearance.] Accordingly, the fact that the plaintiff has been successful in a quasi in rem action does not obviate the need for the plaintiff to prove his or her case again in a second action, whether jurisdiction is quasi in rem or in personam and whether the cases were in the same or in different jurisdictions. Conversely, if the plaintiff loses in the first action, it does not bar further quasi in rem actions against different property or an in personam action against the defendant. Fortunately, this type of wasteful relitigation is rare.

7.   **Threat of Multiple Liability. [§3.4700]**

The problem discussed in §3.3550 regarding the threat of multiple liability when there is more than one claimant is particularly acute when the object of the claim is intangible property, such as a debt, and the res or the debtor may be subject to attachment by several plaintiffs in different states.

8.   **Continued Utility of Jurisdiction Based on Property. [§3.4800]**

Many commentators argue that the contemporary notions of jurisdiction, since they are based on considerations of fairness, minimum contacts, and affiliating circumstances, render the old categories of in personam, in rem, and quasi in rem obsolete and, in particular, suggest the abolition of quasi in rem jurisdiction.

F.   NOTICE AND AN OPPORTUNITY TO BE HEARD. [§3.5000]

Constitutional requirements of due process require that reasonable notice and an opportunity to be heard must be given to the defendant before any type of jurisdiction over his or her person, property, or the property to which he or she has a claim properly may be exercised. A judgment rendered without reasonable notice to a person will be unenforceable against that party. Appropriate notice and an opportunity to be heard are additional requirements rather than a substitute for jurisdiction. Because jurisdiction based on minimum contacts requires many more people to defend lawsuits far from their domiciles, courts have become much more cognizant of the importance of these two elements.

1. Notice: Reasonableness Standard. [§3.5100]

To meet the constitutional test of reasonable notice, the statutes or rules relating to service should require the plaintiff to make a bona fide attempt to give actual notice to every defendant. This means delivery of the papers, in person or by some appropriate alternative procedure such as registered or certified mail, to every defendant whose name and address can be ascertained after diligent efforts. **"The means employed must be such as one desirous of actually informing the absentee, might reasonably adopt to accomplish it"** [*Mullane v. Central Hanover Bank & Trust Co.* (1950)]. If, but only if, reasonable investigation fails to reveal the address of a potentially interested party, it will be proper to give that party notice by the publication of announcements in a newspaper of general circulation. However, when proper, notice by publication is binding on anyone to whom it is directed, even if that person does not actually learn of the action until it is too late to defend against it.

Illustration 1. [§3.5110] P brings suit against D whose name and address are not known by P at the time the action is instituted but which can readily be ascertained since P knows D is a county employee. Service is made by publication in a newspaper of general circulation in the county where D works. Process will be held invalid as not being reasonable under the circumstances.

Illustration 2. [§3.5120] In a proceeding for a trustee's settlement of accounts, service is made by ordinary mail on the 10,000 beneficiaries of the trust whose addresses are known. D argues that each beneficiary should have been personally handed notice or at least that registered mail should have been utilized. The

---

CHAPTER III

argument will be rejected because the notice is reasonable under the circumstances. It will reach the vast majority of the beneficiaries interested in the proceeding and the interest of those not reached presumptively will be protected by those who do receive notice. Furthermore, the costs of D's proposed methods for giving notice would have been prohibitive because of the number of beneficiaries involved.

2. **Case-By-Case Analysis. [§3.5200]**

As the foregoing illustrations suggest, the facts of each case must be analyzed to determine the permissible ways in which notice may be given. The key is what is **reasonable under the circumstances.** For example, when there is a default, the circumstances require that the best possible means for giving notice should be employed before entering judgment.

3. **Requirement of Express Statutory Provision for Notice. [§3.5300]**

Since notice is now a constitutional requirement in practically all situations, express statutory provision for it is probably no longer necessary. However, one Supreme Court case decided in the era of non-resident motorist statutes held that the statute must explicitly order the registrar of motor vehicles to send notice to the defendant; the failure of the statute to do so rendered it invalid even though the defendant actually received notice from the "agent."

4. **Notice: Class Actions. [§3.5400]**

Class actions provide an important exception to the obligation to provide each and every litigant with notice. In certain class actions, typically those in which all members of the class have identical or joint interests, publication plus actual notice to at least a sample of class members may be held adequate [compare **§3.5120**]. However, the Supreme Court has held that when the class action is based solely on the presence of common questions of law or fact that predominate over individual questions, the language of Federal Rule 23 requires that personal notice be given to every member of the class who can be identified [*Eisen v. Carlisle & Jacquelin* (1974)]. However, if the class is large, notice by ordinary mail will suffice. More recently, the Supreme Court has recognized a constitutional requirement of notice to every identifiable class member in an action for money damages [*Phillips Petroleum Co. v. Shutts* (1985)]. [Notice in class actions is discussed at length in **§8.1500–§8.1550.**]

5. **Notice in Cases Involving Jurisdiction Over Property. [§3.5500]**

Historically, adequate notice in quasi in rem or in rem cases could be given by constructive service—either publication or physically posting the notice on the defendant's property—even when the litigant's name and address were known. Justification for this procedure was based on the metaphysical notion that an individual has a symbiotic relationship with his or her property and somehow is aware of what is going on with regard to it, and further, that the owner would have a caretaker overseeing the property who would inform the owner of the institution of the action and of the posting of notice. The unrealistic character of these justifications and increased sensitivity to due process concerns have led courts to require the same kind of reasonable notice that is needed for in personam actions. Unfortunately, a number of unconstitutional statutes authorizing notice by posting or publication remain on the books of many states.

a.   **Notice Requirement Applied. [§3.5510]**

In *Mennonite Board of Missions v. Adams* (1983), the Supreme Court required notice reasonably calculated to apprise all interested parties, stating that constructive notice by publication was not enough. The Court also appeared to be insisting upon a certain amount of diligence on the plaintiff's part in locating the defendant.

6.   **Opportunity to Be Heard. [§3.5600]**

The Due Process Clause of the Fourteenth Amendment of the United States Constitution requires that a defendant be given an opportunity to appear and present his or her defenses to the action.

a.   **Prejudgment Attachment, Garnishment, and Replevin. [§3.5610]**

The popular creditor's remedies of prejudgment garnishment, attachment, and replevin may violate due process if the defendant is not afforded notice of the proceeding and a fair opportunity to be heard. [See the discussion of these procedures in Chapter Seventeen.] In *Sniadach v. Family Finance Corp.* (1969), the Supreme Court struck down a state statute that provided for prejudgment garnishment of a wage earner's income. In *Fuentes v. Shevin* (1972), the *Sniadach* principle was extended to an ex parte prejudgment replevin procedure. In a case of significance decided two years later, *Mitchell v. Grant* (1974), a divided Court held that a Louisiana prejudgment replevin procedure satisfied the due process requirement and seemed to retreat from, if not overrule, *Fuentes*. However, in *North Georgia Finishing, Inc. v. Di–Chem, Inc.* (1975), the Court indicated that *Fuentes* has survived *Mitchell* by striking down a Georgia garnishment procedure in a commercial and non-consumer setting. [The *Mitchell* decision probably has no effect on *Sniadach* since the deprivation of a wage earner's livelihood is of substantially greater significance than the deprivation of chattels.]

(1) Analysis of Fuentes and Mitchell. [§3.5611]

The *Mitchell* Court distinguished *Fuentes* on the grounds that (a) the replevin order in *Mitchell* was granted by a judge, whereas in *Fuentes* the writ was issued by the court clerk; (b) the applicant in *Fuentes* was not required to make a convincing showing of need for the prejudgment seizure, whereas in *Mitchell* the grounds for the seizure had to be set forth in a verified affidavit; (c) the statute struck down in *Fuentes* at best afforded the defendant a delayed opportunity for a hearing on the issues involved in the seizure, whereas an immediate post-seizure hearing was available under the statute involved in *Mitchell*; and (d) in *Mitchell* the admissible facts for determining the propriety of granting the replevin were issues capable of documentary proof, whereas in *Fuentes* a broad and less objective "fault" standard was the ground for replevin. Furthermore, in *Mitchell*, as a result of Louisiana law, the "vendor's privilege" (the right to repossess) ceased upon the vendee's transfer of property to a third person, thereby creating a greater risk to the creditors than was present in *Fuentes*. Taking the cases together, the test seemed to be whether the deprivation of the debtor's right to possession prejudgment outweighed (1) the debtor's possible inability to make the creditor whole for wrongful possession, (2) the risk of destruction and alienation if notice and a prior hearing were granted, and (3) the protections provided by the statute against wrongful seizure by creditors. An important question that remains somewhat in doubt due to this line of cases is whether prejudgment attachment for purposes of asserting quasi in rem jurisdiction can survive constitutional scrutiny.

(2) Three-Part Test. [§3.5612]

The balancing test suggested above has largely been confirmed by the Supreme Court. In *Connecticut v. Doehr* (1991), the defendant challenged the constitutionality of a Connecticut attachment statute after the plaintiff sought attachment of the defendant's $75,000 home to ensure that assets would be available to satisfy the judgment in a civil assault and battery case that the plaintiff was instituting against the defendant. The statute authorized prejudgment attachment of real estate without a hearing. It required the plaintiff to swear that his claim was based on probable cause, but did not require him to post a bond and did not provide for pre-attachment notice to the defendant. Ruling on the defendant's constitutional challenge, the Supreme

Court drew upon precedent regarding the due process requirements for government seizure of property as well as upon *Sniadach, Fuentes, Mitchell,* and *Di-Chem* to articulate a three-part test for scrutinizing prejudgment attachment and similar procedures. The Court balanced (1) the debtor's property interest, (2) the risk of erroneous deprivation and the probable value of additional or alternative safeguards, and (3) the interest of the party seeking the prejudgment remedy. The Court invalidated the Connecticut statute, determining that the attachment of real estate interfered with significant property interests—making it more difficult for defendant property owners to clear title and sell their property and tainting their credit ratings. The Court also found that the probable cause standard was not strict enough to avoid a substantial risk of erroneous deprivation of property and that safeguards including a post-attachment hearing and the imposition of damages on the plaintiff if probable cause was not shown were insufficient when (unlike in *Mitchell*) the claim at issue was not a simple one that the property owner could defend easily with documentary evidence. The Court also concluded that the plaintiff's interests in the attached property were minimal because he was not claiming a right to the property itself and made no showing that the defendant was likely to remove his assets from the state.

b. Cognovit Notes. [§3.5620]

In *D.H. Overmyer Co. v. Frick Co.* (1972), the Supreme Court held that cognovit notes, which contain a confession of judgment provision [see **§3.2140**], and authorize a creditor to enter judgment against a defaulting debtor without service of process or notice, are not per se violative of due process. However, the Court did indicate that it will look with some care at the use of these procedures and examine the relative bargaining positions of the parties and any other elements that might destroy the debtor's ability to engage in a knowing and voluntary waiver of the right to notice and an opportunity to be heard.

G. SERVICE OF PROCESS. [§3.6000]

Except when notice by publication is permitted, the defendant is notified by service, either by hand delivery or by mail, of a paper called a "summons"; in many states and in the federal courts the complaint accompanies the summons. Service of process **informs the defendant of the institution of the suit** and of his or her opportunity and obligation to defend the action.

1. By Whom Process Is Served. [§3.6100]

The traditional practice was that process had to be served by the sheriff, or some corresponding official, such as the marshal in federal practice, or his or her deputy. Other persons could be specially appointed by the court, particularly if doing so would result in a saving of travel fees, if the defendant might be difficult to serve, or if the sheriff's other duties might prevent him or her from serving the process within a reasonable period. In those jurisdictions that still follow this practice, personal service by someone other than the sheriff or a court appointed agent is ineffective. But in a growing number of jurisdictions, including the federal courts, service may be made by anyone of mature years who is not a party to the action.

2. Return of Service. [§3.6200]

After delivering the papers to the defendant, the process server is required to file a return of service with the court. This document contains the basic facts relating to the service, stating that the defendant actually has been served as required. Although the return is strong evidence that proper service was accomplished, it is not necessarily conclusive and generally may be challenged by a showing that the facts alleged therein are inaccurate.

Illustration. [§3.6210] A process server hands the summons and complaint to X, whom the process server believes is an agent or officer of the defendant corporation. The return identifies X as the person served and purports to show his association with the corporation. D can successfully challenge service by showing that X is not one of its agents or officers.

---

3. Methods of Service. [§3.6300]

A variety of different types of service may be utilized depending on the statutes applicable to a given action or in a given situation. Of course, the method used must meet the constitutional requirements of due process. A number of these methods already have been discussed in connection with giving a defendant notice [see **§3.5000–§3.5510**], long-arm statutes [see **§3.3200–§3.3360**], and an opportunity to be heard [see **§3.5600–§3.5620**].

a. Personal Delivery. [§3.6310]

The most common method of service is personal delivery of the summons and complaint to the defendant. When a natural person is the defendant, service may be accomplished by personal delivery to him or her. When a corporation, partnership, or unincorporated association is the defendant, service typically may be effectuated by delivering the process to an officer or managing agent. Individuals, corporations, partnerships, and unincorporated associations may be served by delivering a copy of the summons and complaint to an agent authorized by appointment or law to receive service of process.

b. Substituted Service. [§3.6320]

Methods of delivery of process short of personal delivery to the defendant, which are called substituted service, sometimes may be utilized to establish personal jurisdiction. The term "substituted service" may apply either to leaving process at the defendant's residence or to the use of the mails or publication.

c. Leaving at Defendant's Home. [§3.6330]

Most jurisdictions have a provision similar to Federal Rule 4(e)(2)(b), which provides that service can be effected on an individual defendant by leaving copies of the summons and complaint "at the individual's dwelling place or usual place of abode with someone of suitable age and discretion who resides there. . . ." This form of substituted service is fully as effective as personal delivery in giving the court personal jurisdiction.

d. Registered or Certified Mail. [§3.6340]

Some states permit service by mailing the summons and complaint to the defendant by registered or certified mail, return receipt requested. This technique often is permitted to serve defendants who are subject to the court's jurisdiction but reside outside the forum state. In the federal courts, service by first-class mail is authorized, in effect, by Federal Rule 4(d) [see **§3.6370**].

e. Publication. [§3.6350]

State statutes provide that service may be accomplished by publication of the contents of the summons in a newspaper for a prescribed number of times when the plaintiff has demonstrated that the defendant cannot reasonably be served by any other method. Use of this method of process is carefully circumscribed to avoid due process violations.

f. Service in Federal Courts. [§3.6360]

Federal Rule 4 authorizes the modes of service described above (except publication) for actions brought in the federal courts and includes special provisions for service on individuals in foreign countries [Rule 4(f)], upon minors and incompetent persons [Rule 4(g)], upon the United States [Rule 4(i)], and upon foreign, state, or local governments [Rule 4(j)]. In addition, Rule 4(e)(1) permits service to be made pursuant to the law of the state in which the district court is located or in which service is effected.

g. Request for Waiver of Service. [§3.6370]

Plaintiffs may elect to request that the defendant waive formal service of the summons by providing the defendant with notice of the action, a copy of the complaint, and a written request for waiver. These documents may be sent by first-class mail or "other reliable means," which may include electronic methods. Rule 4(d) gives the defendant two incentives to acquiesce to the plaintiff's request: (1) if formal service is waived, the defendant is given 60 days (or 90 days if the defendant is not within the United States) to answer the complaint instead of the usual 20 days, and (2) if not waived, the defendant must bear the cost of formal service. However, plaintiffs may not request waivers of service from foreign or domestic government entities, from infants, or from incompetent individuals.

4. Territorial Range of Service. [§3.6400]

In actions brought both in the federal and state courts, process issued by a court of general jurisdiction usually may be served anywhere within the forum state. The propriety of service outside the state generally depends on the particular terms of the forum state's long-arm statute or the existence of a federal statute authorizing nationwide service of process. Extraterritorial process is authorized in any case in which the court has jurisdiction under the statute. Usually, no distinction is drawn between service in a sister state and in a foreign country regarding the geographic reach of process.

a. Service Outside of State. [§3.6410]

As discussed earlier [see **§3.2100**], service of process on a defendant outside of the forum state will not, in itself, confer personal jurisdiction on the court. Only when the court has some constitutional and statutory basis for asserting personal jurisdiction—such as express or implied consent, domicile, or minimum contacts—will service outside of the state enable a court to exercise jurisdictional power.

b. Special Provisions for the Federal Courts. [§3.6420]

In actions in the federal courts, persons joined under Rule 14 or Rule 19 may be served in a judicial district outside of the state in which the action is brought if service is made within 100 miles of the place from which service issues [Federal Rule 4(k)(1)(B)].

5. Timing of Service. [§3.6500]

Federal Rule 4(m) requires that service be made within 120 days after the filing of the complaint but provides for an extension of the time period upon a showing of good cause by the plaintiff. In addition, some courts have provided discretionary extensions of time for service even when the plaintiff made no showing of good cause.

6. Immunity from Process. [§3.6600]

In certain situations in which the efficient operation of the courts or the other branches of government might be furthered, immunity from process is conferred, so that individuals can enter a state without the risk of being subject to its personal jurisdiction. Since the purpose of immunity is to promote the convenience of the court or governmental agency rather than to benefit the individual involved, it may be denied or withdrawn if the policy is not served by extending it in a particular situation. Although states vary considerably in their treatment of immunity, it commonly is granted to witnesses, attorneys, and parties to other actions.

a. Limitations on Immunity. [§3.6610]

Immunity may not be extended to a plaintiff who voluntarily enters the state to further his or her own interests by bringing an action, since there is no governmental interest in encouraging litigation by foreigners. Moreover, when immunity is granted it lasts only as long as is necessary to carry out its purpose. If the out-of-state witness, for example, unduly extends his or her stay in the forum, the immunity will expire.

b. Impact of Long–Arm Statutes. [§3.6620]

With the extension of personal jurisdiction principles and the increased opportunity to serve process extraterritorially under a long-arm statute, the notion of immunity from process within the forum state has declined in importance.

7. Fraud in Procuring Service. [§3.6700]

When the defendant's presence in the forum state is procured by fraud, a court normally will refuse to exercise jurisdiction. Should the forum court take jurisdiction and proceed to judgment, another court called upon to enforce that judgment may hold that the original court's decision to proceed was improper and that the resulting judgment is a nullity.

> **Illustration. [§3.6710]** Without identifying himself, the plaintiff's lawyer telephoned the defendant, who was aware of the threat of litigation against him, and invited him to a football banquet in a neighboring state. The defendant accepted the invitation, crossed the state boundary, and was served when he arrived at the banquet. The court may decline to accept personal jurisdiction obtained in this manner if any of the representations made to the defendant on the telephone were false.

a. Defendant in Hiding. [§3.6720]

However, if the defendant is present in the forum state but is attempting to evade process, it generally is permissible to use any method that does not involve criminal conduct to "flush" such a person out of hiding and to serve him or her.

H. CHALLENGING THE COURT'S JURISDICTION. [§3.7000]

The technique and timing of a challenge to a court's jurisdiction over persons and property vary considerably, although they share the characteristic of **requiring this threshold defense to be raised promptly.**

1. State Practice. [§3.7100]

All states now permit a defendant to make a **special appearance** in the action by which he or she can object to the assertion of personal jurisdiction without actually subjecting himself or herself to the court's jurisdiction. Some states take the position that if the defendant makes a special appearance, and proceeds to defend on the merits, he or she waives the jurisdictional objection and cannot assert it on appeal. Most courts, however, allow the defendant to make a full defense on the merits following an unsuccessful special appearance without the defendant losing the right to appeal on the ground that the trial court lacked personal jurisdiction.

a. Former Practice: Special Appearance Not Allowed. [§3.7110]

A very small number of jurisdictions formerly took the position that the defendant impliedly consented to the court's jurisdiction if he or she made any appearance in the action whatsoever—even if it was for the sole purpose of asserting the absence of jurisdiction! An 1890

Supreme Court decision upheld the constitutionality of this practice of prohibiting jurisdictional challenges by special appearance [*York v. Texas* (1890)]. This practice placed the defendant in the dilemma of abandoning an objection to jurisdiction in order to defend on the merits or abandoning a defense on the merits and allowing a default judgment to be entered. The latter alternative left the defendant with the possibility of objecting to the court's lack of jurisdiction by way of collateral attack. Now that Texas and Mississippi permit special appearances, the right to make some form of an appearance to contest in personam jurisdiction exists in all states.

2. Federal Practice. [§3.7200]

Federal Rule 12(b) provides that a defense of lack of jurisdiction over the person may be asserted in a pre-answer motion under Rule 12 or in the answer. The distinction between the general and special appearance has been eliminated from federal practice, and a properly raised objection to personal jurisdiction is preserved for appeal even if the defendant proceeds to a defense on the merits. However, if the objection is not asserted by motion or in the answer, it is waived [Federal Rule 12(h)(1)]. Unlike subject matter jurisdiction, personal jurisdiction need not be considered by a court on its own initiative.

3. Finality. [§3.7300]

In both state and federal practice, once the question of the trial court's jurisdiction has been fully litigated between the parties, whether in connection with a special appearance procedure or otherwise, it may not be raised again by the defendant in another case by way of collateral attack.

4. Limited Appearance in Quasi In Rem Actions. [§3.7400]

If the defendant enters a general appearance to defend against a quasi in rem action, the litigant naturally submits to the general jurisdiction of the court and may become liable for the full value of the claim beyond that of the attached property. Conversely, if the defendant stays out of the action entirely, he will lose by default, although the judgment will affect only the attached property [see **§3.4600**]. To ease this dilemma, some courts permit the defendant to make a limited appearance, which enables a party to defend the personal claim on the merits without increasing his potential liability beyond the attached property. Other courts hold, some pursuant to specific statutory provisions, that any defendant who appears in a quasi in rem action to contest the merits submits to the court's in personam jurisdiction.

*

CHAPTER IV

DETERMINING THE GOVERNING LAW

A. GOVERNING LAW: INTRODUCTION. [§4.0000]

Problems of determining what law applies in a case inevitably arise whenever a dispute touches two or more jurisdictions. These difficulties are magnified in our federal system because of the presence of federal as well as state tribunals in each jurisdiction. This chapter will explore some of the basic governing law questions that are germane to an understanding of our dual system of courts. Other governing law issues must be left to the conflict of laws course.

B. GOVERNING LAW IN THE FEDERAL COURTS. [§4.1000]

Whenever a specific federal statute, treaty, or constitutional provision governs all or part of an action, that provision must be applied. However, when a case, or part of a case, does not involve any provision of federal law, as is usually true of diversity of citizenship actions or claims brought in federal courts under their supplemental jurisdiction [see **§4.4600**], the federal court is required to apply the same law that would have been applied had the action been brought in a court of the state where the federal tribunal is located. Generally speaking, this rule governs only matters of substantive law. Thus, federal law governs procedural matters in all cases in the federal courts, whatever the source of subject matter jurisdiction. In order fully to understand just when a federal court must apply state law, it is necessary to explore the historical development of the principles stated above.

1. The Early History of Choice-Of-Law Regulations. [§4.1100]

Section 34 of the Judiciary Act of 1789, the so-called "Rules of Decision Act," which is still in force today as 28 USC 1652, provided that except when the Constitution, a treaty of the United States, or a federal statute requires or provides otherwise, "the laws of the several states" shall "be regarded as rules of decision" in federal civil actions. This seemingly simple provision gave rise to a major question of construction. Did the reference to "laws of the several states" apply only to statutory and constitutional provisions, or did it also encompass the common law decisions of the state courts?

2. Rule of Swift v. Tyson. [§4.1200]

In *Swift v. Tyson* (1842), the Supreme Court held to the narrower view of the word "law," thus permitting federal courts to apply "federal common law" to matters not covered by state statutes, even though the federal common law might be substantially different from the common law of the courts of the forum state. The Supreme Court hoped that two major benefits would result from the *Swift* decision. First, all federal courts would follow federal decisions, thereby establishing uniformity among federal courts. Second, all state courts would follow the federal model, thereby establishing a single body of substantive law for the entire nation.

3. Difficulties With the Early Law. [§4.1300]

The hoped for benefits of the *Swift* decision did not materialize. First, the decision was held not to apply to a major category of cases, those involving so-called "local actions." These actions, among others, involved title to or injury to realty in the forum state, historically matters perceived by the states as being strictly within their judicial power [see **§2.7300**]. Thus, the possibility of uniformity among the federal courts was seriously eroded. Second, state courts failed to follow federal common law decisions. Indeed, in most situations the reverse was true; a federal court formulated its common law decisions on the basis of the state common law decisions in the jurisdiction in which the federal court sat, which often produced inconsistent results among the federal courts. Nevertheless, federal judges were free to and did sometimes exercise their power to ignore state decisions with which they did not agree. This had the predictable result of encouraging plaintiffs to "forum shop"—that is, to decide between a state and a federal forum on the basis of which tribunal was more likely to apply favorable substantive law. In extreme cases plaintiffs who could not prevail in state courts even changed domicile to create diversity of citizenship in order to benefit from favorable federal decisions.

a. Manipulative Techniques. [§4.1310]

A demonstration of the problems raised by the application of the *Swift* doctrine came in 1928 in *Black & White Taxicab Co. v. Brown & Yellow Taxicab Co.* (1928). A Kentucky corporation had contracted with a railroad for the exclusive right to provide taxi service at a particular station in Kentucky. Another taxicab company subsequently began operations at the same station, but because it was well settled under Kentucky law that exclusive contracts of this type were unenforceable, relief was unavailable to the first company in a state court action. Consequently, the Kentucky corporation was dissolved and another company under the same name was formed in Tennessee. The exclusive contract was assigned to the new company, which thereupon brought a federal diversity action to enjoin the competing taxicab company. The Supreme Court said that the issue was one of "general" law on which Kentucky law was not binding and that the common law as developed and applied by the federal courts permitted enforcement of the exclusive contract.

C. REVERSAL OF EARLY POSITION: THE *ERIE* DOCTRINE. [§4.2000]

In *Erie Railroad Co. v. Tompkins* (1938), the Supreme Court overruled the *Swift* decision and held that in the absence of explicit, governing federal law, a federal court must follow state common law decisions as well as state statutes and constitutional provisions. Justice Brandeis' opinion for the Court offered three reasons for disapproving *Swift* and reconstruing the word "laws" in Section 34 of the Judiciary Act of 1789 to embrace state rules of decision as declared by the forum state's courts. (1) Scholarly research indicated that the *Swift* construction of Section 34 was erroneous and that Congress in 1789 had intended that, except as to matters controlled by federal law, state law—written or unwritten—should be applied by the federal courts. (2) *Swift* had been a failure in that the hoped for national uniformity of law had not developed at either the state or the federal level. Indeed, *Swift* had resulted in a grave discrimination by non-citizens against citizens, since a non-citizen plaintiff, by selecting the forum, had the option of choosing between federal and state law. (3) The *Swift* interpretation of Section 34 (although not the statute itself) was unconstitutional.

1. Constitutional Basis. [§4.2100]

Although the Court's opinion does not specify which provision of the Constitution had been violated by the *Swift* interpretation of the Rules of Decision Act, it is clear from his references to rights reserved to the states that Justice Brandeis had in mind the Tenth Amendment, which preserves state power in areas not expressly delegated to the federal government by the Constitution. The Court found no basis in the Constitution for allowing federal courts to depart from the law of the forum state by declaring a general common law. Many commentators have been critical of Justice Brandeis' constitutional argument as unnecessary to the *Erie* decision and incorrect. They argue that it fails to give proper weight to the constitutional dimension of diversity jurisdiction and the independent status of the federal courts. They further contend that the federal government's power to create national courts, coupled with the Necessary and Proper Clause in Article I of the Constitution, should be read to permit federal courts to exercise the traditional power of courts to declare the common law. Their

109

view was reinforced by the fact that for 15 years following *Erie* the Supreme Court did not again refer to a constitutional basis for the *Erie* doctrine.

D. JUDICIAL DEVELOPMENT FOLLOWING THE *ERIE* DECISION. [§4.3000]

The *Erie* case involved a simple, purely substantive law question as to the obligations owed by a railroad to a person who walked along a path adjacent to its tracks. The Supreme Court offered no clues as to what law should apply to other types of issues that might be considered matters of state procedure but that might conflict with specific federal policies or practices.

1. The Outcome Determinative Test. [§4.3100]

In *Guaranty Trust Co. v. York* (1945), the Court, in an equity case, was called upon to determine whether or not to apply a state statute of limitations, which would bar plaintiff's action, or the more flexible rule of laches, which federal courts, prior to *Erie,* had traditionally applied in suits for equitable relief. The Supreme Court held that under *Erie* the state statute had to apply. In its opinion the Court stated that even though a federal tribunal was not bound to give the identical equitable relief that a state court would give [see **§4.3400–§4.3440**], it could not award any relief if the action would have been completely barred had it been brought in a state tribunal. The Court then went on, in apparent contradiction to what it had said about equitable remedies, to state that in diversity of citizenship cases, the outcome in a federal court should not differ materially from the result that would have ensued had the case been tried in a state forum.

a. Policies Underlying the Outcome Determinative Test. [§4.3110]

Three concerns led to the *York* outcome determinative test. First, the desirability of having a uniform application of substantive law within a state, embracing both state courts and federal courts sitting in diversity jurisdiction, clearly motivated the Supreme Court. Notice the complete abandonment of the *Swift* philosophy of achieving "horizontal" uniformity of the rules of decision. Second, a non-citizen plaintiff should not be able to forum shop for the more favorable law between federal and state courts in the same jurisdiction, which often are located only a city block apart. Third, it is fundamentally unjust to permit the result in a lawsuit to vary merely because the litigants come from different states, rather than the same state, and the dispute is adjudicated in a federal, rather than a state, tribunal.

b.   Deficiencies of the Outcome Determinative Test. [§4.3120]

A test that tries to determine whether the application or non-application of a particular rule might have substantial effect on the outcome of a case is very difficult to apply since prediction at the outset of a lawsuit may simply be guesswork. In addition, the *York* case's emphasis on the limited role of federal courts sitting in diversity jurisdiction appeared to destroy the independence and creativity of the federal courts in this class of cases and to reduce the federal court to what one federal judge referred to as "a ventriloquist's dummy." The *York* approach also created concern about the viability of the Federal Rules of Civil Procedure because almost any procedural rule might affect the outcome of a case if used in lieu of a different state practice. The specter of this result caused many commentators to criticize *York* sharply.

Illustration. [§4.3121] In *Ragan v. Merchants Transfer & Warehouse Co.* (1949), a federal diversity of citizenship suit was filed within the Kansas statute of limitations but process was not served until after the period had run. Kansas law required that service be made within the statutory period. The Supreme Court held that the action must be dismissed despite Federal Rule 3, which provides that a federal court action is commenced merely by filing the complaint. The Court concluded that applying the Federal Rule to the question whether the action was commenced within the limitation period would affect the outcome of the case—the federal court would hear a case that would not be heard in a state court. The federal court therefore would be enforcing a state-created right that no longer would be enforced by the state judiciary. [Further discussion of the *Ragan* case is found in **§4.3341**.]

---

c.   Misinterpretation of the Outcome Determinative Test. [§4.3130]

In retrospect, it seems clear that many courts and commentators overreacted to the *York* case. When carefully analyzed, the Supreme Court's opinion suggests a number of limitations on the outcome determinative principle that significantly moderated its threat to the independence of the federal courts and the viability of the Federal Rules. For example, Justice Frankfurter's opinion indicated that the federal courts could continue to administer the historic system of federal equitable remedies [see **§4.3400–§4.3440**], and his opinion has several passages indicating that the federal-state difference must **significantly affect the result** before the application of state practice becomes mandatory.

2. The Balancing Approach. [§4.3200]

The Supreme Court sought to clarify the scope of the *Erie* decision, and to lay to rest fears that *York* required a rigid application of the outcome test, in *Byrd v. Blue Ridge Rural Electric Cooperative, Inc.* (1958). The federal trial court in *Byrd* had submitted to the jury an issue that would have been decided by the judge had the case been tried in a state court. In upholding the lower court decision, the Supreme Court compared competing federal and state policies to determine whether the former were sufficient to overcome the desirability of a uniform practice in state and federal cases. The Court held that the strong policy favoring jury trial in federal courts (it did not rely directly on the Seventh Amendment's jury trial right) outweighed the state practice of allowing the judge to decide the particular issue. The result was easy to reach since the state practice appeared to have resulted from historical accident rather than reflect a substantial state policy. Articulating a broader principle, the Court said that state law "could not disrupt or alter the essential character or function of a federal court." The Court also emphasized that there was no reason to believe that a judge and a jury would come to a different conclusion on a particular issue, which meant that the nature of the trier could not be said to "significantly affect" the outcome. This also meant that following the federal practice would not produce forum shopping.

a. Difficulties With a Balancing Test. [§4.3210]

The balancing test set forth in *Byrd* has proved difficult to administer because there is no yardstick by which to weigh the "competing considerations." Every federal practice or procedural rule continued to be subject to challenge in a diversity case if the state rule differed. Conceivably, a Federal Rule could be held applicable in one state and inapplicable in another, depending upon the level of justification that could be found in each state for applying the competing local rule.

(1) Application of the Test: Personal Jurisdiction. [§4.3211]

The question of whether a federal court sitting in diversity must apply the forum state's long-arm statute or a federal standard for personal jurisdiction provides an interesting historical example of *Byrd's* balancing test. In *Jaftex Corp. v. Randolph Mills, Inc.* (1960), the Second Circuit held that federal policies emanating from the Article III grant of diversity jurisdiction, federal service of process provisions, subject matter jurisdiction and venue statutes, and Supreme Court decisions interpreting the due process limitations on state jurisdictional power justified following a federal standard for personal jurisdiction. The court also found that using a federal amenability standard was not outcome determinative, as a defendant always could be sued in her home state. In *Arrowsmith v. United Press International* (1963), however, the same court sitting en banc reversed direction. It found that although Congress could create a federal standard of personal jurisdiction, no statute or Federal Rule addressed the issue. Therefore, the court felt obliged to honor the local policies embodied in the personal jurisdiction statutes of the forum state. Subsequent amendments to Federal Rule 4 and surrounding case law have resolved this question in favor of applying the long-arm provisions of the forum state [see **§3.3600**].

(2) Application of the Test: Door–Closing Statutes. [§4.3212]

In *Szantay v. Beech Aircraft Corp.* (1965), the Fourth Circuit held that a district court in South Carolina may entertain a suit by an Illinois citizen against a Delaware corporation on a cause of action arising in Tennessee despite a South Carolina statute barring that class of "foreign" suits from its courts. The Fourth Circuit could not find a weighty state policy underlying the statute. On the other hand, it did find countervailing federal considerations, including the policy of avoiding discrimination against non-residents, embedded in the Article III grant of diversity jurisdiction, the philosophy inherent in the Full Faith and Credit Clause of maximum enforcement in each state of rights created by other states, the federal interest in encouraging efficient joinder in multiparty actions, and the general interest in providing a convenient forum for the adjudication of the plaintiff's action. Accordingly, the federal standard was applied.

3. The *Erie* Doctrine and the Federal Rules. [§4.3300]

The fears concerning the continued vitality of the Federal Rules in diversity cases under *York's* outcome determinative test, although somewhat assuaged by the balancing notions of *Byrd*, were not completely laid to rest until the Supreme Court decided *Hanna v. Plumer* (1965). The case involved a confrontation between then Federal Rule 4(d)(1), now Rule 4(e)(2), and a Massachusetts service-of-process statute requiring in-hand delivery. The Court abandoned the balancing test, holding clearly that a Federal Rule regulating procedure applies even in the face of a competing state rule, even when there may be strong state policy reasons underlying it.

a. Application of Federal Rule Not Outcome Determinative. [§4.3310]

The Supreme Court in *Hanna* allowed the action to proceed in federal court despite the fact that the method of serving process authorized by then Federal Rule 4(d)(1) would not have been permitted had the action been brought in a state court of Massachusetts. The Court, although recognizing that it could be plausibly argued that the application of the Federal Rule was outcome determinative (since the case would go forward in the federal court but not in a state court), nevertheless held that the outcome determinative test did not apply because there would be no difference in result as long as process was served in accordance with the rules of the chosen forum, whether that be state or federal. The same analysis would apply to other procedural matters and utilizations of the Federal Rules.

b. Reinterpretation of Erie Doctrine. [§4.3320]

The Supreme Court in Hanna indicated that the outcome determinative test should be applied with reference to the twin aims of *Erie,* which it described as (a) discouraging forum shopping and (b) avoiding the inequitable administration of the laws. As to the first, the difference between the two procedures for service of process clearly would not have been important enough to influence counsel's choice of a court in *Hanna* at the time the forum was chosen. Therefore, permitting federal practice to be followed did not create a realistic risk of encouraging forum shopping. As to the second, the Court made it clear that there must be a substantial alteration in the enforcement of the state-created right before the equal administration of the law considerations alluded to in *Erie* would arise. The minimal difference between the state and federal procedures for service of process involved in *Hanna* would not result in any significant benefit to a noncitizen who is able to choose between a state and a federal forum. Therefore, the application of the federal practice posed no risk of unequal administration of the law.

c. Federal Interest in Uniform Application of Federal Rules. [§4.3330]

According to the Supreme Court's alternative holding in *Hanna,* there is a strong federal interest in having a body of uniform procedural rules for the federal courts. This interest is reflected in the Rules Enabling Act [28 USC 2072], which is based on the Constitution's express grant of power to Congress to create federal courts as supported by the Necessary and Proper Clause. As a result, the constitutional problem referred to by Justice Brandeis in *Erie* [see **§4.2100**] is not present and the *Erie-York* analysis [see **§4.3100– §4.3130**] should not be employed when the application of a Federal Rule is at issue. Instead, the following analysis must be undertaken.

(1) The Scope of the Applicable Federal Rule Must Be Defined. [§4.3331]

The Federal Rule must first be analyzed to determine whether it actually conflicts with state law in the context of the case before the court. If the Rule actually has a narrower construction or scope than that contended for by the litigant seeking its application, there often will be no conflict with state law and both the federal and the state provisions may be applied.

Illustration: No Conflict between State and Federal Procedures. [§4.3331–1] Federal Rule 23.1 requires that the plaintiffs in a shareholder derivative suit have been stockholders in the corporation at the time of the events that form the basis of the action. A federal court sitting in a state that does not have a comparable "contemporaneous-ownership" requirement will apply Rule 23.1. Moreover, if the forum state requires that the plaintiff own a certain percentage or a minimum dollar value of the company's securities, that requirement will be enforced along with the contemporaneous-ownership requirement of Rule 23.1 since it is not in conflict with a Federal Rule and represents a significant state policy that should be honored under *Erie-York*.

Illustration: No Conflict Between State and Federal Procedures. [§4.3331–2] In the post-*Hanna* case of *Walker v. Armco Steel Corp.* (1980), the Supreme Court addressed whether Federal Rule 3 or a state statute determined when a federal action commenced for statute of limitations purposes. If the state law at issue applied, the statute of limitations would have barred the action. Following the *Ragan* decision [see **§4.3121**], the Court found that Federal Rule 3 functioned only as an internal timing mechanism for the Federal Rules and was not designed to measure time for determining whether a statute of limitations had run. The state statute, however, addressed when the state statute of limitations was to be tolled. Therefore, as the state statute at issue was broader in scope than Rule 3, the forum state's law applied, and the statute of limitations barred the action.

Illustration: Effect of Federal Judgment. [§4.3331–3] In *Semtek International, Inc. v. Lockheed Martin Corp.* (2001), the Supreme Court considered whether Federal Rule 41(b) governed the effect that state courts must give to federal judgments. Characterizing the Rule as a mere default provision regulating internal judicial procedures, the Court concluded that Rule 41(b) did not require state courts to bar cases that were dismissed under the Rule. The Court also noted that interpreting the Rule as governing the effects of federal judgments would arguably affect the substantive rights of parties and render it invalid [see **§4.3332**].

(2) **The Validity of the Federal Rule Must Be Determined.**
   [§4.3332]

   If a conflict does exist, the next step is to determine whether the Federal Rule represents a legitimate exercise of the rule-making power delegated to the Supreme Court by the Rules Enabling Act. In *Burlington Northern Railroad Co. v. Woods* (1987), the Court stated that the Federal Rules do not violate the Act if they incidentally affect the substantive rights of the parties and are reasonably necessary to maintain the integrity of the system of rules as a whole. Moreover, since the Federal Rules were approved by the Supreme Court's Rules Advisory Committee, the Judicial Conference, the United States Supreme Court itself, and not overriden by Congress, the results of this activity will be held constitutional and a proper exercise of the rule-making power unless it can be said that all of these groups were mistaken in their evaluation of a particular Rule's validity. To date, the Supreme Court has never invalidated a Federal Rule. If the Federal Rule is valid, it applies despite the conflict with state law.

Illustration. [§4.3332–1] In a personal injury diversity action in a federal court in State X, D seeks a physical examination of P under Federal Rule 35. P objects on the ground that physical examinations are not permitted in civil actions in the courts of State X and that Federal Rule 35 is invalid because it exceeds the Supreme Court's rule-making power. The physical examination will be ordered because Rule 35 is a valid regulation of procedure and does not transgress any substantive right. Because the Rule is valid, *Hanna* renders state practice irrelevant.

d. Vitality of Erie After Hanna. [§4.3340]

Insofar as basic state substantive rules of law are involved, the vitality of *Erie* is unimpaired by *Hanna*. This also is true of state procedural regulations that necessarily have an effect on outcome and do not conflict with any specific Federal Rule.

Illustration: Federal Rule Inapplicable. [§4.3341] The *Walker* Court held that the *Ragan* case (see §4.3331–2) was good law because Federal Rule 3 apparently was not intended to define commencement of a federal action for purposes of tolling state statutes of limitation. Since this is true, then state limitations provisions will continue to be applied in diversity cases for measuring state-created rights. This is sound since the state provision may reflect significant state policies. Moreover, ignoring the state provision may promote forum shopping.

Illustration: State Statutory Law Applicable. [§4.3342] In *Gasperini v. Center for Humanities, Inc.* (1996), the Supreme Court held that a federal court had to apply a state statutory standard for review of damage awards. The statute at issue required courts to use a less deferential standard of review when examining damage verdicts than at common law and to order a new trial when the recovery was excessive. Following *Hanna's* reinterpretation of the *Erie* doctrine, the Court found that if federal courts failed to apply the state standard, substantial variations in recovery would arise between federal and state courts, thereby undermining the twin aims of *Erie*—the discouragement of forum shopping and the avoidance of the inequitable administration of the laws. Therefore, just as *Erie* precluded a federal court from giving a state-created claim longer life than it would have had in a state court, so *Erie* precluded a recovery in federal court that was significantly larger than a recovery that a state court would have tolerated. Note that under this *Erie* analysis, federal courts must follow state statutory caps on damages.

e. **Vitality of Byrd After Hanna. [§4.3350]**

The *Byrd* analysis is still applicable to matters not directly dealt with in the Federal Rules.

Illustration. [§4.3351] P files suit in a federal district court in Kentucky but the action is barred by the Kentucky statute of limitations. P then sues in a federal district court in Virginia. Unfortunately, that state's statute of limitations had run while the original action was pending in Kentucky and a Virginia court would hold that the Virginia statute was not tolled by the Kentucky federal court action. Employing a *Byrd*-type analysis, it was held in *Atkins v. Schmutz Manufacturing. Co.* (1970), that the tolling effect of the pendency of an identical suit in another federal court was to be determined as a matter of federal, rather than state, law. The court, reasoning that Virginia's tolling rules were peculiar to the operation of the state court system, gave considerable weight to the fact that the federal courts are a unitary court system and should have their own rules for determining the effect of the pendency of an action. The court ultimately concluded that the Virginia federal action was merely a continuation of the suit begun in the Kentucky federal court.

Illustration. [§4.3352] P brings a products liability action against a manufacturer in federal district court in Texas. The manufacturer moves for summary judgment under a Texas discovery rule for measuring the statute of limitations period. P's cause of action accrued when she linked her symptoms to the product at issue. P urges that the federal court begin the running of the statute of limitations upon the filing of the suit, which is the custom among federal courts. The court applies a *Byrd*-type analysis to decide that the Texas discovery rule manifests a substantive policy decision by the Texas legislature, compelling the assertion of a right of action within a reasonable time. The court therefore decides that the policy rationale of Texas' discovery rule outweighs the countervailing considerations in favor of federal court uniformity.

Illustration. [§4.3353] P brings a diversity action against D in federal court asserting breach of contract and various business torts. The federal court dismisses P's action as barred by the forum state's statute of limitations [see **§4.3100**]. P then brings a state action against D in another state. The statute of limitations period in the second state does not bar P's claims. Upon review, the Supreme Court holds that the state court must apply federal law to determine the effect that must be given to the prior dismissal by the federal diversity court. The Court argued that there was a strong federal interest in determining the effect of all federal court judgments [*Semtek International, Inc. v. Lockheed Martin Corp.* (2001)].

4. Equitable Remedial Rights Doctrine. [§4.3400]

One of the interesting aspects of *Erie-York–Byrd* is the effect it has had on federal diversity cases in which equitable relief is sought.

a. Historical Background. [§4.3410]

The federal courts have a long history of applying principles of equity jurisprudence in diversity cases without reference to state law. Traditionally, once federal equity jurisdiction was properly invoked, the court could grant an equitable remedy pursuant to federal standards even though the remedy would not be available under state law. This principle was so firm that under the regime of *Swift v. Tyson* [see **§4.1200**], federal courts would refuse to apply a state statute when doing so would be inconsistent with the availability of a federal equitable remedy.

b. Current Status. [§4.3420]

The continued vitality of the equitable remedial rights doctrine is unclear today because the Supreme Court has not directly addressed the question of how the doctrine has been affected by *Erie, York*, and *Byrd*, or the promulgation of the Federal Rules.

c. Arguments against the Continued Vitality of the Doctrine. [§4.3430]

If the goal of the *Erie* doctrine is to require federal courts to treat state-created substantive rights in the same manner as would state courts, allowing a federal court to award a type of relief that is unavailable in a state court seems to affect the enforcement of that right in a material way. Moreover, an independent federal law of remedies might well encourage certain litigants to shop between

119

federal and state courts in the same state, thereby giving rise to an unequal administration of the law.

d. Arguments for the Vitality of the Doctrine. [§4.3440]

The outcome determinative test arguably applies only to the ultimate result of the litigation—who wins and who loses—not the nature or amount of the relief that may be granted. If this is true, the availability or unavailability of an equitable remedy does not "significantly affect" the result within the meaning of *York* [see **§4.3100**]. The Supreme Court's decision in *Gasperini* [see **§4.3342**], however, weakens this argument. In that case the potential for substantial variations between state and federal damage awards justified requiring a federal court to apply the forum state's statutory standard for review of verdicts. However, it may be argued that a federal court's power to award or withhold equitable relief is part of its "essential character or function" and represents a countervailing consideration of the type recognized in *Byrd* [see **§4.3200**].

5. Federal Rules of Evidence. [§4.3500]

The statutory status of the Federal Rules of Evidence makes it reasonably certain that their content would control in a diversity action on the basis of the *Hanna* decision.

E. SELECTING THE APPROPRIATE STATE LAW. [§4.4000]

After it has been decided that state substantive law must be applied to an issue in a diversity suit, the question remains as to which state's law is to be followed.

1. Law of the Forum State Applied. [§4.4100]

In *Klaxon Co. v. Stentor Electric Manufacturing Co.* (1941), the Supreme Court decided that the *Erie* doctrine requires a federal court to apply the same substantive law that a state court in the same jurisdiction would apply, including the forum state's choice of law rules. In *Erie* itself, the case was remanded to the New York federal court for the application of Pennsylvania law, the place of the alleged tort, presumably on the theory that New York state courts, in accordance with the New York conflict of laws rule, would have applied Pennsylvania law. The *Klaxon* decision eliminates forum shopping between state and federal courts in the same jurisdiction by preventing a federal court from applying its own choice of law rules, which could result in the application of the law of a state other than the one that would be applied if the action had been brought in a state court.

2. Application of the Forum's Conflicts Law. [§4.4200]

The federal courts are obliged to apply the forum state's conflicts principles in precisely the same manner as the state courts would. Thus, for example, if the forum state's conflicts principles require the application of the law of the place where the tort occurred, a federal court must decide how a court of the forum state would determine where the tort occurred and when called upon to do so, interpret the law of the other state as would a court of the forum state.

a. Application of *Klaxon* to Interpleader. [§4.4300]

In *Griffin v. McCoach* (1941), decided the same day as *Klaxon*, an administrator sued an insurance company in a Texas federal court to collect the proceeds of an insurance policy on the deceased's life. The company responded with a bill of interpleader, thereby bringing in other claimants to the proceeds. [Interpleader is discussed in **§8.4000–§8.4900**.] The policy had been issued in New York to members of a syndicate, three of whom subsequently assigned their interest to individuals who thereafter paid portions of the premiums. The Supreme Court held that if a Texas state court would apply that state's own unique rule regarding the assignment of insurance policies to an insurance contract that had been made in another state, a Texas federal court had to do the same and was not free to apply New York law. In *Griffin* the assignees were made parties to a suit in a federal court in Texas only because of a special nationwide service of process provision in the Federal Interpleader Act [see **§8.4760**]. Therefore, even though the assignees were not subject to the personal jurisdiction of a Texas state court without their consent, they were held by the federal court to be bound by whatever law a Texas state court would have applied in a case it probably never could have heard.

b. Criticism of Current Rule. [§4.4400]

The *Klaxon* result has been subject to intense criticism. Many writers feel that the federal courts, being national in character and outlook, are more likely to be neutral and disinterested than state courts in deciding questions of conflict of laws, and therefore are in a particularly advantageous position to develop a rational body of conflicts doctrine. These critics are willing to accept the forum shopping that would result when the federal court would apply a different body of law than would a state court in the same jurisdiction. Nonetheless, the Supreme Court reaffirmed the *Klaxon* rule in *Day & Zimmermann v. Challoner* (1975).

3. **Governing Law in Transferred Cases. [§4.4500]**

When an action has been transferred under 28 USC 1404(a) pursuant to a defendant's motion [see **§2.7630–§2.7632**], the transferee court must apply the same law as the original federal court would have applied. If it were otherwise, the defendant would attempt to forum shop for favorable law and the policy of *Klaxon* would be undermined. A change in forum therefore only means a change of courtrooms, not a change of governing law.

    a. **Unresolved Situations. [§4.4510]**

    It is still not settled definitively what law applies (a) when the plaintiff successfully makes a Section 1404(a) motion, (b) when the original court would have dismissed the action on grounds of forum non conveniens, (c) to the rights or liabilities of parties who are added after a transfer, and (d) when a transfer is granted under Section 1406(a) because of a lack of venue in the original forum [see **§2.7510**]. Reasonable arguments can be made for applying the law of either the original or the transferee forum in each of these situations.

    b. **Forum Selection Provisions. [§4.4520]**

    Federal courts must apply a federal standard when deciding whether to enforce forum selection provisions by transferring the case to the forum named in the contract. *Hanna* dictates that since the federal transfer statute, Section 1404(a), is sufficiently broad to cover the issue of forum selection, federal case law, not state contract law, should govern [*Stewart Organization, Inc. v. Ricoh Corp.* (1988)].

4. **Supplemental and Pendent Claims. [§4.4600]**

Although an argument can be made in favor of the application of federal law along the lines suggested in **§4.4400,** state law controls supplemental claims in the absence of any applicable federal statute, treaty, or constitutional provision. This result seems to be required by the policies underlying *Erie* and *York* and by the language of the Rules of Decision Act. [Supplemental and pendent claims are discussed in **§2.5000–§2.5640.**]

Illustration. [§4.4610] P, a railroad worker, sues D, his employer, under the Federal Employer's Liability Act for personal injuries received in the course of employment. In turn, D brings a third-party action against S, who owns land adjacent to the railroad's

---

right of way and is a co-citizen of the railroad, claiming indemnification for any liability the railroad may incur. Since the indemnification right is state-created, the *Erie-York* principle requires the application of state law to D's claim against S.

F. DETERMINING THE CONTENT OF THE APPLICABLE STATE LAW. [§4.5000]

After a federal court ascertains which state's law is applicable, the next step is to determine the content of that law.

1. Highest State Court Rulings. [§4.5100]

A federal court is bound by the relevant rulings of the highest court of the state and will look to these first for the governing principles of the forum state's substantive law. If a pronouncement of state law is handed down after the district court has decided a case, the federal court of appeals or the Supreme Court must apply the latest state precedent.

2. When No Rulings on Point Have Been Issued by the Highest State Court. [§4.5200]

When the state's highest court has not dealt with the point in issue, a federal court may consider the same source material that a state court would use in an effort to determine how the state's highest court would decide the case. This typically entails reliance on the decisions of lower state courts.

3. No Lower State Court Rulings. [§4.5300]

When there are no relevant judicial precedents, a federal court must "find" state law by examining relevant dicta in state court opinions or reason from rulings on analogous subjects. It also may look to scholarly writings or the law of other jurisdictions, particularly neighboring states. However, the federal court must choose the rule it believes the state court would choose, not the rule it would adopt for itself were it free to do so.

4. Anticipating a Change in State Law. [§4.5400]

Some federal courts have held that they can follow a recent state court's dictum discrediting an ancient ruling by the state's highest court or even disregard a state court decision that has been ignored, though not expressly overruled, in later state court opinions. However, there must be reason to believe the earlier case no longer is a sound precedent in the particular state.

a. Rationale of Practice. [§4.5410]

Unless a federal judge is permitted some flexibility in anticipating changes in state jurisprudence, a lawyer would forum shop based on whether an old or questionable state precedent was favorable to his or her client's position. For example, if the federal courts were bound to apply an archaic state precedent even though it might not be adhered to by a state court, a plaintiff's lawyer would choose a federal court if the ancient rule favored her client and a state court if it was unfavorable and its rejection was necessary for her client to prevail on the merits.

Illustration. [§4.5411] Plaintiff brought suit in a federal court in Mississippi for damages for personal injuries sustained as a result of the alleged negligence of defendant manufacturer in marketing a defective product purchased by the plaintiff from a retailer. The Mississippi rule, declared by the state supreme court almost 30 years earlier, had been that a manufacturer was not liable unless privity of contract existed between it and the user. Subsequently, however, adherence to privity has been rejected in most states and a recent dictum by the Mississippi Supreme Court indicated an awareness and approval of the movement away from that doctrine. The federal court should feel free to apply the modern rule.

---

5. Certification to State High Court. [§4.5500]

A final option for a federal court faced with a difficult issue of state law is to certify a question to the applicable state high court. The certification procedure enables a federal court to obtain an authoritative and binding statement on state law from the state's highest court. Certification is only available if the forum state's high court accepts such questions; most, but not all, states allow it, although the particulars of the procedure vary greatly by state. Finally, a federal court's invocation of the certification procedure does not guarantee a response. For various reasons, including an overburdened docket or the fact-dependent nature of the inquiry, state high courts often refuse to answer certification inquiries.

G. FEDERAL COMMON LAW. [§4.6000]

Extremely difficult problems of determining the applicable law arise when the substantive rights at issue have their source in federal law but questions are presented as to how to interpret that federal law, which may or may not be in statutory form, or how to fill in some of the gaps in coverage that often exist in federal statutes, treaties, or constitutional provisions. Since state-created rights are not in issue, the Rules of Decision Act [see **§4.1100**] and the *Erie* doctrine are not controlling and the federal court is free to develop federal common law.

1. Types of Common Law Distinguished. [§4.6100]

The federal common law now under discussion differs from the federal general common law applied by federal courts under the rule of *Swift v. Tyson* [see **§4.1200**] in three ways: (1) federal common law preempts state statutory as well as state decisional law; (2) if an issue is governed by federal common law, it is binding on both state and federal courts, not simply the latter; and (3) federal courts may apply federal common law only on matters of significant national concern that fall within the powers given the federal government by the Constitution.

Illustration. [§4.6110] In one significant case, the issue before the federal court was whether the water of an interstate stream had to be apportioned between two states. Because of the national interests involved, the Supreme Court held that this was a question of "federal common law," and the federal courts were not bound by the statutes or court decisions of either state.

---

2. State Law Sometimes Applied. [§4.6200]

State law may be applied by a federal court as federal common (or interpretive) law when a federal statute "incorporates" state law by specifying that the latter is to control. A federal court also may adopt state law, rather than develop federal common law: (1) if a substantial state interest exists, (2) as a matter of equity, (3) if federal and state law are closely interwoven, or (4) merely as a matter of convenience when federal law is silent on a particular matter. However, it must be remembered that since these applications of state law are not compelled by *Erie*, the federal court has much greater flexibility in utilizing and interpreting local law in these contexts than it does in pure diversity cases.

Illustration 1. [§4.6210] The Supreme Court has applied the federal common law of nuisance in an action between two states based on the pollution of a lake. However, it added that one state's high water quality standards might be deemed relevant so as not to compel that state to lower its standards to those of its neighbor.

Illustration 2. [§4.6220] If a federal statute creating a cause of action does not contain a limitations period, as a matter of convenience a federal court may use the forum state's statute of limitations that governs the most analogous cause of action.

Illustration. [§4.6230] The Supreme Court has incorporated state law into the federal common law that determines the effect that must be given to federal diversity judgments. The Court noted that state substantive laws were applied in these cases, making the need for a uniform federal rule less urgent.

---

3.   **When Resort to Federal Common Law Is Proper. [§4.6300]**

There is no easy formula for determining when a federal court should apply federal common law rather than the law of the forum state. The following sections illustrate some of the situations in which it has been appropriate for the federal courts to develop uniform national standards.

a.   **Foreign Relations. [§4.6310]**

A financial agent of the Cuban government brought suit in a federal court claiming the value of a certain shipment of sugar because the Cuban government had expropriated the shipment and all of the defendant corporation's other property. The Supreme Court held that as a matter of federal common law, the act-of-state doctrine prohibited challenging the Cuban expropriation decree. The Court reasoned that an issue involving a choice between the respective competence and functions of the judicial and executive branches in the field of foreign relations must be treated as exclusively within the ambit of federal law [*Banco Nacional de Cuba v. Sabbatino* (1964)].

b.   **Statutory Construction and Congressional Delegations. [§4.6320]**

Because statutes cannot be written with sufficient detail to cover every possible contingency, federal courts often are obliged to construe vague statutory terms or supply omitted elements and they do so as a matter of federal common law. Moreover, Congress occasionally may provide a skeletal statutory scheme and permit the federal courts to develop a detailed body of substantive federal common law under the legislation.

Illustration. [§4.6321] An employer sues a labor union in a state court for damages sustained as a result of an allegedly unauthorized strike. Congress has enacted a legislative scheme indicating a federal interest in industrial peace and a policy in favor of the smooth functioning of the collective bargaining process. The Supreme Court has held that the federal courts must fashion, from the legislative outline provided by the national labor laws, a body of substantive principles of federal labor law. Furthermore, state courts are obliged to apply this judicially created law, regardless of the content of local law [see **§4.7000**].

c.   **Proprietary Interests of the Federal Government. [§4.6330]**
Uniform federal law clearly is essential in determining and defining the government's property rights.

Illustration. [§4.6331] A check issued by the United States was stolen and cashed by means of a forged endorsement. The government then sued the bank that had presented the check for payment and had guaranteed prior endorsements. The Supreme Court ultimately held that the rights and duties of the United States on its commercial paper are to be governed by federal common law, not state law.

d.   **Matters Drawn by Implication from the Constitution. [§4.6340]**

In several substantive the federal courts have held that the Constitution implies the development of federal common law. Examples of these areas include controversies between states, admiralty, and Native American relations.

Illustration. [§4.6341] In 1985, an Indian tribe sued a county in New York State for violation of their possessory rights in their tribal land, stemming from an unlawful conveyance of the property in 1795. The Supreme Court noted that, under the Constitution's Indian Commerce Clause, disputes involving relations with Native Americans were exclusively the province of federal law. The Court

> ultimately held that the tribe could maintain a federal common law action for the violation of their rights.

4. Mixture of State and Federal Common Law. [§4.6400]

Occasionally, both state and federal common law will be applied in a single action.

> **Illustration. [§4.6410]** A bank sued to recover money A obtained by cashing federal bonds that had been stolen from the bank. One issue was whether the bonds, which were not yet mature but had been called in by the government for redemption, were "overdue." Another issue was whether A acted in good faith in redeeming the bonds. The Supreme Court held that the "overdueness" issue was governed by federal law since it went to the nature of the rights and obligations created by the United States' commercial instruments. But the burden of proof and good faith questions were considered to pertain to "essentially a private transaction" and had to be decided under the law of the state where the transaction took place.

5. Subject Matter Jurisdiction. [§4.6500]

Federal common law may be applied in both diversity and federal question cases. However, a case "arising under" federal common law presents a federal question that in and of itself provides a federal subject matter jurisdiction base and renders the existence of diversity of citizenship unnecessary [see **§2.2520**].

6. Personal Jurisdiction in Federal Question Cases. [§4.6600]

There is no federal common law regarding the exercise of personal jurisdiction over non-resident defendants. In a case arising under a federal statute that does not provide for nationwide service of process, the Supreme Court held that a federal court must apply the standard of amenability to process articulated in the long-arm statute of the state in which the action is located [*Omni Capital International, Ltd. v. Rudolf Wolff & Co.* (1987)] [see **§3.3610**]. That has been modified by rule amendment. If the state long-arm statute's jurisdictional reach is not coterminous with due process, Federal Rule 4(k)(2) authorizes federal courts to exercise federal question jurisdiction to the fullest extent permitted by the Constitution and statute if the defendant cannot be subject to the general jurisdiction of any state [see **§3.3620**]. [For a discussion of personal jurisdiction in diversity cases, see **§4.3211**.]

H. STATE ENFORCEMENT OF FEDERAL LAW. [§4.7000]

Because there is concurrent jurisdiction in the state and federal courts with regard to many federally created rights, state courts often are required to construe and apply federal law. This means that state courts must attempt to achieve results consistent with federal jurisprudence, which obliges them to act like federal courts in many respects. Not surprisingly, this practice occasionally is referred to as the inverse-*Erie* doctrine.

1. Federal Statutory Right. [§4.7100]

Congress has created several statutory causes of action that can be asserted in a state court—for example, actions under the Federal Employers' Liability Act. When a state court adjudicates a claim under a federal statute, the Supremacy Clause of the federal Constitution requires the application of federal law.

2. Federal Defense. [§4.7200]

A federally created right also may become relevant in a state court action when it is interposed as a defense to a claim based on the state law.

Illustration. [§4.7210] In a state court breach of contract action for non-payment of royalties due under a contract licensing the use of a federal copyright, the defendant asserts two defenses: (1) the copyright is invalid under the substantive tests prescribed by the federal Copyright Act, and (2) the plaintiff's copyright has been used in violation of the federal antitrust laws. Federal law will control the two defenses.

---

3. Federal Interest. [§4.7300]

Federal law also may become relevant in state court litigation because the action involves a federal interest or policy or because a party has asserted a constitutional right.

4. State Procedure. [§4.7400]

The Supreme Court has stated that a state court may use its own procedural rules even though a federally created claim is being litigated. However, to prevent state procedure from being applied to subvert federal substantive law, the Supreme Court has placed limits on the use of some state procedural rules, particularly in FELA actions. For example, in one FELA case, the Supreme Court has held that a state court may not apply its usual rule that pleadings are to be construed strictly against the pleader.

Illustration. [§4.7410] In *Dice v. Akron, Canton & Youngstown R. Co.* (1952), the Supreme Court held that in a FELA case a state could not follow its practice of allowing the court, sitting without a jury, to decide whether a release is invalid because of fraud. Trial by jury was found to be too substantial a part of the substantive rights accorded railroad workers by the federal statute. Note that the effect of this holding is to require state courts to adhere to federal notions of the judge-jury relationship. *Dice* should be compared with the Supreme Court's decision in *Byrd v. Blue Ridge Rural Electric Cooperative, Inc.* [see **§4.3200**], which held that federal courts in diversity cases need not honor state judge-jury practices but were free to adhere to their own procedures.

UNIT TWO

PRETRIAL PROCESS

*

CHAPTER V

MODERN PLEADING

A. MODERN PLEADING: INTRODUCTION. [§5.0000]

At common law the pleadings were central to the procedural system and were relied upon to **give notice** to the opposing party, **crystallize the issues,** and **identify the relevant facts.** Modern procedural systems have reduced the importance of the pleading process by relying on discovery, pretrial conferences, and summary judgment to perform many of the functions formerly discharged by the pleadings.

B. PURPOSES OF PLEADING. [§5.1000]

Contemporary pleading systems are designed to provide a basis for eliminating legally defective contentions and to notify the litigants and the court of each party's allegations regarding a case.

1. Elimination of Legally Defective Contentions. [§5.1100]

Effective utilization of the pleadings allows the court to dismiss alleged claims and defenses that have no legal significance, thus avoiding the unnecessary expenditure of time, energy, and money.

Illustration 1. [§5.1110] P alleges that he was injured when D gave P a vicious, dirty look. Under the applicable substantive law, P has no right to redress for injuries of this type. The court, on motion of D, will dismiss the case immediately.

Illustration 2. [§5.1120] P alleges that he was injured when he was struck intentionally by D. In response, D alleges that P is an atheist. Since P's religious beliefs do not provide D with a defense

---

to P's claims, the court, on P's motion, will strike the purported defense so that it will form no part of the parties' preparation and presentation of the case.

2. Notice to Opposing Party. [§5.1200]

Pleadings inform a party of what the opposing party intends to prove, thereby **eliminating surprise** and allowing the parties **a fair opportunity to prepare for trial.**

Illustration. [§5.1210] X is struck by an automobile driven by Y, who was making a delivery for Y's employer, Z. Y immediately quits his job without telling Z about the accident. Thereafter, X sues Z. X's pleading should inform Z how Z might be liable for the injuries to X.

3. Notice to Court. [§5.1300]

Pleadings inform the court of the matters in dispute, thereby narrowing the scope of pretrial preparation and trial, and enabling the court to make appropriate rulings on matters of discovery and evidence.

Illustration. [§5.1310] P alleges that she incurred medical expenses and experienced pain and suffering as a result of an automobile accident that occurred because of D's negligent driving. D responds admitting the negligent driving but disputing the amount of P's damages. At trial, P seeks to introduce evidence showing that D was negligent. The court may reject this evidence since D has admitted negligence and hence there is no dispute about it.

C. TYPES OF PLEADINGS. [§5.2000]

The types and sequence of the pleadings are as follows.

1. Complaint. [§5.2100]

Plaintiff files a complaint stating one or more claims against defendant.

2. Answer. [§5.2200]

Defendant files an answer denying or admitting specific allegations in the complaint and adding allegations regarding any defenses defendant may have.

3. Counterclaims, Cross–Claims, and Third–Party Claims. [§5.2300]

Defendant may also file a counterclaim, which sets forth any claims defendant has against plaintiff. Defendant also may file a cross-claim, which is a pleading setting forth any claims defendant has against a co-defendant in the action. Or, defendant may file a third-party complaint against someone defendant believes may be liable to defendant if defendant is held to be liable to plaintiff.

4. Answer to New Claims. [§5.2400]

A party against whom a counterclaim, cross-claim, or third-party claim is asserted files an answer to such a pleading denying any untrue allegations and setting forth any available defenses.

5. Reply. [§5.2500]

In some courts there must be a reply to any affirmative allegations contained in an answer. In most jurisdictions, however, **a reply is not required** unless specifically ordered by the court. In these jurisdictions allegations in the answer are treated as having been denied or avoided.

6. Demurrer. [§5.2600]

In a few jurisdictions, a demurrer, which is **a challenge to the legal sufficiency** or to the form of another pleading, is itself considered a pleading. Most courts, however, use the term "pleading" to cover only those listed in **§5.2100** to **§5.2500.**

D. GENERAL PLEADING REQUIREMENTS. [§5.3000]

In the United States there are essentially two basic systems of pleading: One is known as "fact" pleading, and is utilized by state courts that follow the so-called **"code pleading" system** first adopted in New York and California in the middle of the nineteenth century and followed in most jurisdictions until the late 1930's. The other is known as **"notice pleading,"** and is practiced in the federal courts and those state courts that have adopted procedures similar to the Federal Rules. Notice pleading does away with the formalities of previous pleading systems, which were used to force a plaintiff to narrow the issues before coming to court, and instead allows the discovery process to frame the issues in dispute.

1. Requirements of Notice Pleading. [§5.3100]

Under Federal Rules 8(a) and 8(b), and their state counterparts, a pleader need only set forth "**a short and plain statement of the claim showing that the pleader is entitled to relief**" or a short and plain statement of any defense. If a plaintiff does not put forth a sufficient claim, his claim can be dismissed pursuant to Federal Rule 12(b)(6) and its state counterparts for failure to state a claim upon which relief can be granted. At the federal court level, the oft-cited rule, stemming from *Conley v. Gibson* (1957), is that "a complaint should not be dismissed for failure to state a claim unless it appears beyond doubt that the plaintiff can prove no set of facts in support of his claim which would entitle him to relief." A recent Supreme Court case, *Bell Atlantic Corp. v. Twombly* (2007), has called this language in *Conley* into question [see **§5.3421**]. Yet in a per curiam opinion in *Erickson v. Pardus* (2007), issued after *Twombly*, the Court cited *Twombly* quoting *Conley v. Gibson* to reiterate that FRCP 8(a)(2) "requires only 'a short and plain statement of the claim showing that the pleader is entitled to relief.' Specific facts are not necessary; the statement need only 'give the defendant fair notice of what the . . . claim is and the grounds upon which it rests.' " It is thus necessary to be aware of *Twombly* and the fact that there is some confusion as to just what it stands for.

a.   Sufficiency of Notice. [§5.3110]

Allegations under a notice pleading regime must adequately inform the opposing party as to the nature of a legally cognizable claim or defense. If the allegations do not do so, the pleading may be challenged as insufficient.

Illustration. [§5.3111] P files suit against D, alleging as follows: "On or about December 1, 1960, P entered into a contract with X to purchase Greenacre for the sum of $50,000. Both P and X complied with all the requirements of the contract. Thereafter, on or about February 10, 1975, D committed a trespass on Greenacre, all to the damage of P in the amount of $12,000." Under code pleading rules the complaint would be defective in that ownership is alleged only by evidentiary facts and "trespass" would be considered a conclusion of law. Under notice pleading rules, however, the complaint would be held sufficient, since P has adequately notified D of the precise date of the offense and its general nature.

Illustration. [§5.3112] P alleges a claim for relief that could be allowed under either a contract or tort theory. D's answer contains an allegation that "P's claim is barred by the statute of limitations."

Although P is informed as to the nature of the defense, there is no way of telling if the defense goes to relief under the contract theory, the tort theory, or both. A motion for a more definite statement thus would appear to be appropriate. However, in many jurisdictions P is not required to reply to D's allegations which are taken as denied; in that situation the motion will be denied.

b. Relationship Between Notice Pleading, Discovery, and Sanctions. [§5.3120]

The rules of notice pleading, sanctions, and discovery may give competing incentives to plead with particularity and may influence how a plaintiff will plead. In the federal courts, Rule 8, which allows alternative and hypothetical pleading and only requires the plaintiff to put the defendant on notice, gives very little incentive to plead with particularity, since most issues can be refined in discovery. However, the mandatory disclosure requirements of Rule 26 [see **§9.2400**], gives a plaintiff some incentive to narrow the issues right away. Moreover, Rule 11 [see **§5.3311**], imposes sanctions for frivolous claims and allegations that are not likely to have evidentiary support after a reasonable opportunity for discovery. Thus, Rule 8 does not require particularity, but Rule 26 encourages it, and Rule 11 prevents abuse.

c. Motion for More Definite Statement Available When a Responsive Pleading Required. [§5.3130]

A pleading may be sufficient generally to notify the opposing party and yet be so vague as to some details that the **opposing party cannot frame a required answer or reply.** Only in this relatively unusual situation will the opposing party be able to move successfully for a more definite statement to secure greater specificity [see Federal Rule 12(e)].

2. Requirements of Code Pleading. [§5.3200]

Under the typical code pleading standard, each party is required to allege a **"statement of facts setting forth a cause of action or defense** in ordinary and concise language."

a. Meaning of "Facts." [§5.3210]

Perhaps no question has been the subject of more litigation, with less definitive or satisfactory results, than the determination of what are "facts" for code pleading purposes. This is the major reason why many jurisdictions have switched to a notice-pleading system.

(1) The Required "Facts" Are "Ultimate Facts," Not Evidence. [§5.3211]

Under the code system, a party is not permitted to plead evidence; only the "ultimate" facts may be set forth. The purpose of this rule is to avoid "book length" pleadings that detail every minute fact that might bear on the resolution of the case. Unfortunately, however, the distinction between ultimate facts and evidentiary facts has never been quite clear to courts and lawyers, although it can be drawn in simple situations.

Illustration. [§5.3211–1] A vital fact in a trespass action is whether P is the owner of the land. P alleges that for 25 years she has openly and exclusively occupied the land and has exercised all rights of ownership including payment of taxes. This pleading technically is improper because P has alleged facts by which title can be proven, not the ultimate fact, which is simply that "P is the owner" of the land in question.

---

(2) Conclusions of Law Are Not "Ultimate Facts." [§5.3212]

A party is not permitted to plead conclusions of law. The purpose of this limitation is to ensure that the court and the parties will receive notice of the matters that are involved in the case as opposed to a simply uninformative statement such as "defendant is liable to plaintiff." Not only has the distinction between ultimate facts and conclusions of law been the subject of constant litigation, but the courts often cannot agree on how to classify certain basic allegations. In most situations a pleader simply must rely on common sense and on what the courts in the particular jurisdiction have determined to be "facts" in prior cases.

Illustration 1. [§5.3212–1] P sues D on the basis of the negligent acts of D's employee, who, it is alleged, "was operating within the scope of his employment." Although the allegation appears to be clearly an ultimate fact, at least some courts have held that

---

because "scope of employment" has legal overtones, the allegation is an improper conclusion of law. Note, however, that any more detailed allegation seems to run afoul of the rule against pleading evidence [see §5.3211].

Illustration 2. [§5.3212–2] P alleges only that "D is liable to P for money due and unpaid." This allegation is a classic example of an improper conclusion of law since it gives none of the operative facts showing why liability exists and states only the legal consequences. Even so, one could argue that the statement is simply an allegation of fact, and indeed, the ultimate fact in the case.

b. Meaning of "Cause of Action" or "Defense." [§5.3220]

In a code pleading jurisdiction, a pleader must allege **every essential factual element** required by the substantive law to justify relief or to establish a defense [see §5.3200].

Illustration. [§5.3221] P, in an action for personal injuries, alleges that "D struck P in the face, causing P substantial pain and suffering and further causing P damages in the form of medical expenses." The complaint fails to allege that D's act was either intentional or negligent. Without an allegation of legal wrongdoing, the complaint fails to state a cause of action and can be challenged by the opposing party.

c. Consequences of Improper Pleading of Facts. [§5.3230]

Courts have developed two separate approaches regarding improper fact pleading, one more stringent than the other. Recent decisions take the more liberal view, particularly with regard to the pleading of evidence.

(1) Strict View: Improper Allegations Ignored. [§5.3231]

In a number of decisions, courts have refused to consider conclusions of law in a pleading and, to a lesser extent, the pleading of evidence. If the allegations improperly pleaded are essential to state a cause of action or defense, the pleading is considered deficient and subject to challenge by the opposing party at any time before or during trial.

(2) Liberal View: Improper Allegations Subject Only to Challenge for Uncertainty. [§5.3232]

If a pleading, as a whole, notifies the opposing party as to the claims or defenses being advanced, many courts take the position that improperly pleaded allegations can be challenged only if they are indefinite. Moreover, such a challenge is waived if not raised at the earliest opportunity.

> **Illustration. [§5.3233]** P alleges that "D slandered P by stating that P had embezzled $100,000 from D." Publication to a third person, which is a vital element of slander, is not specifically alleged. However, the allegation of "slander," which is a conclusion of law, necessarily implies publication. Under the liberal view, the conclusion of law can be challenged by D only for being uncertain. If D fails to make a challenge at the earliest opportunity permitted by local rules, the pleading will be upheld as stating a cause of action, since D has been notified sufficiently as to the nature of P's cause of action.

3. Truth and Consistency Required in All Pleadings. [§5.3300]

Every jurisdiction requires that all pleadings be made in good faith. Bar Association Cannons of Ethics invariably state that attorneys may not file false pleadings for any reason, including harassment, delay, or tactical advantage. This requirement of truth and consistency in pleading yields the requirement of signatures and the verification of pleadings.

a. Signature of Attorney or Party. [§5.3310]

Most jurisdictions require the attorney to sign the pleadings, thereby certifying that he or she has read them and reasonably believes them to be interposed in good faith. (A party who is handling his or her own case without an attorney signs in place of an attorney.) In other courts, the party may sign the pleadings, which means that the attorney need be less concerned about the truth of the facts stated. However, an attorney cannot file pleadings that are known to be false.

(1) Federal Court Requirements. [§5.3311]

Federal Rule 11, which contains the signature rule requirement for federal pleadings, motions, and other papers, has undergone significant changes since 1983. Until that time, courts could impose sanctions only when the moving party could show that the attorney did not believe there were good grounds to support the allegations in the pleading. This subjective standard proved unworkable in practice, and was replaced by an objective standard in 1983 when the rule was amended. [See *Business Guides, Inc. v. Chromatic Communications Enterprises, Inc.* (1991) (rejecting a "good faith" standard and applying a "reasonableness under the circumstances" test).] Additionally, the amended rule made sanctions mandatory when a violation occurred, but left determination of the appropriate sanction up to the trial judge and provided for a larger range of sanctions. Rule 11 was **amended again in 1993** to address the dramatic increase in motions for sanctions. The imposition of sanctions was made discretionary by the 1993 amendment. The difficult determination of whether sanctions should be calibrated to deter unprofessional conduct or to compensate harassed litigants was resolved in favor of deterrence. Thus, awarding attorney's fees has diminished as the sanction of choice, and fines paid into court correspondingly have increased. The amended rule also includes a **safe-harbor** provision, requiring a party to submit a sanctions motion to an opponent first, then allowing the opponent 21 days to withdraw the offending document before the motion is filed with the court. Finally, in contrast with previous versions, the current Rule 11 makes the **signature obligation a continuous one**, so that a party must stop advocating a pleading or motion that is frivolous or without evidentiary support, even if it was non-frivolous or likely to have evidentiary support when signed. For example, if a defendant denied an allegation for lack of information but later obtains information sufficient to form a belief that the allegation is true, the defendant should not continue to insist on that denial. In general, a court will be less forgiving with respect to improper legal contentions, as opposed to improper factual contentions, because a lawyer has no excuse for insufficient knowledge of the law.

b. Verification. [§5.3320]

A verified pleading is one that is sworn under oath to be true. However, verification of pleadings is not required in all jurisdictions; indeed many jurisdictions do not provide for verification at all.

(1) Verification Usually at Plaintiff's Discretion. [§5.3321]

In courts that provide for verification, plaintiff usually has the choice to verify or not verify the complaint. If he verifies the

141

complaint, all subsequent pleadings must be verified. **Voluntary verification has two tactical advantages**: (a) all subsequent pleadings must be verified; (b) a simple one sentence general denial [see §5.5210] is prohibited. **There are, however, tactical disadvantages of voluntary verification.** A pleading verified by a party is considered a statement of fact that can be introduced into evidence by an opponent at trial. Unverified pleadings are considered allegations, not statements of fact, and generally are not admissible. **The utility of voluntary verification is questionable** since attorneys and parties have an ethical obligation to be truthful in their pleadings at all time. It is thus questionable whether verification adds anything of substance to the pleading process. Indeed, if verification is designed to guarantee that the pleadings are made in good faith, it could be implied that a non-verified pleading need not be in good faith. It is for this reason that FRCP 11 and some state rules provide only that all pleadings must be signed.

Illustration. [§5.3321–1] P sues D on an overdue note. The transaction is a simple one and D has no defense. P knows, however, that D wants to delay paying P for another six months. P will verify the complaint forcing D to answer each allegation specifically and under oath. Although D might have been willing to file a general denial in order to delay a decision in the case, he will be far less likely to commit perjury by denying under oath specific facts that he knows to be true.

Illustration. [§5.3321–2] P, who was injured in an accident, files a verified complaint erroneously alleging that X was the driver of D's vehicle. At trial P identifies Y as the driver. D will introduce P's complaint to refute P's testimony. Although P can explain that he erred in the complaint, the error, made under oath, casts doubt on his credibility and tends to prejudice the jury against him.

---

(2) Verification Required in Particular Actions [§5.3322]

Some jurisdictions require verification in various types of actions. These may be cases in which parties are more likely to be untruthful (e.g., divorce cases) or in which the institution of suit could be used as a form of coercion to secure a quick settlement (e.g., shareholder derivative actions).

(3) **Violation of Signature or Verification Requirements. [§5.3323]**

A pleading that is not signed or verified as required will be stricken on the motion of an opposing party. However, the defect can be cured by amendment [see **§5.9000**] and will be deemed **waived** unless raised at the earliest opportunity. A false verification could result in prosecution for perjury, but such a severe sanction is rarely, if ever, applied. An attorney who signs or verifies in bad faith may be disciplined by the Bar Association and could be suspended from practice. If a party is guilty of false verification or signing in bad faith, the party's pleading may be stricken, and that party will lose the case (such a sanction should not, however, be applied if the attorney, and not the party, is at fault).

c. **Allegations Based on Information and Belief. [§5.3330]**

Because a party or attorney often cannot be certain of the facts at the pleading stage, nearly all jurisdictions permit pleadings that state certain allegations or denials are based on information and belief. Pleadings containing these allegations, if made in **good faith**, may be verified. However, there is **an exception**: a pleading cannot be based on information and belief if the pleader knows the facts, has the ability to ascertain the facts, or the facts are a matter of public record. An allegation or denial improperly based on information and belief will be ignored in determining whether or not an issue has been raised or admitted.

d. **Alternative and Inconsistent Allegations. [§5.3340]**

In general, a party may plead alternative or inconsistent claims if they are made in good faith. This liberality reflects the reality that a pleader may be uncertain as to the facts at the beginning of litigation and should be allowed to "hedge his or her bets."

Illustration. [§5.3341] In an action to recover an alleged loan of $10,000, in a first defense, D alleges that P made a completed gift of the money to D. In a second defense, D claims that the $10,000 was in payment for services rendered by D to P. As long as D may allege in good faith that the facts support both theories, D may allege both and pursue both at trial.

---

(1) **Minority Rule: Election at Trial. [§5.3342]**

Some courts require an election between inconsistent facts or theories prior to submission to the trier of fact. The great majority of courts, however, permit the case to go forward without an election and allow the trier of fact to decide between the facts or theories, since it is unfair to force a party who is acting in good faith to abandon what may be a meritorious allegation.

Illustration. [§5.3342–1] P claims damages for injuries to her father in an auto collision. Shortly after the collision her father dies. Under the applicable law, if the death occurred due to the accident, P's remedy is solely under a wrongful death statute; if the death was unconnected with the accident, P can recover only under a survival statute. The cause of death is subject to conflicting evidence. If P must choose between her allegation that death occurred due to the accident and her inconsistent allegation that death occurred due to other causes, there is a risk that she may pick the wrong allegation and will recover nothing even if D's negligence is clear. However, if the trier of fact is allowed to decide the cause of death, P can obtain a verdict whichever way the decision is made.

---

(2) Separate Statements: Two Basic Views. [§5.3343]

In some code pleading jurisdictions inconsistent allegations cannot be made in a single paragraph. Inconsistent allegations must be made in separate "counts," each giving a complete statement upon which relief may be granted. However, Federal Rule 10(b) and many state rules provide for separate statements only when they facilitate a clear presentation of the case. An opposing party may move for a separate statement if this general guideline has been abused.

4. Matters Subject to Special Pleading Rules. [§5.3400]

It is important to note that many jurisdictions have idiosyncratic rules regarding the pleading of particular facts. The most significant of these special provisions is illustrated by Federal Rule 9, which is generally followed in states that have adopted notice-type pleading. The rule requires special pleading of fraud and mistake and special damages.

a. Fraud and Mistake. [§5.3410]

Federal Rule 9(b), and its many state counterparts, requires the complaint to set forth with particularity the circumstances underlying an allegation of fraud or mistake. This requirement of particularity does not apply to allegations of malice, intent, knowledge, or other states of mind. Rule 9(b) appears to require more than the usual "notice" standard. Some of the reasons for the heightened pleading burden are that allegations of fraud are easy to make and hard to disprove and can be very damaging to a person's or business' reputation. Yet another reason why requiring detailed pleading of fraud and mistake is justified is that these grounds normally are asserted to avoid or rescind written agreements. Since the law favors enforcement of written private arrangements, actions to avoid contractual obligations and consequences should not be lightly entertained without special assurances that the plaintiff can present facts to support the relief sought. Courts in notice pleading jurisdictions typically interpret their versions of Rule 9(b) liberally so as to uphold very general allegations, negating much of the rule's possible impact. Most courts prefer discovery to the pleadings as a means of obtaining detailed information necessary to eliminate non-meritorious cases or to prepare for trial. However, in recent years, the federal courts have tended to demand **highly specific pleading** under Rule 9(b), to deter nuisance suits and suits filed solely for discovery purposes.

(1) Securities Fraud Legislation Governing Pleading. [§5.3411]

In 1995, Congress, dissatisfied with the application of Rule 9(b) in securities fraud cases, enacted the Private Securities Litigation Reform Act. It requires a plaintiff to set forth sufficient detail to show that it is at least as likely as any other explanation that defendant acted intentionally when it distributed misinformation to the public [see *Tellabs, Inc. v. Makor Issues and Rights, Ltd.* (2007)]. Moreover, under the Act plaintiff must specify each misleading statement and the reason why it is misleading.

b. Other Heightened Pleading Rules. [§5.3420]

There has been some tendency in the federal courts to apply heightened pleading standards even in some types of cases not mentioned in Rule 9(b), such as civil rights and governmental liability, as a means of **managing increasingly crowded dockets.** However, with the possible exception of antitrust cases [see *Bell Atlantic Corp. v. Twombly* (2007)], the Supreme Court has affirmed and reaffirmed that notice pleading is the standard to which Rule 9(b) is a specific, narrow exception [*Swierkiewicz v. Sorema, N.A.* (2002)].

(1) Heightened Pleading Standards in Antitrust Cases. [§5.3421]

In *Bell Atlantic Corp. v. Twombly* (2007), the Supreme Court held that plaintiffs in antitrust cases under the Sherman Act must put forth "a complaint with enough factual matter (taken as true) to suggest that an agreement was made." A pleading merely alleging interdependence or parallel conduct of defendants is insufficient. Given language in *Twombly* decrying the cost of discovery in frivolous cases involving complex issues, it is as yet unclear the extent to which *Twombly* may require the pleading of detailed facts in other types of actions [see **§5.3100**].

c. Conditions Precedent. [§5.3430]

Federal Rule 9(c) reflects the pleading rule generally applied in contract actions in both notice pleading and code pleading jurisdictions. Under that rule, the plaintiff need only plead generally his or her performance of all conditions precedent in the contract. The purpose of the rule is to **eliminate** from the pleadings, and hence from trial, **matters about which there is no dispute.** It is the defendant's obligation to specify in the answer those conditions, if any, that the plaintiff allegedly failed to meet. The plaintiff need then introduce evidence only as to those issues that the defendant has raised. There is no need for the plaintiff to waste time proving performance of conditions that the defendant concedes were met.

(1) Exception: Excuse for Performance. [§5.3431]

When the plaintiff intends to rely on an excuse for performance, rather than on performance itself, courts have divided on whether the plaintiff may rely on a general pleading of performance or whether the excuse must be pleaded in the complaint. The decision turns on whether the court believes that a general allegation of performance provides sufficient notification that the plaintiff may introduce evidence of an excuse at trial.

d. Special Damages. [§5.3440]

Federal Rule 9(g) states the general rule applicable in all jurisdictions that the plaintiff cannot collect special damages unless they have been specifically pleaded. Special damages are those that are recoverable under the relevant substantive law, but would not usually be suffered in the type of case pleaded. General damages, which need not be specifically pleaded, are damages that normally flow from the cause of action alleged. The obvious purpose of the special damage rule is to ensure that the defendant is not surprised at trial by evidence of damages that he had no reason to suspect had been incurred.

> **Illustration 1: Tort Action. [§5.3441]** P sues D for personal injuries suffered in an auto collision. P seeks to recover for pain and suffering, for doctor and hospital bills, and for the costs of a housekeeper required to care for him during the period of recovery. P can collect for pain and suffering under a general allegation of injury, but P cannot collect for the other items unless he specifically pleads them in the complaint. If P is not certain of the ultimate total amount of the medical bills, he may so state in the complaint and will be permitted to amend when the bills are received.

> **Illustration 2: Contract Action. [§5.3442]** P sues D for the latter's failure to deliver a rental car as promised. P had specifically informed D that failure to deliver would result in P's loss of a $5,000 fee. In order for P to collect the $5,000, P must plead specifically the notice to D and the subsequent loss, since this type of loss is not a normal result of the breach of a car rental agreement.

E. REQUIREMENTS OF THE COMPLAINT. [§5.4000]

In addition to the general requirements relating to the detail with which the claim or cause must be stated, a complaint must meet some specific pleading requirements. These vary somewhat among jurisdictions, although most courts follow the same pattern as to basic matters.

1. Statement of Subject Matter Jurisdiction in Federal Courts. [§5.4100]

In the federal courts, the basis of the court's subject matter jurisdiction must be set forth in the complaint. This rule stems from the fact that federal courts have **limited jurisdiction,** and a federal court, on its own motion, must dismiss a case if federal jurisdiction does not exist [see **§2.1220**]. However, the Supreme Court has held that the district court may dismiss a case for lack of personal jurisdiction over the defendant without first deciding a difficult question of subject matter jurisdiction. State courts normally do not require a jurisdictional statement in the complaint; if a case is brought in an improper court within a state, it merely will be transferred to another court within the state that has jurisdiction, except in those rare situations when federal jurisdiction is exclusive [see **§2.1300**].

2. Statement of Claim. [§5.4200]

As noted previously [see **§5.3220** and **§5.3100**], a plaintiff must allege sufficient information to establish a right to relief. The question of what is

147

sufficient depends upon the particular requirements of the substantive law or laws that are involved, and the way in which the particular jurisdiction allocates the burden of pleading among the various issues that are presented by the action.

a. **Complaint Generally Must Allege Matters Upon Which Plaintiff Has Burden of Proof. [§5.4210]**

Generally speaking, the plaintiff's burden of pleading follows the burden of proof. Thus, if a matter is one that the defendant must prove as a defense, the plaintiff normally need not raise the issue in the complaint; the burden of pleading is on the defendant who must raise the issue in the answer.

(1) **Exceptions. [§5.4211]**

In a few cases, in some jurisdictions, the plaintiff must plead the nonexistence of defenses on which the defendant has the burden of proof. These are usually matters that must be pleaded if the complaint is to make sense or in order to show that the plaintiff has seriously considered fundamental aspects of the law prior to making the claim.

Illustration 1. [§5.4211–1] P sues D on an overdue note. Payment generally is considered a defense that must be proved by defendants, who normally have receipts showing payment and are in the best position to come forward with the evidence. However, without an allegation of non-payment the complaint would not make sense. Therefore, P must allege nonpayment even though D has the burden of showing that payment has been made.

Illustration 2. [§5.4211–2] P sues D for defamation. The fact that D's statements were true is a defense, which in most jurisdictions D must plead and prove. Some courts, however, require P to allege in the complaint that the statements were false, even though the burden of proving truth remains on D. The purpose is to force plaintiffs to consider the matter of truth before filing suit, in the hope that frivolous defamation actions can be avoided.

---

(2) Caveat: Burdens of Pleading and Proof Vary Among Jurisdictions. [§5.4212]

The burdens of pleading and proof, although generally the same from jurisdiction to jurisdiction, may vary with respect to specific issues.

Illustration. [§5.4212–1] P sues D for personal injuries resulting from D's negligence. Although in most jurisdictions P's contributory negligence is a defense that will be in issue only if raised by D in the answer, in a number of courts P has the obligation to plead and prove the lack of contributory negligence in order to recover.

---

3. Prayer for Relief. [§5.4300]

Every complaint must contain a prayer for relief, asking for a specific amount of damages and/or other relief the pleader may desire, such as an injunction or specific performance of a contract. Parties may inflate, deflate, or carefully select the relief sought in order to achieve various desired tactical results.

a. Prayer May Determine Subject Matter Jurisdiction. [§5.4310]

When the jurisdiction of a court depends upon the amount in controversy or the type of relief sought, the prayer for relief provides the prima facie basis for jurisdiction, and is accepted at face value unless specifically challenged as a sham [see **§2.4200**].

Illustration. [§5.4311] P and D are citizens of different states. P wants to sue D in a state court in the state where P lives because the courthouse is located near P's office. P's attorney also wishes to prohibit D's attorney from removing the case to a federal court that sits some 150 miles away. Therefore, P's prayer will request damages not to exceed $75,000, so that the federal court will not have diversity jurisdiction [see **§2.4200**].

---

b. Prayer May Limit Recovery. [§5.4320]

In a default case, a party cannot recover more than the amount or type of relief specifically requested. This rule is designed to encourage defendants not to contest actions in which the claims are legitimate. However, in litigated cases, most courts follow Federal Rule 54(c) that permits a party to recover all the relief to which he or she is entitled according to the evidence, regardless of the prayer. Under the minority rule, which makes the prayer binding even in litigated cases, a party often is permitted, in the discretion of the court, to amend the prayer to conform to the proof in order to obtain the full amount awarded by the trier of fact [see **§5.9300**].

c. Prayer May Determine Right to Trial by Jury. [§5.4330]

In most jurisdictions, the right to trial by jury depends on the extent to which the relief sought is "legal" or "equitable". Therefore, the court will determine the nature of the case by examining the prayer, unless it is obvious that the relief sought is unavailable and that some other type of remedy will have to be substituted.

Illustration. [§5.4331] P is upset because D, a neighbor, constantly drives his car over P's lawn, destroying the landscaping. P's attorney believes that P is better off before a judge than before a jury. Therefore, P seeks only injunctive relief in equity and refrains from asking for damages at law. In most jurisdictions this tactic will deprive D of a right to jury trial.

F. THE ANSWER. [§5.5000]

A defendant responds to a complaint by filing an answer. The answer may deny some or all of the allegations of the complaint and add allegations setting forth defenses. The general rules of pleading govern answers in the same way that they govern complaints. Thus in code pleading states, defendants must set forth ultimate facts; in notice pleading jurisdictions, the pleadings need only apprise plaintiffs of the defenses to be relied upon at trial.

1. Admissions. [§5.5100]

An allegation in a complaint that is not denied, or is denied ineffectively, is admitted. When an allegation is admitted, it is then binding on the parties and; no evidence is admissible on the matter. If an admission results from a pleading mistake, the party who erred may seek an amendment to cure the defect. [The ability to amend is discussed in **§5.9000**.]

a. Conscious Admissions. [§5.5110]

A party must respond in good faith to the opposing party's allegations. If allegations are known to be true, they must be admitted. For tactical reasons, a party also may admit facts that may not be true (e.g., to keep harmful evidence from reaching the jury).

Illustration. [§5.5111] P, a pedestrian, is struck by a vehicle driven by D. P sustains only mild bruises. P files suit for the injuries, claiming a large sum for damages. P believes that strong evidence of D's intoxication at the time of the injury will inflame the jury and induce a large verdict for P. Although D's attorney has significant evidence to show that D was driving with care, D may admit liability in order to confine the trial solely to issues regarding the amount of P's injuries. The jury thus will not learn of D's drinking.

---

2. **Denials. [§5.5200]**

There are two types of denials—general and specific.

a. **General Denials. [§5.5210]**

A general denial is a single sentence that reads: "Defendant denies each and every allegation in Plaintiff's complaint."

(1) **When Allowed. [§5.5211]**

In federal courts [see Federal Rule 8(b)] and in many states, a general denial is improper unless defendant intends to refute every allegation in the complaint, including matters regarding jurisdiction. As a result, the use of a general denial usually is restricted to very few situations, since it is rare that no allegations in a complaint are true. In a minority of jurisdictions, however, a general denial is permissible if a defendant refutes the general substance of the complaint even though some specific details are true.

(2) **Not Permitted in Response to Verified Pleadings. [§5.5212]**

In those jurisdictions that permit a plaintiff to elect whether or not to verify the complaint, a plaintiff who verifies may obtain a tactical advantage since the defendant is not permitted to utilize a general denial in response to a verified complaint. The jurisdictions that follow this practice are usually those that permit a general denial even when some minor allegations are known to be true.

b. **Specific Denials. [§5.5220]**

In a specific denial, a pleader responds to a complaint paragraph by paragraph, denying only those matters legitimately controverted, thereby admitting all allegations known to be true.

(1) May Controvert All Allegations by Paragraph. [§5.5221]

To deny a complete paragraph a pleader need only state: "Defendant denies each and every allegation of paragraph I of the complaint." To deny all of the allegations in the complaint, the pleader need only expand this one sentence statement by adding the numbers of the other paragraphs in the complaint. Such a pleading amounts to little more than a general denial but it can be interposed only by a party who in good faith wishes to controvert every allegation in the preceding pleading.

(2) Admissions by Defective Specific Denials. [§5.5222]

There are a number of technical defects that may render a specific denial ineffective. In notice pleading states, these defects are often of no significance since it is clear from the pleading that a denial is intended, and that is all that is required. In states with strict code pleading rules, however, defects of form may have potent consequences because an intended denial may be ignored and thus be held to be an admission instead. The court has discretion, however, to permit an amendment to cure a defective denial.

c. Denials on Information and Belief. [§5.5230]

A specific denial may be based on information and belief. However, if the issue is a matter of **public record,** or if it involves information that the pleader is **presumed to know,** such a denial is ineffective.

Illustration. [§5.5231] P alleges that D personally ordered and received goods from P and never paid for them. D denies on information and belief that she ordered the goods. This denial will be ineffective since, absent special circumstances, D knows whether or not she ordered the goods.

---

d. Denials Based on Lack of Knowledge or Information. [§5.5240]

The availability of the denial of knowledge or information sufficient to form a belief meets the dilemma of a pleader who lacks sufficient data to justify his interposing either an honest admission or a denial of an opponent's averment.

e. Argumentative Denials. [§5.5250]

An argumentative denial is one in which the pleader, instead of denying an allegation, affirmatively alleges the opposite to be true.

The vast majority of courts treat argumentative pleading as an appropriate denial, but a few code pleading jurisdictions follow a common law rule that held these "denials" to be defective and to result in admissions.

(1) Minority View: Argumentative Denial Shifts Burden of Proof. [§5.5251]

A few courts have held that a party who makes an argumentative denial must bear the burden of proof on the issue involved. This drastic result is unjustified since the burden of proof should not be determined by the manner of pleading.

f. Negative Pregnants and Conjunctive Denials. [§5.5260]

A negative pregnant or conjunctive denial occurs when a defendant denies an allegation so specifically that if the denial is taken literally, either the general substance of the allegation or one of its major elements is not controverted. In notice pleading jurisdictions, negative pregnants and conjunctive denials generally are treated as mere defects of form, and thus are held to be effective denials of the allegations to which they are addressed.

Illustration 1: Negative Pregnant. [§5.5261] P alleges that D purchased goods from P, the reasonable value of which is $11,000. D denies that "the reasonable value of the goods is $11,000." Taken literally, this could mean that D does not deny—that D admits—that the goods were reasonably worth any sum other than $11,000. In fact, courts that apply the negative pregnant rule hold that in cases of money damages, a denial of this type admits that the sum asked, less one cent, is due. The one cent is then disregarded as a trifling amount. The net result is an admission that the reasonable value is the amount alleged by P.

Illustration 2: Conjunctive Denial. [§5.5262] P alleges that D intentionally cut and dug up P's shrubbery. D denies that he "cut and dug up" the plants. Taken literally, this means that D could have either cut the plants or dug up the plants. Since either one is sufficient to support a judgment in favor of P, D is deemed to have admitted a crucial issue of liability.

153

Illustration 3: Avoiding Negative Pregnants and Conjunctive Denials. [§5.5263] In a case in which P claims damages in a certain sum or alleges that an event occurred at a specific place, D may avoid the negative pregnant rule merely by denying that the sum asked, "or any other sum," is justified or by denying that the alleged event occurred at the place specified or "at any other place." In a situation in which P pleads in the conjunctive that D did acts "A" and "B," D may avoid a conjunctive denial merely by denying that D "did either A or B."

g. Evasive Denials. [§5.5270]

A denial must controvert the allegation or allegations to which it is directed. It cannot be equivocal or ambiguous. If it is, all jurisdictions, including the federal courts and other notice pleading jurisdictions, hold the denial to be defective.

Illustration. [§5.5271] P alleges that D intentionally struck P in the nose. D's answer states, "D refuses either to admit or deny P's allegations, but puts P to proof on the matters alleged." This pleading is defective as a denial and will result in an admission of the allegations in P's complaint.

3. Affirmative Defenses. [§5.5300]

If the defendant wishes to rely on a defense based on facts not pleaded in the complaint, defendant must plead those facts in the answer. If a denial of plaintiff's factual allegation's only raises an issue as to the truth of those averments, then it is not an affirmative defense. It is not the nature of the defendant's proof that counts in deciding whether an affirmative statement is necessary, but whether the defendant merely is refuting one of plaintiff's allegations or whether a totally new issue is being raised. Examples of affirmative defenses include: assumption of risk, contributory negligence, res judicata, fraud, and duress, among others.

Illustration 1. [§5.5310] P alleges that D entered into a contract with P to deliver goods to P. The goods were delivered but proved defective and P claims damages. D, merely by denying P's allegations, can show that the goods delivered were not defective.

However, if D wishes to show that P and D have entered into a binding settlement of the allegations, D must allege the subsequent settlement contract as an affirmative defense.

Illustration 2. [§5.5320] P alleges that she owns a piece of property upon which D now lives. P seeks to eject D and to recover damages for trespass. D denies P's allegations but does not set out any affirmative allegations. At trial D seeks to show that a third party, T, owns the property in question. P objects on the ground that this is an affirmative defense. The court will hold for D. D's proof is designed not to raise a new issue but merely to refute P's essential allegation that P is the owner of the property. D's denial of that allegation should permit any evidence to show that the allegation is untrue.

a.   Minority View: Affirmative Pleading to Avoid Surprise. [§5.5330]

Even though the defendant presents evidence on a point merely to refute an allegation of the complaint, if the nature of that evidence would surprise plaintiff, a few courts require defendant to plead the matter affirmatively.

Illustration. [§5.5331] In the illustration in **§5.5320,** D's evidence that a third person, T, has a competing, superior claim of title to the property could result in substantial surprise to P. The situation is unlike a case in which D merely challenges the validity of documents that P puts forward to show her title. The few courts that follow the "surprise" rule do so out of concern that otherwise P may never know prior to trial the nature of the evidence she must face and hence could be deprived of the opportunity to conduct effective pretrial discovery.

b.   Defense Waived If Not Pleaded. [§5.5340]

An affirmative defense is waived if it is not raised in the answer. The rationale for this rule is that there are myriad possible defenses to nearly every claim and from a practical point of view the only defenses that should be subject to the litigation process are those considered by defendant to be important to the case, as expressed in

155

the answer. An inadvertent omission of an important defense often can be cured by amendment [see **§5.9000**].

c. Confusion between Counterclaims and Affirmative Defenses [§5.5350]

A defendant may wish to bring his own claims (a "counterclaim") asking for affirmative relief against the plaintiff. It may not always be clear whether the defendant's affirmative allegations constitute an affirmative defense, a counterclaim, or both. If only a defense is alleged, most courts do not require a response [see **§5.6100**]. However, if a counterclaim is set forth, a failure to answer will result in an admission of the facts and the liability alleged in the counterclaim. Federal Rule 8 tries to avoid this problem by only requiring a response to a counterclaim "denominated as such" by the defendant. Courts, however, avoid unfairness by permitting amendment whenever confusion has resulted in an honest misunderstanding.

Illustration. [§5.5351] P sues D for injuries in an auto accident. D's answer alleges affirmatively that P and D entered into a settlement agreement under which P agreed to drop the suit upon payment of a sum of money that has been paid. P believes that these allegations constitute an affirmative defense that requires no reply in the particular jurisdiction. P intends to show at trial that D did not pay and never intended to pay the money. D, however, claims that his allegations constitute a counterclaim for damages due to P's failure to drop the case, and that P has admitted D's allegations by not filing a timely answer. If the court finds that P acted in good faith and believed that no counterclaim had been set forth, P will be given additional time to respond to D's allegations.

G. THE REPLY AND SUBSEQUENT RESPONSES. [§5.6000]

If an answer contains only a denial of allegations in the complaint, there are no allegations to which a response is possible. If, however, the answer contains an affirmative defense, logically, the plaintiff should respond, either by admitting or denying the allegations, and perhaps by adding new allegations to avoid the defense. Although some courts do require such a response in the form of a reply, most courts do not.

1. **Majority View: Allegations in Answer Deemed Denied or Avoided. [§5.6100]**

    In the federal courts, under Rules 7(a)(7) and 8(b)(6), and in most states, affirmative allegations in an answer automatically are treated as denied or avoided and no reply is permitted except by court order.

    Illustration. [§5.6110] P files suit against D, alleging a breach of contract. D answers, raising as a defense the running of the applicable statute of limitations. P intends to overcome the statute of limitations defense by showing that D defrauded P by false promises to pay if P would not file suit. The fraud issue is essentially an "affirmative defense to the affirmative defense." In most courts P can present any proof on the issue without a reply. These courts rely on discovery to allow the parties to learn precisely what claims will be made at trial.

    ---

2. **Minority View: Reply Required. [§5.6200]**

    A number of courts still require a reply to affirmative allegations in an answer. The defendant's allegations will be taken as true if they are not denied. The sufficiency of denials in a reply is determined by the same rules as is the sufficiency of denials contained in an answer. A reply not only should deny facts to be controverted at trial; in addition, it should allege any new facts necessary to overcome an affirmative defense.

3. **Pleadings Beyond the Reply Prohibited. [§5.6300]**

    Even though a reply contains affirmative allegations, a response to the reply is not permitted. Allegations in the reply are taken as denied or avoided. The number of situations in which affirmative allegations will be appropriate to overcome affirmative allegations in a reply is extremely small and the discovery process can be used to obtain necessary information as to an opposing party's position in those cases.

H. PLEADING COUNTERCLAIMS, CROSS–CLAIMS, AND THIRD–PARTY CLAIMS. [§5.7000]

Counterclaims, cross-claims, and third-party claims—asserted by a defendant against a plaintiff, a co-defendant, or an outsider to the action—are dealt with in Chapter Seven. However, it is important to recognize at this point the relationship between these claims and the general rules of pleading.

1. **Counterclaims, Cross–Claims, and Third–Party Claims Treated As Complaints. [§5.7100]**

    For pleading purposes, a counterclaim, cross-claim, or third-party claim is treated as if it were an original complaint that must be responded to by an answer. This is true even though in most jurisdictions these claims may be pleaded in the original answer as well as in a separate document. The rules governing an answer to an original action also apply to answers to counterclaims, cross-claims, and third-party claims.

I. CHALLENGES TO PLEADINGS. [§5.8000]

Pleadings can be challenged on the ground that they are substantively insufficient, that they are irregular or improper in form, or that they reveal some defect in procedure that should result in an abatement of the action.

1. Methods of Attacking Substantive Sufficiency. [§5.8100]

The traditional challenge to a pleading is called a **demurrer** and charges that a complaint fails to state a cause of action or that an answer fails to set forth a defense. The Federal Rules, as well as many state courts, have eliminated the demurrer in favor of the functionally similar but more flexible **motion to dismiss** for failure to state a claim and the **motion to strike** an insufficient defense. In addition, most jurisdictions allow a motion for a **judgment on the pleadings,** which serves as an alternative to the demurrer or motion to dismiss. This motion usually is filed only after all the pleadings are completed; it raises the identical questions as does a demurrer or motion to dismiss.

a. Different Challenges Raise Same Question. [§5.8110]

The nomenclature of the challenge to a pleading is of little significance. What is important is that each method raises the same question: has the party whose pleading is under attack adequately stated a claim or defense as required by the rules of pleading in force in the jurisdiction?

b. Challenge to Part of a Pleading. [§5.8120]

If one of several claims or defenses in a pleading is defective, that claim or defense can be eliminated to narrow the issues that must be tried. In most jurisdictions a general challenge to a pleading is satisfactory to eliminate any defective portion of the pleading. In some jurisdictions, however, the courts will uphold a general challenge only if the entire pleading is defective; to eliminate a defective claim or defense, that specific portion of the pleading must be challenged directly.

> **Illustration. [§5.8121]** P sues D, interposing a complaint containing two counts (or sections), one alleging a claim based in contractand the other in tort. D demurs to the complaint on the ground that it fails to state a valid cause of action. The court finds that the allegations in tort do state a cause but those in contract do not. In some courts the challenge will be dismissed since the complaint does state one valid claim for relief. If D had demurred separately to each count, the defective count would have been eliminated.

c. Only the Pleading Itself Considered. [§5.8130]

It normally is improper for a court to look beyond the pleading itself to determine whether or not a challenge should be upheld. It is not the obligation of the court to determine whether the allegations are true, but only whether, if true, they state a legally sufficient claim or defense. (Note that the pretrial procedure by which a pleading may be attacked as substantively without merit is the motion for summary judgment.) In jurisdictions that follow the Federal Rules, a motion to dismiss for failure to state a claim [Federal Rule 12(b)(6)] or a motion for judgment on the pleadings [Federal Rule 12(c)], may, in the discretion of the court, be converted into a motion for summary judgment when the moving party submits affidavits in accordance with Federal Rule 56, the summary judgment provision [see **§11.1000** and **§11.1100**].

(1) Exception 1: Subject Matter Jurisdiction. [§5.8131]

In the federal courts, unlike the situation in most states, the plaintiff must allege facts that would establish the court's subject matter jurisdiction. If the court itself or any of the parties challenge the existence of those facts, the court is allowed to go outside the pleadings to determine if, in fact, subject matter jurisdiction exists. In such a situation, a motion to dismiss is not converted to a motion for summary judgment.

(2) Exception 2: Facts Judicially Noticed. [§5.8132]

On a challenge to a pleading the court will consider unpleaded matters so universally known that they cannot be refuted, including scientific principles, historical events, and matters of local record.

> **Illustration. [§5.8132–1]** P sues for damages suffered in an automobile accident. D challenges the complaint for failure to state a claim on the ground that P already has brought suit on the matter and lost. Obviously allegations regarding the prior suit do not appear in P's pleading. Nevertheless, the court may judicially notice the records of its own court, and if it appears in those records that the identical matter already has been adjudicated, the action will be dismissed.

(3) Exception 3: Challenging Party's Own Pleadings. [§5.8133]

On a challenge to a pleading the court will consider the effect, if any, of the challenging party's own allegations, since the latter may "aid" or "cure" any defects in the pleading under attack.

> **Illustration. [§5.8133—1]** P alleges that D promised to pay $5,000 to P and that D has failed to do so. D challenges the sufficiency of the complaint on the ground that it fails to allege any consideration on behalf of P and hence no contract is shown. However, in addition to challenging P's complaint, D files a counterclaim against P stating that the $5,000 was in exchange for goods delivered to D, and that these goods were defective. D's allegations cure the defect in P's complaint by showing that there was consideration. Therefore, the complaint will not be dismissed and the case will go to trial.

2. Methods of Attacking Irregularities or Improper Form. [§5.8200]

Each jurisdiction provides a number of devices to challenge technical aspects of pleadings. Courts generally are wary of permitting challenges on non-substantive ground's, since cases normally should not be decided nor time wasted on procedural niceties.

a. Motion for More Definite Statement. [§5.8210]

As already noted, in certain situations a motion for a more definite statement may be available to require a pleader to clarify a complaint or answer. In many courts, including the federal courts [see Rule 12(e)], a motion is allowed only when necessary to enable the challenging party to file a response to the challenged pleading.

b. Motion to Strike. [§5.8220]

Almost all jurisdictions allow a motion to strike **unnecessary matters** in a pleading if they are **defamatory or otherwise may be**

harmful. Courts grant these motions only when the allegations being challenged are so unrelated to the plaintiff's claims or defendant's defenses as to be **unworthy of any consideration** and when their presence in the pleading throughout the proceeding will be **prejudicial to the moving party.** If the allegations are material to the claims or defenses set forth, courts always will deny these motions. A motion to strike is also the method of attacking a pleading that has been filed too late, or without approval of the court when that is necessary, or if other rules or court orders have not been satisfied. The court, in its discretion, normally will allow the defect to be corrected unless the opposing party would suffer undue prejudice.

3. **Methods of Raising Matters of Abatement. [§5.8300]**

Pleas in abatement do not concern the merits of the action. Rather, they are addressed to procedural irregularities involving jurisdiction over the subject matter, jurisdiction over the person, service of process, venue, joinder of parties and claims, and lack of capacity to sue. In many courts a plea in abatement can be raised either in the answer as an affirmative defense or by special motion before the answer is filed [see, e.g., Federal Rules 12(b) and 21].

   a. **Exception: Special Rules. [§5.8310]**

   In some jurisdictions a special motion is required to raise a particular plea in abatement. For example, in some courts a challenge to venue must be made by a motion to transfer to a proper court and a challenge to personal jurisdiction can only be raised by a motion to quash service interposed before the answer is filed.

   b. **Early Hearing on Abatement Issues. [§5.8320]**

   Whether a plea is raised by motion or in the answer, most jurisdictions provide for an early hearing to determine the matter. There is little justification for proceeding with a trial that will be useless because threshold procedural details have not been satisfied. In many cases the defects can be cured easily.

   c. **Deferred Hearing until Trial. [§5.8330]**

   Federal Rule 12(i), and its state counterparts, provide for an early hearing on abatement matters unless the court specifically defers the matter until the trial. On occasion, deferral will save time and cost.

> **Illustration. [§5.8331]** P is injured in a vehicle collision in California, where suit is brought. X, the driver of the other car, was killed. P alleges that X was acting within the scope of her employment with D, who lives in Ohio and has no other contact with California. D challenges jurisdiction over him on the ground that X was on vacation and not on D's business at the time of the accident. There is no question that the accident resulted solely from X's negligence, and the amount of P's damages is conceded. The only major issue at trial is whether X was acting within the scope of employment, and that is the identical issue that will determine jurisdiction. The court undoubtedly will not have a separate hearing on jurisdiction but will defer the matter to trial.

4. Waiver of Challenges. [§5.8400]

Many pleading defects are waived if they are not subjected to a timely challenge in accordance with the rules of the court.

a. Exception: Substantive Challenges. [§5.8410]

A challenge to the sufficiency of a claim or defense can be raised at any time up to and during trial. The policy is to prevent one party from prevailing on an issue that is not recognized by the applicable rules of law.

(1) Courts Split on Number of Substantive Challenges. [§5.8411]

In the federal courts, and in some states, a pleading may be challenged as insufficient by a motion to dismiss or to strike and later, on the same ground, by a motion for judgment on the pleadings. The value of avoiding an unnecessary trial is thought to outweigh the waste of time that can result from successive identical challenges. Other courts permit only one challenge. Once the motion is denied, the issue can be raised again directly only on appeal although in a jury case it may surface as an objection to the instructions.

b. Challenges to Form and Pleas in Abatement. [§5.8420]

Under the rules of most jurisdictions, challenges to the form of pleadings as well as most pleas in abatement must be made at the earliest opportunity or they are waived. For example, an attempt to raise a plea in abatement for the first time in an amended answer normally will fail. Sound policy requires these matters to be raised and decided at the earliest time; once preparation of the case has begun, it is wasteful to terminate the action on technical grounds.

(1)   Exception 1: Lack of Subject Matter Jurisdiction. [§5.8421]

The lack of subject matter jurisdiction may be **raised at any time,** even on appeal, by the court as well as by the parties [see **§2.1220**]. This provision is embodied in Federal Rule 12(h)(3), which requires the court to dismiss whenever the lack of subject matter jurisdiction is discovered. Even a Court of Appeal must dismiss the case if it is discovered that the trial court did not have subject matter jurisdiction. The reason is that the parties do not have the power to waive the constitutional and legislative prerogatives regarding the distribution of judicial business among courts.

(2)   Exception 2: Failure to Join Indispensable Party. [§5.8422]

By definition, an indispensable party is one without whose presence the case should not proceed [see **§6.6000**]. Like subject matter jurisdiction, then, this defect **cannot be waived** by the parties and can be raised at any time during trial or on appeal.

5.   Choices Available to Party Losing a Motion Challenging Pleading. [§5.8500]

In theory, the party who has lost a motion challenging a pleading will have a choice either to appeal the court's ruling or to accept the decision and proceed with the case at the trial level. A number of tactical considerations must be weighed in deciding what course to follow.

a.   Availability of Interlocutory Appeal. [§5.8510]

Most jurisdictions restrict the right to appeal an interlocutory decision. In some jurisdictions the courts in special situations may, in their discretion, permit such appeals. However, courts are extremely reluctant to do so on matters of pleading. Therefore, in order to appeal, a party must permit an adverse judgment to be entered. This entails substantial risk, for if the ruling on the pleading challenge is upheld on appeal, the case normally will be at an end, and the adverse judgment will stand. In the few jurisdictions that permit interlocutory appeals, the sole tactical question is whether an appeal is worth the expense.

b. Decision If Challenge Overruled. [§5.8520]

If a pleading challenge is overruled, the losing party usually will decide not to appeal but to proceed to trial, and may attempt to preserve the challenge by other means.

(1) Exception: Clear Legal Error. [§5.8521]

If the court overrules a challenge to a complaint with the result that a long and costly trial will ensue, the defendant may decide to allow a judgment to be entered in order to appeal. This tactically is sound when the defendant is confident that the trial judge is wrong. A party who guesses incorrectly and loses the appeal normally will have no recourse; the judgment entered against the party will stand. In some jurisdictions appellate courts have the power to grant relief by ordering the judgment set aside so the case can proceed on the merits, but this power is exercised only in very rare circumstances to prevent a gross miscarriage of justice.

> **Illustration. [§5.8521–1]** P files suit against D alleging facts that D does not believe entitle P to recover. D's motion to dismiss is overruled, however. D believes that he can win the case before a jury, even as it is pleaded. Nevertheless, at the time the jury is charged, D objects to all instructions that would permit relief, claiming that the law does not permit recovery. If the jury finds for P, D then may appeal on the ground that the instructions were improper.

c. Decision If Challenge Upheld. [§5.8530]

When a pleading challenge is sustained, the losing party typically will exercise the option to amend the pleading so as to continue with the case, particularly if the defect is not material and can be cured easily.

(1) Amendment Eliminates Right to Appeal. [§5.8531]

In most jurisdictions if a party amends a pleading after a successful challenge, the original pleading is superseded and the right to appeal the ruling on the challenge is lost. Thus the choice between amendment and appeal is of substantial significance. There are some tactical ways, however, to amend and still preserve the right to appeal in the event of an adverse judgment.

> **Illustration. [§5.8531–1]** P sues D, alleging an intentional infliction of emotional distress. The trial court grants D's motion to dismiss for failure to state a claim on the ground that P's action is not recognized in the jurisdiction. P amends to state an action for assault, which may be difficult to prove but which cannot be challenged as insufficient. P also includes a second count in the new complaint re-alleging the initial cause for distress. If this count is deleted on court order, an amendment no longer is necessary and the case can proceed on the assault claim without jeopardizing a later appeal on the emotional distress issue.

(2) Redress by Appeal When Good Faith Amendment Impossible. [§5.8532]

If a pleading is successfully challenged and the losing party cannot in good faith file an amendment but must stand or fall on the cause alleged, then that party will permit an adverse judgment to be entered in order to appeal.

J. AMENDMENT OF A PLEADING. [§5.9000]

Most pleading defects can be and are cured by amendment. There are two basic pleading defects to which amendments are directed. The first type occurs when the pleading is successfully challenged by an opposing party. The second occurs when the pleader realizes that a pleading, although it states a valid claim or defense, fails to state properly an important claim or defense that the pleader believes he or she can prove or, indeed, has proved at trial.

1. Amendments When Leave of Court Not Required. [§5.9100]

A party may amend its pleading once without leave before a responsive pleading is served or, if no response is required, within a specified number of days after serving the pleading to be amended.

2. Amendments With Leave of Court. [§5.9200]

If a party wishes to amend a complaint or answer after the right to amend has passed, he or she must obtain the consent of the court. This will be the situation in almost all cases. Courts take a very liberal stance in granting permission. Under Federal Rule 15(a), leave to amend should be given "when justice so requires;" state courts are generally as liberal as federal courts. On appeal, in most jurisdictions a trial court will be reversed for abuse of discretion if it denies leave to amend when there is no substantial justification for doing so.

a. **Denial upon Showing of Prejudice. [§5.9210]**

If an opposing party can show that an amendment will cause undue prejudice, the court may deny leave. But prejudice does not occur simply because new issues will be raised that may hurt the objecting party's legal position.

Illustration: Prejudice. [§5.9211] P sues D for breach of a contract to sell goods. P alleges that the machinery delivered to P by D was defective. After the parties have engaged in considerable discovery, P seeks leave to amend to allege that D negligently installed the machinery in P's plant. At the time the suit originally was filed, the men who installed the machinery were still in D's employ. Subsequently, however, they drifted to other places and other jobs. The foreman is dead; his deputy works for another company in Libya. The whereabouts of the others are unknown. The court, in its discretion, could decide that the delay in claiming improper installation resulted in sufficient prejudice to D so as to deny the amendment.

---

b. **When Prejudice Can Be Alleviated. [§5.9220]**

If the court can find a means of eliminating or easing prejudice that would result from an amendment, then it should grant leave to amend under proper terms.

Illustration. [§5.9221] P sues D on a single cause. Thereafter, P seeks to amend to add an additional cause. D objects on the ground that a key witness to the second cause recently has left the jurisdiction and D does not know where he has gone. The court may grant leave on the condition that P first locate the witness, assure the court that a deposition of the witness can be taken at the place where he is located, and, finally, agree to pay D for the cost of taking the deposition, including attorney's fees and expenses.

---

c. **Special Factors in Determining Prejudice. [§5.9230]**

There are several specific factors that have proved important in decisions whether to grant leave to amend.

(1) **Time of the Motion. [§5.9231]**

If a motion to amend is made early in the case, it is more likely to be granted than if it is made just prior to or during trial, although amendments during trial are not automatically rejected.

Illustration. [§5.9231–1] P is badly injured when struck by an automobile driven by D's 17–year old son. P sues D under a statute making the owner of a vehicle liable up to $10,000 for injuries due to the negligence of a person driving the vehicle with the owner's permission. During the course of trial P moves to amend his complaint to allege that D negligently entrusted the vehicle to his son, a cause that does not carry the $10,000 limit. Such an amendment, if made early in the case, almost surely would be granted. It even may be granted during trial since it is not such a great departure from the facts alleged and because D himself is the key witness on the matter. However, D may argue, perhaps successfully, that leave to amend should be denied because if he had known of the increased exposure, he would have handled the case differently, perhaps by hiring more experienced counsel or even by settling out of court.

(2) Number of Prior Amendments. [§5.9232]

If a party's original pleading was held insufficient and the party has since filed successive amended pleadings, each of which in turn has been held insufficient, the court can **refuse to grant leave for further amendments.** The nature of the case and the court's belief as to whether the party, in good faith, can cure the defects will determine the point at which the court will refuse further amendment.

(3) Sufficiency of Proposed Amendment. [§5.9233]

Some courts require a pleader to file the proposed amendment along with the motion for leave to amend. These courts will deny leave if the amendment would not be sufficient to withstand a challenge. Most courts do not determine the question of leave on the basis of whether the amendment will or will not be sufficient, since once leave is granted, the pleader will be able to concentrate on drafting an amendment that will avoid challenge. **Caveat:** All courts will look to the general subject of the amendment for purposes of deciding if the amendment will be prejudicial.

(4) Raising Disfavored Defenses. [§5.9234]

As already noted [see **§5.8420**], most pleas in abatement cannot be first raised in an amended answer. Failure to raise these issues at the outset results in a **waiver** of the defects. In addition, many courts treat the running of the statute of limitations as a disfavored defense that is waived if not raised in the initial answer. Other courts may permit an amendment to raise the statute of limitations issue but are prone to deny it on the ground of prejudice if the defendant did not have sufficient reason for not raising the issue in the original answer.

(5) Code Pleading Restrictions on Adding a New Cause of Action or Defense. [§5.9235]

In a minority of those courts that adhere to code pleading rules, an amendment is prohibited if it establishes a new cause of action or defense. The courts are very permissive in broadly defining "cause of action" for this purpose. Only if the new matter to be pleaded bears virtually no relation to the original pleading will courts find that a new cause or defense is stated. This would occur, for example, if the plaintiff first alleges a claim for personal injuries and later seeks to substitute an entirely unrelated claim for breach of contract. If the plaintiff's amendment is rejected on the ground that it states a new cause, the plaintiff need only file a separate action. Denial of an amendment, therefore, only serves to increase the number of cases and the fees and costs engendered by them. Of course, recovery in a new lawsuit will be held barred if the statute of limitations has run prior to the filing of the complaint.

3. Amendments to Conform to Evidence. [§5.9300]

After evidence is presented, a party may seek to amend to conform the pleadings to the evidence, that is, to add those issues that were not included in the pleadings but in fact were tried.

a. Majority Rule: Automatically Include Issues Actually Tried. [§5.9310]

The modern rule, epitomized by Federal Rule 15(b), treats the pleadings as including all issues tried by the consent of the parties, whether consent is express or implied. A party may formally amend to include these issues but it is not necessary to do so. However, the parties must have consciously tried the issues in question; the fact that evidence is introduced by one party that might bear on an unpleaded issue is not in itself sufficient.

> **Illustration. [§5.9311]** P sues D for personal injuries sustained in an auto collision. At trial, as part of P's case in showing that D was negligent, P introduces pictures of the location of the vehicles after the accident. P also introduces a mechanic who testifies as to how the damages to P's car demonstrate that D was responsible for the collision. On cross examination D elicits the facts that the mechanic was paid an additional $1,500 for repairs he made to P's car, over $1,000 of which was profit, and that the mechanic was given an additional $1,000 "expense money" to testify. At the conclusion of all the evidence, P argues that the pleadings should be read to include a claim for damages to his vehicle, noting that the pictures plus the testimony of the mechanic clearly revealed the extent of the damage and the cost of repairs. The court should reject P's arguments; the evidence was admitted solely in reference to D's liability and the issue of vehicle damages was not tried by consent.

b. Minority Rule: Reject Any Amendment Establishing a New Cause or Defense. [§5.9320]

In some code pleading jurisdictions, the rule that prohibits amendments establishing a new cause or defense [see **§5.9235**] also applies to amendments to conform to the proof, even though it can be argued that the parties tried the issues by consent. This defect is referred to as a "fatal variance" or "a failure of proof" and is applied to protect the integrity of the code pleading system.

4. Amendments Supersede Original Pleading. [§5.9400]

An amended pleading stands on its own. If a response was required to the original, a new response will be necessary to meet the allegations of the amended complaint, unless the alterations were so minor that the original answer will suffice.

a. Exception: Running of Statute of Limitations on New Claim. [§5.9410]

An important question is the extent to which an amendment to a complaint is barred by the statute of limitations if the statute ran prior to the filing of the amendment. The answer depends on whether the original complaint was filed before the statute ran and on the nature of the amendment.

(1) When Statute Ran Prior to Original Pleading. [§5.9411]

If the limitations period ran on a claim prior to the filing of the original complaint, that claim cannot be saved merely because it is first introduced by an amendment. Otherwise, the limitations period could be thwarted in any situation.

(2) Time of Original Pleading Governs Amendments Arising out of the Same Transaction. [§5.9412]

If the content of an amendment arises out of the same transaction or occurrence as set forth in the original complaint, then the amendment will be deemed filed at the same time that the original complaint was filed. Thus, if the limitations period ran between the time of the original filing and the time the amendment was filed, the statute will not be a bar to the new claim. In federal courts the amendment is said to "relate back" to the original pleading and thus satisfy any statute of limitations problem. Federal Rule 15(c), and many state provisions, expressly provide for the timing of such amendments. Most courts take a very liberal position in finding that an amendment arises from the same transaction or occurrence as an original pleading. The rationale for this rule is that the policies underlying statutes of limitations have been fulfilled. The defendant is already on notice about the suit and has begun to prepare his or her case.

Illustration. [§5.9412–1] P sues D, in timely fashion, alleging that D negligently drove his truck over P's child, who was killed. During discovery, and just after the statute of limitations on wrongful death actions has run, P learns that it will be extremely difficult to prove that D was driving negligently. However, P can establish that after the accident D negligently failed to stop and give proper aid, which could have saved the child's life. P's amendment to set forth the latter claim, in most courts, will be held to arise from the same transaction or occurrence as that originally claimed and therefore the statute of limitations will not bar recovery.

---

b. Bringing in New Parties by Amendment. [§5.9420]

The traditional rule for bringing in new parties held that they could not be added to an action by a pleading amendment after the applicable statute of limitations period had expired unless their actions misled the plaintiff into filing against the wrong defendant. In an increasing number of jurisdictions, including the federal system under Rule 15(c), courts **will not automatically bar an action** against an added defendant **because of the statute of limitations** even though the amendment bringing the new defendant into the action was filed after the limitations period had run. Instead, in certain specific circumstances, the amendment is deemed to "relate back" to the date of the original complaint. The purpose of these rules is to **give relief to a plaintiff who has made a mistake or has been misled** into suing the wrong defendant in cases in which the proper defendant is not prejudiced. A number of courts still do not have such rules and apply the statute of limitations strictly to all new defendants.

(1) Knowledge of Defendant Prior to Running of Limitations Period. [§5.9421]

Federal courts and many state courts permit plaintiff to avoid a statute of limitations defense on behalf of a newly named defendant if two prerequisites are satisfied: (a) the new defendant must have had notice of the action prior to the time the limitations period ran, and (b) the new defendant must have known or should have known that but for a mistake concerning the identity of the proper defendant, the suit would have been filed originally against the new defendant.

(2) Liberal Federal Rule [§5.9422]

Under Rule 15(c)(1)(C) an amendment to join a new defendant after the statute of limitations has run even without the defendant knowing about the suit will still not be subject to a statute of limitations defense if, within the period plaintiff has to serve the summons and complaint on the original defendant, the defendant learns about the suit and the fact that except for plaintiff's mistake it should have been the original defendant. Normally that period is 120 days after the original complaint is filed, although the district judge can for good cause increase the time for an appropriate period.

Illustration. [§5.9422–1] P sues Dr. X, alleging medical malpractice in connection with an operation on P's arm. Sometime later after the statute of limitations has run, but before the expiration of 120 days from the time that the complaint was filed, P learns that the operation was performed by Dr. Y. At the same time Dr. Y first learns of the suit and realizes that except for a mistake of P, he (Dr. Y) was the proper defendant. P, if he acts before the end of the 120

---

days, can amend the complaint to name Dr. Y as the defendant and avoid a statute of limitations defense.

(3) State Statute of Limitations in Federal Court. [§5.9423]

If a case in federal court is governed by a state statute of limitations, and, under Federal Rule 15(c)(3), an amendment would not relate back to the time that the complaint was filed, then under Federal Rule 15(c)(1)(A), if a state rule would permit the amendment to relate back, the state rule will apply.

(4) State "John Doe" Provisions [§5.9424]

A few states avoid the problem of relation back for new defendants by permitting the plaintiff to name "John Doe" defendants in the original complaint, stating that plaintiff does not presently know who they are. Subsequently, when plaintiff learns the name of a true defendant, the latter may be substituted for a John Doe defendant and the new defendant is treated as if it were in the case from the time that the complaint was filed. Federal courts have split on the question whether Rule 15(c) makes such John Doe provisions applicable to cases in federal courts. It is argued that Rule 15(c)(1)(C) does not apply because plaintiff has not made a mistake. On the other hand, it appears that Rule 15(c)(1)(A) would apply if, but only if, the state statute of limitations is applicable.

(5) Correction of Misnomer Distinguished From Naming New Party. [§5.9425]

If a plaintiff files suit against the proper defendant, but uses an incorrect name, an amendment interposed after the limitations period has run will relate back to the time the original complaint was filed. The policies underlying the statute of limitations do not apply to this situation.

Illustration. [§5.9425–1] P files a personal injury suit naming as defendant the "Northfield Community Hospital," which is the name that appears over the main entrance to the hospital and is the way in which the hospital generally is referred to in the community. After the statute of limitations runs, P learns that the true name of the hospital is "Community Hospital of Field County." P should be permitted to amend the complaint to alter the name of the defendant without giving rise to a statute of limitations defense.

(6) Substitution of Successor to Party. [§5.9426]

The rules of amendment with regard to the statute of limitations do not apply to cases of proper substitution of parties, when the newly named party is the successor to the original party. For example, if one party dies, the party's estate may be substituted. Or, if a government officer, acting in his or her official capacity, is a party and resigns the office, the successor to the office may be substituted. Obviously, the situation differs materially from one in which a different, non-successor party is joined.

5. Supplemental Pleadings. [§5.9500]

A supplemental pleading is one that adds new facts that were not in existence at the time of the original pleading. Frequently, a supplemental pleading is used to present claims for additional damages.

a. Curing Defective Original Pleading. [§5.9510]

Most courts today take the position that a supplemental claim can cure a defective pleading. Some, however, take an opposite view and require an entirely new action to be filed. In these latter courts, if P fails to recognize the defect until after the statute of limitations has run, the new action will be barred.

Illustration. [§5.9511] P sues D on an overdue note. At the time the suit was filed the note was not yet overdue. Sometime thereafter, the note became due and was still unpaid. Most courts would permit P to correct the defect in the original complaint by filing a supplemental pleading stating the new facts. Some courts, however, would require P to file a new action.

*

CHAPTER VI

JOINDER OF PARTIES AND JOINDER OF CLAIMS

A. JOINDER OF PARTIES AND CLAIMS: SCOPE NOTE. [§6.0000]

The materials in this chapter deal with the basic rules that govern the dimensions of a lawsuit in terms of who may litigate and what claims may be adjudicated within the framework of a single action. This theme is continued in the next two chapters, which deal with some of the more sophisticated joinder procedures.

B. JOINDER OF PARTIES: AN OVERVIEW. [§6.1000]

In analyzing joinder-of-parties problems, five basic considerations must be kept in mind: (a) Has the action been brought by the "real party in interest" [see **§6.2000**]? (b) Do the parties to the action have capacity to sue or be sued [see **§6.3000**]? (c) Is the party whose joinder is contemplated a "proper party" so that his or her addition to the action is permissible [see **§6.4000**]? (d) Is there someone not yet a party whose relationship to the dispute is such that he or she must be joined if feasible and joinder will be compelled [see **§6.5000**]? (e) Is there someone outside the litigation whose presence is "indispensable" or so essential that in equity and good conscience the suit should be dismissed if, for some reason, joinder is impossible or the non-party's presence in the litigation would defeat the subject matter jurisdiction of the court [see **§6.6000**]?

C. REAL PARTY IN INTEREST. [§6.2000]

The real party in interest is the person who, under the applicable substantive law, has the right to enforce the claim that is the subject matter of the action. The real party in interest may or may not be the individual who ultimately benefits from the litigation.

1. **Historical Development. [§6.2100]**

   The real-party-in-interest rule has developed from a conceptualistic identification of the party possessing legal title to a claim to a more pragmatic identification of the party who really has a direct stake in the outcome of the litigation.

a.   Common Law. [§6.2110]

In order to bring an action at common law, a party must have had legal title to the right to be asserted. Persons having a mere beneficial or equitable interest, such as subrogees and assignees, had to rely upon the party possessing legal title to enforce their rights.

Illustration. [§6.2111] D is sued for injuries sustained by P's wife as a result of the failure of D's revolving door to function properly. The suit is prosecuted in the name of the husband. At one time, in states that followed the common law rule, he would have been the proper plaintiff inasmuch as according to the law of those jurisdictions, the husband possessed the substantive right to recover for a wife's injuries.

---

b.   In Equity. [§6.2120]

The more permissive rules of equity allowed persons with equitable interests in the subject matter of the dispute to sue in their own names. The legal title holder, however, usually had to be joined in order to bind him or her to the decree.

c.   Under the Codes. [§6.2130]

The merger of law and equity effected by the procedural codes of the nineteenth century abolished the often cumbersome requirement that actions at law be brought by the holder of the legal title and provided simply that suit be brought in the name of the "real party in interest."

d.   Modern Practice. [§6.2140]

The modern practice, typified by Federal Rule 17, also requires that the action be brought in the name of the real party in interest but extends the right to bring suit to representative parties. Thus, the rule lists, by way of example, executors, administrators, guardians, bailees, trustees of an express trust, parties with whom or in whose name a contract has been made for the benefit of another, or parties authorized by statute as persons who may sue in their own names without joining with them the party for whose benefit the action is brought.

2.   Criticism of the Real-Party-in-Interest Rule. [§6.2200]

The real-party-in-interest rule has been criticized as being an unnecessary procedural complexity. If the real party in interest simply describes the individual possessing the substantive right to be enforced in the litigation, the rule is superfluous, since it is extremely unlikely that a stranger to the dispute would attempt to prosecute the suit. Moreover, even if such a person brought suit it certainly could be dismissed promptly for not stating a claim upon which relief can be granted [see Federal Rule 12(b)(6)].

3. Defense of the Real-Party-in-Interest Rule. [§6.2300]

Despite the logic of the foregoing criticism, some people contend that the rule has some justification. If a suit is brought by someone other than the real party in interest, it is argued, the defendant might be forced to bear the burden of defending the action without obtaining any of the benefits of res judicata should the defense prove successful, since the real party in interest will not be bound by the first suit [see the discussion in Chapter Sixteen]. To avoid the possibility of relitigation, therefore, the defendant should be allowed to insist that the real party in interest be joined in the original litigation. But the availability of a motion to dismiss seems to undercut this contention.

4. Assignments. [§6.2400]

An assignee may sue in his or her own name on an assigned contractual right of action. Not only is it unnecessary for the assignee to sue in the assignor's name but the modern rule is that an assignor who has transferred all of his or her rights no longer is a real party in interest. If the assignment is partial, both the assignor and assignee are real parties in interest.

Illustration. [§6.2410] Farmer delivers a quantity of milk to D. Before Farmer is paid, he suffers some financial embarrassment and assigns his rights under the contract with D to a local bank. D fails to pay the contract price and Farmer brings suit for breach of contract. Farmer is not a real party in interest and the action should be dismissed on D's motion unless the bank is properly substituted as the plaintiff.

---

a. Defendant May Insist upon Joinder. [§6.2420]

If there has been a partial assignment, a defendant who is sued by either the assignor or assignee may insist upon the joinder of the other so that both are parties to the action [see **§6.5000**]. This avoids the possibility of the defendant being harassed by two lawsuits concerning a single obligation.

Illustration. [§6.2421] P brings suit for patent infringement asking for an accounting, an injunction, and damages. D's answer asserts that P has assigned an undivided 15 percent interest in the patent to a third person, who is not a party to the suit. The assignee originally declined to join in the infringement action, and P made no attempt to join her. D has a right to insist that both assignor and assignee be parties to the litigation if that is possible. If the assignee is not joined, the suit should be dismissed.

5. Subrogation. [§6.2500]

The real-party-in-interest principles applicable to assignments also govern subrogation. Thus, if a subrogee has paid the subrogor the amount to which the latter is entitled, the subrogee must sue in its own name. If, however, the subrogee succeeds to only part of the subrogor's rights, as, for example, by paying only part of the sum to which the subrogor is entitled, both subrogor and subrogee are real parties in interest.

Illustration. [§6.2510] P sues D for personal injuries of $8,000 and property damages of $2,000 as a result of an automobile collision. The suit is brought in P's name. As a result of pretrial discovery D learns that P's losses have been totally paid by his collision insurer. Thereafter, D moves to have P's action dismissed since he is not a real party in interest. The motion should be granted because, having been fully compensated for his losses, the insured no longer had a sufficient interest in the litigation to permit his prosecution of it. The insurance company is the real party in interest. However, if P's insurance policy covered all his losses except an initial payment of $100, the motion should be denied because P continues to have some interest in the litigation.

a. Loan Receipt. [§6.2520]

Insurance companies often will use a device known as a loan receipt to avoid the necessity of suing in their own names and thereby avoid the possibility of jury prejudice against them. Instead of paying the insured's losses, the insurer lends a comparable sum of money to the insured who must repay the loan in an amount not exceeding the recovery from the defendant. If it appears that the transaction is a bona fide loan and not merely designed to keep the insurer's name out of the litigation, the defendant may not insist that the insurer be named as a plaintiff.

(1) Indicia of Sham Loan Receipt Agreements. [§6.2521]

If an inspection of what purports to be a loan receipt agreement reveals that there was no unconditional promise by the insured to repay, no certain date set for the repayment, and no provisions for the accumulation of interest, the court should grant the defendant's motion to join the insurer as a real party in interest, since it seems apparent that the only purpose for executing the loan receipt was to evade the requirement that the litigation be prosecuted in the name of the real party in interest. This conclusion seems particularly appropriate if the litigation is financed and controlled by the insurance company.

6. Effect of Failure to Join Real Party in Interest. [§6.2600]

If the real party in interest has not been joined, the court should allow a reasonable time for his or her substitution. If he or she is not joined during this period, the suit should be dismissed. Dismissal should be a last resort, however. The parties should be allowed to amend freely to substitute the real party in interest, and when the naming of the wrong person was an honest mistake, the amendment should relate back to the date of the original filing if the statute of limitations has run since the commencement of the action. [See **§5.9420** for a discussion of relation back of amendments.]

7. Burden of Proving Real Party in Interest. [§6.2700]

Since the burden of proving a right to relief almost invariably is upon the plaintiff, it follows that the burden of proving that he or she is a real party in interest is upon the plaintiff.

a. Waiver: Real Party in Interest. [§6.2710]

Objections based on real party in interest generally relate to the existence of a claim upon which relief may be granted. Accordingly, some systems [see, e.g., Federal Rule 12(h)] permit the defect to be raised at any time. Other systems, however, see the real party in interest defect as a threshold matter that must be raised in the initial responsive pleading. The better practice, of course, is to raise the defense early in the action to avoid the possibility of waiver.

D. CAPACITY TO SUE OR BE SUED. [§6.3000]

Capacity to sue or be sued refers to an individual's ability or inability to represent his or her interests in a lawsuit without assistance. Problems of capacity generally arise in the context of litigants who are infants or incompetents, or otherwise incapacitated.

1. Distinction between Capacity to Sue or Be Sued and Real Party in Interest. [§6.3100]

A person who is not a real party in interest is one whose interest in the litigation is so slight that he or she should not be permitted to prosecute the action or be named as a party to it. A person lacking capacity to sue or be sued is one who is unable to prosecute or defend an action even though he or she has a direct stake in the outcome of the litigation, but must be represented before the court by someone else.

Illustration 1. [§6.3110] P, a minor, sustains personal injuries in an automobile collision and brings suit alleging that the defendant's negligence was the proximate cause of the accident. Under the law of the forum state, actions on behalf of minors must be prosecuted by a guardian ad litem appointed by the court. Unless this is done, the suit should be dismissed since, even though the minor is the real party in interest, she lacks capacity to sue.

Illustration 2. [§6.3120] P, an eccentric inventor, brings suit for patent infringement. In a recent hearing to determine P's competency to manage his own affairs, he was adjudged legally sane and competent. However, D discovers that P has assigned away his rights under the patent that is the subject matter of the suit. A motion to dismiss the action will succeed because even though P has capacity to sue, he is not a real party in interest.

---

2. Burden of Proving Capacity. [§6.3200]

Modern pleading rules similar to the Federal Rules place the burden on the defendant to assert lack of capacity at the pleading stage. The actual burden of proof is on the party whose capacity is challenged.

a. Waiver: Capacity. [§6.3210]

Objections as to a party's capacity should be raised early in the action since a guardian will have to be appointed if the plaintiff lacks capacity. If this defense is not raised in a timely fashion, it will be waived. In the federal courts, however, if the objection to capacity bears on the court's subject matter jurisdiction in diversity of citizenship cases, it may be raised at any time.

3. Capacity to Sue or Be Sued in the Federal Courts. [§6.3300]

Federal Rule 17 states that a litigant's capacity to sue or be sued is governed by state law, unless the case falls within several listed exceptions. Rule 17 also articulates which state's law should be used in determining the capacity of various types of litigants.

E. PERMISSIVE JOINDER OF PARTIES. [§6.4000]

Before joinder of a party is allowed, it must be determined whether that individual is a proper party. Someone whose interests are closely related to the litigation is a proper party and may be joined at the option of one of the parties already in the action. Modern procedural rules [see, e.g., Federal Rule 20] often require that two questions be answered affirmatively before joinder is permitted: (a) Does the right to relief asserted by or against the person to be joined relate to or arise out of a single transaction or occurrence or a series of related transactions or occurrences that are the subject matter of the action? and (b) Is there some question of law or fact common between or among the parties who are to be joined and those already in the action? Once the first requirement is met, the second almost always follows. The latter requisite is included more as a safety valve to ensure that the subject matter of the dispute between the parties is the same.

1. Historical Development. [§6.4100]

Historically, no joinder of parties was possible since the case was governed entirely by the pleadings and the restrictive rules surrounding the forms of action. The writ system allowed only one plaintiff, one defendant, and one cause of action. Now that the traditional emphasis on the pleadings has been reduced dramatically and the scope of the action much increased, courts have adopted broad, permissive rules allowing the joinder of parties with related interests. Thus, today it is common for a court to resolve all doubts in favor of joinder. When the joinder of parties might lead to confusion or prejudice, the court has the power to sever claims and parties or order separate trials to simplify the lawsuit [see **§6.9200–§6.9400**].

a. Joinder at Common Law and in Equity. [§6.4110]

At common law, joinder of persons who asserted rights that were "several" was unknown. On the other hand, if the rights of the party to be joined were "joint" with the rights of the other parties, joinder was compelled. The practice with respect to joining defendants was more permissive in that joint tortfeasors and defendants whose contract obligations were both "joint" and "several" could be sued

181

jointly or severally. In equity, rules were developed to render complete justice among all persons interested in the litigation and to avoid multiplicity of suits; hence, all persons having an interest in the subject matter of the action or in the relief sought were allowed to join as plaintiffs or defendants.

b. Joinder under the Original Codes. [§6.4120]

Early code provisions were construed as requiring that a party be interested in both the subject matter of the action and in all the relief sought. These requirements meant that two contiguous landowners could not join in an action against a defendant whose tortious conduct had injured their respective properties since both were not interested in all the relief that might be awarded. However, the court would allow the landowners to join in an action for an injunction against the defendant's tortious conduct because both plaintiffs would have an interest in all the relief.

c. Modern Joinder Practice. [§6.4130]

The modern rules of party joinder, illustrated by Federal Rule 20 and followed today in most state courts, permit liberal joinder of plaintiffs or defendants. The rules generally require that the claims by or against the person to be joined present common questions of fact or law, and that they arise out of the same transactions or occurrences as the claims of the other parties litigating the matter [see **§6.4200–§6.4320**].

2. Party Joinder Test 1: Same Transaction or Occurrence. [§6.4200]

Most courts have adopted a case-by-case approach rather than trying to establish a generalized standard for ascertaining when the factual similarities are so numerous that the "same transaction or occurrence" test has been met. Accordingly, the particular facts of each case must be analyzed to determine whether joinder should be permitted.

a. Logical Relationship Standard. [§6.4210]

The judicial approach used in defining "transaction" and "occurrence" in the context of permissive party joinder is similar to the analysis used in the context of compulsory counterclaims [see **§7.1400–§7.1510**]. In both situations, courts typically view the claims of the parties in terms of whether they are logically related to each other. The question in each case is whether there is enough factual overlap so that it would be efficient to allow the parties to litigate jointly.

> **Illustration. [§6.4211]** P brings suit against an insurance company for fraudulently delaying payment of his claim until after the expiration of the statute of limitations. P also joins his former attorney as a defendant alleging that the lawyer was negligent in permitting the statute of limitations to expire before filing suit. The defendants challenge their joinder, claiming that there is a clear separation between the action for fraud and the action for negligence. The motion should be denied. Even though different legal causes of action are involved, the facts of the case show that there is a reasonable connection between them, and adjudicating both together would promote judicial economy.

3.   Party Joinder Test 2: Common Question of Law or Fact. [§6.4300]

The second test that must be met for joinder of parties is that there be a common question of law or fact respecting the claims asserted by or against the party to be joined and those asserted by or against the other parties to the action.

a.   Only One Question Need Be Common. [§6.4310]

Since the modern policy toward joinder of parties is extremely liberal, it is not necessary that all, or even a majority, of the questions in the action be common to all the parties. As long as there is one basic question of law or fact concerning the claims asserted by or against the parties to the action, joinder should be permitted. Moreover, the common question need not actually be in controversy; the issue may have been stipulated to or agreed upon by all the parties in the action.

> **Illustration 1. [§6.4311]** P brings suit against A, B, C, and D for alleged violations of the federal antitrust laws, alleging that the four defendants have engaged in a conspiracy to fix the price of compact discs. In additional counts, P alleges that A has conspired with B to set uniform prices on all Capitol discs, and that C has conspired with D to set uniform prices on all Decca discs. The defendants challenge the joinder, claiming that the fact necessary to show a conspiracy between A and B would be different from the facts required to show a conspiracy between C and D. The

challenge should be rejected. Even though there may be numerous questions of fact not common to all parties, there is at least one question of fact common to all—the existence of a conspiracy among all four defendants.

Illustration 2. [§6.4312] A and B join in an action to recover for personal injuries and property damage resulting from an automobile collision. Both allege that the defendant negligently drove onto a highway in the path of plaintiff A, and that seconds later, B had crashed into the rear of A. B's liability to A was settled out of court. The defendant moves to separate the actions against her asserting that there clearly are separate issues as to damages and a separate issue as to B's contributory negligence. Since there is one common question, the issue of the defendant's negligence, the motion should be denied.

b. Common Questions of Law. [§6.4320]

It has been argued, with limited success, that for purposes of joinder of parties the common question of law must relate directly to the particular facts of the case rather than be a general legal principle. The rationale is that bizarre and inequitable results would follow from permitting joinder when only a general principle of law tenuously connects the parties. This argument overlooks the limiting effect of the first requirement for permissive joinder of parties—that the claims arise out of the same transaction or occurrence. Furthermore, the common question of law requirement is not a rigid rule; it is a flexible concept designed to promote judicial economy and the achievement of complete justice with a minimum of litigation.

4. Several and Alternative Joinder. [§6.4400]

The modern philosophy exemplified by Federal Rule 20 permits joinder of plaintiffs or defendants when the claims asserted by or against them are joint, several, or in the alternative, so long as they meet the two criteria for permissive joinder described in the preceding sections. This represents a significant expansion of the common law practice.

Illustration 1. [§6.4410] A bus driven by one defendant and owned by another defendant—a bus company—failed to stop at a busy intersection and crashed into a brick structure. Thirty of the passengers were injured. They all seek to join in one action against the two defendants. The defendants move to separate the actions claiming that the rights asserted by the plaintiffs are "several" in nature. The motion should be denied. Even though the rights asserted were "several," the joinder of the passengers would promote judicial efficiency and avoid multiplicity of suits.

Illustration 2. [§6.4420] P, the wife of a deceased railroad worker, brings suit against three different insurance carriers under the Federal Employers' Liability Act. Since P is unsure of the identity of her husband's employer at the time of his death, she alleges that he was employed by at least one of three companies, and, therefore, that she should recover from at least one of the companies' insurers. A challenge to this alternative joinder should be rejected since it permits P to settle her claim in one action. Denying joinder would force P to bring separate suits and risk inconsistent jury verdicts.

5. **State Statutes. [§6.4500]**

The joinder rule in some states differs from that set out in Federal Rule 20 and is similar to that permitted in equity prior to the merger of law and equity [see **§6.4110**]. Thus, some states permit joinder whenever the parties have an interest in the property or controversy that is the subject of the action. However, the results reached usually are the same as those achieved under Federal Rule 20 and its counterparts.

F. PERSONS WHO MUST BE JOINED IF FEASIBLE. [§6.5000]

When is a non-party's relationship or involvement in the litigation so strong that his or her presence will be compelled, assuming that this is feasible? Courts apply two tests for determining the degree of interest that a person must have before joinder will be compelled. First, a non-party must be joined if, in his or her absence, complete relief cannot be accorded among those already parties. Second, a non-party's joinder will be compelled if he or she has an interest in the subject matter of the action, and is so situated that rendering a judgment in his or her absence, as a practical matter, may impair or impede his or her ability to protect that interest, or if any of the existing parties would be subject to a substantial risk of incurring inconsistent obligations in separate suits [see Federal Rule 19(a); **§6.5300–§6.5510**]. Non-parties meeting either of these tests must be joined in the litigation, unless their joinder would destroy the subject matter jurisdiction of the court or personal jurisdiction over them cannot be obtained [see **§3.2000–§3.3620**]. In certain circumstances, if the non-party cannot be joined, the action must be dismissed for lack of an "indispensable" party [see **§6.6000–§6.6710**].

1. **Judicial Weighing of the Competing Interests. [§6.5100]**

   Competing interests are raised by the two tests in Rule 19 for compulsory joinder. As the preceding section demonstrates, a court must consider the parties before the court, the absentee parties, and judicial efficiency, when deciding whether or not joinder should be compelled. The right of a plaintiff to select an adverse party or parties and secure an adjudication of his or her claim within that chosen framework of parties may be overridden. This will be the case when the defendant or the potential but absent plaintiffs or defendants might be prejudiced by the outcome, or the judicial system's interest in the orderly, expeditious administration of justice and the entry of final and effective judgments requires the addition of one or more non-parties.

2. **Distinction between Permissive and Necessary Parties. [§6.5200]**

   The difference between a "proper party," who may be joined, and a "party who must be joined if feasible," is really only one of degree. A "party who must be joined if feasible" is only a "proper party" whose interest in the pending litigation is so strong that it would be unfair and inefficient to litigate without him.

Illustration. [§6.5210] P filed an action alleging that four competing shippers had conspired to restrain trade in violation of the Shipping Act of 1916. Only three of the shippers were named as defendants. They promptly moved that the fourth shipper be joined as a defendant alleging that they would be prejudiced if their competitor were not also named a defendant. The three defendants claimed that the absentee was a "party who must be joined if feasible." Because the damage that the present defendants might suffer is not a result of any interest asserted by or against the

---

absentee relating to the subject matter of the litigation, the test for compulsory joinder is not satisfied. P could voluntarily have joined the fourth shipper, however, because the tests for permissive joinder are met—there is a claim that may be asserted against the absentee arising out of the same transaction or occurrence as the claims advanced against the present defendants, and there are common questions of law and fact.

3. **Application of Compulsory Joinder Test: Complete Relief Cannot Be Accorded Those Already Parties. [§6.5300]**

The compulsory joinder requirement is designed to protect the interests of the present litigants against the possibility that despite a full trial on the merits, the court will find that it cannot award effective relief to those before it. It also furthers society's interest in avoiding multiplicity of suits, since, if complete relief cannot be granted, there is a likelihood of subsequent litigation.

Illustration. [§6.5310] P brought suit against her employer's insurer without joining the employer in an action for work-related personal injuries. The insurance policy only covered losses in excess of $25,000. Therefore, a jury verdict for less than $25,000 would be ineffective as against the insurance company. In order to protect the insurance company by avoiding a subsequent and largely duplicative suit against the employer, the latter's joinder should be compelled.

4. **Application of Compulsory Joinder Test: Impairment of Non–Party's Interest. [§6.5400]**

Joinder of a non-party is mandatory when the non-party's interest in the subject matter of the litigation would be impaired if the litigation went forward in his or her absence. The test for determining whether there is a threat of impairment is a practical one and joinder is not limited to situations in which there is a legal handicap. Thus, for example, joinder may be compelled even though the doctrine of res judicata will not be applied to a non-party. All that is necessary is that the adjudication in the non-party's absence threatens the non-party's ability to prosecute or defend a subsequent action.

Illustration. [§6.5410] A and B sue an insurance company after they were injured in an automobile accident involving X's vehicle, which was driven by Y, who allegedly had X's permission. The plaintiffs claim that the insurance company, which was X's insurer, was directly liable to them since the policy, by its terms, covered any person driving with X's permission. The insurance company claims that X must be joined as a defendant since a judgment in his absence might impede X's ability to protect his interests in the dispute. If there is a real possibility that X might be liable as Y's "principal," X has an interest in preserving the insurance fund to cover this potential liability. X's inclusion in the action should be compelled because his ability to protect himself in a subsequent action would be substantially impaired if the insurance fund were exhausted in the present suit [cf. *Provident Tradesmen's Bank & Trust Co. v. Patterson* (1968); see **§6.6310**].

5. Application of Compulsory Joinder Test: Threat of Multiple Liability. [§6.5500]

A party must be joined in an action if he or she claims an interest in the subject matter and is so situated that the rendering of a judgment in his or her absence would subject the parties already litigating the matter to the threat of multiple liability. Of the three standards that may be used in identifying a "party who must be joined if feasible," this test is the easiest to apply. It is similar to the test for interpleader [see **§8.4100**].

Illustration. [§6.5510] P brings suit against D, a bank, for conversion of shares of stock allegedly owned by P. P claims that he and another party, B, jointly purchased stock and that he had requested that B direct the bank to issue some shares reflecting P's half ownership. Nonetheless, all the shares were issued in B's name. The bank, however, claims that it has superior rights to B in the stock and that it had no knowledge of P's alleged ownership. B must be joined if feasible because an adjudication of the plaintiff's half ownership of the stock without B would subject the bank to the threat of double liability since B would not be bound by the judgment in the action and could bring a subsequent action against the bank claiming all the stock [*Haas v. Jefferson Nat'l Bank of Miami Beach* (1971)].

6. Joinder Feasible. [§6.5600]

After it has been determined that a non-party's interest in a lawsuit requires his or her joinder, it is necessary to determine whether joinder can be compelled. Joinder may not be feasible if the plaintiff is unable to obtain personal jurisdiction over the outsider or if joinder would destroy the court's subject matter jurisdiction. Also, there must be proper venue as to the absentee, although if this defense is not asserted in timely fashion, it will be deemed waived [see §2.7120].

7. Procedure for Compulsory Joinder. [§6.5700]

After ascertaining that a non-party's joinder should be compelled and that his or her joinder is feasible, a party seeking joinder normally is given a reasonable opportunity to serve the non-party and bring him or her into the action. If the non-party is not joined, the court may order joinder itself. Dismissal of the action for non-joinder should be the last resort and should be reserved for situations in which a party willfully refuses to comply with the court's orders.

8. Compulsory Joinder of a Non–Party As a Defendant. [§6.5800]

If a non-party's interest in the subject matter of the litigation is such that the non-party should be included in the suit as a plaintiff but he or she refuses to join in the action, the non-party may be joined as a defendant (assuming, of course, that the non-party is subject to the court's jurisdiction).

a. Realignment. [§6.5810]

Normally, someone who naturally would be a plaintiff who has been joined as a defendant should be realigned as a plaintiff, particularly for diversity of citizenship purposes, since his or her interests are the same as those of the original plaintiff. This will avoid the collusive invocation of federal jurisdiction. Sometimes, however, the interests of an involuntarily joined party make that litigant hostile to the plaintiff and he or she should be allowed to remain as a defendant.

Illustration. [§6.5811] P, a stockholder in X Corporation, brought a stockholder's derivative suit against the president of the company for breach of trust. P asked that an accounting be made and that compensation be paid to the company for the president's wrongful conduct. Thus, X Corporation stood to benefit from P's action. The company originally was named as a defendant and realigning it as a plaintiff would destroy diversity of citizenship. Because X Corpora-

---

> tion was under the control of someone whose interests are antagonistic to those of P, realignment should not be ordered.

9.   Compulsory Joinder of an Involuntary Plaintiff. [§6.5900]

In a few special circumstances, if a non-party who should be joined as a plaintiff refuses to enter the suit, he or she may be joined as an involuntary plaintiff. The joinder of an involuntary plaintiff is limited to cases in which the party to be added is not subject to the court's jurisdiction and hence cannot be joined as a defendant [see **§6.5800**]. Involuntary plaintiffs need not be served with process and need not be present in the action for a judgment to have a res judicata effect against them.

a.   Origin and Application of the Involuntary Plaintiff Procedure. [§6.5910]

The involuntary plaintiff practice developed as an attempt to mitigate the harsh results that flowed from the rule that licensees of patents and copyrights could not bring infringement suits without joining the owner of the patent or copyright as a co-plaintiff. If the owner refused to join as a plaintiff, the suit had to be dismissed. Today, the involuntary plaintiff procedure largely is confined to infringement suits by exclusive licensees of patents and copyrights. In the federal courts, Rule 19 limits the application of involuntary plaintiff joinder to a "proper case," which has been interpreted to mean when the non-party whose joinder is sought has a legal duty, typically contractual, to allow the plaintiff to use the non-party's name in the action.

G.   INDISPENSABLE PARTIES. [§6.6000]

If it is not feasible to join a non-party whose presence otherwise would be compelled, it must be determined whether, in equity and good conscience, the action should be dismissed or allowed to proceed without that person. If it is determined that the non-party is indispensable, then the action must be dismissed. Procedural rules often list various factors to be considered in deciding whether the outsider's presence in the action is indispensable to its continuation. Federal Rule 19(b) lists the following: (a) the extent to which a judgment rendered in the non-party's absence might be prejudicial to that person or to those already parties; (b) the extent to which the prejudice can be lessened or avoided by protective provisions in the judgment, shaping of relief, or other measures; (c) whether a judgment rendered in the non-party's absence will provide adequate relief to the existing parties; and (d) whether the plaintiff will have an adequate alternative remedy if the action is dismissed for non-joinder [see **§6.6200–§6.6610**].

1.   **Historical Development of Indispensable Party Concept. [§6.6100]**

The foundation for determining whether a non-party is indispensable to an action or merely necessary or desirable is *Shields v. Barrow* (1855). The Court defined "necessary parties" as persons whose interest in the litigation was sufficiently substantial that joinder should be compelled, but not sufficiently substantial that if joinder would destroy the subject matter jurisdiction of the court or if personal jurisdiction were unobtainable, the action would be dismissed. "Indispensable parties" were defined as persons whose interest in the litigation was so substantial that an action should be dismissed rather than adjudicated in their absence. The codes adopted these labels and spelled out criteria for deciding whether a party was necessary or indispensable. It was said that both necessary and indispensable parties are those whose interests are "joint" with the interests asserted by those already litigating. The difference between the two was that the former's interests were severable so that if a necessary party could not be joined, the suit nevertheless could proceed to judgment in his absence.

Illustration 1. [§6.6110] P, a citizen of Maine, sues D, a citizen of Vermont, in federal district court on a debt. D and his partner, a citizen of Maine, were jointly liable on the debt. D moves to dismiss, asserting that his partner is an indispensable party and that compelling her joinder would destroy the diversity jurisdiction of the court. D's interests are severable, thus, she is merely a "necessary party." The suit should not be dismissed.

Illustration 2. [§6.6120] P, a member of a popular singing group, filed an action to dissolve the partnership agreement that had existed between her and her fellow vocalists. Two of the three other members of the group lived in New York, where the suit was filed; the third lived in California. Process could not be served on the Californian. Since the Californian's interests in the litigation are not severable, any judgment in her absence would prejudice her; therefore, the action should be dismissed.

---

2.   **Modern Indispensable Party Practice. [§6.6200]**

Today, courts usually take a pragmatic approach toward indispensable parties and examine the particular circumstances of each case. This is

191

illustrated by Federal Rule 19. This provision replaces the conclusory labels "necessary" and "indispensable" with four practical considerations that are believed to be more useful in effectuating modern joinder policies—to render complete justice with a minimum of litigation and to maximize judicial economy. The new Rule's designation in subdivision (a) of "parties required to be joined if feasible" roughly corresponds to the old classification of "necessary parties." Subdivision (b), captioned "when joinder is not feasible" eliminates any reference to "indispensable parties" and is intended to describe the conclusion reached after analyzing the factors set out in the Rule. Federal Rule 19(b) lists the following considerations: (1) the extent to which a judgment rendered in the non-party's absence might be prejudicial to that person or to those already parties; (2) the extent to which the prejudice can be lessened or avoided by protective provisions in the judgment, shaping of relief, or other measures; (3) whether a judgment rendered in the non-party's absence will provide adequate relief to the existing parties; and (4) whether the plaintiff will have an adequate alternative remedy if the action is dismissed for non-joinder.

3. First Factor: Prejudice. [§6.6300]

One obvious factor in determining whether the suit should proceed without an absentee is the possibility of prejudice to either the non-party or the parties already litigating the controversy. This possibility should be real, not merely theoretical.

Illustration. [§6.6310] Plaintiffs A, B's administratrix, and C's administrator bring suit against a car owner's (O) insurer (I) for damages arising out of an automobile accident. O allegedly had given the driver (E) permission to drive the car. The terms of the policy covered the liability of persons driving with O's permission. O was not joined and a verdict was rendered against I. The insurance company now moves to dismiss the action asserting that O is an indispensable party, particularly since there is a possibility that O can be held liable to the plaintiff as E's "principal." If the insurance policy limits are exhausted in paying off the verdict in the first action, O's ability to defend an action against him as E's "principal" would be significantly impaired. However, although O might well be a party who should be joined if feasible [see §6.5000], the likelihood of prejudice is not substantial enough to warrant dismissal of the suit because he cannot be joined as a

---

party. As a non-party, O is not bound by the judgment in the action, the threat of his personal liability is neither large nor unavoidable, his vicarious liability as E's principal is unlikely under local state law, and he can raise the issue of lack of permission defensively in any action against him and claim credit for the earlier payments made on E's behalf out of the insurance fund [*Provident Tradesmen's Bank & Trust Co. v. Patterson* (1968)].

4. Second Factor: Minimizing Prejudice by Shaping Relief. [§6.6400]

The extent to which parties or absentees may be prejudiced by non-joinder may be minimized by the inclusion of protective provisions in the judgment. The court is obligated to shape relief whenever it can and thereby preserve the action, especially when it determines that the equities are evenly balanced on the question of dismissal or going forward with the action.

Illustration. [§6.6410] The executor of a will seeks to have the residuary clause of the instrument declared invalid. This action clearly would affect the interest of one absent heir. Rather than dismiss the action, the court could direct the retention by the executor of a sum sufficient to protect the absentee's interest, which would be adjudicated in another suit, or it could require the executor to give adequate security to protect any interest that the absentee may have. Since a decree may be shaped to protect the absentee's interests and yet do justice to the parties before the court, the outsider should not be regarded as indispensable.

5. Third Factor: Ability to Render an Adequate Judgment. [§6.6500]

The court must determine whether adequate relief can be granted in the non-party's absence prior to deciding whether to proceed with the case. If all or a substantial portion of the work to be done in the present action would be nullified by subsequent litigation, then the current action should be terminated. This would be the case if the non-party has a substantial stake in the action, and his or her absence would render the judgment unenforceable and require a second action. Of course, the threat of subsequent litigation is less of a justification for dismissal of the first action once that proceeding has reached judgment.

Illustration. [§6.6510] P brings suit against a corporation in which he owns stock to compel the issuance of dividends. The court neither has jurisdiction over corporate property nor over a majority of the members of the company's board of directors, and as a result, is powerless to compel the issuance of dividends. Any relief that might be ordered, therefore, will be inadequate. The suit should be dismissed because the absentee directors must be regarded as indispensable parties.

6.   **Fourth Factor: Effect of Dismissal on the Adequacy of Plaintiff's Relief. [§6.6600]**

The fourth factor requires the court to consider whether dismissal of the action will deprive the plaintiff of an adequate remedy. Often the plaintiff will be able to file suit in another court. But if dismissal will leave a party without recourse to any court, dismissal should be avoided if at all possible. However, the other factors may be such that it will be appropriate for an action to be dismissed even though the plaintiff will be left without a remedy.

Illustration. [§6.6610] P brings an action involving a labor dispute against several individuals. A local union is determined to be a party that must be joined if feasible. However, venue is improper in the forum state as to the union and joinder would not be feasible. Moreover, the applicable statute of limitations has expired in the only state in which venue is proper as to the union. But it appears that the union's absence will substantially prejudice several parties to the litigation and there is no way to shape a remedy to protect everyone's interests. After giving due weight to the fact that P may not be able to secure a remedy elsewhere, it still is preferable to dismiss the suit than to allow it to proceed.

7.   **Defects in Party Joinder. [§6.6700]**

A defect in joinder will result in dismissal only when an indispensable party cannot be joined; although, as the preceding sections demonstrate, it will not be ordered until after it has been determined that joinder actually is not feasible and the action cannot proceed without the absentee. Dismissal never should be ordered because improper or unnecessary parties have been joined in the action. Any prejudice caused by the presence of improper parties may be avoided by the court severing them from the action or ordering separate trials [see **§6.9200–§6.9330**].

a. **Timely Motions to Dismiss. [§6.6710]**

Motions to dismiss for failure to join an indispensable party may be made at any time by a party, the non-party, or the court. If the prejudice to be prevented relates to someone who is already a party to the action, however, the court may deny a late motion to dismiss, holding the objection to have been waived by the delay.

H. SPECIAL JOINDER PROBLEMS IN THE FEDERAL COURTS. [§6.7000]

Certain joinder of party problems are peculiar to the federal courts because of their limited subject matter jurisdiction.

1. Governing Law. [§6.7100]

In *Provident Tradesmen's Bank & Trust Co. v. Patterson* (1968), the Supreme Court rejected the contention that a party's classification as "necessary" or "indispensable" is substantive in nature under the *Erie* doctrine. It held that a federal court need not follow state joinder practice in diversity cases and that Rule 19(b) is a valid exercise of the rule-making power delegated to the Court by the Rules Enabling Act [see **§4.3332**].

2. Jurisdiction and Venue. [§6.7200]

As amended in 1990, 28 USC 1367 confers supplemental jurisdiction over claims and parties joined to a civil action that is based on federal question jurisdiction. In diversity cases, however, the court does not have supplemental jurisdiction over claims by plaintiffs against non-diverse persons made parties under Rules 19 and 20, or over non-diverse parties joined as plaintiffs under Rule 19. The usual rules of diversity jurisdiction apply, and aggregation of claims ordinarily is permitted for purposes of satisfying the jurisdictional amount only if the parties on one side have a common undivided interest [see **§2.4300**]. Federal venue requirements also must be satisfied [see **§2.7400–§2.7490**].

I. JOINDER OF CLAIMS. [§6.8000]

The sections that follow discuss the basic rules relating to the joinder of claims by one party against an opposing party. This discussion is augmented by the analysis of counterclaims [see **§7.1000**], cross-claims [see **§7.3000**], and third-party claims [see **§7.5000**].

1. Historical Development of Joinder of Claims. [§6.8100]

At common law, the determination of whether claims could be joined depended upon the application of the forms of action, rather than on considerations of judicial efficiency or party convenience. This meant that related claims arising from a single transaction or occurrence could not be joined if they fell under different forms of action. Conversely, completely unrelated claims could be joined as long as they were within the same form of action. In equity, unlimited joinder of claims was permitted in suits between a single plaintiff and a single defendant. In multi-party suits, the chancellor usually would allow claims to be joined if it would be more efficient to litigate the claims in one action.

a. Effect of Merger of Law and Equity. [§6.8110]

The union of law and equity under the codes resulted in a compromise as to when claims could be joined. Claims could be joined so long as they involved the same type of injury, whether or not they arose out of a single transaction. Accordingly, two unrelated contract claims could be joined but a contract claim and a tort claim could not. A plaintiff who sued for personal injuries could not join a claim for property damage. An early modification in many codes was the inclusion of a provision permitting joinder of all claims arising from a single transaction or occurrence.

2. Scope of Modern Claim Joinder. [§6.8200]

Modern procedural rules usually place no restrictions on joinder of claims. This is true in the federal courts, but only if subject matter jurisdiction prerequisites are satisfied. Thus, Federal Rule 18(a) provides that a party asserting a claim to relief on an original claim, counterclaim, cross-claim, or third-party claim may join as many claims—legal, equitable, or maritime—as he or she has against an opposing party. In order to prevent actions from becoming unduly complicated and diffuse, the court has the discretion to sever claims and issues, or order that they be tried separately pursuant to Rule 42(b) [see **§6.9000–§6.9330**].

a. Joinder in the Alternative. [§6.8210]

Claims may be asserted in the alternative; consequently, an election of legal theories or remedies will not be required at the pleading stage.

Illustration. [§6.8211] P, who was injured by a drill press manufactured by D, brings suit, alleging that his injuries are the direct result of D's negligent manufacture of the machine. P also alleges that D had breached its warranty of merchantability and fitness for a particular

---

purpose. D moves to require P to elect between the tort theory and the contract theory. The motion should be denied. There is no reason to force P to select between two theories asserted in good faith. If P must select and loses on the theory of his choice, either he can sue again on the other theory, assuming that the statute of limitations has not run in the interim, or the principles of former adjudication will prevent him from bringing a second suit. Neither of these possibilities serves justice.

b. Joinder of Prospective Claims. [§6.8220]

Modern procedural rules also permit the joinder of claims even though, had they been prosecuted separately, the rendition of a favorable final judgment on one of them would have been necessary before litigation could proceed on the other.

Illustration. [§6.8221] A creditor brings suit against D to recover on a loan. She also joins X, to whom D transferred property that was supposed to provide security for the loan, and requests that the transfer be set aside as fraudulent. At one time the creditor would have been required to obtain a money judgment before calling upon the court to set aside a fraudulent conveyance. Today, both claims may be joined in one suit.

3. Permissive Character of Joinder of Claims. [§6.8300]

Almost all procedural systems permit joinder of claims; most do not compel it. However, doctrines of former adjudication often work to compel the joinder of claims that are factually related [see §16.3110].

4. Joinder of Claims and Joinder of Parties Distinguished. [§6.8400]

Procedural rules governing the joinder of claims are independent of the rules pertaining to joinder of parties. Before the 1966 amendment of Federal Rule 18, this proposition was by no means clear in the federal courts. The amendment makes it clear that once a party has been joined in an action, he or she may assert any claim against an opposing party and, in turn, is subject to any claim asserted by the opposing party. This is not the case in all states, although many have adopted federal-type joinder rules.

Illustration. [§6.8410] P, an owner of property contiguous to a small stream, sues three riparian owners, A, B, and C, claiming damages as a result of their pollution. The claims asserted against each defendant contain common questions of law or fact and stem from the same transaction or occurrence. Thus, A, B, and C are proper parties and their joinder is proper [see **§6.4000**]. In a jurisdiction that follows federal-type joinder rules, the plaintiff may assert a claim against A for breach of contract, even though it is not within the same transaction or occurrence as the claim for nuisance, and even though similar actions for breach of contract are not asserted against B and C.

5.   Federal Subject Matter Jurisdiction. [§6.8500]

In the federal courts, Rule 18(a) does not, in and of itself, satisfy the requirements of subject matter jurisdiction. Thus, the additional claims to be asserted must meet jurisdictional requirements, either independently or through 28 USC 1367. A case based on diversity jurisdiction usually is not affected by Rule 18(a) because the diverse parties already are before the court, and when a single plaintiff is suing a single defendant, the value of all the claims of one party may be aggregated to satisfy the amount in controversy requirement. Aggregation is possible even though the claims are completely unrelated; however, claims among multiple parties may not be aggregated. [Aggregation is discussed in **§2.4300**.] If a federal question forms the original basis of jurisdiction, Section 1367 provides that supplemental jurisdiction will apply only to claims that are so related to the original action that they form the same case or controversy. Additionally, if the initial claim was based on supplemental jurisdiction, a claim under Rule 18(a) cannot be joined without independent subject matter jurisdiction. [Supplemental jurisdiction is discussed in **§2.5000–§2.5530**.]

6.   Personal Jurisdiction and Venue in Federal Actions. [§6.8600]

Although there is some doubt on the point, personal jurisdiction must be proper as to each claim. Problems of personal jurisdiction usually arise only when a party has been properly served with process pursuant to a statute with regard to one claim, but the defendant is not subject to process under that statute for purposes of the joined claim. In some cases, even though the defendant could not have been served with process as to that claim if it were sued upon alone, courts have held that adjudication of the additional claim is permitted as an extension of supplemental jurisdiction [see **§2.5600**], as long as the claim is based on the same transaction and occurrence as the original action. If venue is proper for one of the claims asserted by the plaintiff, the same policies of judicial economy that underlie what is now called supplemental subject matter jurisdiction should lead a court to disregard a defect in venue as to the joined claim.

Illustration. [§6.8610] P brings suit for violation of a federal statute which contains a nationwide service of process provision. P attempts to join a state claim; if sued upon alone, P would not have been able to serve D with process. However, the same basic facts are necessary to prove the federal and state claims. The court has supplemental subject matter jurisdiction over the state claim and may have a form of supplemental personal jurisdiction over D for purposes of the state claim.

J. CONSOLIDATION, SEVERANCE, AND SEPARATE TRIALS. [§6.9000]

Modern procedural systems provide three devices to deal with claims and parties that either should have been joined in a single action, should not be adjudicated together, or should not be tried jointly. These devices are orders of consolidation, orders of severance, and orders of separate trial. In deciding whether to use any of these procedures, the court will consider the convenience of the parties, the need to do justice for each litigant, and the desire to maximize judicial economy.

1. Consolidation of Actions. [§6.9100]

Contemporary procedural regulations, exemplified by Federal Rule 42(a), permit the consolidation of separate actions if there is a common question of law or fact between them. The court's power may be exercised partially. Thus, a joint hearing or trial of only the common issues may be ordered, or the consolidation may extend only to the pretrial phase of the litigation. Complete consolidation is not permitted in the federal courts when the suits are filed in different judicial districts, although the possibility of consolidation may be a factor in determining whether an action will be transferred under 28 USC 1404 [see **§2.7630**]. Furthermore, the consolidation of litigation pending in more than one district may be ordered for pretrial purposes by the Judicial Panel on Multidistrict Litigation pursuant to 28 USC 1407 [see **§2.7700**].

a. Discretion of the Court. [§6.9110]

A question of consolidation may be raised either on the court's initiative or by a party's motion. The consolidation decision is entirely a matter for the discretion of the court; the consent of the parties is not required. If consolidation would lead to delay or to prejudice, or if the common question is not a central one, the court may refuse to order consolidation even though there is some overlap among the claims. When actions are consolidated, the court is empowered to appoint one of the lawyers in the case as "lead" counsel to help coordinate litigation in order to prevent needless delay and expense.

b. Party Joinder, Consolidation, and Claim Joinder Distinguished. [§6.9120]

With respect to joinder of claims against a single party, a judge's power to order a joint trial or consolidation is limited by the requirement that there be a common question of law or fact; thus it is more limited than a party's right to join claims against an opposing party, which is unrestricted [see **§6.8200**]. On the other hand, the judge's power to order a joint trial or consolidation of claims by or against different parties is greater than the right of a party to join different parties because the judge requires only a common question of law or fact whereas a party requires both that the claims involve a common question of law or fact and arise out of the same transaction or occurrence [see **§6.4000**].

2. Severance of Claims. [§6.9200]

Because contemporary joinder procedures tend to encourage joinder of parties and claims, severance is permitted whenever it appears that the continued joint litigation of actions would be inefficient or prejudicial [see, e.g., Federal Rule 21].

a. Separate Trials and Severance of Claims Distinguished. [§6.9210]

The severance of claims leaves them totally independent of each other so that a separate judgment will be entered on each. A separate trial is a more limited decision and still results in the entry of one judgment.

b. Uses of Severance in Federal Courts. [§6.9220]

Severance may be employed to separate claims when some of the parties joined in the action have valid venue objections and the claims asserted against them are separable. The severed claims then may be transferred to a district in which venue would be proper pursuant to 28 USC 1406 [see **§2.7510**], or the claims may be severed in such a fashion that the defendant can implead one of the parties to the original action [see **§7.5000**]. Another use of severance arises in situations in which one of the representative plaintiffs in a class action states an independent claim in an individual capacity against the defendant. The severed claim may proceed even if the class action is dismissed.

Illustration. [§6.9221] A driver and her passenger bring a joint suit against the defendant for damages sustained in a collision between the plaintiff's automobile and one of the defendant's buses. The defendant attempts to implead the plaintiff-driver as the third-party defendant claiming that the driver's negligence makes her liable to the bus company for any liability the bus company may have to the passenger. Because impleader is not allowed when the potential third-party defendant is already a party to the action [see **§7.5000**], the court may order the driver's claim severed and then permit her to be joined as a third-party defendant in the remaining action by the passenger against the bus company.

---

3. **Separate Trials. [§6.9300]**

Separate trials will be permitted: (a) to further the convenience of the parties, (b) to avoid prejudice, and (c) to promote an expeditious and efficient adjudication of the dispute [see, e.g., Federal Rule 42(b)]. If one issue would be dispositive of the case and if separate adjudication of that issue would save time and money, a separate trial may be appropriate. However, if one issue is so interwoven with the other issues that it could not be independently submitted to a single jury without causing confusion, a separate trial on that issue will not be permitted. Separate trials may be ordered either upon motion of a party or on the court's own initiative. Because only the trials are separate, a single judgment will be entered.

Illustration. [§6.9310] P brings suit for personal injuries and joins a request that the court enjoin D from interposing a statute of limitations defense, asserting that D's fraudulent conduct had caused P to permit the limitations period to expire. D moves for a separate trial on the issue of fraud. A separate trial may be ordered if the court believes that a jury trying both the fraud and personal injury claims would be likely to inflate the damages as a result of hearing evidence of D's fraud.

---

a. Jury Trial. [§6.9320]

The separation of issues for separate trials cannot defeat a party's right to a trial by jury on any of the issues [see generally Chapter Thirteen]. If the issues are unrelated, the court has discretion to set the order of the trials; however, if there are overlapping legal and equitable issues, and if a jury trial is requested, the legal issues must be tried first to a jury [see **§13.4420**]. Although it is preferable to try the separate legal issues to the same jury, it probably is not constitutionally necessary that this be done.

b. Separate Trials on Liability and Damages. [§6.9330]

The evidence to establish liability often is distinct from that necessary to prove damages. When it is, separate trials may be ordered without any substantial loss of judicial efficiency. In fact, studies indicate that separate trials of liability and damages in personal injury cases take less time than the more conventional single trials in which issues of damages and liability are simultaneously submitted to the jury. This is because a decision of no liability obviates any need for a trial on damages. If, however, the evidence relating to liability is overlapping, this justification for separating the issues is vitiated.

(1) Constitutionality of Separate Trials for Liability and Damages. [§6.9331]

In light of data indicating that defendants are more likely to win in cases in which issues of liability and damages are handled in different trials, a question has been raised as to the constitutionality of this practice under the jury trial guarantee. Many writers have spoken of the wisdom of allowing the jury to do overall justice in a case. This concern led the Advisory Committee on the Federal Rules to warn that the separation of liability and damages issues should be used only in cases in which the procedure has a demonstrated usefulness.

4. Appealability of Orders. [§6.9400]

Orders granting or denying consolidation, severance, or separate trials are not final judgments. Hence, there is no appeal from these orders in jurisdictions that adhere to the final judgment rule [see **§15.1000**]. Furthermore, attempts to obtain review by writ of mandamus usually fail and certification for appeal under rules similar to Federal Rule 54(b) rarely is permitted.

CHAPTER VII

COUNTERCLAIMS, CROSS–CLAIMS, AND THIRD–PARTY CLAIMS

A. SCOPE NOTE. [§7.0000]

The material in this chapter deals with the special procedures for joinder of claims and parties by way of counterclaim, cross-claim, and third-party (or impleader) claim. These terms will be used throughout this discussion rather than the more generic and less precise term "cross-complaint." The next chapter will discuss three additional joinder devices—class actions, intervention, and interpleader.

B. COUNTERCLAIMS: DEFINITION. [§7.1000]

A counterclaim generally is described as any affirmative claim for relief that a pleader asserts as part of his or her defensive pleading against an opposing party.

1. Origin of the Counterclaim. [§7.1100]

The modern counterclaim is a direct descendant of two common law procedures—**recoupment and set-off.** Recoupment involved any claim the defendant had against the original plaintiff arising out of the transaction that formed the basis of the plaintiff's claim. The set-off was any claim for a liquidated amount the defendant had against the plaintiff, whether or not it arose out of the same transaction as the plaintiff's claim (the requirement that it be for a liquidated amount severely limited the set-off's utility). Both recoupment and set-off were completely defensive and relief could be awarded only to offset an amount the plaintiff recovered on the original claim.

2. Development of the Counterclaim. [§7.1200]

The counterclaim was substituted for recoupment and set-off during the nineteenth century. Most state codes, however, limited the pleader to certain specified types of counterclaims. The most common types of counterclaims were those that arose out of the same transaction as did the plaintiff's claim, for liquidated sums and for specified causes of action, such as contract or certain tort claims. The contemporary counterclaim provision, typified by Federal Rule 13, does not limit the nature or the subject matter of the counterclaim in any way and permits the defendant to recover any relief to which he or she is entitled regardless of the disposition of the plaintiff's claim.

3. **"Opposing Party." [§7.1300]**

Most counterclaim rules limit the availability of the counterclaim by providing that it must be asserted against an "opposing party," although additional parties may be added [see **§7.4000**]. In general, this means that there must be an adversarial relationship between the two litigants. Thus, a counterclaim usually is improper between co-parties (e.g., between co-plaintiffs or co-defendants). Moreover, if a party sues or is sued in one capacity, that litigant cannot counterclaim or be counterclaimed against in another capacity because the required "opposing-party" relationship would not exist.

Illustration 1. [§7.1310] A sues B and C for injuries arising out of a three-car collision. B and C file separate counterclaims against A, based on A's negligence. Both counterclaims satisfy the opposing-party requirement. However, if B asserts a claim against C, it will not be a counterclaim because the "opposing-party" requirement is not satisfied—they are co-defendants. The B v. C claim will be a cross-claim [see **§7.3000**].

Illustration 2. [§7.1320] An action is brought against a city tax official on the ground that she allegedly caused the unlawful arrest and detention of the plaintiff for non-payment of taxes. The tax official will not be permitted to assert a counterclaim on behalf of the city for the recovery of those taxes inasmuch as the suit was brought against the official in her individual capacity and the counterclaim would be asserted in her official capacity.

---

4. **Permissive and Compulsory Counterclaims Distinguished. [§7.1400]**

Federal Rule 13, and the rules of a number of states, distinguish between **permissive and compulsory counterclaims.** A compulsory counterclaim is one that arises out of the same transaction or occurrence or series of transactions or occurrences as does the claim previously asserted by the party against whom the counterclaim is interposed. Parties are required to assert any compulsory counterclaim that they may have against opposing parties; if they fail to do so, the claim cannot be brought as a separate action [see §7.1700]. A permissive counterclaim is any counterclaim that does not arise out of the same transaction or occurrence as does the claim originally asserted by the opposing party. Parties are not required to assert a permissive counterclaim and can bring it as a separate suit.

Illustration 1. [§7.1410] Drivers A and B are involved in a two-car collision. Subsequent to the collision, A meets B on the street and strikes him out of anger over the accident. A then sues B for personal injuries and property damage. Any claim that B might have against A for personal injuries or for damages to his car caused by the accident would be a compulsory counterclaim since it would arise out of the same transaction or occurrence as did the plaintiff's claim. B's claim against A for assault and battery would not be compulsory since it arose out of a separate event that occurred at a different time and place; it would be a permissive counterclaim.

Ilustration 2. [§7.1420] A agrees to manufacture and deliver to B ten automobiles, which are to be used as taxicabs. After the vehicles are delivered, A sues B claiming that B has failed to pay the agreed upon purchase price. B counterclaims against A for breach of warranty and negligent manufacture of the taxicabs. Most courts would consider this a compulsory counterclaim to A's action for the purchase price because it stems from the same contract. The same conclusion also might be reached even if the defects in the taxicabs became apparent as a result of the failure of the taxicabs to function properly some time after their delivery to B. However, any counterclaim that B might have against A for breach of warranty relating to a different contract for the purchase of other vehicles would be permissive only, even if the contract was identical to the contract involved in A's claim for non-payment.

---

5. **Compulsory-Permissive Distinction Analyzed. [§7.1500]**

Because there is no precise definition of what constitutes a single transaction or occurrence or a series of transactions or occurrences, in many situations it is difficult to determine whether a counterclaim is compulsory or permissive. Courts usually approach the problem in a pragmatic fashion. Thus, many courts say that if there is a significant overlap in the evidence required to establish the original claim and that needed to prove the counterclaim, the requisite nexus exists and the counterclaim should be deemed compulsory. The theory is that efficiency and economy would be served by adjudicating the two claims together. However, complete identity of proof between the claim and the counterclaim is not necessary. Thus, for example, differences in damage elements or standards of liability will not normally defeat the application of the compulsory counterclaim rule.

a. Logical Relationship Test. [§7.1510]

The most widely accepted test for determining whether a counterclaim should be classified as compulsory or permissive is the **logical relationship test.** If a counterclaim is logically related to the original claim, the two are said to be within the same transaction or occurrence and the counterclaim is compulsory. The flexibility and generality of this test gives the court an opportunity to label a claim compulsory whenever it can be profitably litigated simultaneously with the opposing party's claim and would be reasonable for the parties to do so.

6. Separate Trial of Compulsory or Permissive Counterclaims. [§7.1600]

In theory, jurisdictions that broadly define the right to counterclaim permit any unrelated claim a pleader has against an opposing party to be asserted as a permissive counterclaim. However, the court always has authority to separate a permissive counterclaim from the main claim and order separate trials when it appears that confusion or prejudice will result from trying the claims together. This is a special risk when a jury trial is involved. Furthermore, even though the court also has the power to order a separate trial of a compulsory counterclaim, this power is rarely utilized.

7. Effect of Failing to Assert a Compulsory Counterclaim. [§7.1700]

A party who does not interpose a compulsory counterclaim generally is prohibited from asserting the same claim in a subsequent action, whether it be as a plaintiff seeking affirmative relief or as a compulsary **or** permissive counterclaim in another action brought by the same plaintiff.

a. Rationale of Practice. [§7.1710]

The prohibition against the subsequent assertion of an omitted compulsory counterclaim is in the nature of an estoppel or waiver based on the culpable conduct of the litigant who failed to raise the counterclaim as required by the rule. The estoppel will not be applied in all cases. For example, if the defense of the first action was controlled entirely by the defendant's insurance company but the insured had no knowledge of the opportunity and obligation to interpose a compulsory counterclaim, he will be permitted to assert it in a subsequent action. It should be understood that the barring effect of failing to assert a compulsory counterclaim is not necessarily the result of any principle of res judicata or collateral estoppel. [See Chapter Sixteen for a discussion of former adjudication.]

b. **Limitations on the Effect of Failing to Assert a Compulsory Counterclaim. [§7.1720]**

A party who fails to assert a compulsory counterclaim will be prevented from asserting that claim affirmatively or by counterclaim in an action in any federal court. Although there is some uncertainty on the matter, most state courts will apply the waiver or estoppel principle described in the preceding section even to actions in which the original action was instituted outside their system. However, some state courts may allow the defaulting litigant to assert it in a subsequent state court proceeding. State court decisions have been divided over whether to give effect to the federal compulsory counterclaim rule; several have held that the failure to assert a compulsory counterclaim in a federal court action bars the subsequent assertion of that claim in a state court. To date it has not been definitively determined whether the application of one court's compulsory counterclaim rule must be given effect by all other courts under the Full Faith and Credit Clause of the Constitution nor whether the application of the federal rule must be given effect by all state courts under the Supremacy Clause of the Constitution.

c. **Assertion of Counterclaim in a Separate Action. [§7.1730]**

A separate action filed in the same court system will be dismissed if the claim asserted therein should have been interposed as a compulsory counterclaim in an earlier action. If the initial action is still awaiting trial, the court, in its discretion, may consolidate the two cases or allow the new claim to be asserted as a counterclaim. When the action asserting the counterclaim is brought in another court system, the court in which the initial suit was brought will not enjoin the counterclaimant from pursuing the second claim because of the natural desire not to interfere with the functioning of another court system. However, the original plaintiff, who is the defendant in the action involving the counterclaim, may apply for a dismissal or a stay of the second action in the court that is hearing it.

> **Illustration. [§7.1731]** A brings suit against B in a federal court for damages resulting from an automobile collision. B then sues A for personal injuries in a different federal court for personal injuries sustained in the same collision. B also brings suit against A in a state court for damages to his automobile arising out of the accident. The federal court having jurisdiction over A's claim will enjoin B from proceeding further with his personal injury claim in the other federal court, but will not attempt to enjoin B from proceeding in the state court action.

d. Exceptions to the Requirement of Asserting Compulsory Counterclaims. [§7.1740]

The obligation of a party to assert a compulsory counterclaim is subject to certain commonly recognized explicit exceptions such as those contained in Federal Rule 13. For example: (a) a party does not have to assert a counterclaim that does not exist at the time he or she serves a responsive pleading. (b) The counterclaim need not be asserted when it necessitates the joinder of third parties over whom the court cannot acquire jurisdiction for its proper adjudication. "Jurisdiction" in this context refers to personal jurisdiction, rather than subject matter jurisdiction, inasmuch as compulsory counterclaims fall within the "supplemental" jurisdiction of the federal courts [see **§7.2100**]. (c) A counterclaim will not be treated as compulsory if it is the subject of another pending action, as long as the other action was pending at the time the action in which the counterclaim should be asserted was filed. If a party prefers, he or she may abandon the initial action in order to assert that claim as a counterclaim in the second action. (d) A counterclaim need not be asserted when the jurisdictional basis of the main action is attachment or garnishment because it is considered unfair to require a defendant to assert a counterclaim when the court does not have jurisdiction over the defendant's person but merely has jurisdiction over his or her property. This exception will be inapplicable, however, if the defendant does assert a counterclaim against the opposing party. Thus, for this category of cases, if any counterclaim is interposed, all compulsory counterclaims must be asserted.

Illustration 1. [§7.1741] A brings suit against B on a sham and frivolous theory of relief. B's compulsory counterclaim for abuse of process based on A's lawsuit need not be asserted in many jurisdictions because a claim for abuse of process does not come into existence until the original sham action has been terminated.

Illustration 2. [§7.1742] A sues B for non-payment of the agreed upon purchase price for a shipment of a certain kind of transistors. B believes that A and X have artificially rigged the price of these transistors. If the court cannot acquire personal jurisdiction over X, however, B need not interpose a compulsory counterclaim for damages in the contract action.

e. **Judicially Created Exceptions to the Compulsory Counterclaim Rule. [§7.1750]**

In addition to the exceptions in the rule, there are some judicially created exceptions to the compulsory counterclaim rule. For example, a court has the inherent authority to allow an omitted counterclaim to be interposed. This power is exercised by allowing the late assertion of the claim in the same action in which the counterclaim should have been advanced or by allowing the assertion of the claim in a separate action. Typically, this discretion is exercised in situations in which doing so would further some other policy, such as the efficiency of the system or the assurance of justice.

Illustration. [§7.1751] A, a door manufacturer, sues B, a builder, in a New York federal court for non-payment for 10,000 doors delivered to B in that state and also in a Maine federal court for non-payment for 10,000 doors delivered to B in that state. The doors were the subject of a single integrated contract between the parties. B believes that all of the doors are defective. Since B has a single compulsory counterclaim to the two suits pending in different jurisdictions, it may assert the counterclaim in either litigation; it is not obliged to assert the counterclaim in the first suit filed [see *Southern Construction Co. v. Pickard* (1962)].

8. **Counterclaims for Declaratory Relief. [§7.1800]**

A pleader may seek declaratory relief by way of counterclaim and the claim will be treated as compulsory or permissive depending upon

209

whether it arises out of the same transaction or occurrence or the same series of transactions or occurrences that form the basis of the original claim.

C. PROCEDURAL ASPECTS OF COUNTERCLAIM PRACTICE. [§7.2000]

The modern counterclaim creates a number of procedural difficulties that always must be kept in mind in analyzing a counterclaim problem.

1. Supplemental Jurisdiction: Compulsory Counterclaims. [§7.2100]

It is now well established that **a federal court has supplemental jurisdiction over a compulsory counterclaim**. [See §2.5500–§2.5510 for a discussion of supplemental jurisdiction.] Thus, for example, if the plaintiff's claim is based on federal question jurisdiction, the federal court may assert jurisdiction over a compulsory counterclaim even though it does not involve a federal question and there is no diversity of citizenship between the litigants. Supplemental jurisdiction also extends to compulsory counterclaims for less than the requisite amount in controversy. Those states that draw the compulsory-permissive counterclaim distinction also have special provisions or judicial practices that automatically extend a court's subject matter jurisdiction to embrace compulsory counterclaims.

Illustration. [§7.2110] A of New York sues B of New York alleging that B has violated the federal antitrust laws by engaging in contracts that are in restraint of trade. B counterclaims for A's non-performance of one of the contracts that is the subject of A's suit and asks for $6,000 in damages. The counterclaim is compulsory and there is supplemental jurisdiction over it even though it fails to satisfy the federal question, diversity of citizenship, and amount in controversy requirements for federal subject matter jurisdiction.

---

2. Supplemental Jurisdiction: Permissive Counterclaims. [§7.2200]

Supplemental jurisdiction does not extend to permissive counterclaims in the federal courts. In the ordinary course, then, a defendant must establish that she could assert her counterclaim (or claims) as an independent action. Nevertheless, invoking the common law recoupment and set-off practices [see **§7.1100**], some state and federal courts have allowed jurisdiction over permissive counterclaims in the absence of an independent basis for subject matter jurisdiction when they were asserted to offset an opponent's claim rather than for affirmative relief.

3. Jurisdiction over the Person and Venue. [§7.2300]

A court with personal jurisdiction over the defendant and venue as to the original claim normally is held to have personal jurisdiction over the plaintiff and venue with regard to any counterclaim that might be interposed. Once the plaintiff has invoked the jurisdiction of the court for purposes of bringing the original action, the plaintiff has consented to the court's power for purposes of any claims asserted against him or her by the defendant. This is true even if the original plaintiff is not a resident of the forum and would not have been subject to jurisdiction had the counterclaim been an original action. The conclusion may not be the same, however, when the counterclaim is asserted by someone not originally sued by the plaintiff, such as an intervenor; the law is unsettled on the point.

4. Pleading Counterclaims. [§7.2400]

A party asserting a counterclaim, whether compulsory or permissive, is obliged to satisfy all of the pleading rules applicable to the statement of a claim [see **§5.4000–§5.4342** and **§5.7000–§5.7210**]. Since a counterclaim normally is included in a responsive pleading, it should be labeled as a counterclaim in order to distinguish it from the pleader's defenses to the original action. Moreover, a plaintiff must respond to a defendant's counterclaim only when the counterclaim is labeled as such. Most procedural systems give the trial judge discretion to ignore any mislabeling or non-labeling of the counterclaim [see **§5.7200**]. A counterclaim is subject to the same challenges as is any other claim for relief. [Challenges to pleadings are discussed in **§5.8000–§5.8422**.]

a. Counterclaim in a Reply. [§7.2410]

If the defendant's answer contains a counterclaim to which the plaintiff has a counterclaim—usually a compulsory counterclaim—the plaintiff's counterclaim may be asserted in a reply. Perhaps the better practice is for the plaintiff to amend the original complaint to assert the claim, assuming, of course, that there is an independent basis for subject matter jurisdiction.

5. Effect of a Counterclaim on the Statute of Limitations. [§7.2500]

The difference between compulsory and permissive counterclaims is important for statute-of-limitations purposes. When the plaintiff files a claim against the defendant, most courts hold that the statute of limitations ceases to run on any compulsory counterclaims that the defendant later may impose in the responsive pleading. The rationale is that the courts do not want to force the defendant to rush to file an answer simply because the statutory period is about to expire. That policy is far less persuasive when the counterclaim is permissive. The situation is more complicated, however, when the plaintiff commences the action after the statute of limitations on the counterclaim has already run. Although there is some authority to the effect that compulsory counterclaims may be maintained in such a situation, it is settled that permissive counterclaims cannot. In some states, special statutes provide that the defendant's claim for money damages, even though barred when the plaintiff's suit was filed, may be asserted as an offset to any damages awarded the plaintiff, but affirmative relief is not allowed. In addition, the Supreme Court has held that, unless Congress has clearly and expressly provided otherwise, a defendant may raise a claim by recoupment even when the claim, if brought independently, would be barred by the applicable statute of limitations.

6.   Jury Trial. [§7.2600]

The fact that a claim is asserted by way of counterclaim does not affect the right to trial by jury. As is discussed in the material on jury trial [see **§13.4000–§13.4431**], it is settled in the federal courts and in a number of state courts that asserting a legal counterclaim to an equitable claim does not result in a waiver of the counterclaimant's right to a jury trial.

7.   Appealability of Rulings Relating to Counterclaims. [§7.2700]

In a jurisdiction following the final judgment rule [see **§15.1000**], an appeal cannot be taken from a refusal to dismiss a counterclaim. The court's order is interlocutory and must await the rendition of a final judgment. The same is true of an order dismissing a counterclaim. In courts following the federal practice under Rule 54(b), however, the judge may direct the entry of a final judgment on a counterclaim and this will be appealable immediately if the court determines that there is no just reason for delaying the entry of that judgment [see **§15.1310**].

D.   CROSS–CLAIMS: DEFINITION. [§7.3000]

A cross-claim is a claim asserted by one party against a co-party.

1.   Theory and Purpose of Cross–Claims. [§7.3100]

The cross-claim procedure is designed to avoid multiple litigation between or among the parties to the action by allowing co-parties to adjudicate some or all of the claims they may have against each other. Since cross-claims generally must arise from the same transaction or occurrence as the original dispute [see **§7.3240**], another major objective is to determine all controversies having a significant evidentiary overlap in a single proceeding.

> **Illustration. [§7.3110]** A sues B and C for injuries arising out of a three-car collision. B may cross-claim against C for damages B has sustained in the accident. Suppose, however, that B seeks only to cross-claim against C for breach of a contract to buy and sell Blackacre. The cross-claim will be disallowed if the jurisdiction only permits transactionally related cross-claims.

2. Requirements for Cross–Claims. [§7.3200]

In most jurisdictions a cross-claim must (a) be asserted against a co-party, (b) seek affirmative relief from that party, (c) be asserted by a party against whom a claim already has been asserted, and (d) arise out of the same transaction or occurrence as the original claim or any counterclaim in the action, or relate to property that is the subject of the action [see Federal Rule 13(g)].

a. Co–Parties. [§7.3210]

A cross-claim may be asserted only against **someone who already is a co-party of the cross-claimant,** although additional parties may be added [see **§7.4000**]. This permits cross-claims between plaintiffs, defendants, third-party defendants, and, possibly, between intervenors. Since a cross-claim may be asserted only against a co-party, it should be distinguished from a counterclaim, which may be asserted only against an opposing party in the action [see **§7.1300**].

> **Illustration. [§7.3211]** A brings an action against B and C. B then asserts a claim against D, who is added as a party to the action. Most jurisdictions would conclude that this is not a proper cross-claim since a cross-claim may be asserted only between parties on the same litigation level—that is, only between B and C. Because D is not on the same level of litigation as B and C, no cross-claim may be asserted between B and D or C and D. These claims might be proper third-party or impleader claims, however [see **§7.5000– §7.5910**].

b. Nature of Relief Available. [§7.3220]

A cross-claimant may seek any relief that he or she would have sought had the claim been brought as an independent lawsuit. In addition, under the rules of most jurisdictions, the cross-claimant may assert that the co-party against whom the cross-claim is brought is liable for all or part of any judgment awarded to the plaintiff against the cross-claimant.

Illustration. [§7.3221] A sues B and C for breach of contract. A claims damages from B due to B's negligent manufacture of goods sold to A. A alleges C is liable for late delivery of the goods to A. C files a cross-claim against B in which she alleges that B's failure to finish the goods on time was the sole cause of C's late delivery to A. C prays that B should be required to indemnify C for any award A obtains against C. B's motion to dismiss the cross-claim as improper will be denied.

---

c. **Right of One Co–Plaintiff to Cross–Claim against Another. [§7.3230]**

Although co-plaintiffs technically come within the language of the typical cross-claim rule, it has been held that a cross-claim cannot be asserted between co-plaintiffs unless a claim has been asserted against them. This means that a cross-claim is proper only after a defendant interposes a counterclaim against the plaintiffs.

Illustration. [§7.3231] Plaintiffs A, B, and C join in an action against D. D asserts a compulsory counterclaim against A and B. A cross-claims against B for contribution. B cross-claims against C for indemnity on the claim asserted by A against B. If it meets the transaction or occurrence requirement [see **§7.3240**] A's cross-claim is proper because a counterclaim has been asserted against him. However, B's cross-claim against C might not be proper because D's counterclaim was only against A and B, which means that B and C were not co-parties to it. Similarly, A's cross-claim was only against B, which means that B and C were not co-parties to it.

---

d. **Transaction or Occurrence Test. [§7.3240]**

Most jurisdictions limit the scope of the cross-claim to disputes arising out of the **same transaction or occurrence that forms the basis of the original claim or a counterclaim in the action** [see, e.g., Federal Rule 13(g)]. The test that is applied appears to be identical to that used to define compulsory counterclaims. Accordingly, the discussion of the transaction or occurrence test in the counterclaim context applies to cross-claims [see **§7.1400–§7.1510**].

214

Illustration 1. [§7.3241] Upon a seller's failure to consummate a contract to sell Blackacre, the purchaser deposits the contract price with a stakeholder. Finding that there are inconsistent claims to the fund deposited with him, the stakeholder institutes an interpleader action against both the purchaser and the seller. A cross-claim by the purchaser against the seller, both of whom are now co-parties, seeking specific performance of the contract would be proper.

Illustration 2. [§7.3242] An insurer brings an action for a declaration of non-liability under an automobile policy against the insured and the person driving the car at the time of the accident. A cross-claim by the insured against her co-defendant alleging that the vehicle involved had been loaned to the co-defendant and seeking a declaration that the vehicle was not under the control of the cross-complainant at the time of the accident would be proper.

Illustration 3. [§7.3243] The United States brings an antitrust action against several companies alleging a conspiracy in restraint of trade. One defendant attempts to cross-claim against another defendant to recover royalties paid under an allegedly invalid patent licensing agreement. If the antitrust suit involves activities by the parties not directly related to the contract, the cross-claim is not proper. The key is whether the cross-claimant's action for royalties would involve entirely different issues and evidence from the government's antitrust action and whether the cross-claim might simply confuse or prejudice the trial of the main action.

3. Federal Jurisdiction and Venue over Cross–Claims. [§7.3300]

The federal courts generally have held that cross-claims, because of their transactional relationship to the main claim, fall within the supplemental subject matter jurisdiction of the court and independent jurisdiction need not be established over them. [See **§2.5000–§2.5530** for a discussion of supplemental jurisdiction.] Of course, if the original claim fails for lack of subject matter jurisdiction, the cross-claim will have to be dismissed as well. Since the parties to the cross-claim are already before the court, problems of personal jurisdiction do not arise. Finally, if venue over the original action is proper, the court also will have supplemental venue over a cross-claim, even though venue would not exist if the cross-claim were an independent action.

4. Other Procedural Matters. [§7.3400]

A cross-claim is treated like any other claim for relief with regard to pleading, discovery, jury trial, declaratory relief, appealability, and other procedural matters.

5. State Practice. [§7.3500]

In some states, a cross-claim is denominated a cross-complaint and is considered a separate and distinct pleading from the defendant's answer. If the cross-complaint is filed simultaneously with the answer, it may be submitted without leave of court; otherwise, leave of court must be obtained before a cross-complaint may be interposed. In other aspects, the rules pertaining to cross-complaints between co-parties are similar to the rules governing cross-claims.

6. Cross–Claims and the Statute of Limitations. [§7.3600]

As is true with regard to compulsory counterclaims [see **§7.2500**], the filing of the plaintiff's complaint tolls the statute of limitations for any cross-claims between co-parties. As long as the plaintiff's complaint was filed prior to the time the statute ran on the cross-claim, the cross-claim will be timely. If, however, the limitations period on the cross-claim lapsed before the plaintiff filed the action, the cross-claim will be barred.

E. JOINDER OF ADDITIONAL PARTIES TO COUNTERCLAIMS AND CROSS–CLAIMS. [§7.4000]

Modern counterclaim and cross-claim rules typically provide that persons other than those who are parties to the original action may be added as parties to a counterclaim or cross-claim to ensure that those claims are fully adjudicated in a single action [see, e.g., Federal Rule 13(h)].

1. Practice Relating to Additional Parties to Counterclaims and Cross–Claims. [§7.4100]

Provisions for the addition of new parties to a counterclaim or cross-claim generally allow the joinder of anyone who could have been joined under the applicable permissive joinder rule [see **§6.4000**] had the counterclaim or cross-claim been brought as an original action. The added party will be aligned with regard to the counterclaim or cross-claim phase of the action in accordance with his or her actual interest in that dispute. A party may not be added unless the claim against that person also is asserted against someone who already is a party to the counterclaim or crossclaim. The joinder of an additional party to a counterclaim or cross-claim should be distinguished from the addition of a third-party complaint or impleader claim [see **§7.5000–§7.5910**].

Illustration. [§7.4110] A and B are involved in a two-car collision. A sues B for personal injuries and property damage. B counterclaims against A for property damage and personal injuries arising out of the same accident, and seeks to add C as an additional party to the counterclaim on the ground that C also was involved in the collision. Joinder of C will be permitted.

---

2.   Jurisdiction and Venue over Additional Parties. [§7.4200]

In jurisdictions that distinguish between compulsory and permissive counterclaims, supplemental subject matter jurisdiction typically extends to additional persons brought into the action to facilitate the complete adjudication of a compulsory counterclaim. This is not true of persons joined to litigate a permissive counterclaim. Additional parties to cross-claims, whose claims by definition arise from the same transaction as the original claim, usually are held to fall within the court's supplemental jurisdiction. Personal jurisdiction must be acquired over an additional party to a compulsory or permissive counterclaim or to a cross-claim. As is true of subject matter jurisdiction, the principle of common nucleus of operative facts normally applies to give the court "supplemental" or "pendent" venue over compulsory counterclaims and cross-claims but not to permissive counterclaims.

3.   Additional Parties and the Statute of Limitations. [§7.4300]

Unlike the situation with regard to the original parties in the suit [see **§7.2500** and **§7.3600**], the date on which the plaintiff files the initial action does not affect the running of the statute of limitations on claims against additional parties to counterclaims and cross-claims. The statute of limitations continues to run until the time the action is commenced against such individuals, which in most jurisdictions means the filing of a counterclaim or cross-claim naming them as parties. In a few jurisdictions the statute runs until the time the new parties are served with process. It would be grossly unfair to permit a counterclaim or cross-claim to override the statute of limitations by allowing a claim against an additional party that would have been barred by the statute of limitations had it been asserted in a separate action.

217

F. THIRD–PARTY CLAIMS. [§7.5000]

Third-party practice, sometimes called **impleader**, permits a defendant (the third-party plaintiff) to join a person who was not originally a party to the suit (the third-party defendant) **when the defendant believes that the impleaded party is primarily liable for all or part of the original plaintiff's claim against the defendant**. This process is intended to avoid circuity of actions, to facilitate the adjudication of all disputes arising out of a single factual setting, and to eliminate the possible time lag between the plaintiff's judgment against the defendant and a judgment in the defendant's favor against the third-party defendant.

1. Historical Development. [§7.5100]

Modern third-party practice, typified by Federal Rule 14, is the descendant of the English common law practice of "vouching to warranty." This technique enabled a defendant who was sued by a plaintiff for the recovery of property to call upon a third party to defend the action when the third party had given the defendant a warranty of title at the time the property was sold to the defendant. An analogous, but expanded, practice found its way into American law in admiralty suits. From these beginnings, some state codes fashioned a procedure permitting any defendant to bring in an outsider who was liable to him or her for any liability that the defendant had to the plaintiff on the plaintiff's claim.

2. When a Third–Party Action Is Proper. [§7.5200]

A third-party claim is proper when the third-party defendant is alleged to be liable to the third-party plaintiff for all or part of the original claim. The theory of the third-party claim may be indemnity, subrogation, contribution, or breach of warranty. On the other hand, a third-party claim is inappropriate when the third-party defendant's liability to the third-party plaintiff is direct rather than derived from the defendant's claim.

Illustration. [§7.5210] P brings suit for personal injuries resulting from a malfunctioning door on a boxcar that had been delivered by D, a railroad company. P alleges that D's employee had negligently placed the boxcar. D claims that the workers who had located the car and were unloading it at the time of the injury to P were in the employ of a third party and that, as a consequence, the third party

---

and not the defendant was liable to the plaintiff on the theory of respondeat superior. The third-party claim will not be allowed since the liability asserted is not derivative in nature.

a. **Necessity That Derivative Liability Be Recognized by Governing Law. [§7.5220]**

A third-party claim will not be allowed if the governing substantive law does not recognize the particular kind of derivative liability asserted by the third-party plaintiff. A federal court sitting in diversity of citizenship jurisdiction will look to the forum state's law to see if it recognizes the substantive claim being asserted. If it does, impleader will be proper in a federal court even though the governing state law does not permit third-party practice [see also **§7.5330**].

Illustration. [§7.5221] A sues B in a federal court diversity action in State X alleging that she has been injured as a result of B's negligent driving. B seeks to implead C, another driver who was involved in the accident, seeking contribution to A's potential recovery. If the law of State X does not recognize contribution between joint tortfeasors or requires that they be sued together and a joint judgment obtained against them before a right of contribution arises, the third-party claim must be dismissed.

b. **Contingent Liability. [§7.5230]**

There is no requirement that the liability of the third-party defendant be fixed or certain at the time impleader is sought. Thus, a defendant may bring in a third party who may be liable for the plaintiff's claim as long as the defendant's claim will accrue if the plaintiff succeeds in the action against the defendant or when the plaintiff's claim is satisfied.

Illustration. [§7.5231] P brings suit in a federal court for damages resulting from the consumption of allegedly contaminated meat purchased from D. D seeks to implead its supplier. The third-party defendant resists its inclusion in the action, asserting that a federal court sitting in diversity jurisdiction must look to the forum state's substantive law, and that the applicable state law requires that a defendant satisfy the claim against it before a cause of action can be asserted against a third party on the basis of derivative liability. Permitting the third-party claim will only accelerate in time the determination of the liability of the third-party defendant and therefore it is proper. Furthermore, a conditional judgment may be entered against the third-party defendant even though it will not become effective until after the original defendant satisfies the judgment on the main claim.

c. Discretion of the Court. [§7.5240]

The court has discretion to disallow a technically proper third-party complaint, although this discretion is rarely used. However, if at any point in the case it appears that the continued joint litigation of the claims either is not in the interest of judicial economy or would result in prejudice to one or more of the parties, the court may order the claim stricken, severed, or tried separately.

Illustration. [§7.5241] P sues a trucking firm to recover for personal injuries resulting from a collision between P's automobile and D's truck. D seeks to implead the driver of the truck, D's employee, whose negligence allegedly caused the accident. Even though D may have a right of indemnity against the driver, the court may deny the third-party claim if, for example, the driver is insolvent and the only reason for his inclusion is to arouse juror sympathy by encouraging them to think that the driver would have to bear the judgment.

3. Procedure for Asserting a Third–Party Claim. [§7.5300]

To interpose a third-party claim, a litigant serves a summons and third-party complaint upon the third-party defendant. If the defendant acts expeditiously (e.g., including the cross-claim with the answer), leave of court usually is not required; otherwise, leave of court is necessary.

a. Who May Assert a Third–Party Claim. [§7.5310]

Although third-party practice typically is used by the original defendant, contemporary procedural rules permit a plaintiff against whom a counterclaim has been asserted to implead a third party who is or may be liable for all or part of the original defendant's counterclaim. Moreover, the third-party defendant may implead a person claimed to be liable on the defendant's third-party claim— usually called a fourth-party defendant. This might occur, for example, in a products liability case in which liability ultimately may fall on a component-part manufacturer.

b. **Persons against Whom a Third–Party Claim May Be Asserted. [§7.5320]**

Third-party claims are asserted only against persons who are not already parties to the litigation. Counterclaims and cross-claims are the proper procedures to be invoked against those who already are parties to the action.

c. **Impleading Persons Who Could Not Be Sued Directly. [§7.5330]**

Although there has been some confusion over whether a third-party plaintiff may implead an outsider who could not have been sued directly by the original plaintiff, the practice now appears to be accepted since the benefits of the third-party action inure to the third-party plaintiff, not the original plaintiff. Thus, it has been held that a defendant can implead the plaintiff's employer in a federal court action even though the forum state's compensation act would have prevented the plaintiff, an employee, from suing her employer directly. Furthermore, there are cases holding that a person may be impleaded even though the statute of limitations would have barred an action against him or her by the original plaintiff because a right of indemnity or subrogation does not arise until the third-party plaintiff has been held liable on the original claim. On the other hand, a third-party claim against a member of the plaintiff's immediate family, such as a spouse or child, is not permitted in jurisdictions that require a joint judgment respecting a family unit or in jurisdictions that prohibit actions between family members [see also **§7.5220**].

Illustration. [§7.5331] P brings a tort action more than two years after the relevant conduct occurred. D impleads the United States government on an indemnification theory. Although the two-year statute of limitations has run, thereby barring P's claim against the government, D's third-party claim did not accrue until he was sued by P and should not be barred.

---

4. **Rights of a Third–Party Defendant. [§7.5400]**

The third-party defendant may interpose any defenses that he or she has against the third-party claim, and under Federal Rule 14 and similar state provisions, may assert any available counterclaims against any defendant or any cross-claims against any co-third-party defendants. In addition, any defenses that the third-party plaintiff may have against the plaintiff's original claim may be advanced by the third-party defendant [see also **§7.5600**].

5. **Plaintiff's Rights against a Third–Party Defendant. [§7.5500]**

Many third-party practice rules permit the original plaintiff to assert a claim against the third-party defendant as long as that claim arises out of the same transaction or occurrence as does the plaintiff's claim against the original defendant [see Rule 14(a)(3)].

Illustration. [§7.5510] A purchaser of a nightgown brings suit against the store from which the garment was bought for injuries sustained when it burst into flames. The store brings in the manufacturer of the gown by way of third-party complaint. The original plaintiff may now assert a claim directly against the third-party defendant based on the latter's negligent manufacture of the nightgown.

---

6. **Third–Party Defendant's Rights against an Original Plaintiff. [§7.5600]**

Third-party practice rules often permit a third-party defendant to assert a claim against an original plaintiff so long as it arises out of the same transaction or occurrence as the plaintiff's claim against the original defendant. Because Federal Rule 14(a)(2)(D) omits the words "may be liable" from the sentence governing the third-party defendant's rights against the original plaintiff, it has been thought that a third-party's claim against the plaintiff need not be contingent in nature.

7. **Federal Subject Matter Jurisdiction. [§7.5700]**

If each third-party claim were required to satisfy all subject matter jurisdiction requirements, third-party practice would be severely restricted. Thus, the federal courts have applied supplemental jurisdiction to some, but not all, of the claims that may arise as part of third-party practice. [Supplemental jurisdiction is discussed in **§2.5000–§2.5530**.]

a. **Third–Party Claims. [§7.5710]**

If a third-party claim arises out of the common nucleus of operative fact that gave rise to the original claim, then a court having jurisdiction over the main claim may assert supplemental subject matter jurisdiction over the third-party claim. Virtually all third-party claims will satisfy this criterion because it is almost certain that the evidence adduced concerning the plaintiff's original claim will overlap substantially with the evidence relating to the third-party claim. In keeping with the limitations on supplemental jurisdiction [see **§2.5430**], most federal courts will dismiss a third-party claim if the main claim is dismissed before reaching trial. A court does have discretion not to dismiss, however, and will consider the fairness and judicial efficiency of retaining or terminating the ancillary action.

Illustration. [§7.5711] A of New York sues B of New York for $6,000 in a federal court under the Federal Patent Act for infringement of A's patent on a certain product. B impleads C, also of New York, on an indemnification theory alleging that C supplied B the allegedly infringing items. Despite the absence of a federal question or diversity of citizenship or the requisite amount in controversy for diversity cases, the federal court has supplemental jurisdiction over the third-party claim.

---

b.   Other Claims against a Third–Party Defendant. [§7.5720]

Modern procedural rules permit a defendant to join with a third-party claim any other claims he or she may have against the third-party defendant. If such an additional claim arises out of the same transaction or occurrence as does plaintiff's claim against the defendant, the usual principles of supplemental jurisdiction will apply. Otherwise, a claim added against a third-party defendant must have an independent jurisdictional base.

Illustration. [§7.5721] A sues B for injuries arising out of the malfunction of a lawn-mower sold by B. B impleads C, the lawn-mower manufacturer, claiming that the latter's negligence makes C liable for all or part of A's claims against B. B also joins a claim against C for lost profits resulting from bad publicity about the lawn-mower accident, and a claim for breach of a contract to deliver a shipment of garden tillers. The claim for lost profits probably is within the same transaction or occurrence as A's claim

---

and supplemental jurisdiction will apply. The contract claim, however, is transactionally unrelated to A's claim, and must be dismissed unless there is an independent basis for subject matter jurisdiction.

    c.   **Other Third–Party Practice Claims. [§7.5730]**

Even though the plaintiff's claim against the third-party defendant will satisfy the usual test for supplemental jurisdiction—the same transaction or occurrence—federal courts generally require independent subject matter jurisdiction over these claims. This apparently is because of the possibility that plaintiff and defendant will collusively use the mechanism of the third-party claim to obtain a federal forum for an action against the third-party defendant that otherwise could not be brought in a federal court. In the diversity context, the Supreme Court has held that the use of supplemental jurisdiction when the plaintiff and the third-party defendant are co-citizens would violate the complete diversity requirement [*Owen Equipment & Erection Co. v. Kroger* (1978)]. Similarly, some courts have refused to extend supplemental jurisdiction to a third-party defendant's claim against the original plaintiff. The propriety of this result seems very dubious since there is virtually no chance of collusion between the third-party defendant and the original defendant.

8.   Personal Jurisdiction. [§7.5800]

It is settled that personal jurisdiction must be obtained over parties added to the litigation by way of third-party practice. Federal Rule 4(k)(1)(B), however, creates a small exception to the normal requirements of personal jurisdiction [see **§3.3630**]. Federal courts can assert jurisdiction over third-party defendants served within a 100–mile radius of the court issuing the summons regardless of territorial boundaries, so long as service occurs within a United States judicial district.

9.   Federal Venue. [§7.5900]

Since it would be absurd to dismiss a third-party suit because of the third-party defendant's venue objections when the constitutional requirements of subject matter jurisdiction have been subordinated in favor of the judicial efficiency policies underlying supplemental jurisdiction, it has been held that supplemental venue extends to third-party claims.

    a.   **Venue over Plaintiff's Claim against Third–Party Defendant. [§7.5910]**

Since independent subject matter jurisdiction grounds are required for a plaintiff's claim against a third-party defendant [see **§7.5730**], venue must be proper between the original plaintiff and the third-party defendant. An examination of the policies behind venue provisions indicates that this requirement is unnecessary. There would be no added inconvenience to the third-party defendant in making her defend against the original plaintiff's claim in the original forum, since she already is obliged to defend the third-party action there. Arguably, therefore, supplemental venue should be extended to a plaintiff's claim against a third-party defendant.

*

CHAPTER VIII

CLASS ACTIONS, INTERVENTION, AND INTERPLEADER

A. SCOPE NOTE. [§8.0000]

Along with the expansion of joinder of parties and joinder of claims [see Chapters Six and Seven], procedural systems have developed a number of special devices for the handling of litigation involving multiple parties. This chapter discusses the three most significant of these procedures—class actions, intervention, and interpleader.

B. CLASS ACTIONS. [§8.1000]

The class action is a device by which suit may be brought by or against large numbers of individuals whose interests are sufficiently related so that it is **more efficient** to adjudicate their rights or liabilities in a single action than in a series of separate individual suits. The propriety of a particular class action usually should be analyzed in two stages. First, it must be determined whether certain procedural prerequisites for the class suit have been met [see **§8.1200**]. Second, it must be decided whether the particular suit **falls within the definition of the class action** set out in the applicable rule [see **§8.1300–§8.1334**].

1. Development. [§8.1100]

The class action was developed by the English equity courts in order that mere numbers would not prevent groups of individuals who were united in interest from enforcing their equitable rights nor give them immunity from being sued to rectify their equitable wrongs.

a. Class Actions under the State Codes. [§8.1110]

Many state codes simply define the class action procedure in general terms. Others specifically describe three types of class actions. First, the so-called "true" class action, in which the interests of all class members are "common and undivided." Second, the "hybrid" class action, in which the subject of the action is a specific fund or property, but the interests of the class members are "several." Third, the "spurious" class action, in which a common question of law or fact links the interests of each class member together; again, the interests of the class members are said to be "several." Until 1966, these three types of class actions also were provided for in the then existing text of Federal Rule 23.

b. Class Actions under Present Federal Rule 23. [§8.1120]

Dissatisfaction with the conceptualistic and arbitrary tripartite division of class actions described in the preceding section led the federal rulemakers to revise Federal Rule 23 in 1966. The former categories have been replaced by the three types of class actions described in **§8.1300–§8.1334**, which reflect an attempt at a more functional definition of when a class action is appropriate.

c. Controversy over the Class Action. [§8.1130]

For more than four decades the class action has been an extremely popular and controversial procedure, particularly in the federal courts. It has been used extensively in antitrust, securities, products, environmental, discrimination, and welfare benefits litigation. The enormous increase in class action activity often is attributed to the liberalizing revision of Federal Rule 23 in 1966. However, the trend probably also reflects changes in the substantive law in the areas mentioned above, increased attention to social action litigation, and the attractiveness of class action attorney's fee awards. Whatever the cause, the class action has imposed burdens on the judiciary and corporate defendants and has led some to challenge it as a "Frankenstein monster." On the other hand, the procedure may represent the only viable method for people with small claims to vindicate their rights or with civil rights claims to litigate important social issues. Supreme Court decisions [see **§8.1520** and **§8.1820**] have reduced the ability to bring class actions in the federal courts, particularly in diversity cases, adding fuel to the controversy. Ultimately, the rulemakers or Congress may continue to adjust the scope of the class action in the federal courts. One example of such efforts is the Class Action Fairness Act (CAFA), passed in 2005, which expanded access to the federal courts for certain actions [see **§8.1800–§8.1832–1**].]

2. Prerequisites for a Class Action. [§8.1200]

Before a class suit of any type may proceed, all of the following questions must be answered in the affirmative. (a) Is there an identifiable class [see **§8.1210**]? (b) Is the class representative a member of that class [see **§8.1220**]? (c) Is the class large enough to make joinder impracticable [see

§8.1230]? (d) Are there common questions of law or fact concerning the claim of each class member [see **§8.1240**]? (e) Are the claims or defenses of the representatives of the class typical of the members of the class [see **§8.1250**]? (f) Will the representatives adequately represent and protect the interests of the absent class members [see **§8.1260**]?

a. **An Identifiable Class Must Exist. [§8.1210]**

The first two requirements do not actually appear in Rule 23 but have been developed by the courts. First, the **outlines of a group must be recognizable** enough at the outset of the litigation in order to determine which class members will benefit from relief and which will be bound by an adverse ruling. Although it is not necessary that every class member be identifiable at that time, a class description that is devoid of objective factors will be insufficient. On the other hand, a plaintiff may err on the side of specificity, making the class description too complex. Typical classes include: purchasers of a particular security who claim they were defrauded; a group of alleged patent or copyright infringers; purchasers of a defective product; all those victimized by age, race, or sex discrimination; and owners of land along a river suing an upstream owner for pollution.

b. **The Representative Must Be a Member of the Class. [§8.1220]**

The second requirement that courts have developed is that **the class representative must be a member of the class**. The theory is that as long as the representative has the same general interests and/or injuries to be redressed, the representative will protect the interests of the absentee members. The representative's membership is essentially a standing requirement, and if the plaintiff's claims already have been satisfied at the time of class certification, or if the plaintiff has no claim against the defendant, the case may be dismissed.

c. **Size of the Class—Numerosity. [§8.1230]**

Rule 23(a)(1) requires that the **number of class members is so numerous such that joinder of all members is impractical**. There is no magic number of class members that will make joinder impracticable. Regardless, the federal courts generally require that the class be at least 30 to 40 in number. For the class to be large enough, impossibility of joinder is not necessary; extreme difficulty or impracticability of joinder is sufficient. Factors such as geographical dispersion and size of the claims will affect the practicability of joinder.

d. **Common Questions of Law or Fact—Commonality. [§8.1240]**

Rule (23)(a)(2) dictates that a class action may be maintained only when **common questions of law or fact** exist among the class members. This does not mean, however, that all of the questions of law or fact in the action must be common to the class members. Courts must balance efficiency gains from joint adjudication with possible fairness losses. Ultimately, the common-question requirement has given the courts little difficulty since common questions almost always exist.

Illustration. [§8.1241] A class action is brought by five owners of stock in Widget, Inc. on behalf of all those who purchased stock in the company between January 1, 2006 and June 30, 2007 in reliance on certain allegedly fraudulent public statements issued by the corporation. The facts relating to the content of these statements and their legal effect present questions that are sufficiently common to all members of the proposed class to satisfy this class action prerequisite.

---

e. **The Claims or Defenses of the Representatives Must Be Typical—Typicality. [§8.1250]**

According to Federal Rule 23(a)(3) the claims or defenses of the representatives **must be typical** of the claims or defenses of all the members of the class. However, the representatives' claims do not have to be substantially identical to those of the absent class members. Thus, for example, differences in damages respecting the representatives and the absentees.

f. **Adequacy of Representation. [§8.1260]**

Since a class action judgment binds persons who were not before the court, Rule 23(a)(4) requires **the named representatives and attorneys to be adequate protectors of the interests of the absent class members**. Of course, the representatives themselves must be members of the class. Furthermore, they must not have interests that conflict with those of the class they seek to represent. It is the quality of the representation, not the quantity, that is important; thus, one representative may be sufficient if that representative and his or her counsel have the incentive, the resources, and the character to prosecute or defend the rights of the other members of the class. The Private Securities Litigation Reform Act (PSLRA) has placed a particular emphasis on the qualifications of the class representative in actions covered by that statute. An absent member of a class cannot be bound by a judgment if he or she was not adequately represented in the suit, and a deficiency in representation may be challenged under the Fifth and Fourteenth Amendments to the Constitution. This has been announced by the Supreme Court on several occasions, most recently in *Amchem Products, Inc. v. Windsor* (1997) and *Ortiz v. Fibreboard Corp.* (1999).

Illustration. [§8.1261] Z Law School automatically rejects all applicants who do not have a Law School Admission Test score exceeding 165, regardless of other qualifications. Several persons who were rejected by Z file a class suit on behalf of all applicants for the following academic year, challenging the school's standard for admission. The court holds that the test score requirement is arbitrary and capricious and orders Z to revoke all prior admissions and reconsider the records of all the applicants. Prior to the determination of this case, M had been notified by Z that she was admitted for the following year and in reliance thereon had notified other law schools to which she was admitted that she would not attend. M seeks to challenge the revocation of her admission. M is not bound by the class suit since the named plaintiffs' interests diverged so radically from her own that these plaintiffs cannot be held to have adequately represented her [compare *Hansberry v. Lee* (1940)].

---

g. Adequacy of Representative's Attorney. [§8.1270]

To insure that the absent class members are protected, courts increasingly are scrutinizing the competence and motivation of the counsel selected by the class representative. Realistically, the adequacy of the class' lawyers is more critical than whether the representative party is rich or smart. The court will look at the competence of the class' lawyers and whether they can protect all of the class members adequately and even-handedly.

h. Continuing Duty. [§8.1280]

The court has a continuing duty to ensure the adequacy of representation even after certification. If it falls below the required standard, the court must decertify the class action.

3. Cases Subject to Class Action Treatment: Federal Rule 23(b). [§8.1300]

Federal Rule 23(b) describes three types of cases that are appropriate for class action treatment. Although many state class action provisions do not contain express definitions of proper classes, the Federal Rule does represent an excellent model of the kinds of cases that most courts will accept for class action treatment.

a. **Adverse Effects on Class Members or Opposing Party—Rule 23(b)(1) Classes. [§8.1310]**

The first of the three types of class actions provided for in Rule 23(b) permits a class action (a) when the prosecution of separate actions might result in inconsistent or varying adjudications that would establish incompatible standards of conduct for the party opposing the class or (b) when separate actions might result in judgments that would be dispositive of the interests of nonparty class members. A class action under Rule 23(b)(1) is proper if either of these requirements is met.

(1) **Effect on the Opposing Party—Rule 23(b)(1)(A) Classes. [§8.1311]**

The requirement that individual adjudications may result in incompatible standards of conduct for the party opposing the class presupposes that there is a real possibility that separate actions will be filed against the non-class party. Thus, pragmatic considerations, such as the size of each class member's claim, will be relevant in determining whether there is a threat of multiple litigation. If such a threat exists, the court must decide whether incompatible standards of conduct are likely to result. The most common example of incompatible standards of conduct is when the party opposing the class is legally required to act in the same manner respecting each member of the class so that differing results in separate cases would be unworkable or would put an intolerable burden on the non-class party.

Illustration. [§8.1311–1] A patent owner brings suit against a class of alleged patent infringers. The patent's invalidity is raised as a defense. Inconsistent individual judgments on this issue would mean that the patentee could protect his rights against infringement by some but not against others. Assuming the other criteria of Rule 23 are met, a class action is proper.

---

(2) **Effect on the Class Members—Rule 23(b)(1)(B) Classes. [§8.1312]**

The possibility that the prosecution of separate independent actions would result in adjudications that would be dispositive of the interests of absent class members—the second class action standard in Rule 23(b)(1)—does not presuppose that there is a likelihood of multiple litigation. In fact, even if a single action would impair the rights of other class members, the test for a class action is met.

Illustration. [§8.1312–1] A brings an action against a corporation to compel the distribution of dividends. Although it can be argued that each stockholder has an individual claim to dividends, any decree that might be issued in A's action certainly will have some effect on all stockholders. Consequently, the class action device is proper.

---

(3) Limited Fund Cases. [§8.1313]

Perhaps the most common type of action that is certified under Rule 23(b)(1)(B) because of the impact individual actions might have on absent class members involves the situation in which they are seeking relief out of a fund, such as a trust or insurance policy, and the aggregate amount of the class members' claims exceeds the value of the fund. An example would be a group of creditors whose total claims are greater than the debtor's assets available to pay them. Class certification in that instance is designed to ensure an equitable distribution of the fund and avoid its exhaustion by the first claimants to sue. In *Ortiz v. Fibreboard Corp.* (1999), the Supreme Court restricted the availability of this type of class action under Rule 23(b)(1) to situations in which it has been established that the fund is inadequate to pay all of the claims, the entirety of the inadequate fund is to be devoted to the class members' claims, and the claimants are to be treated equitably. Understandably, post-*Ortiz* cases have exhibited a reluctance to use Rule 23(b)(1)(B).

b. Actions for Injunctive or Declaratory Relief—Rule 23(b)(2) Classes. [§8.1320]

According to Federal Rule 23(b)(2), a class action is permitted if (a) the party opposing the class has acted or refused to act on grounds generally applicable to the class as a whole, and (b) the class representatives are seeking final injunctive relief or corresponding declaratory relief. Unlike a class action under Rule 23(b)(1), both requirements for a Rule 23(b)(2) class action must be satisfied for certification purposes.

(1) Grounds Generally Applicable. [§8.1321]

As long as the conduct of the person opposing the class would affect each member of the class, even in a general way, the requirement is met; he or she does not have to act directly against each member of the class. Moreover, every class member does not have to be affected adversely by the conduct of the opponent of the class. Common examples of proper Rule 23(b)(2) class actions are African American parents seeking to enjoin racial discrimination in a school district, riparian landowners attempting to stop water pollution, and prisoners attempting to restrain a particular practice in a penitentiary.

Illustration. [§8.1321–1] Several persons relocated as a result of an urban renewal project bring a class action on behalf of all those who have been relocated, alleging that the defendant has discriminated against them in connection with their relocation. Some of the members of the class, however, are satisfied with their relocation. Nevertheless, a Rule 23(b)(2) class action will be permitted since a general pattern of conduct, applicable to the class as a whole, is all that is required. Furthermore, the fact that the alleged discriminatory scheme did not actually discriminate against all class members should not defeat the action.

---

(2) Injunctive or Declaratory Relief. [§8.1322]

The second requirement for a Rule 23(b)(2) class action is that the class representatives must seek final injunctive or corresponding declaratory relief; thus, Rule 23(b)(2) will not apply when the plaintiff seeks primarily money damages. In actions seeking both an injunction and monetary compensation for harm already caused, a court may scrutinize the plaintiffs' pleadings to determine whether the equitable relief is indeed the primary aim of the suit. It does not matter whether the relief sought is mandatory or prohibitory. However, the declaratory or injunctive relief sought must be final; a request for a temporary restraining order alone is insufficient. Because the Rule calls for "corresponding" declaratory relief, the requested declaratory judgment must lay the foundation for a judicial order in the nature of an injunction. A suit requesting a declaration that certain conduct constitutes a breach of contract would be insufficient, since it only sets the stage for a later action for damages.

c. Common Questions Predominate over Individual Questions—Rule 23(b)(3) Classes. [§8.1330]

A class action under Rule 23(b)(3)—the so-called common-question class action—is permitted when (a) the **common questions of law or** fact **predominate** over questions only affecting individual class members, and (b) **the class action device is superior** to other means of adjudicating the controversy. These special requirements reflect the fact that the class members in a Rule 23(b)(3) action are very loosely affiliated and the rights of the absent members must be protected.

(1) Predominance of Common Questions. [§8.1331]

The requirement that common questions predominate is designed to achieve the judicial economy associated with class actions. The common questions need not be identical as to every class member, nor do they need to be dispositive of the entire action. There simply has to be a significant common nucleus of issues to ensure the utility of the class action procedure. Note, however, that it is not enough that some common questions exist, as was true of the class action prerequisite discussed in **§8.1240**; they must predominate in an action under Rule 23(b)(3).

Illustration. [§8.1331–1] A, a discharged African American public school teacher, brings suit on behalf of himself and others similarly situated to compel the school board to issue teaching contracts on a non-discriminatory basis to those discharged. The ultimate issue respecting each member of the class is whether his or her discharge was for constitutionally justifiable reasons. Although the question of the school board's racial discrimination may well arise in connection with the proof of each teacher's claim, a consideration of the facts surrounding each teacher's discharge is necessary. Since the individual questions predominate over the common class questions, the case should not proceed as a class action.

---

(2) Superiority of Class Action over Other Methods of Adjudication. [§8.1332]

This requirement obliges the court to consider the other procedures, if any, that exist for resolving the controversy and to determine whether any of them would be more advantageous than a class action. If a comparison of the alternative adjudicatory techniques reveals that the benefits of a class suit are sufficient to warrant both the expenditure of judicial energy necessary to manage it and the possible procedural unfairness to class members, the class suit should be permitted to proceed.

(3) Factors to Be Considered. [§8.1333]

To help guide the court in determining whether the requirements for a common-question class action are met, Federal Rule 23(b)(3) lists four factors that should be considered. (a) The interest that individual class members may have in controlling the prosecution or defense of a suit involving their rights. It must be apparent that individual members have valid reasons for prosecuting individual suits before the class action will be rejected on this basis. (b) Whether other actions concerning the controversy are already pending. The purpose of this inquiry is to avoid multiple litigation since, if the other suits cannot be enjoined or stayed, the class action simply will add to the amount of litigation; furthermore, scrutiny of the existing actions may help the court to determine whether class issues predominate. (c) The desirability of having the litigation concentrated in one forum. The relevant concerns here are avoiding inconsistent judgments in individual actions and minimizing duplication of effort. Also relevant is a consideration of whether the forum chosen for the class action is an appropriate one in light of the citizenship of the interested parties, the availability of witnesses and evidence, and the condition of the court's calendar. (d) The management difficulties that might be encountered if the suit is permitted to proceed as a class action. Relevant considerations that must be weighed against the benefits of consolidated dispute resolution include the size of the claims of its individual members and the class itself, the existence of special individual issues, and the onerousness of compliance with the notice requirements.

Illustration. [§8.1333–1] A, B, and C bring a class action under the antitrust laws on behalf of all persons who have rented automobiles from 15 defendant car rental agencies in the New York City area, alleging that the defendants have illegally agreed to impose a $1 surcharge to cover unpaid parking tickets received by some customers. In deciding whether to allow the case to proceed on a class basis, the court will take account of the management difficulties caused by the large size of the class and the problems of identifying and giving notice to its members, the small amount that will be recovered by each class member should the action

---

succeed, the time and money that will be consumed in adjudicating the dispute, and the possibility that the defendants will assert counterclaims against many class members to recover the amount of unpaid parking tickets. Factors in favor of class action treatment are the gravity of the alleged antitrust violation, the inability of class members to prosecute the action on an individual basis, and the absence of other pending actions.

(4) Right of Absent Class Members to Opt Out. [§8.1334]

The members of common-question classes are given **the right to opt out of the action** by Rule 23(c)(2)(B). Any class member who does so will not be bound by the judgment in the action [see **§8.1600**], and will be free to pursue his or her rights on an individual basis. The United States Supreme Court has extended this right to plaintiffs in state class actions wholly or predominantly for money damages. The Supreme Court did not decide whether this applies to non-monetary class actions, such as those typically associated with Rule 23(b)(1) and Rule 23(b)(2) [*Phillips Petroleum Co. v. Shutts* (1985)]. On the one hand, the due process concerns that prompted the adoption of an opt-out provision for common-question classes seem similarly applicable to other classes. On the other hand, allowing plaintiffs to opt out of subdivision (b)(1) or (b)(2) classes would defeat the very object of their use: consistent adjudication and the availability of injunctive or declaratory relief on a classwide basis. [See **§8.1335–§8.1336** for a discussion of common-question class actions; see **§8.1500–§8.1560** for a discussion of adequacy of notice.]

(5) Class Actions in the Mass Tort Context. [§8.1335]

Due to concerns that the mere possibility of class certification induced defendants to settle rather than go to trial, the federal system in the mid–1990s began to disfavor the certification of mass torts. A number of attempts during that time to certify class actions for mass torts under Rule 23(b)(3) were largely unsuccessful. For example, in *Castano v. American Tobacco Co.* (1996), the court reversed a district court's conditional certification of a class action under Rule 23(b)(3) on behalf of all nicotine-dependent persons and their families. The appellate court asserted that conditional certification does not obviate the need to decide if the class fulfills the Rule 23 prerequisites, and that this class failed to meet the requirement that common questions predominate. First, the variations among applicable state standards overwhelmed issues common to the class. Second, without deciding how to conduct the trial, the district court could not determine whether individual issues, such as reliance and choice-of-law, would outnumber common issues. Finally, because no court has tried the injury-as-addiction claim, it is impossible to discern whether a class action would save judicial resources or whether common issues would predominate. The Fifth Circuit declared that "immature" torts are inappropriate for class actions because a court needs experience with a claim in order to conclude that the requirements of Rule 23 are fulfilled.

Illustration. [§8.1335–1] The Sixth Circuit in the mid–1990s decertified a Rule 23(b)(3) class in *In re American Medical Systems (AMS)* (1996). The court held that the case was certified erroneously because no demonstration had been made to the district court that the class met every requirement presented by Rule 23. Like *Castano*, the court felt that common questions could not predominate because the negligence law to be applied differed in each jurisdiction. Both *Castano* and *In re AMS* cited the Advisory Committee's 1966 observation that class actions are inappropriate for mass torts and both decisions reveal a heightened scrutiny of whether common issues predominate.

Illustration. [§8.1335–2] The Seventh Circuit decertified a Rule 23(b)(3) class in *In the Matter of Rhone–Poulenc* (1995) on a writ of mandamus, reversing the district court's certification of a class that had been based on the issue of negligence. The Seventh Circuit was concerned with the Seventh Amendment protection of jury trial, and the risk of entrusting a potentially multi-billion dollar verdict to one jury. The court also addressed the problem of nationwide class actions and rejected the notion that a court could merge conflicting laws from fifty states; in fact, the court doubted the constitutionality of such a practice in light of the *Erie* doctrine [see the discussion in **§4.2000–§4.3351**]. The Seventh Circuit also commented that the plaintiffs' claim appeared to lack merit, since twelve out of thirteen individual cases had concluded in favor of the defendants. The court's inquiry into the likelihood of a claim's success is not permitted on a certification motion under Rule 23; however, some judges have begun to allow limited discussions of the merits to enter into their certification decisions, and a reversal of that rule has been contemplated by the Federal Rules Advisory Committee [see **§8.1337**].

(6) Settlement Classes. [§8.1336]

Prior to the mid–1990s, courts had certified many class actions, knowing they would never go to trial, in order to allow a defendant to settle with the class [see **§8.1710**]. A reaction developed in the federal courts against this procedure based on concerns that the settlements were unfair and standards for certification too loose. The Supreme Court in the late 1990s attempted to settle this dispute in two decisions [*Amchem Products, Inc. v. Windsor* (1997); *Ortiz v. Fibreboard Corp.* (1999)], which clarified that although a class action may be certified for settlement purposes only, both the Rule 23(b)(3) requirements of predominance and superiority, and the Rule 23(a) requirement of adequacy of representation must be given heightened attention in order to protect absent members from misrepresentation and conflicting class interests. When considering certification, the prospects of a fair and efficient settlement are relevant, but not determinative.

Illustration. [§8.1336–1] In *Amchem Products, Inc. v. Windsor* (1997), The Supreme Court affirmed the Third Circuit's decertification of a Rule 23(b)(3) class consisting of potentially over one million persons who had been exposed to asbestos and who were the subject of an attempt to achieve a global settlement of present and future injury claims. A plethora of individual issues characterized the settlement class, such as the members' unique medical histories, varying levels and forms of exposure to different asbestos-containing products, and the availability of widely ranging causes of action. The settlement class also was plagued by diversity of interest since it consisted of at least three types of plaintiffs: those who (1) already suffer from asbestos-related injuries and are interested in generous immediate compensation; (2) have yet to experience any adverse effects, but are aware of their exposure and are interested in ensuring an ample fund for future compensation should they become seriously ill; and (3) have yet to experience any adverse effects, are unaware of being exposed, and lack the ability to make an informed decision whether or not to be bound by the settlement. The Supreme Court held that the enormously diverse class before it could not satisfy Rule 23(b)(3)'s predominance and superiority standard, and that it is not enough to base class cohesion upon a common interest in receiving compensation, especially when those interests can be antagonistic or can determine the rights of unknowing members. If a common interest in a fair compromise could satisfy the predominance and superiority requirement, Rule 23(b)(3) would be stripped of any meaning in the settlement context. The Court held that the inherently divisive objectives of the diverse groups and individuals affected by the *Amchem* settlement deprived it of any structural assurance of fair and adequate representation. The Court reiterated many of these points in *Ortiz v. Fibreboard Corp.* (1999).

(7) Proposed Amendments to Federal Rule 23. [§8.1337]

For a number of years, the Federal Rules Advisory Committee has been considering amending Rule 23. It has proposed incorporating the likelihood of a claim's success as a factor in the certification decision and that Rule 23(b)(3) require a class action not only to be the "superior" but also the "necessary" method of adjudication. Because of substantial opposition, both of these proposals were withdrawn. In addition to these matters, the Committee has under consideration proposals for a small-claims common question class and for a fourth type of class, the settlement class. The small-claims proposal has produced much controversy, and the Committee has deferred treatment of the settlement class proposal in order to digest the Supreme Court's decision in *Amchem Products, Inc. v. Windsor* (1997). New proposals that were adopted in 2003 increased the court's control over the class action process regarding notice, the appointment of class counsel, and attorneys fees. The changes to the Federal Rules of Civil Procedure adopted in 2007 contained only stylistic changes to Rule 23.

(8) Judicial Panel on Multidistrict Litigation. [§8.1338]

One method of handling suits filed in several districts appears in 28 USC 1407, which allows the transfer of scattered actions into one district court for pretrial proceedings. If the actions share common questions and their consolidation will promote efficiency, a panel of seven specially appointed judges may consolidate the pending litigation in a single district. Although the statute authorizes transfer for pretrial proceedings only and provides that the actions "shall" be remanded to their original districts for trial, federal courts for many years followed the practice of retaining those cases for trial, either by obtaining the consent of the parties or pursuant to a transfer procedure. However, the Supreme Court invalidated this practice in *Lexecon, Inc. v. Milberg Weiss Bershad Hynes & Lerach* (1998), holding that the Judicial Panel on Multidistrict Litigation was under a clear statutory obligation to remand the cases, and that the transferee courts could not prevent the Panel from fulfilling this obligation [see **§2.7720**].

4. Determination Whether Class Action Is Maintainable. [§8.1400]

Pursuant to Rule 23(c)(1)(A), at an early practical time after a suit has been commenced as a class action, the court will hold a hearing to determine whether the litigation should proceed as a class suit. The court may make the determination on its own initiative and is not required to wait for a motion by one of the parties. If the judge is convinced it is appropriate, he or she will certify the class action status of the case.

a. Determination Not Final. [§8.1410]

The initial decision regarding the maintainability of an action as a class suit is not final. If, in the course of a certified class action, it becomes apparent that the suit should not be continued on a representative basis, Rule 23(c)(1)(C) allows the class suit aspect of the case to be stricken.

Illustration. [§8.1411] A, B, and C institute a common-question class action against a vendor on behalf of 100 purchasers of a product alleged to be defective. After certifying the action as a class action, notice is sent to the 97 other members of the class. Upon learning that 85 members of the class have exercised their right to opt out, the court may decide to revise its earlier order and strike the class action allegations.

---

b. Partial Class Action Order. [§8.1420]

The court may determine that the action should proceed as a class suit only with regard to certain issues or as to certain parties. In that event, individuals, at their option, may prosecute their claims in the same or separate suits.

c. Formation of Subclasses. [§8.1430]

If it is determined that some class members have interests that are antagonistic to or divergent from those of other class members, the court has the power under Rule 23(c)(5) to divide the class into subclasses, each having its own representative(s). If the original class has been divided into subclasses, the court must repeat the procedure of determining whether the suit is maintainable as a class action as to each subclass. If any of the prerequisites for the class action is not satisfied with regard to one of the subclasses, the class suit allegations must be dismissed respecting that subclass, unless the court can correct the situation. Members of the original class who were not included in the newly created subclass will not be subject to the res judicata effect of any resulting judgment.

Illustration. [§8.1431] In *Amchem Products, Inc. v. Windsor* (1997) [see **§8.1337**], the Supreme Court affirmed the Third Circuit's decertification of a Rule 23(b)(3) class consisting of potentially over one million persons exposed to asbestos. The Supreme Court held that a fair and representative settlement could not be achieved given the divergence between short-term and long-term compensation interests, between exposure victims with current injuries and exposure victims with latent injuries, between smoking and non-smoking class members, and between those members aware of their exposure and those unaware of their exposure. The Supreme Court did, however, leave the door open for devising a mass tort class for settlement purposes that would be in accordance with Rule 23 by subtly inviting the district court to divide the sprawling class into subclasses, in which members would be grouped according to common qualities, interests, and levels of awareness. However, that was not done.

---

d. Conditional Orders. [§8.1440]

The court may enter an order requiring the litigants to meet certain conditions before the suit will be permitted to continue on a class basis. For example, the class representatives may be required to amend the complaint in order to delimit more clearly the membership of the class or the court may require the class to have better representation.

e.   **Appealability. [§8.1450]**

Because a court's certification decision is not a final judgment, prior to the 1998 amendment to Rule 23, it was not ordinarily appealable. This situation produced an anomalous result because for those plaintiffs whose claims were small enough to preclude individual actions, the failure to secure certification meant an end to lititgation. Similarly, for those defendants who faced a potential windfall loss if the class action were certified, settlement often seemed the best option. Thus, although a certification decision was not a final judgment in these cases, it did effectively finalize lititgation. Rule 23(f) was added in 1998 in order to address this anomaly. The amendment permits a Court of Appeals, at its discretion, to grant an appeal of a certification decision. Although the rule itself does not set forth any guidelines for determining when a grant of appeal is proper, the Advisory Committee Notes hint that the amendment is intended to affect those cases in which a district court's decision regarding certification (a) is dependent on a new or unsettled question or law, or (b) is likely to preclude further litigation.

Illustration. [§8.1451] In *Waste Management Holdings, Inc. v. Mowbray* (2000), the court delineated three situations in which it would ordinarily grant leave to appeal an order granting or denying class certification. First, when a denial of class status effectively ends the case. Second, when the grant of class status raises the stakes of the litigation so substantially that the defendant likely will feel irresistible pressure to settle. Third, when an appeal will permit the resolution of an unsettled legal issue that is important to the particular litigation as well as important per se and is likely to escape effective review if left unsettled. The court, however, was careful not to limit the appealability of certification decision to these specific categories. In fact, in *Waste Management*, no category was strictly met; however, the court granted appeal largely because the merits of the certification decision had already been briefed.

---

5.   **Notice to Absent Class Members. [§8.1500]**

Federal Rule 23 and comparable state provisions require that **the best notice of the institution of the action practicable under the circumstances**

must be given to the absent class members if the class action is based on Rule 23(b)(3) or is of the so-called common-question type [see **§8.1330–§8.1334**]. Notice is crucial to these class actions since the members of the class are tenuously affiliated and without it the requirements of due process would not permit the judgment to bind unnotified absentees. Although such notice is explicitly required by Rule 23 only in common-question class actions, the requirements of due process would be violated by an attempt to bind members of a Rule 23(b)(1) or Rule 23(b)(2) class if notice is not given. Thus, Rule 23(c)(2)(A) indicates that a federal court may order that notice be given in these types of class suits as well. Another difference may be in the quality of the notice and the efforts required to transmit it. [Other aspects of notice in class actions are discussed in **§8.1710** (settlement and compromise), and **§8.1720** (judicial management).]

a. Timing of Notice. [§8.1510]

Generally, notice will be given as soon as the initial determination that the suit should proceed as a class action has been made. This is designed to give class members a full and fair opportunity either to intervene in the action with leave of the court or, in the case of common-question class actions, to opt out.

b. Character of Notice. [§8.1520]

For federal class actions under Rule 23(b)(3) and state class actions for money damages, the Supreme Court has held that **individual notice must be given by the class representative to those class members who can be identified and located** [*Eisen v. Carlisle & Jacquelin* (1974); *Phillips Petroleum Co. v. Shutts* (1985)]. This requirement is set out in Rule 23(c)(2)(B). Thus interpreted, the notice requirement constitutes an almost insuperable barrier to class litigation when the class is large and the individual claims are small so that notice to the absentees cannot be financed [see **§8.1560**]. Unless the Supreme Court extends this principle, other class actions fall under Rule 23(c)(2)(A) and the discretionary-notice provision in Rule 23(d)(1)(B), which lets the court decide when notice is appropriate "for the protection of the members of the class or otherwise for the fair conduct of the action."

(1) Manner of Giving Notice. [§8.1521]

The acceptable manner of giving notice may vary according to the type of class action involved. The single point of agreement is that the notice must be reasonably calculated to apprise the class members of the pendency of the action and afford them an opportunity to protect their interests. If the identity or location of class members is unknown and cannot be determined through reasonable effort, notice by publication is permitted [see **§3.5100**]. Some state rules give courts complete discretion to determine the manner of notice, and notice by television or radio has been accepted. Nevertheless, the Supreme Court has interpreted Rule 23(c)(2) to require that individual notice be sent to all reasonably identifiable members of a common question class—regardless of the difficulty caused by class size or cost [*Eisen v. Carlisle & Jacquelin* (1974)].

c. Contents of the Notice. [§8.1530]

According to Federal Rule 23(c)(2)(B), the notice must indicate that: (a) the court will exclude from the class anyone who requests to opt out by a specified date; (b) any class member who fails to opt out will be included in the judgment; and (c) if the class member does not request exclusion from the action, he or she may make an appearance through counsel. For a Rule 23(b)(3) action, the notice must also contain a description of the suit and the issues being litigated.

d. Adequacy of Notice. [§8.1540]

The potential for undermining Rule 23(c)(2) notice is especially tangible when certifying a settlement-only class in the context of mass tort litigation. It is very common that these enormous classes consist of members who, after being exposed to the dangerous condition or substance, possess different levels of awareness of their injuries and exhibit various forms of damage. For members in the exposure-only category who are unaware of their exposure or of the extent of harm they may incur, the significance of class notice, even if it should reach them, is lost, as they may not have the knowledge or foresight needed to decide whether to stay in the class or to opt out. In order to protect oblivious absent members, the Supreme Court demands a cautious outlook in deciding whether to certify a class for settlement purposes in which individual stakes are high and disparities among members are great [*Amchem Products, Inc. v. Windsor* (1997); see **§8.1337**].

e. Mechanics of Giving Notice. [§8.1550]

A fear that permitting notice to be given by the representative plaintiff's counsel will be used as a device for claim solicitation has led some judges to require that the court itself control notice-giving in a common-question class action. The burden on the court's time that would be imposed by this practice has led other judges to require the representatives to draft a notice subject to approval by the court and objection by the defendant.

f. Cost of Giving Notice. [§8.1560]

The economic burden of giving notice usually is not expressly governed by a class rule. The Supreme Court, however, has held that a federal court cannot direct that the cost of giving notice be shifted to the defendant [*Eisen v. Carlisle & Jacquelin* (1974)]. Arguably, the better practice would be to allow the cost burden to be shifted in appropriate cases. The court could consider: (a) whether the claim seems meritorious, (b) whether the defendant desires and would benefit from the broader res judicata effect of a judgment in a class suit, (c) the number and financial position of the named plaintiffs, (d) the proportion of the total recovery that would be received by the named plaintiffs, and (e) the total cost of the notice. The Supreme Court has reinforced the *Eisen* result by indicating that the cost of identifying class members also normally should be borne by the party seeking class action treatment, although that burden may be imposed on the non-class party when it would be significantly easier for it to identify the class members [*Oppenheimer Fund, Inc. v. Sanders* (1978)].

6. Binding Effect of a Class Action Judgment. [§8.1600]

A class action judgment generally will apply to those whom the court finds to be members of the class. In a Rule 23(b)(3) class, those who have opted out will not be bound by the judgment; however, they also will not be able to take advantage of the benefits of a favorable decision by claiming collateral estoppel in suits brought on their own [see **§8.1334**]. The court adjudicating an action cannot predetermine its res judicata effect; that can be determined only when a collateral attack is made upon it in a subsequent action.

a. Practice under Some State Codes. [§8.1610]

State provisions retaining the old "true," "hybrid," and "spurious" classification of class actions [see **§8.1110**] make the binding effect of the judgment depend upon the particular type of class action that is involved. All members of the class in a "true" class action will be bound. In a "hybrid" class suit, the judgment will be binding on all members with regard to the fund or property that is the subject matter of the action. In a "spurious" class suit, only those class members before the court originally or who enter by intervention will be bound by the judgment.

b. Limitations on Collateral Attack. [§8.1620]

There is a relatively strong policy in favor of protecting a class action judgment against challenges by class members who did not participate in the original action. Otherwise, the benefits of the class action would be lost and what often has been a time-consuming and expensive litigation would have settled nothing. Moreover, the procedural requirements for a class suit usually are designed to make certain that the application of res judicata and collateral estoppel is fair and equitable. Thus, collateral attack should be limited to situations in which the class member can demonstrate that the representation of his or her interests has been inadequate or that some other basic prerequisite to class action treatment (e.g., notice) has not been satisfied, and enforcement of the judgment would be inequitable.

7. Judicial Management of the Class Suit. [§8.1700]

The highly complex nature of many class actions (particularly in the federal courts) and the danger of violating the due process rights of absent class members have led many rulemakers to provide the trial judge with authority to control and manage numerous aspects of the class suit. For example, Federal Rule 23(d) contains a non-exhaustive list of possible orders that a judge may issue in the conduct of a class action. In addition, the Manual on Complex Litigation issued by the Federal Judicial Center contains an extensive description of various practices federal judges may follow to ensure the effective management of class actions.

a. Settlement and Compromise. [§8.1710]

To provide additional protection for absent class members, class action provisions typically require **court approval of any settlement or compromise** of the class' claims entered into between the class representatives and the defendant [see Federal Rule 23(e)]. This is designed to guard against any unjust or unfair settlements that may occur because the class representatives become faint-hearted or are "bought off" by the opposing party. Judicial approval typically entails giving notice of the proposed settlement or compromise to all class members and holding a hearing to determine whether the terms of the agreement are in the best interests of the class. Since most actions, whether or not they are class suits, are filed in the hope that they will be settled without trial, the elaborate requirements for settlement of class suits have serious practical consequences. Many lawyers shy away from class suits for fear that the costs of securing court agreement, including giving notice to all class members, will inhibit legitimate settlement and be detrimental to the interests of their clients. Courts have found one way out of this dilemma by permitting settlement with individual class members so long as agreement is reached prior to the court's determination that the class suit is proper. This procedure, although practical, has been severely criticized as undercutting the policy underlying judicial approval of settlements and being potentially damaging to the rights of the absentees.

Illustration. [See the discussion of settlement classes in *Amchem* in **§8.1336–1** and **§1337.**]

---

b. Discretionary Notice. [§8.1720]

One power typically provided courts is to order notice to absent class members at any point in the action for any purpose thought appropriate. The court may employ this authority to inform absentees of major developments in the case and to give the absentees an opportunity to provide oversight on the activities of the class representatives.

c. Intervention. [§8.1730]

Unnamed members of the class may seek to intervene in the action and actively participate in it. The court must decide whether their presence in the action is necessary for the protection of absent class members or will tend to make the management of the action more difficult. [Intervention is discussed in **§8.3000–§8.3700.**]

8. Federal Subject Matter Jurisdiction. [§8.1800]

In 2005, Congress passed the Class Action Fairness Act (CAFA) [28 USC §1332(d)], establishing a form of minimal diversity jurisdiction over large, multi-state class actions. Henceforth, federal subject matter jurisdiction in class actions will be determined largely by whether CAFA applies.

a. Does the Class Action Arise Under CAFA? [§8.1810]

CAFA provides the federal district courts with original and removal jurisdiction over class actions involving 100 or more proposed plaintiff class members when any plaintiff is diverse in citizenship with regard to any defendant, and when the sum or value of all class members' claims exceeds $5,000,000. CAFA applies only to class actions initially filed on or after February 18, 2005, and is subject to certain enumerated exceptions. When an action originally is brought in state court, a defendant seeking removal pursuant to CAFA bears the burden of proving that the statute's requirements have been satisfied.

(1) **Are there 100 or more class members? [§8.1811]**

(2) **Is at least one plaintiff from a different state than any defendant? [§8.1812]**

(3) **Does the matter in controversy exceed the sum or value of $5,000,000, exclusive of interest and costs? [§8.1813]**

(4) **Was the class action initially filed—not removed—on or after February 18, 2005? [§8.1814]**

Some courts have held that a defendant added or substituted after CAFA's effective date to a pre-existing action may, in fact, remove the action to federal court, though other courts have reached the opposite conclusion. Most courts have held that state law determines when an action was commenced for purposes of this provision of CAFA.

b. **If the Class Action Arises Under CAFA, Do Any of the Exceptions to Federal Subject Matter Jurisdiction Apply? [§8.1820]**

The legislative history of CAFA suggests that Congress intended the Act to be construed liberally in order to "strongly favor the exercise of federal diversity jurisdiction over class actions with interstate ramifications." Each of the exceptions below is to be construed narrowly. A party seeking remand of an action removed pursuant to CAFA bears the burden of proving that one of the CAFA's exceptions applies.

(1) **"Home State" Exception. [§8.1821]**

Potentially the most expansive exception to CAFA depends upon the proportion of the class that shares the citizenship of the "primary defendants." When two-thirds or more of the class members and the primary defendants are citizens of the state in which the action was filed, the federal court may not exercise jurisdiction over the class action. On the other hand, when more than two-thirds of the members of the plaintiff class or one or more of the primary defendants are not citizens of the forum state, there will be federal diversity jurisdiction over the class action. In the middle are class actions in which both the primary defendants and between one-third and two-thirds of the members of the proposed plaintiff class are citizens of the forum state. In these situations, the federal court may decline to exercise jurisdiction "in the interests of justice" and in view of "the totality of the circumstances."

(2) "Local Controversy" Exception. [§8.1822]

Parties seeking to invoke this exception must run a gauntlet. Federal courts must decline diversity jurisdiction over class actions in which (1) more than two-thirds of the class members are citizens of the forum state, (2) there is at least one in-state defendant from whom "significant relief" is sought and whose conduct is a "significant basis" of the plaintiffs' claims, (3) the plaintiffs' principal injuries were incurred in the forum state, and (4) no other class action asserting similar claims has been brought during the preceding three years.

(3) Eleventh Amendment Exception. [§8.1823]

CAFA prohibits federal diversity jurisdiction over actions in which the primary defendants are states, state officials, or "other governmental entities against whom the district court may be foreclosed from ordering relief" by the Eleventh Amendment, which grants sovereign immunity to the individual states.

(4) Securities Litigation Exception. [§8.1824]

In 1998, Congress enacted the Securities Litigation Uniform Standards Act, which provides that large securities class actions must proceed in federal court. CAFA does not apply to these actions, or to class actions that relate to the internal affairs or governance of a business enterprise when the claim arises under the laws of the state in which the business is incorporated or organized.

c. Class Actions Not Subject to CAFA. [§8.1830]

In *Exxon Mobil Corporation v. Allapattah Services, Inc.* (2005), the United States Supreme Court resolved a longstanding division among the Courts of Appeals regarding the interpretation of the supplemental jurisdiction statute [28 USC 1367]. The Court held that when there is complete diversity of citizenship and at least one named plaintiff's claim satisfies the amount-in-controversy requirement of Section 1332, a district court may exercise supplemental jurisdiction over the jurisdictionally insufficient claims of any other plaintiff with regard to the same "case or controversy." In the class action context, this means that the federal courts will have subject matter jurisdiction over class actions founded solely upon diversity grounds when the class representatives are completely diverse with regard to the defendant and at least one of them states a claim for more than $75,000.

(1) Whose Citizenship Governs? [§8.1831]

The rule is that only the citizenship of the class representatives need be scrutinized in a class action for diversity jurisdiction purposes. In view of the complete diversity requirement, a requirement that the citizenship of all class members must be taken into account would restrict the availability of the class action procedure dramatically. [See **§2.3000–§2.3830** for a discussion of diversity of citizenship jurisdiction.]

(2) Jurisdictional Amount. [§8.1832]

For many years, the United States Supreme Court held that each class member had to be able to assert a claim that would satisfy the amount in controversy requirement, except when the claims of the class members were to enforce a single title or right in which they had a common and undivided interest. Only in that limited situation could the class members aggregate their claims to meet the amount in controversy requirement. [*Zahn v. International Paper Co.* (1973); *Snyder v. Harris* (1969).]

However, Congress, in 1990 enacted a supplemental jurisdiction statute [28 USC 1367] that the Supreme Court has held overrules *Zahn* and *Snyder.* In *Exxon Mobil Corporation v. Allapattah Services, Inc.* (2005), the Supreme Court ruled that claims by parties that fail to meet the amount in controversy requirement may be brought when combined with claims by other plaintiffs that do satisfy that requirement. Only one of the named class representatives needs to satisfy the amount in controversy requirement, giving the court supplemental jurisdiction in the class action context when many other class members may have claims of less than $75,000. However, the Court's conclusion in *Allapattah* does not abolish the traditional doctrine that individual plaintiffs' independent claims may not be aggregated to reach the required jurisdictional amount in controversy except when they sued to enforce a single title or right in which they had a common and undivided interest.

Illustration. [§8.1832–1] One named plaintiff brings a class action against a motor fuel supplier on behalf of itself and approximately 10,000 current and former fuel dealers for damages resulting from

---

251

supplier's systematic and intentional overcharging of the dealers. Subject matter jurisdiction is based on diversity of citizenship. The named representative has a claim for more than $75,000, but many of the other members of the class have claims for far less than the required amount in controversy. According to the Supreme Court's interpretation of Section 1367 in *Allapattah*, the plaintiffs will be able to proceed on a class action basis since the court may assert supplemental jurisdiction over the claims that do not satisfy the amount in controversy requirement, so long as the claims of the unnamed members are sufficiently related to those of the named representatives to satisfy the statute [see also **§2.4330– §2.4331**].

9. State Class Action Practice. [§8.1900]

Class action practice differs from state to state, with some states having extremely limited rules. Probably the most liberal approach to class action litigation is found in Section 382 of the California Code of Civil Procedure, which provides only that "when the question is one of a common or general interest, of many persons, or when the parties are numerous, and it is impracticable to bring them all before the court, one or more may sue or defend for the benefit of all." The most striking difference between this provision and Federal Rule 23 is that California courts are not required to differentiate among different types of class actions as federal courts are required to do [see **§8.1300–§8.1334**].

a. An Identifiable Class. [§8.1910]

In order for a class action to be brought in California, the court must determine that there is an identifiable class. This requirement combines the federal prerequisites that there be an identifiable class and that the class be too large to permit joinder [see **§8.1210** and **§8.1230**]. As in the federal courts, it is not necessary in California that the representatives be able to identify each class member.

b. Community of Interest. [§8.1920]

California courts will not allow a class action to proceed unless there is a sufficient community of interest among the members of the class. This requirement telescopes the federal prerequisites that there be common questions of law or fact [see **§8.1240**], that the interests of the representatives be typical of those of the class [see **§8.1250**], and that the representatives adequately protect the interests of the absent class members [see **§8.1260**]. Furthermore, the community of interest requirement seems to include the first of the two requirements for the so-called common-question, or Rule 23(b)(3), class action in the federal system—that the common questions raised by the class predominate over any questions that have to be adjudicated on an individual basis [see **§8.1240**].

c.   Growth in State Class Action Practice. [§8.1930]

For many years there was a clear trend toward increased state class action practice. This resulted from the liberalization of the class action rules in a number of states and the inaccessibility of the federal courts for small claim diversity-based class actions. This trend undoubtedly has been reversed by the enactment of CAFA in 2005 [see **§8.1800–§8.1824**].

C.   OTHER REPRESENTATIVE ACTIONS. [§8.2000]

Federal Rules 23.1 and 23.2, which have counterparts in most jurisdictions, permit actions to be instituted by the representatives of particular groups. Federal Rule 23.1 deals with shareholder derivative suits and Federal Rule 23.2 deals with actions involving unincorporated associations.

1.   Shareholder Derivative Suits. [§8.2100]

Under certain circumstances one or more shareholders may bring an action for the benefit of the corporation when the board of directors refuses to bring suit to vindicate the corporation's rights. The claimant is treated as the representative of the shareholders and must meet the usual prerequisites for a class action. Federal Rule 23.1 imposes special pleading requirements on plaintiffs in shareholder derivative actions.

a.   State Practice. [§8.2110]

In order to prevent frivolous or sham shareholder derivative suits, a number of states have imposed restrictions on potential plaintiffs in these actions. Among the more common requirements are that the plaintiffs own a certain percentage or dollar amount of the corporation's stock or that they post a bond to cover the expenses of the lawsuit should the plaintiffs lose.

2.   Unincorporated Associations. [§8.2200]

Federal Rule 23.2 is designed to cure special problems relating to the question of whether an unincorporated association, such as a partnership or labor union, is an entity for the purposes of filing a representative suit on behalf of its members. The rule allows a proceeding to be brought in a federal court in the nature of a class action.

a. **State Practice. [§8.2210]**

In some states that have not promulgated a curative provision comparable to Federal Rule 23.2, it often is necessary to join all of the members of an unincorporated association against whom the judgment is to be enforced. Those not joined will not be bound by the judgment.

D. INTERVENTION. [§8.3000]

Intervention permits someone who is not a party to an action to protect his or her interests by joining the litigation. This is thought to be desirable when it would afford the non-party an efficient way to adjudicate a right or liability that is related to the subject matter of the action or when there is a risk that the judgment in the action will have a detrimental effect on the interests of the non-party. Contemporary procedural rules, typified by Federal Rule 24, recognize two different kinds of interventions—intervention of right and permissive intervention.

1. Intervention. [§8.3100]

Modern intervention provisions—which have displaced earlier, more conceptualistic standards—typically contain a tripartite standard that must be met before intervention of right will be permitted. First, the potential intervenor **must have an interest relating to the property or transaction that is the subject of the action.** Second, a disposition of the action in the intervenor's absence, as a practical matter, **must be likely to impair his or her ability to protect that interest.** Third, there must be a showing that the **present litigants do not adequately represent the intervenor's interests.** Rule 24(a) is a typical modern provision, describing when someone has an automatic right to intervene, without leave of the court.

a. Interest in the Subject Matter of the Action. [§8.3110]

There is no clear standard as to how significant an interest a potential intervenor must have in the subject matter of the suit before the first test for intervention of right is met. Some courts have required a direct, substantial, and legally protectable interest. Other courts avoid the often fruitless attempt to weigh the applicant's interest and simply consider the facts of the particular case and decide the intervention request in terms of judicial economy and the conflicting consideration of avoiding overly complex and diffused litigation.

Illustration. [§8.3111] Several inhabitants of a peaceful residential section of a city bring suit to enjoin a railroad from continuing to use certain tracks near their homes for the storage and coupling of freight cars on the ground that it constitutes a nuisance. A manufacturer who claims that the injunction would curtail essential railroad service to its factory has a sufficient interest in the subject matter of the action, permitting it to intervene as of right.

b. Impairment of Interest. [§8.3120]

The requirement that the potential intervenor show a possible impairment of his or her ability to protect an interest in the subject matter of the litigation does not mean that it is necessary that the outsider will be legally bound by the judgment. Indeed, the principles of res judicata and collateral estoppel normally do not extend to non-parties [see **§16.8000–§16.9700**]. Today, intervention often is permitted even if the potential impairment is not very substantial or direct. For example, the adverse effect of stare decisis occasionally has been held to be a sufficient possibility of impairment to justify intervention.

Illustration. [§8.3121] A attempts to obtain permission from the United States government to build a fishing club and hotel on certain reefs off the Florida coast to which A holds title. While A's application is pending, the government brings suit against B for building on some of these reefs without government authorization. B defends on the ground that the reefs are outside the scope of the Outer Continental Shelf Lands Act and therefore are open property. A seeks to intervene. Although A will not be legally bound by the judgment in the government's action against B, the slim prospects of having a decision on the law overruled in a subsequent case are such that a denial of A's application to intervene will make A's claim to the property practically worthless in the event that B loses. Thus, assuming the other criteria are met, A should be permitted to intervene as of right. [See *Atlantis Development Corp. v. U.S.* (1967).]

c. Adequacy of Representation. [§8.3130]

Lack of representation is a ground for intervention in class actions as well as in suits by trustees, executors, and other fiduciaries. Representation clearly is inadequate and intervention appropriate if there is collusion between a party supposedly representing the intervenor and an opposing party, or if the representative has failed to fulfill a fiduciary duty to the person seeking to intervene. These situations, however, do not constitute the only instances of inadequacy of representation. In each case, the positions of the existing parties must be compared with the interests of the applicant seeking intervention. [See also the discussion of adequacy of representation in the class action context in **§8.1260–§8.1261.**]

(1) Burden of Proof. [§8.3131]

Before 1966, Federal Rule 24 allowed intervention when "the representation is or may be inadequate." The rule, after amendment, permits intervention "unless existing parties adequately represent that interest." The amendment of Rule 24 appears to have shifted the burden of showing the inadequacy of the representation away from the potential intervenor and placed the burden of showing its adequacy on the parties opposing intervention.

d. Unconditional Statutory Right. [§8.3140]

In addition to permitting intervention when the three criteria discussed in the preceding sections are met, intervention rules typically permit intervention of right when a statute provides an unconditional right to intervene in specified situations.

2. Permissive Intervention. [§8.3200]

When intervention of right is unavailable, the court may permit an outsider to intervene **when the interest he or she seeks to protect presents a common question of law or fact with the interests of those who already are parties to the litigation.** Unlike intervention of right, which is tested against a fairly precise rule or statutory standard, permissive intervention is addressed to the court's discretion.

a. Conditional Statutory Right. [§8.3210]

Federal Rule 24(b) and its many state counterparts authorize permissive intervention when a statute grants a conditional right to intervene. For example, the United States Attorney General may intervene in a civil rights suit upon certifying that the case is of general public importance. It must be remembered that if the statute grants an unconditional right to intervene, the intervention is of right; thus, every special intervention statute must be analyzed to see if it creates a conditional or unconditional right to intervene.

b. Common Question of Law or Fact. [§8.3220]

The relatively minimal requirement that a common question of law or fact exists between the parties and putative intervenor allows the court to permit someone to intervene even though he or she would not have been a proper party for joinder purposes; there is no requirement that the applicant's claim be transactionally related to any claim in the action, as is true of permissive joinder [see §6.4200]. The common question requirement should be applied to intervention in the same fashion as in other joinder contexts [see §6.4300].

c. Government Officers and Agencies. [§8.3230]

A federal or state officer or governmental agency typically may intervene in an action in which a party has relied upon a statute or executive order administered by that officer or agency or when any regulation, order, requirement, or agreement issued or made pursuant to the statute or executive order is called into question.

d. Discretion of Court. [§8.3240]

After it has been demonstrated that an applicant either has a conditional statutory right to intervene, or raises a question of law or fact in common with the original action, or that the applicant is a governmental officer or agency having a conditional right to intervene under a statute or rule, the applicant must convince the court to exercise its discretion to permit intervention. The issue is whether the benefits of intervention will outweigh the possibility of unduly proliferating the controversy or of causing delay or expense. If the applicant would not significantly benefit from intervention (e.g., if the applicant is a participant in a number of other actions litigating substantially the same controversy) intervention should be denied.

Illustration. [§8.3241] P sues for damages and an injunction, claiming that D is infringing P's patent. X seeks to intervene as a defendant in the infringement suit and to interpose a counterclaim for unfair competition. Since D is wholly disinterested in the unfair competition claim, the court in its discretion may deny intervention or permit intervention on condition that the issue of unfair competition will not be raised. On the other hand, if X's counterclaim has a close transactional relationship with the original action, it may be allowed.

---

3. Timeliness of Intervention. [§8.3300]

Whether the intervention sought is of right or permissive, the motion for leave to intervene must be made in a timely fashion. Since a potential intervenor of right may be seriously harmed if excluded from the action, intervention motions rarely should be denied as being untimely. What constitutes a timely application will be determined by the court on the basis of the circumstances of the particular case. But the time element is only one factor to be considered. All the circumstances should be evaluated and special attention should be given to the possibility of prejudice to those who already are parties.

4. Procedure for Intervention. [§8.3400]

Many contemporary procedural rules call for the service of a motion for leave to intervene upon all parties and require that it state the grounds for intervention. A statement of the claim or defense must accompany the motion that is the basis for intervention. A hearing on the motion ordinarily will be held, but one is not required.

a. Notice to Attorney General in Constitutional Cases. [§8.3410]

If the constitutionality of a federal law affecting the public interest is questioned in any action in which the United States or an officer, agency, or employee thereof is not a party, the court shall notify the Attorney General so that he or she may intervene pursuant to 28 USC 2403.

5. Federal Subject Matter Jurisdiction. [§8.3500]

If the court lacks subject matter jurisdiction over the pending action, it must be dismissed even though the inclusion of an intervenor would cure the jurisdictional defect. Conversely, even if all of its requirements are met, intervention must be denied if it will destroy the court's subject matter jurisdiction. The enactment of the supplemental jurisdiction statute, 28 USC 1367, in 1990 eliminated any possibility of ancillary jurisdiction over claims by an intervenor, or by a plaintiff against an intervenor, in diversity of citizenship cases [see **§2.5000–§2.5530**]. If the case is based on federal question jurisdiction, and an intervenor claims intervention of right, supplemental jurisdiction generally is permitted. However, even in federal question cases, permissive intervenors must demonstrate an independent source of subject matter jurisdiction. Ordinarily, if intervention is sought pursuant to conditional statutory authority [see **§8.3210**], independent subject matter jurisdiction will exist.

Illustration. [§8.3510] A, a vendor of land, and B, the holder of a mortgage on the land, join in an action in a federal court against C,

---

the vendee who has failed to pay the full purchase price. B is dismissed from the action because her citizenship is the same as C's. Since B is not an indispensable party, the action will continue. B cannot avoid the original jurisdictional problems by returning to the suit as an intervenor; thus, intervention must be denied.

6. Personal Jurisdiction and Venue. [§8.3600]

The intervenor cannot object to personal jurisdiction or venue because he or she is voluntarily coming to the forum to enter the action; hence, these defenses are waived by intervention. Venue objections, however, may be raised by someone who is already a party to the action. Thus, in cases of permissive intervention in which concepts of ancillary jurisdiction do not apply, intervention should be disallowed when the inclusion of the applicant would create a venue problem. If, however the intervention is of right, so that ancillary subject matter jurisdiction will apply, the court also should assert ancillary venue over the intervenor.

7. Appealability. [§8.3700]

An order granting leave to intervene is not a final judgment and, in jurisdictions adhering to the final judgment rule, is not appealable until the action is terminated [see **§15.1000–§15.1510**]. When intervention is denied, however, the decision may become appealable if the trial court, finding no just reason for delay, orders the entry of a final judgment [see **§15.1310**]. Some courts, however, hold that a denial of intervention is a collateral order and is appealable as such [see **§15.1320**]. Once the case is properly before the appellate court, it may reverse on the basis of error in cases involving a claim of intervention of right and for abuse of discretion in cases of permissive intervention.

E. INTERPLEADER. [§8.4000]

Interpleader is an equitable procedure by which a person holding property—a stakeholder—who is or may be subject to inconsistent claims, can join all the claimants in a single action. **This protects the stakeholder from multiple lawsuits and perhaps from multiple liability.**

1. Threat of Multiple Liability. [§8.4100]

If the stakeholder had to decide for itself which of several claims to property or a fund under its control is the most meritorious, there would be a serious threat of multiple liability. Interpleader permits a disinterested stakeholder, one who acknowledges liability to one or some but not all claimants, to avoid having to make this kind of risky choice.

> **Illustration. [§8.4110]** An insurance company is faced with claims by the executor of an insured's estate and the insured's widow for the proceeds of certain life insurance policies. Although the insurance company believes that it should pay the executor, it fears that it still might be held liable to the widow should she file suit after the executor is paid. Interpleader is appropriate to protect the company against the possibility of double liability.

2. Vexation of Multiple Suits. [§8.4200]

Even when the stakeholder has a valid defense affording protection against the threat of multiple liability, interpleader protects the stakeholder against the vexation and expense of becoming embroiled in multiple litigation with each of the claimants.

> **Illustration. [§8.4210]** As a result of an accident, three claims totalling $100,000 are advanced by A, B, and C against driver X. X has liability insurance in the amount of $20,000 under a policy obligating the company to defend all claims against the insured. Even though the company does not face any risk of multiple liability because its exposure is limited by the terms of the policy, it may use interpleader against A, B, and C to avoid having to defend the separate lawsuits that otherwise may be brought by each of the claimants.

3. Historical Limitations on the Availability of Interpleader. [§8.4300]

Historically, there were four requirements for a "strict" bill of interpleader: (a) the same thing, debt, or duty had to be claimed by all the parties against whom interpleader was demanded; (b) all of the claimants' adverse titles or rights had to be dependent on or be derived from a common source; (c) the plaintiff-stakeholder could not claim any interest in the subject matter of the interpleader; and (d) the person seeking the remedy must have incurred no independent liability to any of the claimants—the stakeholder had to stand perfectly indifferent among them.

a. Modern Attitude Toward the Availability of Interpleader. [§8.4310]

The four historic limitations on interpleader are no longer of great significance in most jurisdictions. For example, both Federal Rule 22 and the present interpleader statute abolish the first three requirements. [Interpleader in the federal courts is discussed in **§8.4700–§8.4900**.]

b. **No Independent Liability. [§8.4320]**

The fourth historic requirement has proven to be the most resistant to change. It derives from the fear that the stakeholder might not be neutral as between the claimants if it also might be liable to one of the claimants on independent grounds. When this is the case, the stakeholder will favor the claimant to whom it may be liable on other grounds, in order to avoid having to pay twice. However, the modern trend indicates some movement away from the no-independent-liability restriction on interpleader.

Illustration. [§8.4321] A and B assert mutually exclusive claims against an insurance company, S, for the proceeds of a life insurance policy and the latter institutes an interpleader action. However, claimant A asserts that stakeholder S has been negligent in processing a change-of-beneficiary form, and therefore is independently liable to A should B prove to be entitled to the proceeds of the policy. A court that adheres to the fourth historic prerequisite to interpleader will dismiss the interpleader action because S is not neutral between the claimants.

---

4. **The First Stage of Interpleader. [§8.4400]**

The court first must determine whether the prerequisites for the interpleader remedy have been met. This requires a showing that the stakeholder legitimately fears multiple liability or multiple litigation regarding a single fund or property interest under its control. If interpleader is proper and the stakeholder has no further interest in the dispute, it may place the property under the court's control and be discharged from the action.

a. **Adverse Claimants Required. [§8.4410]**

The claimants must be "adverse" to one another. Their claims must be against a single fund and mutually exclusive. Interpleader is improper if the stakeholder may be liable to both claimants under the applicable substantive law [compare **§8.4321**].

Illustration 1. [§8.4411] A liability insurer, facing a large number of claims arising out of a multiple vehicle accident and aggregating more than the insurer's contractual liability, seeks interpleader against the claimants. The remedy is proper because the interests of each are adverse to the others by virtue of the limited nature of the insurance fund.

Illustration 2. [§8.4412] A and B each claim the proceeds of a life insurance policy. A predicates her rights on the basis of having been the designated beneficiary when the policy was issued. B asserts that the deceased changed the beneficiary and designated her in A's place. Interpleader is appropriate because A and B are adverse claimants and the insurance company is not legally obligated to pay both of them.

b. **Requirement of Deposit. [§8.4420]**

Traditionally, the stakeholder either has been required to place the money or property under the control of the court or to post a bond sufficient to ensure compliance with any future order of the court. This has been thought to be a necessary condition to the court's interpleader jurisdiction even if the stakeholder is an interested party, in which case the deposit or bond does not constitute a waiver of plaintiff-stakeholder's contention of non-liability. The present interpleader statute, 28 USC 1335, still requires the stakeholder to deposit the property in question, but Federal Rule 22 does not. [See the discussion of interpleader in the federal courts in **§8.4700–§8.4900**.] A number of jurisdictions no longer expressly require a deposit in court prior to the discharge of a disinterested stakeholder. In these systems the court has general power to require a deposit or bond if it seems necessary for the preservation and availability of the property.

c. **Prospective Claims. [§8.4430]**

Interpleader is available even though some or all of the claims confronting the plaintiff have not yet been asserted. Moreover, the claims, whether in contract or tort, need not be either liquidated or reduced to judgment for purposes of deciding the initial question of whether interpleader should be granted.

> **Illustration. [§8.4431]** In the illustration in **§8.4411,** even if the potential claimants cannot bring suit directly against the insurer because there is no direct action statute, the court will grant an interpleader request by an insurer who ultimately may face multiple claims in excess of its contractual liability.

5. Second Stage of Interpleader. [§8.4500]

The second stage of interpleader consists of the determination of the respective rights of the claimants and, in some cases, claims between the claimants on matters related to the subject matter of the interpleader.

a. Interested Stakeholders. [§8.4510]

With the elimination of the historic requirement of "disinterestedness" on the part of the stakeholder [see **§8.4300**], it is now possible for the stakeholder to assume the position of a claimant once the court authorizes the interpleader. This enables the stakeholder to participate in the second stage of interpleader whenever it claims part or all of the stake.

> **Illustration. [§8.4511]** Several claimants present conflicting claims for the proceeds of a life insurance policy. The insurance company denies liability to any of the claimants, asserting that the policy has lapsed due to non-payment of premiums. The company's request for interpleader will be granted, thereby protecting it from the threat of multiple liability or vexation, and it may participate in the second stage by attempting to establish its non-liability on the policy.

6. Defensive Interpleader. [§8.4600]

The remedy of interpleader is not limited to an original action by a plaintiff-stakeholder. It also is available to any defendant who is threatened with multiple liability in an action by one or more of the claimants. The defendant may assert the interpleader by way of counterclaim, cross-claim, or third-party claim.

7. Interpleader in the Federal Courts. [§8.4700]

Interpleader may be secured in the federal courts in either of two ways: under Rule 22 of the Federal Rules or under the Federal Interpleader Act, 28 USC 1335 (jurisdiction), 1397 (venue), and 2361 (process and procedure). Although these two procedures embody the basic principles of interpleader discussed above, there are some important differences between them.

a.   Subject Matter Jurisdiction: Federal Rule 22. [§8.4710]

An interpleader action under Rule 22 must have an independent basis of federal subject matter jurisdiction. The suit must either present a federal question or diversity of citizenship must exist. [These two bases of jurisdiction are discussed in **§2.2000–§2.3830**.]

(1)   Determining Citizenship. [§8.4711]

In interpleader under Rule 22, it is the citizenship of the plaintiff-stakeholder, whether "interested" or not, that must be diverse from that of the defendant-claimants; the absence of diversity of citizenship among the defendant-claimants is irrelevant.

Illustration. [§8.4711–1] A bank incorporated and having its principal place of business in New York seeks interpleader against two adverse claimants to a bank account who are both citizens of New Hampshire. There is diversity of citizenship for interpleader under Rule 22.

---

b.   Subject Matter Jurisdiction: Statutory Interpleader. [§8.4720]

Subject matter jurisdiction under the interpleader statute is based on diversity of citizenship among the claimants. However, the Supreme Court has construed this statute as requiring only minimal diversity [see **§2.3220**] so that all that is necessary is that at least one claimant be a citizen of a state different from the other claimants; the citizenship of the stakeholder is irrelevant.

Illustration 1. [§8.4721] An insurance company, which is incorporated and has its principal place of business in New York, seeks interpleader against claimants to the proceeds of an insurance policy from New Jersey and New York. There is diversity of citizenship for statutory interpleader but not for interpleader under Rule 22.

Illustration 2. [§8.4722] An insurance company, which is incorporated and has its principal place of business in New York, seeks interpleader against two New Jersey claimants to the proceeds of an insurance policy. A federal court would not have statutory interpleader jurisdiction because of the lack of diversity between the claimants. However, if the insurance company is an interested stakeholder because it disclaims liability on the policy, some courts might realign the stakeholder as a claimant for purposes of establishing diversity jurisdiction under the statute. In any event, interpleader would be available under Rule 22 since there is diversity between the stakeholder and the claimants.

c. **Amount in Controversy: Federal Rule 22. [§8.4730]**

The normal amount in controversy principles apply in rule interpleader cases [see **§2.4000–§2.4510**]. Thus, in a typical interpleader case based on diversity of citizenship, the amount in controversy must exceed $75,000.

Illustration. [§8.4731] An insurance company is liable under a policy for $65,000. Three parties each assert a separate claim under the policy for $30,000. Interpleader will not be available. The court will look to the amount of the fund involved, which is only $65,000; the aggregate of the three claims against the stake is irrelevant.

d. **Amount in Controversy: Statutory Interpleader. [§8.4740]**

Section 1335 of Title 28 requires only that $500 or more be in controversy in statutory interpleader cases, substantially less than is necessary for interpleader under Rule 22.

e. **Personal Jurisdiction and Process: Federal Rule 22. [§8.4750]**

Personal jurisdiction must be secured over all the claimants in an interpleader action under Federal Rule 22. The usual principles of personal jurisdiction apply, and claimants may be served with process in the same manner as in any other civil action within the territorial limits prescribed by Rule 4. Except when all claimants live in the forum state, a plaintiff-stakeholder's ability to utilize Rule 22 effectively will depend upon whether the state in which the federal court is sitting has a long-arm statute. [Jurisdiction and process are discussed in Chapter Three.]

> **Illustration. [§8.4751]** A California Bank brings an action in a federal court in California to interplead two claimants to a savings account. C–1 is a citizen of New York and C–2 is from Ohio. Since California has a long-arm statute that enables the assertion of jurisdiction over people in other states for claims growing out of an interest in property located in California, personal jurisdiction will be acquired over the claimants.

f. Personal Jurisdiction and Process: Statutory Interpleader. [§8.4760]

One of the primary benefits of proceeding under the Federal Interpleader Act is the availability of nationwide service of process on all claimants [28 USC 2361]. However, service may be made only in the districts where the claimants reside or may be found, and therefore the statute technically will not reach claimants who are out of the country or who cannot be found.

> **Illustration. [§8.4761]** If the litigation described in **§8.4751** took place in a federal court in a state that did not have a long-arm statute, there would be no difficulty in acquiring personal jurisdiction under the federal interpleader statute so long as the defendants could be located within the United States.

g. Venue: Federal Rule 22. [§8.4770]

In actions brought under Rule 22, provisions of 28 USC 1391 govern venue [See **§2.700–§2.7710** for a discussion of venue.] Thus, if interpleader jurisdiction is based on a federal question, venue will be proper in: (a) the district where any defendant resides, if all defendants reside in the same State; (b) a district in which a substantial part of the events or omissions giving rise to the claim occurred or a substantial part of property that is the subject of the action is situated; or (c) a district in which any defendant may be found, if there is no district in which the action may otherwise be brought. When interpleader is based on diversity of citizenship, the action may be brought: (a) in a judicial district where a defendant resides if all defendants reside in the same state; (b) in a district in which a substantial part of the events or omissions giving rise to the litigation occurred or a substantial part of the litigated property is located; or (c) in a judicial district in which the defendants are subject to personal jurisdiction at the time the action is commenced, if there is no district in which the action may otherwise be brought.

Illustration. [§8.4771] P, an alleged tortfeasor's insurance company, is a citizen of Texas and has its principal place of business in the Northern District of Texas. The accident occurred in Fargo, North Dakota. One claimant to the insurance proceeds is a Wisconsin resident, and the other claimants are Louisiana residents. The only proper venue for a Rule 22 interpleader suit is the district of North Dakota, the place where a substantial amount of the events giving rise to the claim occurred.

---

h.   Venue: Statutory Interpleader. [§8.4780]

A special venue statute, 28 USC 1397, governs statutory interpleader. This statute provides that venue is proper in any district where one or more of the claimants reside.

Illustration. [§8.4781] If the litigation in the illustration in **§8.4771** were brought under the interpleader statute, proper venue would exist in either Wisconsin or Louisiana.

---

i.   Transfer of Venue. [§8.4790]

Even if venue is proper, an interpleader suit may be transferred pursuant to 28 USC 1404(a) to any other district where it could have been brought as an original matter if it would serve the convenience of the parties and be in the interests of the efficient and just adjudication of the dispute. [Transfer of venue is discussed in **§2.7630–§2.7710**.]

8.   Law Governing Interpleader Actions in the Federal Courts. [§8.4800]

The principle that a federal court sitting in diversity jurisdiction must apply the substantive law of the forum state [see **§4.1000–§4.5411**] is fully applicable to both statutory and rule interpleader. (In the relatively rare instance in which an interpleader action is based on federal question jurisdiction, state law is not controlling.) The question of whether the interpleader remedy is available is a procedural matter and will be decided pursuant to federal interpleader standards.

Illustration. [§8.4810] In a diversity action under Rule 22, multiple claimants seek the proceeds of a life insurance policy, each claiming to be the heir of the deceased. State law will control the construction of the insurance policy and all issues relating to the descent and distribution of the deceased's estate.

---

a. **Conflicts Rules. [§8.4820]**

In interpleader cases involving diversity jurisdiction, whether under Federal Rule 22 or the Federal Interpleader Act, federal courts apply the same law that would be applied by the courts of the forum state [see **§4.4300**].

9. **Injunction Against Parallel State Court Actions by Federal Court. [§8.4900]**

Section 2361 of Title 28 expressly allows a federal district court to enjoin state court proceedings that involve the same subject matter as a statutory interpleader action. Because of the federal-state relations involved, federal courts act with restraint under this provision. A federal court's power to enjoin parallel state actions is much narrower in a Federal Rule 22 interpleader proceeding than it is in the statutory interpleader situation.

CHAPTER IX

DISCOVERY

A. INTRODUCTION AND HISTORY. [§9.0000]

Discovery refers to those procedural devices by which a party or potential party to a lawsuit obtains information relating to the case. The need for some court procedure to allow a party to obtain and preserve evidence was recognized in early English equity practice. Not until the promulgation of the Federal Rules of Civil Procedure in 1938, however, did pretrial discovery, as we know it today, become a vital part of the litigation process. And indeed, the Federal Rules revolutionized trial practice in the United States. Almost every state has adopted a set of regulations for widespread discovery modeled after the Federal Rules.

B. PURPOSES. [§9.1000]

It is generally agreed that there are three basic purposes of pretrial discovery: preserving information for trial, eliminating undisputed facts, and the ascertainment of facts.

1. Preserving Information for Trial. [§9.1100]

If a potential witness is about to die or leave the country, discovery provides a means of obtaining testimony from such a person in a form that permits its introduction into evidence if the individual is unable to testify when the trial takes place.

2. Elimination of Undisputed Facts. [§9.1200]

A matter that appears to be in dispute on the face of the pleadings may not be in dispute at all. Discovery can be used to determine what facts and issues are actually being contested by the parties and thereby avoid unnecessary trial of matters not in dispute.

269

Illustration. [§9.1210] P files a suit to enjoin D from trespassing on P's property. In addition, P seeks damages for alleged past trespasses. In the answer, D raises an affirmative defense that any action for damages from any trespass that occurred more than three years prior to the filing of the complaint is barred by the applicable statute of limitations. Under the pleading rules of the jurisdiction, no reply to D's answer is permitted; thus, D's affirmative defense is deemed to have been denied by P. In fact, P agrees with D's contention and does not intend to pursue such damages. D may utilize discovery to bind P to this position and avoid any need to gather information or proof regarding any time-barred trespass.

---

3.   Ascertainment of Facts. [§9.1300]

Discovery may be utilized to ascertain facts in preparation for trial. This may be accomplished through the testimony of witnesses, physical or mental examination of parties, and inspection of documents or other tangible items, including real property.

C. GENERAL SCOPE OF DISCOVERY. [§9.2000]

Federal Rule 26(b)(1) defines the basic scope of discovery to include all nonprivileged information relevant to the claim or defense of any party. However, for good cause, a court can expand the scope to include any nonprivileged information relevant to the subject matter of the action.

1.   Privileged Matter. [§9.2100]

Privileged matter is strictly defined as information that is protected from disclosure at trial by the rules of evidence. This material is excluded from discovery in order to protect the privacy and secrecy of individuals in certain relationships. The most notable privileges cover communications between attorney-client, doctor-patient, priest-penitent, and husband-wife. Furthermore, certain testimonial limitations also are recognized, such as the privilege against self-incrimination and the privilege not to reveal confidential police informants. Jurisdictions vary in the extent to which they recognize these and certain other privileged matters. Under Federal Rule 26(b)(5), a party who withholds information on the ground that it is privileged must specifically set forth information sufficient to permit the other parties to determine whether in fact the withheld information is privileged.

2.   **Relevant Information. [§9.2200]**

Pursuant to Federal Rule 26(b)(1), information is deemed relevant and hence discoverable if **it appears reasonably calculated to lead to evidence admissible at trial.** The information sought need not itself be admissible.

Illustration: Facts Inadmissible at Trial. [§9.2210] A party in an auto accident case may discover from one eyewitness what a second eyewitness said at the scene of the collision even though the statement of the second would be inadmissible at trial under the hearsay rule. The precise knowledge of the second witness may aid the party in determining how the collision occurred and in establishing the facts; if so, the party may wish to locate and subpoena the second witness to testify at trial.

---

a.   **Facts Concerning Opponent's Case. [§9.2220]**

Historically, a party was limited to discovery of matters regarding those aspects of the case that party was required to plead and prove; discovery of facts regarding the opponent's case was not permitted. Modern rules have eliminated this artificial distinction. Federal Rule 26(b)(1) permits discovery of facts regarding any of the matters in dispute.

b.   **Facts for Impeachment of Witness. [§9.2230]**

In the past, some courts have been reluctant to permit discovery of facts to be used solely for impeachment, arguing that these matters are not "relevant" to the issues in the case. In federal courts and in most jurisdictions with modern procedural rules, discovery of this information is now held permissible.

Illustration. [§9.2231] In a suit for a large amount of damages, in which an eyewitness strongly supports P's version of the facts, D properly may utilize discovery to inquire into the relationship between P and the witness to determine if the latter would benefit from a verdict for P. The answers may reveal important evidence for cross-examination on the ground of bias.

---

c.   **Basis of Contentions in Pleadings. [§9.2240]**

Particularly in jurisdictions in which generalized pleadings are permitted, opposing parties may feel the need to ascertain the facts

271

underlying the allegations in the complaint and answer. Although there is a lack of definitive decisions, **lower courts generally have allowed discovery of facts related to contentions.** A counter-argument may be made that, in effect, such discovery results in a return to the days of structured pleadings, when parties were held to their factual allegations, often with unjust results; thus, a party should be allowed to discover facts related to what occurred, but he should not be permitted to pin down an opposing party to a precise and binding explanation of what is said in the pleadings.

Illustration. [§9.2241] P alleges that D negligently drove a vehicle that struck P's automobile. D seeks to learn upon what specific facts P bases the claim of negligence. The inquiry generally will be allowed, but P's answer will not be held evasive if he truthfully responds in a generalized way since negligence often must be inferred from the result, particularly if an accident results from a driver's inattention rather than a more easily defined cause such as driving through a stop sign or a red traffic light.

---

3.   Irrelevant Information. [§9.2300]

A party cannot discover **facts with no real bearing on the case,** especially those that are sought only to **harass or embarrass an opponent** [see also §9.3300].

a.   Trial Strategy. [§9.2310]

A party **is not permitted to discover the tactics that opposing counsel intends to use** at trial such as the order in which witnesses and exhibits will be presented. However, pursuant to Federal Rule 26(a) each party must reveal before trial the names of the witnesses whom she will call or will call if necessary and the documents and exhibits she intends to introduce.

b.   Defendant's Financial Ability. [§9.2320]

In the ordinary case, a defendant's general financial resources have no bearing on the issues to be presented at trial; hence they are irrelevant for purposes of discovery. There are two notable exceptions however.

(1)   Exception 1: Punitive Damage Cases. [§9.2321]

When plaintiff seeks to recover punitive or exemplary damages, a major element for the trier of fact in determining the proper amount of damages is the financial resources of the defendant. The greater the defendant's ability to pay, the larger the damages must be if the defendant is to be deterred from engaging in improper activities. Thus in such cases, the defendant's finances are admissible in evidence at trial, and therefore subject to discovery.

(2) Exception 2: Insurance Policy Limits. [§9.2322]

One of the most controversial subjects in the discovery field has been the extent to which a defendant must disclose the monetary limits of a liability insurance policy that would indemnify the defendant for any portion of the damages recovered by the plaintiff. Except when punitive damages are sought, such information will not lead to admissible evidence; hence the courts in a number of states have held insurance information to be outside the scope of discovery. On the other hand, disclosure of the existence and extent of insurance coverage is **important to the rational and informed settlement of many cases** (although it is not clear whether discovery actually tends to produce more settlements) and a litigant's appraisal of his case and litigation strategy. Moreover, unlike disclosure of other financial information, **discovery of insurance policy limits does not constitute a serious invasion of privacy.** Thus, a majority of courts have allowed discovery of insurance information as an exception to the relevance standard.

(a) Mandatory Disclosure of Insurance Policies in Federal Cases. [§9.2322–1]

Federal Rule 26(a)(1)(A)(iv) requires parties, **without request**, to disclose any insurance policies for inspection that would cover any amount for which defendant may be held liable to plaintiff.

(b) Insurance Information Is Not Admissible at Trial. [§9.2322–2]

The fact that insurance information is discoverable before trial does not alter the general rule that such information is not admissible into evidence at trial due to the fact that it has no bearing on liability.

4. Required Disclosures. [§9.2400]

Certain information is so important to effective preparation that non-disclosure would tend to place a party at a severe disadvantage at trial or is so basic that its discovery will properly be sought in almost every action. Thus, the Federal Rules employ mandatory disclosure requirements found in Rule 26(a), which place a duty on parties to disclose such information without request.

a. Initial Disclosures. [§9.2410]

As amended in 1993 and 2000, Federal Rule 26(a)(1) lists certain disclosures that must be made within fourteen days of the Rule 26(f) discovery conference [see **§9.3321**]. All of these initial disclosure requirements can be superceded by court order or an agreement of the parties.

(1) Witnesses. [§9.2411]

Parties must disclose the identity of persons likely to have discoverable information relevant to the disclosing party's claims or defenses. The disclosing party also should indicate generally the subjects on which each individual has knowledge in order to assist the other parties in deciding which depositions to take.

(a) Special Rules for Disclosure of Expert Witnesses [§9.2411–1]

Special rules have been developed for the disclosure of a party's expert witnesses and the details of their expert testimony. [The federal regulations are set out at **§9.3200–§9.3232**].

(2) Tangible Things. [§9.2412]

A party must disclose a copy or description (including location) of all tangible things within the control of the party that the disclosing party may use to support its claims or defenses. This includes documents and data compilations.

(3) Damages. [§9.2413]

Parties must disclose any computations of claimed damages as well as the bases for those computations.

(4) Insurance. [§9.2414]

Parties must disclose for inspection and copying any insurance policy that may cover liability in the action.

b. Disclosures Prior to Trial. [§9.2420]

Rule 26(a)(3) lists types of information that parties must provide automatically at least 30 days before trial.

(1) Trial Witnesses. [§9.2421]

The 1993 and 2000 amendments direct disclosure of witnesses who may be called at trial, although they do not require designation of the subject matter of the testimony.

(2) Deposition Testimony. [§9.2422]

The pretrial disclosure rules require each party to designate any witnesses whose testimony will be presented via deposition and, as to those depositions not recorded stenographically, also to provide a transcript of the pertinent portions of the deposition testimony.

(3) Trial Exhibits. [§9.2423]

The rules as amended in 1993 and 2000 call for the identification of each document or other exhibit that the party anticipates using as substantive evidence at trial.

c. Duty to Supplement. [§9.2430]

Rule 26(e) requires parties to supplement or correct any information disclosed pursuant to Rule 26(a). The triggering event for the duty to supplement is that the party learns that in **some material respect the information is incomplete or incorrect.** Excluded from the duty to supplement is information provided at a deposition, except for a deposition of a party's expert witness.

D. SPECIAL LIMITATIONS ON DISCOVERY. [§9.3000]

For important policy reasons, limitations have been imposed on the discovery of certain types of relevant, non-privileged information.

1. Work–Product. [§9.3100]

Federal Rule 26(b)(3)(A) is typical of provisions that limit discovery of materials prepared in anticipation of litigation. Ordinarily, a party may not discover documents and tangible things that are **prepared in anticipation of litigation** or for trial by or for another party or its representative (including the other party's attorney, consultant, surety, indemnitor, insurer, or agent). But those materials may be discovered if: (i) they are **otherwise discoverable** and (ii) the party shows that it has **substantial need** for the materials to prepare its case and cannot, without **undue hardship**, obtain their substantial equivalent by other means.

The policy behind the work-product rule, forcefully enunciated by the Supreme Court in the famous case of *Hickman v. Taylor* (1947), is to allow

275

an attorney to investigate all aspects of a case, whether favorable or unfavorable to the client, without fear that by such thorough preparation the client may be disserved by having to turn the adverse information over to the opposing party. Furthermore, every attorney should be encouraged to investigate each case and not rely on work done by an adversary.

a. Types of Work Product [§9.3110]

(1) Attorney's Notes and Unwritten Ideas. [§9.3111]

Any memoranda, notes, or working papers created by an attorney in anticipation of litigation are within the work product rule. Although Federal Rule 26(b)(3) refers only to "documents and tangible things," the *Hickman* decision made clear that it would be an even worse violation of policy to require an attorney to reveal his unwritten ideas, theories, or opinions regarding a case.

(2) Investigator's or Counselor's Notes and Unwritten Ideas. [§9.3112]

The *Hickman* case was unclear whether work-product included only work done by the attorney or whether it also envisioned material assembled by investigators and others in preparation for litigation. Federal Rule 26(b)(3), like rules in many states, now specifically includes information prepared by non-attorneys for counsel. In some other jurisdictions, however, the rule refers only to "attorneys" and the question must be resolved by judicial decision. Strong policy reasons support the federal provision, for if only attorneys are covered, an attorney would be induced to do a variety of non-legal tasks alone. This would be inefficient, and would deprive clients of the benefit of expert assistance by accountants, insurance brokers, investigators, and various other specialists. Note, however, that information developed for purposes other than litigation, e.g. to promote future safety when a lawsuit is not contemplated, is not protected by the work-product rule.

(3) Statements of Witnesses. [§9.3113]

Written and oral statements of witnesses obtained by an attorney or investigator in anticipation of trial are an important type of work-product information. The *Hickman* case itself was fought over the right of an opposing party to obtain such statements.

b. **Caveat: Relevant Evidence Turned over to an Attorney or Investigator. [§9.3120]**

The work-product doctrine protects only the thoughts, ideas, and theories of the people who gather information for trial; it cannot be used to hide facts relevant to the case.

Illustration 1. [§9.3121] P files suit on the basis of a deed that has been lost. Through diligent search the attorney locates the deed. The opposing party may discover the fact that the deed has been found and will be entitled to inspect it.

Illustration 2. [§9.3122] A party tells his attorney all that the party knows about the incidents involved in the case. Although the attorney will not be required to reveal what the client has said, the client may be interrogated by the opposing party as to all the relevant information in the client's possession.

---

c. **Discovery upon Showing of Necessity. [§9.3130]**

The work-product rules are not an absolute bar to discovery. Courts can require disclosure upon a showing of good cause in order to avoid a possible miscarriage of justice. Good cause generally is satisfied by a showing that the material sought is not otherwise available to the party seeking discovery.

Illustration. [§9.3131] An attorney obtains a written statement of the only known eyewitness to an accident that is the subject of the lawsuit. Sometime thereafter, the opposing party locates the witness who unfortunately claims she can no longer recall any of the details of what occurred. On motion of the opposing party, discovery of the witness' earlier statement will be allowed.

---

d. **Exception: Information Not Discoverable under Any Circumstances. [§9.3140]**

Federal Rule 26(b)(3) and many state work-product provisions specifically prohibit any disclosure of an attorney's conclusions, theories, and mental impressions. The rationale is that lawyers are advocates and should not be put in the position of testifying or providing information adverse to the interests of their clients, which might undermine the attorney-client relationship. The most common problems arise when the attorney's conclusions and mental processes are inextricably linked with otherwise discoverable factual material. In this situation, the court, in its discretion, may redact the privileged sections or issue any protective order [see **§9.3322**] necessary to protect the interests of both parties.

Illustration. [§9.3141] An attorney, in preparation for litigation, takes a written statement from an important witness on a question-answer basis. Just prior to a scheduled interrogation by the opposing lawyer, the witness dies. The latter attorney then seeks a copy of the statement. The first attorney argues against discovery on the ground that his questions reveal his impressions and legal theories of the case. If the answers are sufficiently complete in themselves to convey all of the witness' vital information, the court may permit discovery of the answers but will not allow disclosure of the questions. But if the answers make no sense without the questions, or if the answers necessarily reveal the theories that the questioning attorney was pursuing, many if not most courts either will not require disclosure or will attempt to shape a protective order.

---

e. Certain Information Discoverable on Demand. [§9.3150]

The overwhelming need for some types of information has resulted in special regulations permitting discovery despite the work-product rule.

(1) Party's Own Statements. [§9.3151]

It is a generally accepted rule that a party may discover **any statement he or she has made that is in the hands of the opposing side** without making any showing of need. Federal Rule 26(b)(3) specifically so provides. The reason is that under ordinary rules of evidence, one party always may introduce a statement of an opposing party at trial. Because it is a party's own statement, it often will have a great impact on the trier of fact. It is unfair to preclude the party who made the statement from reviewing it prior to trial in order to be prepared to counter the statement's adverse effects.

> **Illustration. [§9.3151–1]** P, who is claiming damages for permanent leg injuries, seeks to learn the substance of a statement she made to D's attorney three months after the injuries occurred. The statement appears to show that P took part in a tennis tournament in spite of the problems with her legs. At trial P will be able to explain that she attended the tennis tournament as a spectator and was confined to a wheelchair at that time.

(2) Non–Party Witness, Own Statement. [§9.3152]

Federal Rule 26(b)(3) permits any witness to obtain a copy of his or her statement given to any party. The purpose of this provision is to protect the witness from embarrassment at trial since, under the rules of evidence, the statement can be used to contradict the witness' testimony. This provision can be improperly manipulated to undercut the policy of the work-product rule. Thus an attorney, who is thwarted in an attempt to obtain a copy of a witness' statement from the opposing side, may request that the witness ask for a copy of the statement and then turn it over to the attorney for inspection. If the witness is friendly to the attorney who seeks the statement or the party she represents, the witness will cooperate; otherwise the witness may refuse. It seems particularly unfortunate to create a situation in which disclosure depends upon the witness' relationship with the parties to the suit.

2. Expert Information Developed for Litigation. [§9.3200]

Frequently a party or an attorney will employ an expert to assist in the preparation of a case. If an opposing party could freely discover the expert's observations, opinions, and conclusions, many parties would cease to hire any experts but those who guarantee in advance to support the position of the employing party. It would be most damaging if at trial one party presented, as a favorable expert, a witness hired by the opposing side. Each litigant should feel free and be encouraged to prepare its case originally and thoroughly. **One must distinguish those situations in which an expert, at the time he obtained relevant information, had not been hired to assist in preparing for litigation. In such cases the expert is an ordinary witness and there are no special limits on discovery even though the information sought may involve the witness' expertise.**

Illustration. [§9.3210] P is injured in an auto accident and a physician is called to treat him. Subsequently, P files suit to recover for his injuries, and D seeks to take the deposition of the physician concerning the extent of the injuries. Assuming that there is no applicable physician-patient privilege, D will be allowed to do so; the physician obtained his information as a treating doctor, not as one hired solely to assess the injuries for purposes of trial.

---

a. Importance of Whether the Witness Will Testify at Trial. [§9.3220]

Once a party who has hired an expert decides to call the expert at trial, the reasons for restricting discovery are terminated. Obviously, the opposing party will not be attempting to discover information from a witness who has taken a position adverse to the employing party. Moreover, it becomes extremely important that the opposing party have a chance to obtain information so as to be able to prepare for trial. It often is more important to obtain facts from an opposing expert than from any other opposing witness because the adequacy of the expert's training may be subject to challenge and because time usually is needed to prepare effective cross examination of a scientific or technical witness. Indeed, in modern practice, it is common to subject an expert witness to a complete deposition [see **§9.5100**] by the opposing party before trial.

Illustration. [§9.3221] D's attorney hires a doctor to examine P. The doctor concludes that P's condition, although currently serious, will gradually improve with treatment. This opinion is derived from the doctor's direct experience with two patients and from several medical journal articles concerning the type of injuries involved. Without pretrial discovery of the doctor's opinion, P's attorney will be hard pressed to counter the testimony. Because he is able to utilize discovery, however, the attorney may learn that the course of treatment involved has serious side effects and cannot be used at all for certain patients, such as P, who have a history of diabetes or heart trouble.

---

(1) Discovery Regarding an Expert Who Will Testify. [§9.3222]

The Federal Rules provide parties with relatively broad access regarding expert witnesses who are scheduled to testify at trial.

(a) Mandatory Disclosure. [§9.3222–1]

Federal Rule 26(b)(3) requires the disclosure of certain expert information without request. A party must disclose **a list of any expert witnesses who may be called to testify at trial**. Additionally, the parties must provide a report detailing each expert's opinions, the bases for those opinions, and each expert's qualifications.

(b) Further Discovery. [§9.3222–2]

Rule 26(b)(4) governs the discovery of facts known and opinions held by experts and acquired or developed in anticipation of litigation or for trial. **The rule authorizes depositions of any expert whose opinions may be presented at trial.** Note, however, that one rationale for the Rule 26(a)(2) disclosure requirement is to obviate the need to depose all expert witnesses.

(c) Rationale for Open Discovery. [§9.3222–3]

There is little doubt as to the need to know the bases of an adverse party's expert testimony in order to prepare one's case for trial. An expert is unlike an eyewitness to an event. The expert's conclusions, which are evidence, have roots in a myriad of books, educational training, experiments, and personal experiences, and it may take another expert to point out even the most fundamental flaws. Thus, it is reasonable that a party should be permitted automatically to depose any other party's expert whose testimony is to be used at trial.

(2) Discovery from an Expert Who Will Not Testify. [§9.3223]

The reasons for rejecting discovery are greatest when the expert will not be called by the employing party. Even then, however, discovery is allowed if it would be impossible or highly impractical to obtain the information from another source. Thus, Federal Rule 26(b)(4)(B) provides for discovery from a non-witness expert "upon showing of exceptional circumstances under which it is impracticable for the party seeking discovery to obtain facts or opinions on the same subject by other means."

> **Illustration. [§9.3223–1]** Defense counsel pays an expert to undertake certain tests on a machine part that P alleges is defective. The tests destroy or significantly alter the machine part, thus making it impossible for P to have tests made. Even though D does not plan to call the expert at trial, P will be allowed to discover the expert's findings.

b. Sharing the Expert's Fee. [§9.3230]

When expert information prepared for one party is held discoverable by the opposing party, fairness ordinarily requires that the discovering party pay something for the expert advice received.

(1) Compensation of the Expert. [§9.3231]

Federal Rule 26(b)(4)(C) specifically provides that unless manifest injustice would result, the discovering party should give reasonable compensation to an expert who is required to spend time responding to discovery. Compensation is not required, however, for the initial disclosures and report required under Rule 26(b)(2).

(2) Compensation to the Opposing Party. [§9.3232]

When one party is allowed to discover information from an opposing party's expert, Federal Rule 26(b)(4)(C) specifically permits the court to order a splitting of the expert's fee paid by the employing party. The courts have broad discretion to determine just what, if any, portion of the fee should be shifted.

3. Avoiding Harassment or Oppression. [§9.3300]

In recent years much has been said and written concerning abuses of the discovery process. Parties have been accused of making excessive demands for remotely related documents on the mere hope that one or two useful items will turn up among the thousands requested. Similar charges have been made with respect to the service of interrogatories on an opposing party. Courts have long had the power under rules such as Federal Rule 26(c) to protect any person or party from "annoyance, embarrassment, oppression, or undue burden or expense" in the discovery process. However, the inability or unwillingness of trial judges to utilize those powers to control abuses has led to a number of proposed reforms, some of which have recently been adopted in the federal courts.

a. Control by Prohibiting Discovery. [§9.3310]

In situations in which the discovery is being sought to harass the opposing party, the court, in its discretion, may prohibit disclosure.

Pursuant to Federal Rule 26(b)(2)(c), even good faith discovery can be limited if it is "unreasonably cumulative or duplicative," if the information can be obtained from a "more convenient, less burdensome, or less expensive" source, if the "party seeking discovery has had ample opportunity to obtain the information by discovery in the action," or if the "burden or expense of the proposed discovery outweighs its likely benefit, taking into account the needs of the case, the amount in controversy, the parties' resources, the importance of the issues at stake in the litigation," and the importance of the discovery in resolving the issues. This latter clause is the most significant because **it permits a court to keep useful information from discovery when the judge, on balance, finds the cost of disclosure to outweigh its value.** This is especially important when one element of the weighing process is the parties' ability to pay. Finally, the Federal Rules also provide for sanctions if redundant or disproportionate discovery is sought.

Illustration 1: Unjustifiable Cost. [§9.3311] D seeks to discover information from P that P already has supplied in prior discovery proceedings. D's aim appears to be to raise P's legal expenses in order to make P settle at a minimal figure. The court can reject further discovery except as to facts not previously involved in the discovery process.

Illustration 2: Trade Secrets. [§9.3312] In an action brought by P business against D competitor, P seeks to obtain secret lists of D's customers. The chief assets of both parties are their customer lists and if P's discovery is approved, D's business will be destroyed. The court may refuse to allow such discovery unless it is vital to the case. Even then it may restrict the way in which the information is handled [see **§9.3322**].

---

(1) When Prohibition Improper. [§9.3313]

Despite the increased power of the court to avoid harassment and oppression, it still should not exercise its discretion to thwart the basic policy of discovery by failing to require disclosure of information vital to the case.

Illustration. [§9.3313–1] P business sues D competitor, alleging that the latter hired a former employee of P and that the employee took P's secret customer lists and turned them over to D. P demands discovery of D's customer lists to see if they include all the names of P's customers. D answers that P's motive is merely to learn the names of D's customers. The court, without proof of P's bad faith, cannot refuse discovery, although it can take steps to protect both parties [see **§9.3322**].

---

b. Control by Governing Details of Discovery. [§9.3320]

Under Federal Rules 26(c) and (d) and their state counterparts, trial courts are empowered to exercise broad discretion to eliminate abuse of the discovery process by specifying the manner in which discovery shall proceed. The court may govern such aspects as the time and place of discovery, which party must bear the initial expenses, the order in which issues shall be explored and witnesses deposed, and which persons shall have access to the information revealed.

(1) Control through Use of Discovery Conference. [§9.3321]

Rule 26(f) provides that in all cases not exempted by local rule or special order, the litigants must confer as soon as practicable to prepare, among other things, a proposed discovery plan. This required meeting is known as a discovery conference and can, under the federal rules, be accomplished electronically or in person.

(a) Discovery Plan. [§9.3321–1]

The parties must submit a proposed discovery plan to the court, usually during the Rule 16(b) pretrial scheduling conference. The proposal should indicate the parties' views regarding the required disclosures under Rule 26(a), the subjects and timing for discovery, possible limitations on discovery, the means of disclosure of electronic information, and any protective orders that should be entered by the court. Under Rule 16(b)(3)(A), the court normally must issue a scheduling order limiting the time to complete discovery.

(b) Discovery Moratorium Pending Discovery Plan. [§9.3321–2]

Federal Rule 26(d) requires that in general no formal discovery may be undertaken until the parties have met and discussed the discovery plan. This moratorium on discovery may be removed by a court order or an agreement of all parties.

(2) Protective Orders. [§9.3322]

The potential controls over discovery under Rule 26(c) are extremely broad, designed to protect parties from harassment, oppression, and undue expense. Proper imposition of a protective order depends on the particular situation before the court. In all cases, a protective order requires a motion by a party or by the person from whom discovery is sought. **A movant must (i) show good cause and (ii) certify that she has made an honest attempt to resolve the matter with the other parties.**

c. Control by Requiring Signature of Attorney or Party. [§9.3330]

Rule 26(g) requires an attorney representing a party (or the party herself if she is unrepresented) to sign every formal request or response or objection to discovery. The signature constitutes a certification that the request, response, or objection is consistent with the rules, made in good faith, and not duly burdensome given the nature of the issue, the amount in controversy, and the prior discovery in the case. If certification is made in violation of the rule, "without substantial justification" the court "must impose" a mandatory, appropriate sanction. This provision is akin to the required signing of pleadings. Both are designed to eliminate abuses by the imposition of specific ethical standards on attorneys.

d. Limitations on the Quantity of Discovery. [§9.3340]

The discovery rules limit, in various ways, the amount of discovery that can be had without permission of the court. For example, pursuant to Federal Rule 30(a)(2), each side may conduct no more than 10 depositions, including oral and written depositions, without leave of the court. Under Federal Rule 33(a), interrogatories served on a party may not exceed 25 in number without permission of the court. Certain limitations may be altered by local rule or by a court order, which is crucial since the limits proscribed by the Federal Rules do not differentiate between simple and complex cases.

e. Illustrations of Discovery Issues [§9.3350]

Illustration 1: Time and Place. [§9.3351] D seeks to inspect P's financial records, which are used continuously in P's business. The court may order that D must inspect the books at P's place of business and at times and in a manner so as not to interfere seriously with P's normal activities.

Illustration 2: Initial Expenses. [§9.3352] P files suit in the United States against a citizen of England. P demands that D appear in the United States for purposes of discovery. D argues that P's attorney should go to England where D is located. The court must decide where discovery is most appropriate and then determine whether or not to award expenses. For example, the court may decide that D should come to the United States, but order P to pay D's air fare and other expenses. Ultimately, if P wins, these costs may be recovered from D. It is important to realize, however, that the party required to bear the initial expenses may find them so oppressive that the party might be induced to agree to an unfavorable settlement.

Illustration 3: Issues to Be Explored First. [§9.3353] P sues D, a resident of New York, in a California court. D claims that the California court does not have personal jurisdiction over him. Prior to permitting P to engage in widespread discovery of all aspects of the case, the court may limit discovery to facts relating to the jurisdictional issue because, if that issue is decided in favor of D, the case will be dismissed. The court, in making its decision, must consider the likelihood of such a dismissal and whether or not, if the case is allowed to continue, bifurcated discovery will be harassing to the witnesses and costly to the parties. This problem particularly is acute if those who know facts regarding jurisdiction also are potential deponents regarding other aspects of the case.

Illustration 4: Order of Discovery from Parties and Witnesses. [§9.3354] P and D each want the other to submit first to deposition.

Each claims that the other party will change his story after hearing the opponent testify. If the court believes that there is some truth to the charge, it can order the examination to proceed in a series (e.g., first one party being interrogated for 30 minutes, then the other for 30 minutes, and so on).

Illustration 5: Limits on Access to Information. [§9.3355] P soft drink company sues D soft drink company, alleging that D stole P's highly successful formula for its product. P seeks discovery of the formula for D's product in order to see if it in fact matches that of P. D denies that it took P's formula and claims that P only seeks discovery in order to learn and copy D's secret formula. The court may order D and P both to reveal their respective formulae to a neutral third party (who will be bound to an oath of secrecy) to determine if the products are substantially identical. If they are not, discovery will be terminated without harm to either party. Even if discovery is not terminated, the court can limit access to the information by sealing documents, specifying those who can attend depositions, and ordering those who obtain the information not to reveal it to outside persons.

Illustration 6: Limits on Protective Orders. [§9.3356] P non-profit organization sues D newspaper, alleging libel. During discovery, P seeks a protective order against the disclosure of the organization's membership and income for the purposes of publication. D claims First Amendment considerations should allow it to publish the information. The court must decide if there is sufficient justification to authorize a protective order. In this situation, the membership lists will be discoverable for the purposes of the action, but D will be banned from publishing them since it would be unjust to allow D access to information that would not be available to it but for the pending suit. However, this protective order would not restrict the dissemination of information obtained from other sources.

E. DISCOVERY BEFORE SUIT FILED. [§9.4000]

In most jurisdictions, pre-suit discovery is confined to the perpetuation of testimony for a potential subsequent action [see, e.g., Federal Rule 27]. A few courts permit such discovery to aid in the preparation of pleadings.

1. Perpetuation of Testimony. [§9.4100]

Discovery to perpetuate testimony is permitted only when a potential action, which one party reasonably expects to file, cannot currently be brought, and when it reasonably appears that the witness whose testimony is sought may not be available at a later date.

Illustration. [§9.4110] P sues D in an automobile collision case. D's insurer disclaims responsibility and refuses to undertake the defense. P, if successful against D, may then, but only then, file a suit against D's insurer. D's spouse, who was present when D purchased the policy, will be an important witness for P in a suit against the insurer. However, the spouse is gravely ill and may not survive. P may take the spouse's deposition for use at the subsequent trial if the spouse dies or is too ill to attend.

---

2. Preparation of Pleadings. [§9.4200]

In a few jurisdictions, pretrial discovery is permitted to enable a potential plaintiff to prepare a complaint. Thus, if a potential plaintiff does not have important facts at hand, discovery may be proper.

a. Not Allowed for Determining Whether Case Exists. [§9.4210]

Courts that allow pre-pleading discovery normally restrict it to cases in which **plaintiff is certain that a case exists and needs only to fill in factual details before pleading.** Courts are wary of fishing expeditions. If any person could merely demand discovery from anyone else in order to see if a case existed, the result could be a serious invasion of privacy; every individual's business or personal life could become subject to scrutiny by others. In jurisdictions that have adopted notice-type pleading rules under which general allegations in a complaint are sufficient, there seems little need for pre-pleading discovery. In states that adhere to a stricter fact-pleading requirement, discovery may be useful. It is therefore surprising that pre-pleading discovery is more common in jurisdictions where liberal pleadings are permitted than in jurisdictions with stricter rules.

3. Scope Limited to the Specific Purposes Allowed. [§9.4300]

The scope of pre-suit discovery is not as broad as is discovery after an action has been filed. If the purpose is to perpetuate testimony, only admissible testimony may be obtained; if the purpose is to prepare a complaint, only the facts needed may be explored.

Illustration. [§9.4310] A person who has a potential action wishes to preserve the testimony of an aging eyewitness. The witness is asked to repeat hearsay statements of other persons who were present. This information would not be admissible into evidence at trial and its discovery generally is not permitted.

---

4. Notification and Service on Adverse Party. [§9.4400]

An action for pre-suit discovery proceeds just as does a regular case. Potential defendants must be notified of the proceedings and have an opportunity to be present to protect their interests, since such potential parties may be bound later to the testimony of witnesses who become unavailable. Due process requires notice and an opportunity to participate.

F. THE SPECIFIC DISCOVERY DEVICES. [§9.5000]

1. Oral Depositions. [§9.5100]

At an oral deposition, attorneys for each of the parties take turns asking the person whose deposition is being taken (the deponent) questions relevant to the issues in the case. Depositions usually take place in an attorney's office but may be held anywhere. The deponent is placed under oath by the officer in charge of the deposition who can be anyone authorized to administer oaths (very often a notary public) or by anyone upon whom the parties agree. Questions and answers are recorded by a reporter (who almost always acts as the officer as well). Unless the court orders otherwise, the deposition may be recorded by sound, sound-and-visual, or stenographic means. Videotaping has become increasingly popular because it captures much more than can a sterile written record, which may prove useful at trial or to deter sanctionable behavior. Objections may be made for the record throughout the deposition. After the deposition has been concluded and a transcript prepared, the deponent is called upon to sign the deposition. If the deponent refuses, the officer signs, stating the reasons why the deponent would not do so. [For a useful model of the general details governing oral depositions, see Federal Rule 30.]

a. Deposition by Telephone. [§9.5110]

Rule 30(b)(4), provides for the taking of depositions by telephone or other remote electronic means if ordered by the court or stipulated to by the parties. Elimination of the necessity for the lawyers and the deponent to be physically present at a single location can be a significant cost saver in many cases.

b. Refusal to Answer. [§9.5120]

The deponent, usually on advice of counsel, may refuse to answer questions that are considered improper. When this occurs, the deposition normally proceeds on other matters. However, pursuant to Federal Rule 30, except if the information is alleged to be privileged or subject to a prior court order limiting the inquiry, the deponent must answer subject to any objection which may later be considered by the court. If the deponent refuses to answer, the party seeking answers may ask the court to require the deponent to answer and sanctions may be imposed for an unjustified refusal. [see **§9.8100**]. In lieu of continuing a deposition when answers are refused, either the deposing party or the deponent can move the court to rule on the propriety of the inquiry and to make appropriate orders governing the scope of the deposition when it resumes.

c. Court Order Not Normally Required. [§9.5130]

An attorney who wishes to take a deposition need only send a notice (giving a certain number of days advance notice as required by local law) to each of the other parties in the suit specifying the time and place of the deposition and the identity of the deponent.

d. When Permission of the Court is Required. [§9.5140]

Federal Rule 30(a)(2), amended in 1993, lists four situations in which a party must acquire leave of the court in order to conduct a deposition.

(1) Deponent in Prison. [§9.5141]

First, if the witness is confined in prison, the party seeking to take the deposition must obtain leave of the court.

(2) More than Ten Depositions. [§9.5142]

Second, the rule sets out a limit of ten depositions per side, including oral and written depositions, unless leave of the court is obtained to exceed that number or the parties so stipulate in writing. A side refers to plaintiffs, defendants, and third-party defendants. Occasionally, especially in complex litigation, some difficulties may arise in determining which parties are to be considered a "side" for the purpose of applying the rule.

(3) Witness Previously Deposed. [§9.5143]

Third, Federal Rule 30(a)(2) requires leave of the court for a second deposition of a person whose deposition already has been taken, unless the parties stipulate in writing to allow the second deposition. In multi-party cases, the rule does not suggest any limitation on how many parties can interrogate the witness at a deposition.

(4) Prior to Discovery Conference. [§9.5144]

Finally, the rule requires leave of the court for a deposition to be taken before the discovery conference at which the discovery plan is discussed [see **§9.3321**]. One exception is that a deposition may be taken before that time without leave of the court if the witness is about to leave the country and will not return prior to the close of discovery.

e. Order Regarding Time, Place, and Scope of Examination. [§9.5150]

Normally attorneys for the parties accommodate one another by agreeing to the time, place, and nature of each deposition. If no agreement can be reached, the court will decide these matters.

f. Who Can Be Deposed. [§9.5160]

Any individual, whether or not a party, who has information relevant to the case can be subject to deposition.

(1) Minority Rule: Deposition of a Corporation or Association. [§9.5161]

In an innovation that became effective in 1970, Federal Rule 30(b)(6) permits a party to notice the deposition of a corporation or association. The notice must set forth the matters to be explored. The organization must then send to the deposition those persons who have knowledge of the matters to be explored. The purpose of the rule is to eliminate the waste of time and other expense that occurs when a party notices the deposition of an individual member of an organization only to learn that it is someone else who possesses the relevant information.

g. Necessity for Subpoenas and Failure to Appear. [§9.5170]

Different rules apply to party and non-party deponents in terms of assuring their appearance at the examination.

(1) Party Deponents. [§9.5171]

A notice to take a party's deposition is all that is necessary to require that party's attendance. Failure of the party to attend can result in serious sanctions [see **§9.8400**]. Moreover, a party-deponent can be required to bring documents and other items of evidence in his possession merely by including a demand therefore in the notice of deposition. **There is no need for a subpoena.**

(2) Non–Party Deponents. [§9.5172]

A non-party need not be subpoenaed to a deposition, but unless a subpoena has been issued, there is **no penalty against the deponent if the deponent fails to appear.** Furthermore, a non-party deponent need not bring documents or other items in his possession to a deposition unless he has been served with a subpoena ordering him to do so. A deponent who fails to obey a subpoena is subject to a contempt citation. If the party who noticed the deposition fails to subpoena the witness, and the witness does not attend, that party may be ordered to pay reasonable expenses including attorney's fees to an opposing party that has incurred costs due to the wasted appearance. Similarly, if neither the party who called the deposition nor his or her attorney appears, then an opposing party who did attend may request a court order to collect for the expense of the time wasted, including reasonable attorney's fees.

h. Priority of Depositions. [§9.5180]

In some jurisdictions, depositions normally are taken in the order that notice is given. This gives an advantage to a defendant since, in the early stages of the case, plaintiff must obtain a court order authorizing the taking of a deposition, while defendant need not do so. Although the matter does not appear to be of critical importance, many lawyers do prefer to pin down the opposing party's story before their own client is deposed. Federal Rule 26(d), followed in a number of states, reflects a different approach by rejecting any rules of priority per se. Discovery is to proceed at the times requested by the parties in their notices (or by their agreements) regardless of when a notice is sent. In all jurisdictions, the courts have the discretion to alter the normal rules and to establish whatever priorities the circumstances of a particular case require.

i. Advantages of Oral Depositions over Other Discovery Devices. [§9.5190]

Oral depositions allow an attorney to observe the demeanor of the witness, thus giving a strong indication of how she will appear if called to testify at trial. It also permits the attorney to pin down the witness as to essential factual details that are relevant to the case. Most importantly, the attorney is able to "follow up" on the witness' answers, and pursue different lines of interrogation than originally contemplated. None of this would be possible if a witness merely responded to questions while at home or in his or her office, with the benefit of counsel, and with no direct confrontation by the deposing attorney. Unfortunately, the extremely high costs of this procedure often prevent it from being utilized.

2. Written Depositions. [§9.5200]

A written deposition proceeds as does an oral deposition with one major difference. The attorneys, instead of asking questions orally, submit them in writing in advance to the officer. The officer asks the questions of the witness who answers orally. The questions and answers are recorded by a reporter. The party taking the deposition first serves the initial set of questions to be asked. The other parties then submit cross-questions, the first party submits re-direct questions, and finally the other parties submit re-cross questions. Each set of questions is sent to all other parties so that they may formulate their ensuing questions. Each jurisdiction has specific time limits for the submission of questions.

a. Details of Written Depositions. [§9.5210]

Matters as to time, place, need for subpoena, requirement of signature, and objections to the scope of inquiry are all dealt with in the same manner as oral depositions. Typical regulations appear in Federal Rule 31. Leave of the court is required for written depositions under the same circumstances as oral depositions [see **§9.5140– 9.5144**].

b. Advantages of Written Depositions over Other Discovery Devices. [§9.5220]

Although written depositions have the benefit of being **considerably less expensive** than other devices, they have few of the advantages of an oral deposition since there is usually no attorney present during the procedure to observe the demeanor of the witness. As a result, written depositions are used infrequently.

3. Written Interrogatories. [§9.5300]

One party may send to another party a set of relevant questions that the recipient party must answer under oath [see generally Federal Rule 33]. Unlike a deposition, there is no formal proceeding and no officer is present. Interrogatories have many advantages over other discovery devices. They require the responding party to investigate before answering. Thus, the inquiring party is able to obtain all the information known by a corporation without having to take the depositions of numerous individuals. Interrogatories are particularly useful for disclosing basic, non-controversial information. The answering party merely formulates the answers, invariably with the aid of counsel, writes them down, signs them under oath, and sends copies to the court and to the other parties within the time limit specified by the particular rules of the jurisdiction. If a question is considered improper, the answer may so state and give the reasons for the objection. In such case, the party that sent the interrogatories may ask the court to order an answer.

a. For Parties, Not Witnesses. [§9.5310]

Interrogatories may be sent to parties but not to non-party witnesses. A party obviously has the motive and ability to protect its interests when answering questions, particularly since the party knows that the answers sometimes may be used in court [see **§9.7500**]. A non-party witness, however, has no stake in the outcome of the case and it would be inappropriate to require such a witness to answer one-sided questions, since the responses could be misleading. Thus, information from non-party witnesses can be obtained only through depositions when the presence of attorneys for the adverse parties helps guarantee a fair and complete inquiry.

b. Minority Rule: For Adverse Parties Only. [§9.5320]

Some courts permit interrogatories to be sent only to adverse parties. Under established rules of evidence, only an adverse party can introduce the answers at trial. Therefore, it is argued, interrogatories to a co-party may not be answered with the same care as would interrogatories from an adversary. Most courts reject the "adverse party" requirement for the following reasons: (a) even when questions are formulated by a party who is not adverse to the answering party, the answers may be introduced into evidence by a third party who is adverse to the answering party; thus all answers to interrogatories, whatever their source, must be carefully drafted; (b) interrogatories are a relatively inexpensive and useful way of obtaining information from those most knowledgeable about the case; and (c) it has proved difficult to decide who qualifies as an adverse party.

c. Court Order Not Required. [§9.5330]

Ordinarily, one party simply mails the interrogatories to the party from whom answers are sought. As with depositions, no order of the court, generally, is required.

(1) Exception—More Than 25 Interrogatories. [§9.5331]

According to Federal Rule 33(a) the set of written interrogatories served on a party may not include more than 25 questions including all discrete subparts. Exceeding this number requires the permission of the court or a written stipulation. Courts have had difficulty in determining when a set of multiple questions constitutes a single question or a series of discrete subparts. Routine interrogatories asking a party's full name, address and phone number are usually considered to be a single question.

(2) Exception—Early Stages of Litigation. [§9.5332]

Most jurisdictions have tried to protect defendants from having to respond to interrogatories before they have an opportunity to employ counsel, either by requiring a court order for early discovery or extending the time allowed for a response to the discovery requests. The federal rules address this by prohibiting interrogatories (and all other formal discovery) from being initiated prior to the Rule 26(f) discovery conference [see **§9.3321**] without leave of the court or written stipulation.

d. Duty to Investigate before Answering. [§9.5340]

Generally a party has the duty to answer interrogatories not only on the basis of his or her own knowledge, but also on the basis of knowledge that the responding party reasonably can obtain through investigation. However, Federal Rule 33(b)(1)(A) appears not to require an individual who is a party to make such an investigation. When the party is a corporation, association, or governmental agency, interrogatories are an effective way to obtain information that no single individual within the organization holds.

e. Interrogatories Involving Application of Law to Fact. [§9.5350]

Federal Rule 33 specifically permits questions involving the application of law to fact. Some state courts, however, have held that such questions involve work product [see **§9.3100**].

Illustration. [§9.5351] P alleges that D engaged in certain unfair trade practices. One issue in the case is whether federal antitrust standards are applicable. These standards apply only if D was

---

engaged in interstate commerce. P sends interrogatories to D that state: Does D engage in any business activity involving interstate commerce? If so, what are the details of this activity? In many courts these questions are appropriate. D, of course, may answer "No" or explain the nature of its activity in detail. In other jurisdictions, however, the questions are not allowed since they require D to define interstate commerce, which, in this context, is a legal determination.

f. Burden to Ascertain Answers Contained in Business Records. [§9.5360]

Federal Rule 33(d) and its state counterparts permit a party served with interrogatories, the answers to which are contained in the party's business records, simply to notify the interrogating party to do the clerical work necessary to obtain the answers itself. The responding party either must turn the files over to the interrogating party or otherwise provide fair access to them. Moreover, the responding party cannot merely leave the interrogating party to flounder amid a sea of business records; it must designate in sufficient detail where the pertinent information can be located so that the burden on the interrogating party to obtain the answers is not significantly greater than it would be on the responding party.

(1) Exception: Undue Burden on Interrogating Party. [§9.5361]

If there would be a much greater burden on the interrogating party to obtain answers from the files than there would be on the responding party, the latter cannot require the former to ferret out the information.

4. Requests for Admission. [§9.5400]

One party may send to any other party a formal request to admit specific facts in controversy under the pleadings or to admit that certain documents or other items are genuine so as to facilitate their introduction into evidence at trial. The responding party, under oath, must admit, deny, or specify why it cannot admit or deny the matters involved [see generally Federal Rule 36]. Good faith requires the responding party to qualify an answer or make only a partial denial when appropriate.

> **Illustration. [§9.5410]** P brings suit against the estate of T for injuries that P suffered in an auto accident in which T and T's passenger were killed. The complaint alleged that T was the driver of the vehicle which struck P's car. The attorney for D, the executor of T's estate, filed an answer denying that T was the driver, since at the time, there was no evidence as to who was driving the car in which T was riding. Subsequently, however, D obtained clear evidence that T was, in fact, the driver. By use of a request to admit, P can avoid the expense of proving this fact at trial.

a. No Court Order Required. [§9.5420]

A request to admit, much like a set of interrogatories, is sent directly to the party from whom a response is sought. No court order is required.

b. Duty of Responding Party. [§9.5430]

Each jurisdiction prescribes the time within which a response is required. **Failure to respond results in the admission of the facts that the request seeks**, although courts are liberal in granting relief when the failure is not willful. An answering party has a duty to conduct a reasonable investigation before responding; a formal refusal to admit or deny can be based on the insufficiency of available information.

c. Requests on Critical Issues. [§9.5440]

Under Federal Rule 36 and many state counterparts, any disputed issue may be the subject of a request to admit. On the other hand, some courts have taken the position that requests should not be directed to so-called "basic" or "crucial" issues that are disputed in the pleadings. Crucial issues are those upon which the case or a substantial portion of it would turn. The rationale for this latter position is not clear; presumably, it is based on the notion that discovery is to be used to discover facts for trial, rather than to obviate the need for litigation entirely.

d. Requests Involving the Application of Law to Fact. [§9.5450]

Federal Rule 36 and some state counterparts specifically permit requests that involve the application of law to fact (e.g., "Was the defendant engaged in interstate commerce?" "Did plaintiff operate his vehicle in a negligent manner?" etc.) Some courts, however, in the absence of a similar clause in the state rule, take the position that such requests are improper because they involve an element of work-product [see **§9.3100**].

e. Binding Effect of Admissions. [§9.5460]

Under Federal Rule 36(b), and many state counterparts, an admission is binding on the party who made it. Thus, the trier of fact must accept the admission as true. Evidence to counter the admission cannot be introduced at trial.

(1) Minority View: Not Binding. [§9.5461]

In a few courts, admissions have been treated only as an item of evidence that can be refuted at trial. This substantially weakens the utility of admissions, since a party cannot rely upon them and will want to submit additional evidence at trial. Thus, little time and expense are saved.

(2) Amendment of Admissions. [§9.5462]

If a party in good faith admits a fact that it later finds to be untrue, courts in all jurisdictions will entertain a timely motion to amend the admission, just as the courts do with respect to pleadings. Of course, the moving party must show that the matter is of substantial importance to a just determination of the case before relief will be granted.

(3) No Effect in Subsequent Case. [§9.5463]

To avoid unfairness, admissions made in response to requests to admit only affect the case in which they are made and cannot be used in any way in other litigation. Parties would press hard not to admit any fact if serious unforeseen consequences could result.

Illustration. [§9.5463–1] P seeks to authenticate a document of minor importance to the case. D is willing to admit that the document is genuine to avoid time and expense, although a thorough investigation of the facts has not been made. However, if a document might later be the cornerstone of a separate action against D, and the admission were to bind D in such subsequent

---

litigation, D would refuse to admit on the ground that reasonable investigation has not revealed sufficient information to admit or deny.

f. Advantages of Requests to Admit over Other Discovery Devices. [§9.5470]

Unlike other forms of discovery, the primary function of requests to admit is to eliminate undisputed matters for trial. On its face, requests to admit seem quite advantageous since they are inexpensive to use and can save both parties a great deal of time and money if a matter at issue need not be litigated. Further, the federal rules do not limit the number of admissions requests that may be served on a party. Unfortunately, they have not been very effective in practice since responding parties are loath to admit even the most obvious matters and the sanction for a false denial is inadequate [see **§9.8500– §9.8510**].

5. Inspection of Documents and Other Items. [§9.5500]

Any party, on proper request or order, will be permitted to inspect, photograph, or copy any relevant documents or papers and inspect, photograph, and survey any real or personal property that is in the possession of another party to the suit [see generally Federal Rule 34]. Federal Rule 34 specifically allows for the discovery of electronically stored documents and information.

a. Need for Court Order: Split View. [§9.5510]

Federal Rule 34, and comparable rules in some states, permit inspection on notice without a court order. If the party from whom discovery is sought refuses to permit the inspection (for example, on the ground that the items sought are not relevant), the discovering party then must go to court for a determination and appropriate sanction. In other states, however, the discovering party must move for a court order based upon a showing of good cause before discovery is permitted. This requirement stems from the deep-seated belief that interference with a person's property is a serious matter bordering on an invasion of privacy. To establish good cause, it is not sufficient to show that the material sought is useful and relevant. The party seeking discovery must demonstrate that unless discovery is allowed, it would be impossible or highly impractical to obtain vital information.

b.   Requirements of Notice or Motion. [§9.5520]

The party seeking discovery must designate the property to be inspected. Designation of documents, photographs, or other tangible items may be by category; each particular item need not be designated. The request or motion must set forth the time, place, and manner of inspection—for example, whether a land survey is to be made. The court always must arrange these matters if the parties cannot agree.

c.   Requirement of Orderly Production. [§9.5530]

Some litigants, in order to thwart the meaningful production of documents, have turned them over in disarray, without any order whatsoever. To prohibit such practices Federal Rule 34(b)(1)(E)(i) now requires a party to produce documents either "as they are kept in the usual course of business" or organized and labeled to correspond with categories made in the request.

d.   Discovery from Non–Parties. [§9.5540]

In most courts, discovery of items or property in the possession of non-parties is strictly limited to situations in which the individual is summoned to a deposition and served with a subpoena requiring him to bring the designated items with him. Federal Rule 45 authorizes a subpoena to command the production of documents or to permit inspection of the premises, whether or not the person subpoenaed also will be deposed.

(1)   Objections by a Non–Party. [§9.5541]

A non-party can object to a subpoena if it calls for disclosure of privileged or protected matter, such as trade secrets, or if it imposes an undue burden. It is not clear the extent to which a non-party can object solely on the ground that the information sought is not relevant to the case. A non-party who objects to disclosure should seek a court order limiting the scope of the subpoena and the court then has the power to determine whether limitation is in order and to issue an appropriate order to satisfy both the needs of the party who sent the subpoena and the non-party who seeks protection.

(2)   Scope of Discovery from Non–Parties. [§9.5542]

Federal Rule 45 subjects nonparties to the same scope of discovery as parties under Rule 34. Federal Rule 45(a)(1)(D) specifically provides that a party may examine and copy items produced in response to a subpoena. The law is unclear in courts that permit discovery from a non-party only in connection with a deposition of non-party. Some decisions have refused to allow parties to inspect, arguing instead that the witness should be asked questions as to matters that can be answered only by reference to the subpoenaed items. There seems little justification for such a position.

e. Independent Discovery Actions in Equity. [§9.5550]

Modern rules specifically do not limit the traditional suit in equity for discovery. Such an action operated as a separate lawsuit by a party against a person possessing evidence needed in another case. Although independent actions have fallen into disuse, often because they are subject to restrictions, defenses, and limitations that render them useless in many situations, it still may be possible, in some states, to invoke equity proceedings to enter onto and inspect land in the hands of a person who is not a party to the suit for which inspection is necessary.

6. Physical or Mental Examinations. [§9.5600]

Most jurisdictions permit physical and mental examinations based on the model set forth in Federal Rule 35.

a. Limited to Parties or Persons under Their Control. [§9.5610]

The normal rule is that **only a party is subject to a physical or mental examination**. In recent years, however, a number of jurisdictions, including the federal courts, have extended their rules to cover **persons in the custody or under the legal control of a party**. Legal control, however, is defined narrowly to encompass only such groups as minors and incompetents; witnesses, employees, and other persons who otherwise are unconnected with a party are not included.

Illustration. [§9.5611] P, a parent, sues on behalf of her minor child for injuries incurred in an accident. D believes that the child's doctors are exaggerating the nature and seriousness of the injuries; hence D wants his own medical expert to examine the child. In a jurisdiction in which the child is not a formal party, and only parties can be examined, D will not be able to obtain the medical information he seeks. A contrary result will be reached in

---

a jurisdiction that permits examination of persons in the custody or under the legal control of a party.

(1) Minority View: Agents. [§9.5612]

A few jurisdictions permit examination of a party's agents as well as of those over whom the party has legal custody or control. It seems somewhat unfair to place a party in the position of attempting to force reluctant employees to undergo physical or mental examinations. On the other hand, an opposing party should not be victimized by collusion between an employing party and the employee to avoid necessary examination. So far, the issue has arisen only in cases in which the employee can be made a codefendant and therefore is subject directly to an examination. Since the rules of those jurisdictions that allow for an examination of a party's agent do not provide an order directing the agent to undergo tests, it is enough that the party make a good faith effort to induce the agent to submit to an examination; the party will not be subjected to sanctions if the agent refuses.

b. Condition Must Be in Controversy. [§9.5620]

An examination is appropriate only when the mental or physical condition sought to be examined **forms a major element in the case, either as a basis of a claim or of a defense.**

Illustration 1: Contract. [§9.5621] P sues D for breach of contract to provide certain personal services. A clause of the contract specifically excuses performance during any period in which D is sick and confined to bed. D alleges that the failure to perform was due to a serious, continuing illness. P normally will be permitted to obtain a physical examination of D.

Illustration 2: Tort. [§9.5622] A and B are involved in an auto accident that only results in property damage. A sues and B countersues, each claiming that the damages were caused solely by the negligent driving of the other. A alleges that B's eyesight is so deficient that B cannot see other vehicles approaching; B alleges that A has a bad leg that prevents A from stepping on the brakes in emergency situations. It would be appropriate for A to obtain an examination of B's eyesight and B to obtain an examination of the condition of A's leg.

c. **Not Allowed for Impeachment Purposes. [§9.5630]**

One party cannot require an examination of an opponent's eyesight or mental condition merely to show that the opponent's testimony at trial is unreliable. The condition itself is not "in controversy" within the meaning of the discovery rule. Otherwise, in every case a party who intends to testify could be subjected to a series of medical examinations.

d. **Court Order Required. [§9.5640]**

Unless the parties otherwise agree (as is frequently the case), an examination will take place only upon **court order based on a showing of good cause**. The rationale is that an examination involves an invasion of privacy that ought not to be required without serious consideration. Normally, sufficient good cause exists when the party seeking the examination has no other way of checking or verifying the claims of the opposing party as supported by that party's medical experts.

(1) **Specification of Time, Place, and Doctor. [§9.5641]**

The party seeking the examination sets forth in its motion the time, place, name of the examiner or examiners, and any other conditions that are appropriate. The court may approve, disapprove, or modify these conditions after hearing arguments from both sides.

Illustration 1: Limiting Scope to Avoid Pain or Danger. [§9.5641–1] D wishes to verify findings of P's medical experts based on several tests that are painful and dangerous. D seeks to have the tests repeated by doctors of D's choosing. Because there is no reason to suspect the validity of the tests made (as opposed to conclusions to be drawn therefrom), the court will refuse to order a new set of tests.

Illustration 2: Determining Who May Be Present at Examination. [§9.5641–2] P requests that his attorney be present when P is examined by the physician. D objects on the ground that this inhibits the examination. In the absence of any special reason, courts usually refuse to allow the attorney to attend. The court may allow a relative or friend to attend when the examined party, either because of illness or advanced age, is in need of a companion.

e.   **Right of Examined Party to Receive Report. [§9.5650]**

Federal Rule 35(b) provides a model, adopted in nearly all jurisdictions, that permits an examined party to obtain, on demand, a detailed copy of the examiner's report, including all findings, results of tests, diagnoses, and conclusions. The normal limits on discovery of an opposing party's expert information [discussed in **§9.3200**], do not apply to reports of medical examinations under Rule 35. Many examinations are made by agreement of the parties in cases in which it is clear that the court would order an examination if a motion were to be made. To foster agreements and avoid unfairness, discovery rules provide that the examined party has a right to a copy of the report unless the agreement specifically provides otherwise.

f.   **Conditional Right of Examining Party to Prior Reports. [§9.5660]**

Once an examined party demands and obtains a copy of the report, the reports of the examined party's own examiners (regarding the same condition) are subject to discovery. The purpose is to provide a full exchange of medical information. The examined party is specifically held to waive any privilege when he requests and receives the report of the opposing party's doctor.

G. PRACTICAL PROBLEMS IN CONTROL AND OPERATION OF DISCOVERY DEVICES. [§9.6000]

Although most discovery takes place without controversy or court interference, there are a number of problems that do require formal resolution. Some of these are governed by specific rules; others must be determined by the courts on a case-by-case basis [see **§9.3300**].

1.   **Effect of Limited Range of Subpoenas. [§9.6100]**

A subpoena has a limited range, depending upon local rules and constitutional limitations. Thus a deposition of a non-party witness must be taken within the general area where the witness is located (unless the witness volunteers to attend elsewhere), regardless of where the suit is filed. [See generally Federal Rule 45.]

a. Control by Court That Issues Subpoena. [§9.6110]

If a witness does not live within the jurisdiction of the court in which suit is filed, a subpoena may be obtained from the courts of the state where the witness is located. (Every jurisdiction has some provision or ruling that permits its courts to assist in judicial proceedings instituted elsewhere.) However, the scope and details of the deposition are within the control of the court that issued the subpoena and may differ from the rules that apply in the state where suit is brought. One advantage of bringing suit in federal court is that a uniform set of rules applies throughout the nation.

b. Cost of Oral Depositions in Other Jurisdictions. [§9.6120]

If the attorney must travel out of state to take a deposition, the cost can be prohibitive. Sometimes expenses can be curtailed by employing local attorneys to handle the matter, or by using written depositions.

2. Duty to Update Discovery: Split View. [§9.6200]

A serious problem arises when a party who gave a good faith response to discovery later learns that the response was incorrect, incomplete, or otherwise misleading. Courts are split on whether the responding party has a duty to correct the prior answers. On the one hand, it is argued that **a party should not continuously have to worry about what was said in prior discovery**; it is too easy to overlook such matters and it would be unfair to impose sanctions for a party's failure to recognize the significance of new information. Moreover, the other party always may send a later set of interrogatories requesting any supplementary information. The opposing argument is that **it is wasteful to encourage extra interrogatories, which usually will prove useless**. Furthermore, new information of a vital nature (for example, the name of a newly discovered eyewitness) may not be learned until trial, after all discovery has been completed.

a. Scope of Duty to Update. [§9.6210]

Federal Rule 26(e) provides a model for provisions requiring discovery supplementation. It obliges a party to supplement all disclosures required by Rule 26(a) [see **§9.2400**] if they were incomplete or incorrect. In addition, Rule 26(e) requires a party to update its responses to interrogatories, requests for production, or requests for admission if they were incomplete or incorrect. The rule does not require a party to update answers in depositions, except for depositions of experts who may be called to testify. Updating is not required if the other parties already have been made aware of the changes.

H. USE OF DISCOVERY AT TRIAL. [§9.7000]

Federal Rule 32 and its state counterparts specifically provide for the use at trial of some discovery that otherwise would be inadmissible hearsay.

1. **Deposition of a Party: Use by Opponent. [§9.7100]**

   Typically, the evidence rules permit any out-of-court statement of a party to be introduced by an adversary [see Federal Rule 32(a)(2)]. This includes the deposition of a party's director or managing agent who is presumed authorized to speak for the party. Sometimes an ordinary employee is authorized to speak for a party on a particular matter, or is presumed to be authorized under the rules of evidence in force in the jurisdiction. In that case, statements on such a matter in the employee's deposition are considered statements of the party and may be introduced by an opponent. A few courts allow a party to use the deposition of any employee of an adverse party. This position goes beyond the normal rules of evidence and is justified on the ground that in a deposition situation, a party has ample opportunity to consult with employees so that no inadvertent or misleading statements are made. The opposing majority view is based on the notion that an ordinary employee may not be controlled by the employer and should be treated as an ordinary witness.

2. **Deposition of a Witness to Contradict Testimony at Trial. [§9.7200]**

   A general rule of evidence permits a party to introduce at trial any previous statement of a witness that conflicts with the witness' testimony in court for the **sole purpose of demonstrating that the witness is unreliable**. The Federal Rules explicitly provide for the use of depositions to contradict or impeach testimony [see Federal Rule 32(a)(2)]. The rule should and does clearly extend to statements made under oath in discovery. In a few state courts, contradictory statements, including statements in depositions, may be used not merely to impeach a witness but may also be used as proof of the facts set out in the statement.

3. **Deposition of Party or Other Witness Who Is Unavailable at Trial. [§9.7300]**

   Pursuant to Federal Rule 32(a)(4) if the party or other witness is dead, over 100 miles from the place of trial, out of the country, ill, incompetent, imprisoned, or beyond the subpoena power of the trial court, then the witness's deposition may be introduced into evidence. The rationale is that it is better to have a deposition than no evidence at all, particularly since hearsay dangers are minimized by the fact that all parties are present at the deposition to question the witness who testifies under oath. There is an important exception, however; **a party who has procured the witness' absence cannot use her deposition.**

Illustration. [§9.7310] D deposes one of P's employees. The deposition reads favorably to P, who would hesitate to call the witness at trial because the witness is an alcoholic. P transfers the employee to a subsidiary in a foreign country and attempts to use the deposition at trial. The deposition will not be admissible if D objects.

---

a. Party's Use of Own Deposition. [§9.7320]

If a party does not attend the trial because she is ill or lives and works beyond the reach of the court's subpoena power, then the party's own attorney may introduce the party's deposition into evidence. If the party lives within the scope of the court's subpoena power and merely chooses not to attend the trial, her deposition may not be introduced in her absence.

4. Inadmissible Portions of Depositions. [§9.7400]

Because a party can obtain substantial information during discovery that is not admissible at trial, a deposition normally will contain both admissible and inadmissible evidence. When a deposition is to be used at trial, therefore, either party may require the inadmissible matters to be eliminated.

5. Answers to Interrogatories. [§9.7500]

As already noted [see **§9.7100**], out-of-court statements of one party may be put into evidence by an adverse party. Thus one party's answer to an interrogatory, under oath, may be introduced by an opponent even though normally it would be inadmissible hearsay. Of course, since the scope of discovery is broader than the scope of admissible evidence, only those answers that otherwise are admissible can be introduced.

> **Illustration. [§9.7510]** P sends interrogatories to D asking whether D is insured, and if so, the amount of that insurance. P cannot introduce the answers into evidence at trial because information regarding insurance is not admissible under the rules of evidence.

a. Inadmissibility of Party's Own Answers. [§9.7520]

A party's own answers may be one-sided; they are not subject to cross-examination as in a deposition. Therefore, the party cannot introduce them.

6. Admission Made in Response to a Request to Admit. [§9.7600]

Most courts hold an admission to constitute a binding determination of the matter admitted. A few courts have held an admission to be mere evidence subject to refutation. This latter view of admissions weakens their effect without any justification. [For exploration of the effect of admissions, see **§9.5460–§9.5461**]

I. SANCTIONS FOR FAILURE TO COMPLY WITH DISCOVERY. [§9.8000]

Federal Rule 37, and many state counterparts, set forth the various means by which the rules of discovery may be enforced.

1. Motion to Require Response. [§9.8100]

A court order requiring a response may be directed toward any party or witness who fails to answer a question at a deposition or on interrogatories, or who fails to produce items on proper notice, or who fails to admit or deny a request to admit.

a. Certification of Attempt to Resolve. [§9.8110]

Pursuant to Rule 37(a), a party making a motion to compel discovery must certify that he has made an honest attempt to secure the disclosure without court action.

b. Assessing Expenses against Unreasonable Party. [§9.8120]

A party who is unreasonable in demanding or refusing discovery may, in the court's discretion, be ordered to pay the successful party's expenses of the motion to compel discovery, including reasonable attorney's fees.

c. **Sanctions When Deposition Taken in Another Jurisdiction. [§9.8130]**

Any party is subject to the control of the court where suit is pending. By way of contrast, a non-party witness is subject only to the court having jurisdiction over him or her. If a non-party witness refuses to respond to questions, denying the litigants the benefit of a telephone deposition [see **§9.5110**], motions for sanctions must be filed in the court where the discovery is being, or is to be, taken, not in the court where the action was filed.

2. **Motion to Have Matters Deemed Admitted. [§9.8200]**

According to rules governing requests to admit, a party who fails to respond to a request admits the facts involved. However, courts are reluctant, in the absence of a showing of bad faith, to hold a party to a vital admission and usually will grant him or her relief, even at trial. Therefore, to clarify the situation in advance, the requesting party may elect to move for a response or for a determination that the facts are admitted. This allows both parties to begin trial with correct knowledge regarding what has been admitted.

3. **Sanctions for Failure to Comply with Court Order or Subpoena. [§9.8300]**

Sometimes a subpoena or court order is obtained at the outset of discovery, such as on a motion for a physical examination, or when a deponent is ordered to bring documents to the deposition. Other times, an order is obtained only after a party or witness refuses to comply with a proper discovery request. Any willful violation of a subpoena or court order is a serious matter, subject to severe sanctions.

a. **Contempt Order. [§9.8310]**

One who violates a subpoena or court order may be held in contempt, fined, and even jailed until a proper response is made. There is, however, one exception: no one can be jailed for failure to submit to a physical or mental examination. The rules recognize that a person should not be physically coerced into giving up the privacy of his or her body or mind.

b. **Dismissal of All or Part of Complaint or Defense. [§9.8320]**

A party who refuses to obey a court order may be forced to give up all or part of his or her case, or may be prohibited from introducing certain evidence or from refuting certain evidence introduced by the adverse party. **The court has wide discretion to formulate appropriate sanctions depending on the situation.**

c.   **Assessing Expenses of Obtaining Sanctions. [§9.8330]**

In addition to other sanctions, a defaulting party can be ordered to pay the expenses of an opponent incurred in obtaining sanctions, including reasonable attorney's fees.

4.   **Immediate Sanctions When Party Willfully Fails to Appear at Deposition or to Answer Interrogatories. [§9.8400]**

When a party willfully fails to arrive at his or her own deposition or to answer interrogatories, the court, in its discretion, may impose such penalties as striking all or part of the complaint or defense, entering a default judgment, or limiting the evidence admissible at trial. The importance of these sanctions is that they operate immediately; they do not require violation of a prior court order. The sanctions are available against party corporations and associations when their officers or directors willfully default.

a.   **Strict Requirement of Willful Failure. [§9.8410]**

At least in the past, direct sanctions against a party have rarely been assessed, courts being extremely reluctant to find a party's default to be willful rather than negligent. In most cases, the aggrieved party needed to first obtain a court order requiring a response. However, courts have become increasingly distressed with dilatory practices and it is likely that there will be greater willingness to impose sanctions in the future.

b.   **Collection of Expenses of Obtaining Sanctions. [§9.8420]**

In addition to other direct sanctions, the court, in its discretion, may award expenses of obtaining sanctions, including reasonable attorney's fees.

5.   **Special Sanctions When Party Falsely Denies Request to Admit. [§9.8500]**

Under Federal Rule 37(c)(2) and its state counterparts, if a party without justification makes a false denial in response to a request to admit on a significant issue, and the requesting party proves the issue at trial, the requesting party is entitled to the reasonable costs of proving the matter.

a.   **More Severe Sanction Needed. [§9.8510]**

The current sanction as set out in the preceding section is woefully inadequate. Note that it is applied only when a party is guilty of perjury. And even then it often cannot be utilized because the aggrieved party may not be able to demonstrate that the matter at issue was proved, or because the cost of proof may be small or uncertain. So far proposals for an increase in sanctions have not been adopted.

Illustration. [§9.8511] P sues for damages allegedly received in an automobile collision. D claims he was not negligent, that P was contributorily negligent, and that P's claims were extinguished by an executed settlement agreement. P, in a response to a request to admit, falsely denies the existence of a settlement agreement. D puts in evidence as to all three defense claims; the jury brings in a general verdict for D. D seeks to collect expenses incurred on account of P's false denial. P can successfully argue that D cannot establish that the settlement was "proved" since the jury could have decided the case on any one of D's claims.

---

6.   Sanctions for Failure to Perform Automatic Disclosures. [§9.8600]

A party who fails to disclose information as required by Rule 26(a) [see **§9.2400–§9.2414**] normally will be prohibited from presenting such information at trial. Under Federal Rule 37(c)(1), however, the court has the power to substitute other sanctions when appropriate.

*

CHAPTER X

THE PRETRIAL CONFERENCE

A. THE PRETRIAL CONFERENCE. [§10.0000]

A number of major changes in procedure—including expanded joinder of parties and claims, virtually unlimited discovery, less informative pleadings, and increasingly complex and protracted litigation—have created a need for increased judicial intervention in the development of cases prior to trial. In many jurisdictions the response has been the pretrial conference [see, e.g., Federal Rule 16].

B. PURPOSE OF PRETRIAL CONFERENCE. [§10.1000]

A pretrial conference is a meeting of the attorneys with a trial judge or with a magistrate who possesses certain judicial powers. There are two different views as to the primary purpose of such a conference: some courts believe that the conference should be used chiefly to prepare for and streamline the trial; other courts view the conference as a means to avoid trial by inducing the parties to settle the case out of court. Indeed, well over 90% of all cases do not reach trial. The federal provision, Rule 16, emphasizes the significance of case management but makes clear that settlement, when possible, is also an important goal.

1. Preparation for Trial. [§10.1100]

The pretrial conference can be very useful in assisting the court and the parties to prepare for trial. The issues can be clarified, the pleadings can be amended, discovery can be controlled, the parties can agree upon admission of items of evidence and upon the number of witnesses to be called, and the format and sequence of trial can be arranged. Federal Rule 16 underscores the importance of the conference as a means of overall case management, not merely a time for the exchange of information or ritualistic stipulation as to minutiae. The rule makes it clear that the court, not the parties, has the discretion to direct the conference and take action with respect to the items listed. The rule further permits consideration of still other issues including such matters as limits on the proposed use of expert testimony, the possibility of summary judgment, the use of control of the discovery process, and the possibility of using alternative dispute resolution techniques. Other details of discovery, pleading and joinder, evidence and methods of proof, hearings on motions, and the procedures to be used at trial are all appropriate topics for discussion and agreement. The rule suggests the possibility of two or more conferences, the first at the outset of the case to deal with items of preliminary procedure, including planning and scheduling, and a final conference with the court to nail down the issues actually to be tried and the specific details of the trial itself.

2. Settlement. [§10.1200]

The opportunity for settlement is enhanced whenever opposing attorneys meet to discuss a case. In some courts, primarily those with a heavy backlog of cases, the trial judge will be most interested in obtaining a final agreement, and will shape the conference to that effect. Indeed, in some jurisdictions the trial judge can order a separate "settlement conference" whenever it appears that a settlement is possible.

C. MANDATORY OR DISCRETIONARY CONFERENCE. [§10.2000]

In most jurisdictions, pretrial conferences are held at the discretion of the trial judge. In a few courts, usually those in which the conference is viewed primarily as a device to obtain settlements and thus to reduce court congestion, conferences are mandatory in jury trial cases. Mandatory conferences generally are rejected for two reasons. First, unless the trial judge takes an active interest in the conference, little will be accomplished; therefore, nothing is to be gained by forcing judges to hold conferences when they do not want to do so. Second, in many actions conferences are a waste of time. When the case basically is a simple and straightforward one, there may be little that a conference can accomplish; in short cases a conference could take as long or longer than the trial itself. It must be remembered that a pretrial conference requiring attendance of the attorneys is costly to clients who must pay for the time of their counsel.

1. Required Scheduling Order in Federal Courts. [§10.2100]

Federal Rule 16(b), requires the trial court, after receipt of a report under Rule 26(f) [see **§9.3321**], or after consultation with the attorneys for the parties, to issue a scheduling order within the earlier of 120 days after the defendant was served the complaint or 90 days after his appearance, unless the case falls within a specific local rule excepting categories of cases when such order would be unnecessary or otherwise inappropriate.

The rule requires the setting of deadlines for changes in pleading, joinder of additional parties, completion of discovery, and the filing of motions. Dates for other matters, such as the times for other pretrial conferences, may also be part of the order in the discretion of the court.

a. Scheduling Order Imposed by Court. [§10.2110]

The scheduling order required under Federal Rule 16(b) differs from the ordinary pretrial order which is a product of mutual agreement among parties. The court (or magistrate, if sitting pursuant to local rule) must discuss the proposed scheduling order with the parties, but issues the final order on its own, whether or not the parties agree.

D. PROCEDURAL ASPECTS OF PRETRIAL CONFERENCES. [§10.3000]

In most jurisdictions, even those in which conferences are mandatory, the details of the conference are left to the court on a case-by-case basis, although, as we have seen in **§10.2110** with regard to Federal Rule 16(b), certain aspects may be mandated. In general, however, the judge decides when the conference should be held—early in the case to shape the parties' preparation or later, after discovery, to eliminate matters that are no longer in dispute. The court may require two or even more conferences in complex cases. In addition to the timing of the conference, the court also may specify the degree of preparation required by the lawyers before the conference takes place. Some judges have required counsel to meet privately in a pre-pretrial conference to agree, insofar as possible, on such matters as amendments to pleadings and elimination of issues, the extent of the discovery yet to come, the number of expert witnesses to be called at trial, and the admission of documentary evidence without necessity of laying an elaborate foundation. The court may, and often does, require the lawyer who will handle the case at trial to appear at the pretrial conference; this is to avoid a practice by some law firms of sending to the conference a young, inexperienced attorney who has little knowledge of the case and whose authority to enter into stipulations is limited. Further, Federal Rule 16 makes clear that the court may require each party or its representative to be available by telephone in order to consider possible settlements; this effectively circumvents the problem of parties that send representatives to a pretrial conference without any authority to act.

1. Methods of Conducting Conference. [§10.3100]

Courts vary considerably on how a pretrial conference should be conducted. Some judges prefer to hold conferences formally, in open court, perhaps with the clients present. Others handle conferences informally in chambers, sometimes without even a court reporter. The nature of the conference depends to a large extent on the judge's personality and upon his or her view as to the primary goals to be achieved. If settlement is at stake, the conference will more likely be a tense affair, with the trial judge actively pushing each of the parties to give ground; when the conference is focused less on settlement, the atmosphere generally will be more relaxed.

2.   Selection of Pretrial Judge. [§10.3200]

Courts vary as to whether the same judge who will conduct the trial should also handle the pretrial conference. There is an obvious advantage to having a single judge handle all aspects of a case, particularly a complex one; it is a waste of time and energy to have to educate a new judge as to intricate factual and legal problems merely to hold a meaningful pretrial conference. On the other hand, a single judge system has a substantial drawback. Attorneys at a pretrial conference will be reluctant to stand fast on legitimate positions with which the judge seems to disagree for fear that the judge will become angry with them and that this attitude will prove detrimental at the subsequent trial. Moreover, a judge, aware of this subtle coercion, will be reluctant to engage in frank discussions with attorneys regarding weaknesses in their cases for fear that his or her remarks will be misinterpreted. These problems do not exist when the pretrial judge will not preside at trial.

3.   Sanctions for Failure to Carry Out Pretrial Obligations. [§10.3300]

If the plaintiff's attorney continually refuses to attend scheduled conferences, or to obey orders of the court in connection therewith, the case can be dismissed for want of prosecution. Conceivably, a judgment could be entered against a defendant whose attorney similarly failed to cooperate. Courts are reluctant, however, to visit such harsh sanctions on clients for the derelictions of counsel. Certainly lesser sanctions are available, such as requiring a party whose counsel appeared unprepared at a pretrial conference to pay the opposing party's expenses regarding the conference, including attorney's fees. In addition, direct sanctions, including contempt orders, are available against attorneys who fail to cooperate.

E. THE PRETRIAL ORDER. [§10.4000]

The results of the pretrial conference are embodied in a pretrial order signed by the judge. This order is critically important because **it supersedes the pleadings and controls the subsequent course of the action.** The order specifies any amendments permitted to the pleadings and identifies the matters to which the parties have agreed and the issues to which the trial will be limited. Thus the order can preclude trial of issues that appear in the pleadings but are either no longer relevant or no longer in dispute. The pretrial order may even introduce new issues not included within the original pleadings.

Illustration. [§10.4100] P sues D, alleging that P was injured by the negligent driving of T, acting within the scope of his employment for D. D answers merely denying T's negligence. At the pretrial conference, D's attorney requests the court to amend the answer also to deny that T was acting within the scope of his employment at the time of P's injury. The court may simply direct that this "amendment" be reflected in the pretrial order, and P will have to prove the matter at trial.

---

1. Amendment of Order. [§10.4200]

A pretrial order may be amended in much the same way as pleadings are amended [see **§5.9000–§5.9320**]. The party seeking to amend must make a substantial showing of circumstances justifying the request, and must overcome any claim of prejudice to the opposing party. **Modification always requires consent of the judge.**

F. EVALUATION OF THE PRETRIAL CONFERENCE. [§10.5000]

Studies of how the pretrial conference actually functions show that it results in better preparation for trial and hence better conducted trials. The studies do not indicate, however, that trials are shortened. Judges who utilize pretrial conferences primarily to attempt settlements often are successful in obtaining final agreements among the parties. There is no way of knowing, however, how many cases that are settled during pretrial conferences would have been settled anyway. Furthermore, there is no way of telling whether settlements reached as a result of judicial coercion tend unjustly to favor one of the parties at the expense of another.

G. ROLE OF PRETRIAL CONFERENCE IN COMPLEX LITIGATION. [§10.6000]

Over the years litigation has tended to become more and more complex, often involving large numbers of plaintiffs or defendants and a variety of difficult, interrelated factual issues. The management of complex actions has posed a great challenge to the courts, and the use of pretrial conferences has proved an effective method of coping with the problems. Indeed, in the Manual for Complex Litigation, drafted by a panel of federal judges assisted by prominent attorneys and law professors to suggest methods of handling protracted cases, the primary proposal is the use of a series of pretrial conferences and related procedures to keep litigation under control at all times.

CHAPTER XI

ADJUDICATION WITHOUT TRIAL

A. ADJUDICATION WITHOUT TRIAL: SCOPE NOTE. [§11.0000]

A lawsuit may be terminated prior to trial for a number of reasons. Those reasons resulting from pleading defects are discussed in Chapter Five. This chapter deals with the two most significant procedures for adjudicating and ending an action before trial—summary judgment and default judgment.

B. SUMMARY JUDGMENT. [§11.1000]

Summary judgment is a means by which the court and the parties may use information outside of the pleadings in order to dispose of a case (or one or more of the issues in a case) about which there is no real factual dispute. It is designed to avoid the need for a trial when the issues can be resolved by the judge as a matter of law [see generally Federal Rule 56].

1. Relationship to Pleading Challenges. [§11.1100]

Challenges to pleadings—such as motions to dismiss for failure to state a claim, or motions for judgment on the pleadings or, under earlier systems, demurrers—**attack the formal sufficiency of the pleadings only**. If the plaintiff pleads his case properly, a challenge of this type must fail, even though there may be no evidence to support the allegations, because for the purpose of these motions the claims of the plaintiff are assumed to be true. Although a pleading challenge differs from a motion for summary judgment in terms of timing and the legal effect of a dismissal (a pleading dismissal is typically with leave to replead but a summary judgment is "on the merits"), the two devices are closely related in function. Both are designed to determine whether there is **any reason for continuing the law suit**. Therefore, in many jurisdictions, a motion to challenge a pleading **may be converted into a motion for summary judgment** "when matters outside of the pleading are presented and not excluded by the court." [See, e.g., Federal Rules 12(b)(6) and 12(c).] The trial judge has discretion to determine whether this conversion of a pleading challenge to a summary judgment motion is appropriate in each case.

Illustration. [§11.1110] P sues D, alleging that "on June 1, 2000, in Los Angeles, California, D gave P a vicious, dirty look and otherwise assaulted and insulted P." D moves to dismiss the complaint on the ground that it fails to state a valid claim for relief. D's attorney is concerned that the general allegation of "assault" could possibly be held sufficient to avoid a dismissal. She therefore attaches to the motion affidavits of a number of witnesses who state that at the time of the alleged acts, D was in Europe on a two-year study grant and therefore could not have committed the acts alleged, even if those acts would constitute grounds for relief under the applicable tort principles. Given the uncontroverted proof regarding D's location at the time of the events in question, as well as the questionable sufficiency of P's pleading, the court is likely to accept the affidavits and treat the motion as one for summary judgment.

2. Motion Required. [§11.1200]

Summary judgment must be requested in the form of a motion.

a. Timeliness of Motion. [§11.1210]

Some jurisdictions require the moving party, at least if he or she is the party seeking relief, to wait for a period of time, usually the time by which a pleading response is to be interposed, before filing a motion for summary judgment. Under Federal Rule 56, although a defending party may move for summary judgment at any time, a party seeking to recover can so move only after 20 days from commencement of the action or after such a motion has been filed by the adverse party. The purpose of this time limitation is to give the respondent an opportunity to retain counsel and to assess the case against him or her before being forced to reply to a motion that, in effect, could result in an adverse judgment. Other jurisdictions allow the motion to be filed at any time after the action has commenced, relying on the court to delay argument and decision when justice so requires. However, once the initial period has passed, either party may file the motion at any time prior to the beginning of trial.

b. Relationship between Summary Judgment and Discovery. [§11.1220]

In most cases a summary judgment motion will neither be made nor heard until the parties have had an opportunity to engage in

pretrial discovery. The moving party normally will wait in order to obtain the maximum amount of information in order to put forth the strongest arguments possible; the court will not rule on the motion until the responding party has had ample opportunity to ascertain evidence to support his or her position.

3. Partial Summary Judgment. [§11.1300]

Summary judgment may be sought and granted on an **entire case,** or on **a single claim, counterclaim, or defense, or on a portion of a claim,** such as the damages to be awarded in the event liability is established at trial, or on any material factual issue in the case.

Illustration. [§11.1310] P sues D for breach of contract and fraud, requesting both compensatory and punitive damages. Although D recognizes that P has an arguable case for breach of contract, D can see no justification for the allegations of fraud without which the claim for punitive damages will fail. Therefore, D moves for summary judgment on the strength of affidavits showing that no misrepresentations were made. Unless P introduces counteraffidavits, the court can grant summary judgment on the claim of fraud and eliminate the demand for punitive damages, even though the contract action remains unchallenged and unimpaired and will proceed to trial.

---

4. The Moving Party's Burden. [§11.1400]

It is the burden of the moving party to present information that, if believed, clearly demonstrates that there is no factual dispute regarding the matter upon which summary judgment is sought. It is often said that the movant must show "that there is no genuine issue as to any material fact" and that he or she is "entitled to a judgment as a matter of law." [See Federal Rule 56(c).] The idea of a judgment as a matter of law links the summary judgment motion with the trial motion for judgment as a matter of law (the directed verdict motion) since both of them seek to prevent the litigation from going forward. [See **§14.7100.**] Indeed, the Supreme Court of the United States has stated explicitly that a federal court should grant summary judgment if it would grant a directed verdict on the basis of the same evidence at trial [*Anderson v. Liberty Lobby, Inc.* (1986)].

a. Means of Meeting Burden. [§11.1410]

The moving party may support a motion for summary judgment with any **evidence that would be admissible at trial**. [See **§11.1700–§11.1721** for a discussion of the sufficiency of affidavits and other material.] The movant may submit affidavits of potential witnesses stating what they would testify to at trial, or, in the court's discretion, may present oral testimony in open court at the time the motion is argued. There is no requirement in Rule 56, however, that the moving party support its motion with affidavits or other similar materials negating the opponent's claim when the opponent must bear the burden of proof at trial. Summary judgment may properly be granted upon a showing, based on the pleadings, depositions, answers to interrogatories, and admissions on file, that there is an absence of any evidence to support the non-moving party's case [*Celotex Corp. v. Catrett* (1986)].

Illustration. [§11.1411] P sues D for battery, claiming that he was injured during a fist fight. D moves for summary judgment, asserting that P cannot establish that the fight occurred or of any injuries. D makes no affirmative showing to controvert P's allegations, but instead demonstrates, referring specifically to the record including discovery, that P has failed to come up with any evidence that the fight in fact did take place. D's motion will be granted since he has met the requisite burden of showing that there is no genuine issue of material fact.

Illustration. [§11.1412] Plaintiffs, a group of American television manufacturers, alleged that a group of twenty-one Japanese manufacturers and distributors engaged in a long-term conspiracy to fix prices in an effort to monopolize the American market. When the case reached the United States Supreme Court, it concluded that summary judgment was proper because the defendants had shown there was no "plausible motive" for the defendants to engage in the predatory pricing charged against them. In light of the absence of any rational economic motive to conspire, the defendants' conduct in Japan became irrelevant and did not create a genuine issue for trial [*Matsushita Elec. Industrial Co. v. Zenith Radio Corp.* (1986)].

---

b. Result of Failure to Meet Burden. [§11.1420]

If the moving party fails to present information that, if believed, would clearly demonstrate that no factual dispute exists regarding the issue or issues upon which summary judgment is sought, the motion must be denied. It is irrelevant whether or not the responding party is ready to offer contradictory material.

Illustration. [§11.1421] P sues D for battery, claiming that he was injured during a fist fight. D alleges that he acted solely in self-defense and moves for summary judgment supported by numerous affidavits of responsible citizens showing that P has a violent temper, frequently engages in fist fights, and dislikes D because of the latter's political views. D's motion will be denied even if P puts in no contradictory affidavits since D's affidavits, even if true, fail to establish that there is no triable issue of whether D acted in self-defense on the occasion in question.

---

5. Burden of Responding Party to Reply. [§11.1500]

When confronted with a motion for summary judgment, a party may have to respond to avoid it being granted, depending on the strength of the moving party's papers.

a. No Obligation If Moving Party Fails to Carry Burden. [§11.1510]

If the moving party fails to make an adequate showing based on the record or neglects to offer sufficient evidence or other materials to show that a summary judgment should be granted, the motion must be denied even though the responding party makes no reply whatsoever [see **§11.1421**].

b. Obligation When Moving Party Has Carried Burden. [§11.1520]

If the moving party has made a showing based on the record, or has submitted affidavits or other materials that, if believed, would justify summary judgment, the respondent has the burden of replying by submitting contrary information showing that a genuine issue of fact exists. **The respondent cannot simply rely on the allegations in the pleadings**; this is because the very purpose of the summary judgment procedure is to determine if evidence exists to support allegations or denials in the pleadings.

Illustration 1. [§11.1521] P sues D for damages arising out of a vehicle collision. As a defense, D pleads that the suit has been

---

compromised by an executed settlement agreement, a claim that P denies. D moves for summary judgment and supports the motion with a copy of the settlement agreement signed by both parties and an affidavit by D authenticating the signatures. If P does not respond to the motion and evidence, the trial court could properly grant judgment for D, since D's evidence and affidavits, if believed, establish a complete defense.

Illustration 2. [§11.1522] P files a verified pleading alleging that D struck P in the nose. D moves for summary judgment on the basis of several affidavits stating that D did not commit the battery and that at the time it was alleged to have occurred, D was out of the country. P files no counter-affidavits but argues that his pleadings, signed under oath, should suffice to block D's motion. The court will reject P's contention. Even verified pleadings [see **§5.3320**] are insufficient to counter opposing affidavits since they contain only allegations that later investigation may show to be untrue.

Illustration 3. [§11.1523] P files a claim for defamation, but fails to allege that publication, as required for a valid claim, actually occurred. D moves for summary judgment, noting in the motion that by omitting publication, P has failed to plead a prima facie case. P is unable to provide affidavits showing that publication occurred. The court will grant D's motion because of P's failure to meet its burden of going forward.

c. **Nature of Responding Party's Supporting Materials. [§11.1530]**

The responding party, in defending against a summary judgment motion, may submit the same types of evidence and materials, (e.g., affidavits and responses to discovery) that the moving party may utilize to support the motion.

d. **Sufficiency of Response to Defeat Motion. [§11.1540]**

Whenever the respondent's affidavits or other evidence contradict the moving party's affidavits or otherwise show that there is a factual dispute on the matter for which summary judgment is sought, summary judgment must be denied. The court **cannot choose**

between conflicting evidence if it has been shown that a factual dispute exists; that is the role of the fact-finder at a trial on the merits.

Illustration. [§11.1541] P alleges he suffered injuries when D negligently drove his vehicle through a red light and struck the car driven by P. D moves for summary judgment on the basis of his own affidavit and those of five clergymen who witnessed the accident, all of whom state that P went through a red light to strike D. P counters only with an affidavit of an alcoholic who swears she witnessed the collision and that the facts were as alleged in P's complaint. Summary judgment must be denied. It is for a trier of fact to decide which witnesses are telling the truth. Credibility is not an issue of law regardless of how obvious it may appear that one party's affidavits are more reliable than those of the opposing party.

---

6. Special Factors Modify General Summary Judgment Rules. [§11.1600]

Although the foregoing general rules have been established for deciding when summary judgment should or should not be granted, there are special circumstances that require the modification of these rules in order to avoid unjust determinations.

a. Effect of Burden of Proof. [§11.1610]

When the party responding to a motion for summary judgment would have to carry the burden of persuasion at trial [see **§12.3520**], that party's failure to produce evidence to refute the moving party's affidavits demonstrates that the burden could not be met at trial and that summary judgment is appropriate. When summary judgment is sought by the party with the burden of proof, however, the matter is more complex. At trial, the trier of fact may disbelieve the witnesses who testify on behalf of such a party, even though the witnesses are not refuted by contrary evidence. In such a case, the party with the burden will lose. One may argue, then, that even if the responding party does not file contradictory affidavits, summary judgment for the party with the burden of proof is improper. Generally, the courts have rejected this argument; one important reason is that statutes and rules governing summary judgment do not distinguish between parties who bear the burden of proof and those who do not. However, courts are **especially cautious in cases in which the moving party has the burden,** and summary judgment will be denied if there is any indication of unfairness.

b. Burden of Proof and Witness' Bias. [§11.1620]

An affidavit of a witness may be countered solely by affidavits showing that the witness is biased or otherwise unreliable. But such counteraffidavits will be effective only if the original affidavit was presented by a moving party who would bear the burden of proof at trial. That is because if a witness is of doubtful credibility, he or she might be disbelieved by the fact-finder at trial, which means that the witness' affidavit could not justify a summary judgment in favor of a party who bears the burden of proof. If, however, it is the party opposing the summary judgment motion who bears the burden of proof at trial, it should not be sufficient to defeat summary judgment for the respondent merely to attack the veracity of the moving party's witness. The respondent must be able to show that he or she could come forward at trial with some evidence to discharge the burden of proof. Merely casting doubt on the moving party's witness will not assist the respondent in this regard.

Illustration. [§11.1621] P alleges that at a certain time and place, X, now deceased, struck P in the face, causing serious injury. D, the executor of X's estate, moves for summary judgment on the basis of an affidavit of W, X's private secretary, who swears that he was present at the stated time and place and that the alleged incident did not occur. P, who is charged with the burden of proof on all issues, attempts to counter W's affidavit with his own affidavit, which states only that W is a beneficiary under X's will and therefore stands to lose money if the estate is held liable to P for damages. P's affidavit is insufficient to avoid summary judgment. At trial P would have to prove that X's attack took place; if P cannot produce any evidence on the motion that the event occurred, not even his own sworn statement, then summary judgment should be granted.

---

c. Effect of the Level of the Required Burden of Proof. [§11.1630]

When considering a summary judgment motion, it is appropriate for the court to consider the applicable evidentiary burden of proof that the plaintiff must meet at a trial on the merits. The court must ask not whether it thinks the evidence favors one side or the other, but **whether a fair-minded jury could return a verdict for the plaintiff** under the applicable burden of proof on the evidence presented [*Anderson v. Liberty Lobby, Inc.* (1986)].

Illustration. [§11.1631] P sues D newspaper for allegedly defaming his organization. To prevail at trial, P must prove by clear and convincing evidence that D published the defamatory article with actual malice and/or knowledge of its falsity. On a summary judgment motion, the court will view the evidence with due regard for the substantive evidentiary burden that P must meet. If it determines that a reasonable jury could not find clear and convincing evidence of actual malice by D, the summary judgment motion must be granted.

d. **Lack of Opportunity to Obtain Facts. [§11.1640]**

A motion for summary judgment may be denied, or at least delayed, when the responding party demonstrates that more time is needed to obtain facts to counter the motion. Courts are quite liberal in granting delays for this purpose [see Federal Rule 56(f)].

e. **Facts Not Equally Available to the Parties. [§11.1650]**

A motion for summary judgment may be denied when the responding party does not have the same access to evidence as does the moving party. Rarely does this situation occur in a jurisdiction that has broad discovery rules permitting full scale investigation. Nevertheless, cases do exist in which the very nature of the issue, such as an actor's intent, makes equality of access impossible. In these cases courts are reluctant to grant summary judgment; they would rather allow the trier of fact to evaluate the testimony, particularly when the moving party bears the burden of proof.

Illustration. [§11.1651] T, a professor of the French language, seeks to deduct the cost of a trip to France from her earnings for income tax purposes. The government claims the trip was a vacation and hence non-deductible. T moves for summary judgment based on her own affidavit that the sole purpose of the journey was to increase her linguistic skills, which was done by attending plays, operas, and nightclubs. The federal government is unable to respond since it has no effective way to obtain evidence to counter the affidavit on the crucial issue of intent. Therefore, summary judgment will be denied; the question of intent, which

327

> depends solely on T's own testimony, should be determined by a trier of fact only after listening to T.

7. Nature and Sufficiency of Affidavits. [§11.1700]

In most cases, motions for summary judgment are determined on the basis of affidavits, although depositions, answers to interrogatories, and even oral testimony can be utilized.

a. Form of Affidavits. [§11.1710]

Affidavits are statements made **under oath;** they must be based on **personal knowledge,** must state that the affiant is competent to testify as to all matters stated in the affidavit under the rules of evidence, and must set forth **substantive facts that would be admissible in evidence.** However, when a responding party does not have access to the facts that are under the control of the moving party, courts accept respondent's affidavits containing opinions that would not in themselves be admissible as testimony.

> **Illustration 1. [§11.1711]** D is sued for negligently operating an automobile so as to strike P. D moves for summary judgment based solely on the affidavit of M, who swears that "N, a person I know to be reliable and truthful, saw the accident and is positive that D was not operating the vehicle when it occurred." The affidavit will be ignored and the motion will be denied. The affidavit is not based on personal knowledge but on hearsay of a type that would not be admissible at trial.

> **Illustration 2. [§11.1712]** P sues for hospital malpractice resulting in the loss of his leg. D hospital presents affidavits of each nurse and of all other employees who had anything to do with P's case, each averring that no negligent or unusual acts took place. P, who is not certain what did occur, presents only his own affidavit that the hospital "negligently allowed an infection in his leg to go untreated." Although it contains no more than his own layman's opinion, many courts will stretch to accept P's affidavit to allow the

case to proceed to trial in order that P can call the hospital's employees to testify under oath in the courtroom.

b. Use of Information in Depositions and Interrogatories. [§11.1720]

Information in depositions and answers to interrogatories, as well as other similar information sworn to under oath, may be substituted for affidavits but only to the extent the information would be admissible into evidence at trial.

Illustration. [§11.1721] P moves for summary judgment on the basis of his own answers to interrogatories sent to him by D and answered under oath. The interrogatories must be ignored, and the motion denied. Only the opposing party may introduce answers to interrogatories into evidence at trial.

8. Consideration by the Court of a Summary Judgment Motion. [§11.1800]

When considering whether to grant a summary judgment motion, **the court must examine all relevant issues in the light most favorable to the non-moving party**. Therefore, the court will evaluate the evidence and assume credibility issues in favor of the non-moving party whenever possible, and when several inferences may be drawn from the facts, the court will select the inference most advantageous to that party. Furthermore, the summary judgment motion is discretionary, and thus, even if the court believes that the Rule 56 standards have been met, it still has discretion to deny the motion if it believes it would be in the interests of justice to do so.

9. Scope of Review. [§11.1900]

No review of a summary judgment denial is possible in those jurisdictions that follow the final judgment rule [see **§15.1000**] until the disposition of the entire suit is determined. At this point, the moving party must show that the denial of the motion prejudiced his or her suit in some way. If summary judgment is granted on an entire case, the lawsuit is terminated on the merits and an immediate appeal is available. Some appellate courts will submit the judge's decision to plenary review, considering the motion to be an issue of law and therefore according the trial judge no special deference. Other appellate courts view the decision as one of weighing the credibility of evidence and will reverse only if it appears that the trial judge abused his or her discretion. In exceptional circumstances, a decision to deny summary judgment or to grant it only on a portion of the case might be subject to review immediately through one of the exceptions to the final judgment rule [see **§15.1400–§15.1510**].

C. DEFAULT JUDGMENT. [§11.2000]

Default judgments are provided for by Federal Rule 55 and various state counterparts. A default judgment is the appropriate remedy when the allegations of a party seeking relief are unanswered by an opposing party. A default judgment has two parts: the entry of default by the clerk of the court [see Federal Rule 55(a)] and the judgment of default entered subsequently by the court or by the clerk if the sum is certain and computational [see Federal Rule 55(b)]. A default judgment may not be entered against an infant or incompetent unless that party was represented by a guardian who appeared in the action. There are a number of reasons why a party may default. First, the party simply may concede the validity of an opponent's allegations. The law is designed to encourage litigants not to contest legitimate claims. It is for this reason that a plaintiff, in a default case, may not obtain relief beyond that sought in the prayer. Second, a party may not feel that it is worth the time and expense to respond. If a defendant has no assets from which a judgment against her can be satisfied, she may not contest even a claim for substantial monetary relief. Finally, a party may default inadvertently, because he does not understand the significance of the papers served upon him or because he, or his attorney, forgets to take steps necessary to respond. This may be remedied at the discretion of the court; pursuant to Federal Rule 55(c), the court may set aside an entry of default or a judgment of default for good cause. Courts are usually disposed to set aside default judgments due to a party's failure to understand the significance of the documents served or his obligations in regard thereto. Courts are similarly lenient, although somewhat less so, in setting aside default judgments resulting from counsel's inadvertence. If such a default is not set aside, the defaulting party is remitted to an action against the attorney for legal malpractice.

1. **Entry of Default on Failure to Answer or Defend. [§11.2100]**

    When a party fails to answer a complaint within the specified time as provided by local rule, that party's default may be entered on application to the clerk of the court. This will serve as the basis for the later entry of judgment by default.

    a. **Failure to Appear at Trial Distinguished. [§11.2110]**

        Entry of default is not proper simply because a party who has answered the opposing party's allegations fails to appear at trial. The trial must go on, even though the party is absent.

Illustration. [§11.2111] P files suit against D, alleging that the latter breached the terms of a contract with P, causing P to suffer damages. D files an answer denying the existence of a valid contract, and demands a jury trial. At the time the trial is scheduled, neither D nor his attorney appears. A default is inappropriate. The case must proceed; a jury will be selected and evidence will be presented. P must carry the burden of proof or he will lose. P will, of course, have a substantial tactical advantage in the presentation and argumentation of the case.

b. Lack of Defense on the Merits. [§11.2120]

The entry of default is proper if the defendant fails to make a factual defense on the merits even though the defendant has made a procedural or legal challenge to the plaintiff's complaint.

Illustration 1. [§11.2121] P sues D, alleging that D breached a contract with P. D moves to dismiss the case for lack of personal jurisdiction and improper venue. The court overrules the motion to dismiss. D takes no further steps to defend the action by answering the allegations in the complaint. The entry of default is proper.

Illustration 2. [§11.2122] P sues D, alleging a case for intentional infliction of emotional distress. D files a demurrer (or motion to dismiss) on the ground that the complaint fails to state a claim upon which relief can be granted. The challenge is overruled. D takes no steps to respond to the allegations in the complaint. Entry of default against D is proper.

2. Entry of Default Judgment by Clerk or by Court. [§11.2200]

If a default has been entered and it is clear from the complaint that a certain sum and only that sum is due to the complainant, the clerk of the court may enter a default judgment for that sum. Otherwise, the complainant must apply to the court, which will enter a default judgment only after proof as to the appropriate relief has been presented.

Illustration 1: Judgment by Clerk Proper. [§11.2210] P files suit on an overdue note for $10,000. D's default is properly entered. From the pleadings, which incorporate the note, it is clear that P is entitled to $10,000 and only $10,000. The clerk may enter judgment for P in that amount.

Illustration 2: Entry of Judgment by Court Required. [§11.2220] P sues D for $10,000 in damages it allegedly suffered when D failed to deliver goods under a contract with P, which in turn caused P to breach its contract with several third parties. D fails to respond to the complaint and a default is entered. The court clerk cannot enter a default judgment, as the amount due is not clearly a sum certain that can be definitely determined from the pleadings themselves. P must appear in court and make a showing as to the amount of loss actually incurred due to D's failure to perform.

3. Court May Accept Affidavits. [§11.2300]

In many jurisdictions, a court will not require witnesses to appear in person on a motion for entry of a default judgment but will permit evidence to be submitted by affidavit. Usually, however, the party seeking judgment must obtain **prior approval** of the court to utilize affidavits.

4. Notice to Defaulting Party. [§11.2400]

The rules as to when a defaulting party is entitled to notice of an impending default or default judgment vary somewhat among jurisdictions as set forth below.

a. Some Courts Require Notice of Application to Enter Default. [§11.2410]

Some courts require the complainant to send a notice of any application for entry of default to the last known address of the defaulting party. In many courts, however, mere entry of default is appropriate without notice.

b. Application for Default Judgment by the Clerk Requires No Notice. [§11.2420]

When the amount due is clear so that the clerk may enter judgment, notice to a defaulting party is not required. The amount of the judgment is not subject to dispute.

c. **Application for Default Judgment by Court Requires Notice If Defaulting Party Has Appeared in the Case. [§11.2430]**

Most jurisdictions follow a rule similar to Federal Rule 55, which provides for three days notice of a motion for a default judgment from the court, if, but only if, the defendant has appeared in the case. A defendant who has taken any active role in the case is thus given the chance to contest the amount, extent, or type of relief granted.

Illustration 1: No Appearance. [§11.2431] P sues D in an action for personal injury. D not only fails to file an answer, but never appears in the action. P need not notify D of a motion for entry of a default judgment, even though P must appear to establish the extent of the damages suffered.

Illustration 2: When Party Has Appeared. [§11.2432] P sues D in an action for personal injury. D's attorney files a motion to dismiss for lack of personal jurisdiction over D. The motion is rejected and thereafter D takes no steps to defend the case. D must be given timely notice of a motion to enter judgment by default.

---

5. **Remedy Limited by Prayer for Relief. [§11.2500]**

A default judgment cannot give a party relief of a type or in an amount not specifically prayed for in the complaint.

Illustration 1: Type of Relief. [§11.2510] P sues to enjoin D from engaging in certain operations on D's land that allegedly pollute P's adjacent property. D fails to respond and P seeks a default judgment. The court determines, however, that injunctive relief is inappropriate and that P could only be entitled to damages. Because there is no claim for damages in the complaint, relief cannot be granted. This is true even if P has included a general prayer for "all other relief to which P is entitled."

> **Illustration 2: Amount of Relief. [§11.2520]** P sues D for personal injuries, requesting damages in the sum of $5,000. D fails to answer and P seeks judgment by default. At the default hearing, P provides evidence of medical bills in excess of $10,000. The court cannot grant P judgment for any amount greater than the $5,000 pleaded.

6. **Effect of Insufficient Pleading. [§11.2600]**

Normally, courts do not inquire into the substantive aspects of a defaulted case, except as required to determine the amount and nature of relief that is appropriate. However, since the purpose of the court is not to create a windfall victory for a party, even in a case in which no response is filed, a defendant may successfully argue at a hearing on a default judgment that the pleading fails to state a claim or cause of action upon which relief can be granted.

> **Illustration. [§11.2610]** P alleges that D deliberately gave P a vicious, dirty look as a result of which P collapsed and suffered severe physical and emotional injuries. D fails to respond and his default is entered. At the hearing before the court to ascertain damages, D appears and argues correctly that the complaint does not state a claim upon which relief is proper. The court will not enter a default judgment for P.

D. PENALTY DEFAULT JUDGMENT. [§11.3000]

Violation of the court's procedural rules may result in a special type of default judgment. Unlike a default that occurs when there is a failure to defend, this default is imposed as a penalty.

> **Illustration. [§11.3100]** P seeks to take the deposition of D. D continually refuses to appear although the time and place set for the deposition have been approved by the court. If the court determines D's failure to cooperate to be willful, it can then enter a default judgment for P.

1. **Inapplicability of Usual Provisions Governing Default Judgments. [§11.3200]**

   The penalty default is **entirely different from an ordinary default** and the **rules governing the latter do not apply**. In the penalty case, the parties all are before the court and orders are made directly to them.

   Illustration. [§11.3210] P sues D for personal injuries, alleging damages of $25,000. D answers the complaint, denying liability. During the pretrial stage, P learns that her injuries are more serious than first believed and that she probably will need an expensive operation. P does not amend the complaint to increase her prayer because the jurisdiction in which the case is filed follows the majority rule that in a contested case P can receive all the relief to which she is entitled, even if it exceeds the prayer. P seeks to take D's deposition, but D willfully refuses to attend, even after a court order to do so. The court enters a default judgment for P. P requests that the court grant relief for $50,000 rather than for the $25,000 requested. The court may award the full amount of damages shown even though it exceeds the prayer for relief.

E. DISMISSAL WITHOUT PREJUDICE. [§11.4000]

Almost all jurisdictions provide a means by which a plaintiff can **voluntarily terminate an action or part of an action without prejudice to the filing of a new suit on the same cause.**

1. **Dismissal as a Matter of Right. [§11.4100]**

   Jurisdictions vary substantially as to when and in what types of cases a plaintiff may voluntarily dismiss without court approval. In some courts, the plaintiff cannot dismiss as of right after an answer has been filed; elsewhere the plaintiff can dismiss at any time before the case is submitted to a jury or before a verdict is returned. **Court approval** of every dismissal often is **required in certain types of cases,** such as class actions or suits brought on behalf of incompetents. That procedure is designed to protect the interests of those who are not present in court. Pursuant to Federal Rule 41(a), a plaintiff can voluntarily dismiss, without order of the court, at any time before the adverse party serves an answer or a motion for summary judgment or at any time with a signed stipulation of all parties in the action.

2. Dismissal in Discretion of Court. [§11.4200]

Most jurisdictions provide for a dismissal without prejudice **by leave of court** whenever dismissal as of right is not permitted. A court may deny a motion to dismiss or grant it subject to appropriate terms and conditions.

a. Tactical Advantage to Moving Party. [§11.4210]

Leave to dismiss without prejudice should not be denied merely because it gives the moving party a tactical advantage; that is the very purpose of the motion. Thus dismissal is not precluded if a plaintiff realizes during trial that his evidence is insufficient to overcome an expected motion for directed verdict, and he desires to terminate the present action in order to reinvestigate and obtain more proof.

b. Prejudice to Opposing Party. [§11.4220]

Leave to dismiss should be denied if it would result in **undue prejudice** to the opposing party. The later in the action dismissal is sought, the more likely it is that the court will find undue prejudice. For example, a plaintiff's motion for dismissal just before trial is to begin will most likely be denied if the defendant and all his witnesses are from out of state and have appeared for trial at substantial personal expense and inconvenience. Dismissal after trial has begun will rarely be permitted.

c. If a Counterclaim has Been Pleaded. [§11.4230]

Under Federal Rule 41, if a defendant has filed a counterclaim, the court may not grant the plaintiff's motion to dismiss unless the defendant's counterclaim can remain and be adjudicated by the court.

Illustration. [§11.4231] P filed an action in federal court, which has exclusive jurisdiction over patent claims, alleging that D infringed P's patent. D files a counterclaim for breach of contract that D claims involves D's rights to use the patent. Immediately, P files a motion to dismiss the complaint voluntarily and argues that D's counterclaim must also be dismissed because it meets no independent grounds of federal court jurisdiction. If the latter is true, the court cannot grant P's motion to dismiss and the entire action will be adjudicated.

---

d. Terms and Conditions. [§11.4240]

The court may grant leave to dismiss subject to terms and conditions, such as the payment of the opposing party's expenses (including attorney's fees), the production of certain items of evidence, or even an agreement not to make certain claims in a subsequent lawsuit. The purpose of the conditions must be to alleviate prejudice to the opposing party that otherwise would result in a denial of leave to dismiss.

3.   Effect of Second Dismissal on Same Claim. [§11.4300]

Under Federal Rule 41(a)(1) and similar rules in many states, a second dismissal of an action **operates as an adjudication on the merits** of any of the claims affected by both dismissals and bars plaintiff from successfully prosecuting a third suit based upon those claims. **The purpose of this rule is to avoid harassment of defendants and inconvenience and undue expense to the court** through the use of a series of voluntary dismissals.

F.   DISMISSAL FOR LACK OF PROSECUTION. [§11.5000]

Once a case is properly commenced, it remains pending until it is dismissed or decided. However, courts have the power to **dismiss with prejudice** suits that a plaintiff has failed to bring to trial long after they have been filed. A dismissal of this type will act as an adjudication on the merits and will bar any future suit on the same claims.

1.   Dismissal as of Right. [§11.5100]

In a few jurisdictions, a defendant is entitled to a dismissal for lack of prosecution if the case has not been brought to trial within a specific time period. Most jurisdictions, however, do not set rigid time limits.

2.   Dismissal in Discretion of Court. [§11.5200]

Most courts permit dismissal for lack of prosecution in the discretion of the trial judge, without any time limitations. However, some jurisdictions provide a specific time prior to which a dismissal is not allowed. [See Federal Rule 41(b)].

a.   Dismissal Not Generally Favored. [§11.5210]

Trial courts are reluctant to dismiss for lack of prosecution, much preferring to decide cases on their merits. This is particularly true when the failure to move the case along is due to derelictions of counsel rather than the client, who ought not to lose an otherwise meritorious case. Similarly, appellate courts do not favor dismissals for lack of prosecution, and thus are likely to find an abuse of discretion whenever a litigant can show a valid excuse for not bringing the case to trial.

337

Illustration. [§11.5211] P files suit in 1994, and obtains a trial date in 1997. Shortly before the trial is scheduled to begin, D dies, and the case is removed from the trial calendar at the request of the lawyer who represented D, and who promises to notify the court, who in turn promises to notify P, when an executor is appointed. The lawyer does notify the court but the clerk fails to notify P and P takes no action on the case. In early 2000, D's executor first enters the case to move for a dismissal for lack of prosecution, and the motion is granted. On appeal, there is a good chance for a reversal. It is true that P was not diligent in ascertaining the name of the executor and going forward with the lawsuit, but the fault is largely that of the court, which failed to live up to its promise, and of the executor, who should have contacted P directly before moving to dismiss.

G. COMPROMISE. [§11.6000]

Technically speaking, the **settlement** of a lawsuit is **not an adjudication.** However, it **often operates in the same manner** when, as one aspect of the settlement, the plaintiff files a motion to dismiss with prejudice or the parties confirm their agreement by entering into a **consent judgment** (sometimes referred to as a judgment by stipulation or confession). Once a consent judgment is entered, it is treated as any other judgment.

1. Need for Careful Drafting of Consent Judgment. [§11.6100]

A consent judgment is not based upon a case record that can be searched to ascertain the scope and operation of the judgment should it become relevant in another action. The judgment must be carefully drafted, therefore, with an eye to its future effects.

H. TERMINATION WITH PREJUDICE. [§11.7000]

A party normally may dismiss his or her own claim with prejudice—that is, so that it cannot be brought again. This may occur after a motion to dismiss without prejudice has been denied and when the expense of going forward is unjustified. Or it may occur when the party seeks the good will of the party against whom the claim was brought. However, when the party who filed the claim did so wholly or in part in a **representative capacity,** termination usually will require **approval of the court** in order to protect the absentees whose interests will be affected [see also **§11.4100**].

UNIT THREE

TRIAL

*

Chapter XII

THE TRIAL PROCESS

A. THE TRIAL PROCESS: SCOPE NOTE. [§12.0000]

This chapter contains a general description of the sequence of events at trial, the rules of evidence, and burdens of proof. The institution of jury trial and the details of trial, verdict, and the post-trial motions are discussed in Chapter Thirteen and Chapter Fourteen respectively.

B. SETTING THE CASE FOR TRIAL. [§12.1000]

Once the pleadings are completed, any party may move to set the case for trial. Except in special circumstances, in which certain types of matters are given priority, cases are placed on an appropriate **trial calendar** and scheduled for trial in the order that the motions are heard. Different courts maintain different types of trial calendars, often depending upon the nature of the case. In many jurisdictions jury trial cases are placed on one calendar, non-jury cases on another, and a specific number of judges are assigned to each calendar. This often means that non-jury cases are brought to trial much faster than jury actions. In some places the assigned trial date in jury cases may be years in the future. Obviously, a court cannot predict exactly when it will be ready to try a case. Thus, when the assigned trial date nears, the court will periodically inform the lawyers of the state of the calendar and the likelihood of delay. In setting a precise date, the court must take into consideration the fact that the attorneys may be in trial on other cases or that they or their clients may have commitments that prevent their attendance on a day the court would prefer to begin.

C. ORDER OF A TRIAL. [§12.2000]

If a case is to be tried by a jury, the first order of business is **jury selection** [see **§13.7100–§13.7520**]. Thereafter, the usual order is as follows: plaintiff's opening statement, defendant's opening statement, plaintiff's presentation of direct evidence, defendant's presentation of direct evidence, plaintiff's presentation of rebuttal evidence, defendant's presentation of rebuttal evidence, opening final argument by plaintiff, defendant's final argument, closing final argument by plaintiff, the judge's instruction of the jury, jury deliberation, and rendition of the verdict. This sequence will vary slightly from jurisdiction to jurisdiction and can be altered in specific cases at the discretion of the trial judge.

1. Order in Non–Jury Cases. [§12.2100]

The order of trial is usually the same in non-jury cases as in jury cases except that there is no jury selection, nor any instructions. Moreover, the court, as trier of fact, often will request counsel to dispense with opening statements and closing arguments. Rarely will an attorney refuse to accede to such a request.

D. TACTICS OF TRIAL. [§12.3000]

Throughout any trial the attorneys are faced with many situations that call for tactical decisions; often these decisions have to be made immediately without time for reflection. A good trial lawyer will carefully plan the case so as to anticipate as many of these problems as possible.

1. Choice Between a Jury or Non–Jury Trial. [§12.3100]

When a party has a choice between a trial by jury or before the judge, a number of factors are considered. A jury trial is costly and increases the financial gamble for a party uncertain of success; a party who loses normally is required to pay the standard daily fees of the jurors plus a mileage allowance for travel to and from their homes and money for their meals. Furthermore, a party usually must wait considerably longer to get to a trial by jury than to get a trial by the court. Finally, a jury trial requires a special degree of showmanship and psychological sophistication on the part of the trial attorney. On the other hand, a jury decision may be preferable in that it is the product of a consensus of lay people, not the determination of a single judge whose particular philosophy may dictate the result. Moreover, a jury, unlike a judge, will be less likely to indulge in "legalisms." Thus, jurors are more likely to decide the case on an overall notion of fairness than to rely on narrow legal points.

2. Selection of Favorable Jurors. [§12.3200]

The parties' attorneys have a limited opportunity to determine who will sit on the jury [see **§13.7100–§13.7520**]. Both common sense and intuition play an important part in jury selection.

3. Opening Statements. [§12.3300]

The plaintiff's attorney makes the first opening statement, except in the rare situation in which the defendant has the burden of proof on all the issues in the case. The defendant's attorney may deliver an opening statement immediately after the plaintiff's opening statement or may wait until after the plaintiff has presented his evidence. Usually the defendant prefers the earlier statement so that the plaintiff's version of the facts does not become deeply entrenched in the jurors' minds. Sometimes, however, when the defendant's evidence is particularly dramatic, defense counsel may wish to delay addressing the jury in order to increase the impact.

Illustration. [§12.3310] P sues D for a large sum, alleging debilitating personal injuries. D intends to introduce into evidence recent movies showing P engaging in a variety of physically demanding athletic activities. D's counsel is likely to wait until after P's case is completed to make her opening statement informing the jury about this evidence.

---

4. Presentation of Evidence. [§12.3400]

Normally, the plaintiff will introduce evidence first, followed by the defendant. Then the plaintiff and the defendant in turn have the opportunity to present evidence rebutting the opponent's evidence that has been previously introduced. Most evidence is presented through witnesses, who first are examined by the party who calls them and then are cross-examined by the opposing side.

a. Rules of Evidence. [§12.3410]

Specific rules of evidence govern what is and what is not admissible. Evidence normally will not be excluded unless a party **objects** to its admission. Some of the major exclusionary rules are outlined below.

(1) Irrelevant Evidence. [§12.3411]

Evidence that does not aid the trier of fact in deciding an issue will be excluded. This not only saves time and expense, but also prevents a party from conducting a filibuster.

(2) Privileged Information. [§12.3412]

Some evidence is excluded because of an overriding policy against its disclosure. For example, confidential communications between husband and wife, lawyer and client, doctor and patient, or priest and penitent usually are protected in order to foster those relationships. In addition, the privilege against self-incrimination protects individuals from being trapped into confessing criminal conduct. Jurisdictions vary as to the nature and scope of the privileges recognized by their courts.

(3) Hearsay. [§12.3413]

Hearsay is an out-of-court statement offered to prove its truth. For example, it is hearsay when one eyewitness is asked during her testimony at trial what she was told by another eyewitness who is not present. Because it was not made in open court, it is not subject to cross examination to determine its accuracy and thus is generally excluded at trial. The rule excluding hearsay is riddled with exceptions to cover situations in which hearsay is sufficiently reliable to be admitted. Those exceptions include, among others, any statement made by an opposing party, spontaneous statements made at the time of an exciting event, statements made for medical diagnosis or treatment, and entries in business records made in the ordinary course of business.

(4) Evidence That Is More Prejudicial Than Probative. [§12.3414]

Even though none of the specific exclusionary rules apply, evidence still may be rejected at the discretion of the court when its value is overshadowed by the prejudicial effect it may have on the trier of fact. For example, in a civil fraud action in which a major issue is whether the defendant was married, evidence that he was found guilty of wife abuse will be excluded if there is any other means of proving marital status.

5. Meeting the Burden of Proof. [§12.3500]

The term "burden of proof" encompasses two quite different matters—the burden of producing evidence and the burden of persuading the trier of fact. A party who has either of these burdens on an issue must produce sufficient evidence to meet that burden or the issue will be decided in favor of the opposing party. Usually both burdens fall on the same party, but there are important exceptions.

a. The Burden of Production. [§12.3510]

A party who has the burden of production on an issue must introduce sufficient evidence to enable the trier of fact to find in his or her favor on that issue or else the court, as a matter of law, will decide the issue in favor of the opposing party. This rule has its greatest impact in jury cases, for if the burden of production is not met, the court either will grant a judgment as a matter of law or overturn a jury finding for the party with the burden by granting a renewed motion for judgment as a matter of law. [See **§14.7000–§14.7500** for a complete discussion of the standards applicable to judgment as a matter of law.]

b.   The Burden of Persuasion. [§12.3520]

Even though a party meets its burden of production on an issue, that party will not necessarily prevail on the issue. It then becomes a matter for the trier of fact who not only must evaluate the evidence presented by the party with the burden of production, but must weigh it in light of the evidence presented by the opposing party. The decision is made on the basis of whether the party with the burden of persuasion has met that burden. In the **ordinary civil action** the party with the burden of persuasion on an issue must convince the trier of fact that it is more probable than not that the facts are as that party contends; otherwise the issue must be decided for the opposing party. In criminal cases, the prosecution has the burden of persuading the trier of fact that its contentions are true beyond reasonable doubt. Whenever a case is heard by a jury, the court will instruct the jurors as to the burden of persuasion to be applied.

Illustration. [§12.3521] P sues D for personal injuries allegedly due to D's negligence, an issue on which P has the burden of persuasion. After considerable deliberation, the jury decides that the evidence on negligence equally supports P and D. The jury must find for D, since P has failed to carry the persuasion burden. Had the case for P been only slightly stronger, P would have prevailed.

---

c.   Assignment of Burdens between Parties. [§12.3530]

The issues in any case are divided between those matters essential to the plaintiff's action and those matters which are defenses to be raised only if the defendant wishes to pursue them. [See the discussion of burden of pleading in **§5.4210–§5.4212–1.**] In most circumstances the plaintiff has the burdens of both production and persuasion on issues essential to his or her case, and the defendant must bear both burdens on issues pertaining to defenses.

(1)   Assignment Based on Substantive Policy. [§12.3531]

In most situations the burden of proof is assigned according to substantive policy, that is, which party normally should be expected to bear the loss suffered. Courts do not always agree as to particular issues. Perhaps most notable is the issue of contributory negligence; in a majority of courts this is a defense to be proved by defendant, but in a sizable minority of jurisdictions it is considered an integral part of the plaintiff's case.

(2) Assignment Based on Availability of Proof. [§12.3532]

In some situations one party clearly has an advantage in being able to produce evidence on an issue. In such a case, if it does not otherwise interfere with substantive policy, the burden of proof will be placed on that party. Thus, in contract actions for failure to pay money, the burden of proving payment is placed on the defendant who is likely to have receipts or cancelled checks [see also §5.4211–1].

(3) Splitting Burden of Production from Burden of Persuasion. [§12.3533]

In some situations, both for reasons of policy and the relative access to evidence, the burden of production is placed upon one of the parties and the burden of persuasion on another.

Illustration. [§12.3533–1] In a negligence action in which D has complete control of the instrumentality alleged to have caused P's injury, P may carry the burden of production and avoid a directed verdict by introducing evidence as to D's complete control plus evidence that the injury is not one likely to have occurred without negligence of D. This is the so-called doctrine of res ipsa loquitur. In some jurisdictions, D then has the burden of persuading the trier of fact that the injury occurred without negligence.

---

6. Closing Arguments. [§12.3600]

Closing arguments give each party an opportunity to summarize the evidence and its logical implications. Normally the plaintiff argues first, then the defendant, and finally the plaintiff is given an opportunity to rebut what the defendant has stated. This order is reversed if the defendant has the burden of persuasion on all major issues.

a. Improper Argument. [§12.3610]

In the closing, an attorney is not allowed to argue on the basis of evidence excluded or not presented, nor may the attorney appeal to emotion or prejudice. The following statements constitute improper argument: "My client will starve if he loses this case!" "Give plaintiff the damages you would want if you were the plaintiff." "Suppose I were to tell you that the psychiatrist withheld facts in this case."

*

CHAPTER XIII

SELECTING A TRIER OF FACT

A. TRIERS OF FACT. [§13.0000]

Issues of fact may be determined either by a judge or by a jury. Because of the historic commitment of the American legal system to the jury institution, it will be considered in some detail in this chapter. It should be noted, however, that **most civil trials in the United States are conducted before a judge sitting without a jury.** A trial judge will hear a case without a jury when (a) there is neither a constitutional nor a statutory right to jury trial, (b) when the parties fail to request a jury trial or otherwise waive it by their conduct, or (c) when the parties specifically agree to a non-jury trial.

B. NATURE OF THE JURY. [§13.1000]

The modern jury is the product of many centuries of historical evolution. This background is of considerable importance in understanding contemporary practice.

1. Historical Evolution of the Jury: Witness to Stranger. [§13.1100]

Until the mid-fifteenth century, jurors in England often were selected on the basis of their prior knowledge of the facts and were likely to have witnessed the event in controversy. They were empowered to inform themselves by personal observation and sharing of information. This often entailed direct communication with the parties and witnesses to the execution of documents. In effect, jurors were inquisitors who ascertained the facts and then applied them to the dispute. However, gradual erosion of the power of jurors to inform themselves independently of the courtroom process required the jury to rely on materials presented in open court. The obligation to gather the facts therefore shifted from the jurors to the parties and their counsel.

2. Functions of the Modern Jury. [§13.1200]

The contemporary jury performs three main functions: (a) determining what the facts are; (b) evaluating the facts in terms of the legal consequences formulated by the trial judge in the charge; and (c) presenting the result of its findings in the form of a verdict.

Illustration. [§13.1210] A signs and seals a document that reads as follows: "I promise to convey my farm Blackacre to my son Carl within a reasonable time." Should the conveyance be contested after A's death, it is A's meaning and intent gleaned from the facts as determined by the jury that will give legal effect to the document. Some of these factual issues may be: Which piece of property is Blackacre? Did A mean to include the contiguous tract of land that A purchased a year before his death, which he occasionally called Greenacre? Was Carl the illegitimate son with whom A lived or was he A's legitimate son who also was named Carl? What is a reasonable time within the meaning of the document?

---

3. **Jury Does Not Act as a Fact–Finder on Preliminary Questions. [§13.1300]**

The role of the jury as a fact-finder typically does not extend to factual issues raised by questions of admissibility and exclusion of evidence, claims of privilege, and threshold defenses—including jurisdictional and pleading issues—which have been decided, as they usually are, before the trial on the merits [see **§13.2000**]. The determination of the facts in these contexts is within the province of the trial judge unless he or she chooses to use an advisory jury [see **§13.3400**]. This result appears to be primarily based on pragmatic considerations—it is expensive in terms of time and money to convene a jury simply to determine a jurisdiction question.

Illustration. [§13.1310] In a federal court negligence action, the plaintiff alleges that she suffered personal injuries in the amount of $85,000 as a result of defendant's conduct. On a motion to dismiss for lack of the requisite amount in controversy [see **§2.4000**], the court and not a jury will determine whether the alleged injuries might support the plaintiff's claim that the injuries could be valued at more than $75,000.

---

4. **Weighing Open Court Testimony. [§13.1400]**

Both the philosophy of the adversary system and the requirement of fairness to the parties necessitate that evidence be presented to the trier of fact in open court and under oath. Only if one party introduces evidence in open court can the opposing party hope to meet the evidence by cross-examination or by further clarifying or refuting testimony. It is only through this process that the jury will be able to evaluate the evidence and appraise the credibility of the witnesses in reaching a verdict. [See also the discussion of verdicts in **§14.3000–§14.3530**.]

5. Drawing Inference Chains. [§13.1500]

There are times when the jury must infer the existence or non-existence of an important fact from other facts on which evidence has been presented. For example, it appears that X was in Chicago on July 14, at 5:00 p.m.; the jury may infer that X was not in New York at that time. However, occasionally the evidence supports two or more competing or inconsistent chains of inference. Although some courts have held that when none of the competing inference chains seems more persuasive than the others, a judgment must be directed against the party with the burden of proof because any choice by the jury would involve rank speculation, most courts now permit the jury to choose from among competing reasonable inference chains.

Illustration. [§13.1510] A railroad switchman was found unconscious in a dark railway yard. He died, apparently, from a blow in the back of the head, without regaining consciousness. There were no known eyewitnesses to the fatal event. The railroad advanced the theory that the decedent was murdered; the deceased's estate offered the theory that a mail hook negligently left dangling from the side of a mail car on a passing train struck and killed the decedent. Although the facts seem to support both inference chains equally, the jury will be permitted to render a verdict based on what it feels was the more reasonable set of inferences, and to discard or disbelieve facts inconsistent with its conclusion [*Lavender v. Kurn* (1946)].

C. FUNCTIONS OF THE COURT IN A JURY TRIAL CASE. [§13.2000]

The trial judge has the following duties in a case tried to a jury: (a) deciding all preliminary questions relating to jurisdiction and other procedural matters; (b) screening evidence by determining what propositions require proof, what evidence has the requisite degree of relevance and probative value to be admitted, and whether the evidence is sufficient to support a given proposition;

(c) deciding what issues are judicially noticeable and need not be proven; (d) choosing what rules of substantive law should be applied; (e) instructing the jury as to the rules of substantive law; and (f) selecting the type of verdict to be rendered by the jury. [See the discussion of verdicts in **§14.3000–§14.3530.**]

1. Allocation of Functions Between Judge and Jury. [§13.2100]

Although the general categories "matters of law" and "matters of fact" delineate the respective provinces of judge and jury, this division is imprecise, and the functions of the judge and jury necessarily vary with the nature of the litigation and the rules of the particular jurisdiction.

a. Contract Actions. [§13.2110]

The typical distribution of functions between judge and jury in an action on a written instrument is as follows: The jury decides if a contract exists. The trial judge determines whether or not the contract is ambiguous. When the contract is ambiguous, its meaning is decided by the jury based on evidence introduced by the parties; if the contract is unambiguous, the court interprets and applies its language. In an action on an oral contract, however, the terms will be determined by the jury.

b. Negligence Actions. [§13.2120]

In an action for injuries sustained as a result of D's allegedly negligent driving, factual questions such as whether the driver slowed down approaching an intersection or was maintaining a proper lookout at the time of the accident ordinarily are determined by the jury. But if the trial judge considers the evidence to be so clear that no reasonable person could conclude the driver did slow down or had a proper lookout, the issue may be withdrawn from the jury. [Attacks on the legal sufficiency of the evidence are discussed in **§14.7000–§14.7400.**] Whether the driver had the duty to slow down is a question of law to be determined by the judge, as is defining the general standard of conduct of a reasonably prudent person. The application of the particular standard of conduct—namely, was D driving sufficiently slowly in approaching the intersection to meet the reasonable person test in the circumstances of the case—is ordinarily a jury question.

2. Distribution of Power Between Judge and Jury: Jury Control Mechanisms. [§13.2200]

There has been considerable ambivalence over the centuries concerning the proper distribution of decision-making power between judges and juries. This stems from the tension between the desire to preserve the historic Anglo–American commitment to jury trial and a concern as to the capacity of lay people to find facts accurately and without bias or prejudice. Not surprisingly, therefore, the trial judge enjoys considerable flexibility in exercising his or her functions, and consequently has the ability to circumscribe the jury's freedom of action in a number of significant ways. Consider two examples.

a. Control over Evidence. [§13.2210]

Because of his or her control over the evidence that the jury may consider, the trial judge may well shape the conclusion that the jury ultimately reaches. In fact, the exclusion of certain evidence may so narrow the information available to the trier on a crucial issue that the judge is compelled to withdraw the case from the jury and direct a verdict.

b. Jury Instructions. [§13.2220]

The court may formulate the applicable legal standard in general terms when the court instructs the jury. For example, in the case of a motorist who allegedly fails to slow down at an intersection [see §13.2120], it might simply say that a reasonable person would reduce speed at an intersection. This formulation gives the jury wide latitude to determine whether the defendant acted reasonably under the circumstances. On the other hand, the trial judge might well formulate the standard of care with great specificity. For example, the court might state that a reasonable person would approach the intersection at no more than five miles per hour. If it does so, the jury retains only the prerogative to decide whether the defendant did slow down to that speed.

c. Other Controls on the Jury. [§13.2230]

It should be kept in mind that various procedural mechanisms—including summary judgments, directed verdicts, remittitur and additur, new trials, and judgments notwithstanding the verdict [post-trial motions are discussed in §14.6000–§14.7410]—also enable the judge to maintain control over the jury. Moreover, in some jurisdictions, the trial court judge is permitted to comment on the evidence.

3. Criticism of the Jury System. [§13.2300]

Critics of the jury trial argue that society needs precise standards to guide human conduct, standards that derive from the knowledge that given rules will bind all litigants in all future lawsuits in precisely the same fashion. At best, they argue, the jury system produces ad hoc verdicts that are relevant only to particular cases. Jurors, it is said, often ignore the instructions of the court in reaching their conclusions and tend to be plaintiff-oriented in negligence cases. Furthermore, jurors lack the experience and knowledge necessary to perform their functions properly in highly complex cases. The trial judge, the critics urge, brings to a trial both the requisite expertise and a sense of the community standards derived from sitting in numerous, diversified cases over the years; hence a jury is superfluous. Finally, jury trials are costly and time consuming, both to the litigants and to society.

4. Defense of the Jury System. [§13.2400]

Advocates of jury trial counter that the law must conform its standards to the needs and experience of the community and the jury can perform this function far better than a single, sheltered judge. Moreover, the jury tempers the rigors of the law with a "popular" or "communal" sense of justice and acts as a restraint on the potentially arbitrary action of a governmentally paid judge. Finally, there is the historic commitment to jury trial embodied in constitutional mandates—both state and federal— that trial by jury be "preserved" or retained "inviolate." Supporters of the jury system maintain that these provisions should not be debilitated in the absence of an overriding reason to do so, which would have to take the form of an amendment to the constitutional provision.

D. SOURCE OF THE RIGHT TO A JURY TRIAL. [§13.3000]

There are three sources authorizing jury trial: (1) the common law right preserved in constitutional provisions, both federal and state; (2) a right provided by statute for specified causes of action; and (3) the historic discretion of a court to empanel an advisory jury in certain types of cases.

1. Constitutional Right to Jury Trial in the Federal Courts. [§13.3100]

The Seventh Amendment of the United States Constitution guarantees the right to a jury trial in the federal courts in certain civil actions. It provides:

> "In suits at common law, where the value in controversy shall exceed twenty dollars, the right of trial by jury shall be preserved, and no fact tried by a jury, shall be otherwise re-examined in any Court of the United States, than according to the rules of the common law."

[State constitutional jury trial provisions are discussed in **§13.3600**.]

a. **Scope of the Constitutional Right in the Federal Courts. [§13.3110]**

At the time of the Seventh Amendment's ratification in 1791, judicial proceedings were divided between two systems—the courts of law and the courts of equity. Actions at law carried a right to a jury trial; equitable actions were decided by a judge. Not long thereafter, in many jurisdictions, law and equity courts merged so that a single judge would sit on both types of cases. However, for jury trial purposes, the distinction between law and equity remains. Thus the federal courts have interpreted the Seventh Amendment as preserving the right to jury trial as it existed at law in 1791 [see **§13.4000**].

b. **Jury Trial under the Federal Rules. [§13.3120]**

The Rules Enabling Act [28 USC 2072], under which the Federal Rules were promulgated [see **§4.3330**], mandates that the right of trial by jury be preserved. Accordingly, Rule 38(a) provides that the right "as declared by the Seventh Amendment to the Constitution—or as provided by a federal statute—is preserved to the parties inviolate."

c. **No Right to Non-Jury Trial. [§13.3130]**

There is no constitutional right to have an issue or claim, not covered by the Seventh Amendment, tried in a federal court by a judge sitting without a jury. Thus, it would not be inappropriate for a federal judge to empanel a jury in an equity case. In some states, however, courts have held or implied that there is a right to a non-jury trial in equity cases in their courts.

2. **Analyzing Statutorily Created Rights and the Constitutional Right to Jury Trial. [§13.3200]**

A statute cannot deprive a party of a Seventh Amendment right to a jury trial either expressly or by silence. Similarly, the Seventh Amendment is not restricted to those common law actions that actually existed in 1791. **If a statute establishes a legal right analogous to or in the nature of a common law cause of action, then the right is subject to a constitutional right to a jury trial, even though the precise action may not have existed in 1791**. To determine whether a statute is of such a nature, precedent firmly establishes that the federal court must engage in at least three inquiries: (1) the nature of the action, whether it serves the same function as a known common law action; (2) the relief sought, whether the relief requested is one traditionally offered by common law courts; and (3) whether the statutory proceeding takes place in an Article III court [*Curtis v. Loether* (1974); *Granfinanciera v. Nordberg* (1989)]. Jury trial gener-

355

ally does not extend to other tribunals, such as administrative proceedings. On rare occasions, federal courts may consider other factors as well [see **§13.3500**].

Illustration 1. [§13.3210] P, a black woman, brings an action under the Civil Rights Act of 1968 alleging that D, a white landlord, refused to rent an apartment to her in violation of the Act. The statute authorizes the courts to award both actual and punitive damages as well as injunctive relief but does not expressly provide a right to a jury trial. Because the plaintiff seeks actual and punitive damages (relief traditionally offered by courts of law), as well as injunctive relief, and the cause of action is one to enforce legal rights analogous to rights known at common law, either party is entitled to a jury trial [*Curtis v. Loether* (1974)].

Illustration 2. [§13.3220] A landlord brings an action under a District of Columbia statute establishing a summary procedure for recovering possession of real property by evicting a tenant for non-payment of rent. The summary proceeding serves the same essential function as the common law action of ejectment—to enable a plaintiff to evict a person wrongfully in possession of the premises. Actions of ejectment in 1791 carried the right to a jury trial and therefore the summary proceeding statute cannot destroy that right [*Pernell v. Southall Realty* (1974)].

---

a. The Historical Test. [§13.3230]

Of the three inquiries, the first two, taken together, are known as the "historical test," because they examine how the action historically would have been tried in a pre-merger system [*Tull v. United States* (1987)]. According to the Supreme Court, the second inquiry—characterizing the relief sought—is more important than the first—examining the historical nature of the action [*Chauffeurs, Teamsters & Helpers, Local No. 391 v. Terry* (1990)].

(1) Nature of the Action—Eighteenth Century Analogy. [§13.3231]

The first inquiry—examining the nature of the action—involves comparing the statutory action to actions brought in the pre-merger courts of England in 1791. **If the action was unknown**

in eighteenth century England, the court must look for an analogous cause of action. The historical records do not always afford a clear answer as to which actions were tried by a judge and which actions were tried by a jury in 1791.

Illustration. [§13.3231–1] A, a truck driver, sues B, his labor union, and C, his employer, for breach of a collective bargaining agreement pursuant to the Labor Management Relations Act. A alleges that C breached a collective bargaining agreement and that B subsequently failed to protect the interests of its members. A requests a jury trial. Although a suit against a labor union for violating its duty of fair representation was unknown at common law, a suit for breach of a collective bargaining agreement is very similar to a claim for breach of contract, which is a legal claim. Because the issue of B's breach of the agreement is analogous to an eighteenth century suit at common law, the first inquiry suggests that A's request for a jury trial should be granted [*Chauffeurs, Teamsters & Helpers, Local No. 391 v. Terry* (1990)].

---

(2) Relief Sought. [§13.3232]

The second and more important inquiry is determining whether the relief prayed for would have been sought in a court of law or a court of equity in 1791. If the plaintiff seeks a traditional legal remedy, such as compensatory or punitive damages, then the claim normally will be tried by a jury, even if the plaintiff is also seeking equitable remedies. If only an equitable remedy, such as an injunction, is sought, then there probably will be no right to a jury trial. For instance, a monetary remedy typically is considered legal, and a jury trial right usually will attach to a claim for a monetary award. However, the Supreme Court has stated that monetary relief may be deemed equitable when such relief is restitutionary or intertwined with injunctive relief [*Chauffeurs, Teamsters & Helpers, Local No. 391 v. Terry* (1990)].

Illustration 1. [§13.3232–1] The United States sues D, a real estate developer, for dumping waste on wetlands in violation of the Clean Water Act. The government seeks an injunction against D as well as the imposition of the maximum civil penalties allowable

---

under the Act. D requests a jury trial. The civil penalties are a legal, rather than an equitable, form of relief. D's request will be granted, even though the government also seeks equitable relief [*Tull v. United States* (1987)].

Illustration 2. [§13.3232–2] In *Feltner v. Columbia Pictures Television, Inc.* (1998), the Supreme Court concluded that the Copyright Act did not provide for a jury trial on the question of statutory damages, which are an available remedy in lieu of actual damages. Indeed, the Court seemed to conclude that the statute called for a non-jury trial. Nonetheless, the Court concluded that the Seventh Amendment required a jury trial because statutory damages were a legal remedy and there was a long history of jury availability in copyright damage cases in both England and this country.

b.   Statutory Proceeding. [§13.3240]

The federal courts—e.g., a United States District Court—are created by Congress pursuant to Article III of the Constitution. Additionally, Congress has authority under Article I to create other forums for adjudication, such as administrative proceedings and specialized tribunals. **The type of court is an important factor in analyzing the jury trial right in the context of statutory causes of action.** If the historical test reveals that the action is not legal in character, then there is no right to a jury trial, regardless of the tribunal in which the action is enforced. Even when the action is analogous to a suit at common law, however, if the statute provides for the action to be enforced in a non-Article III forum, then a jury trial might not be required.

(1)   Administrative Proceedings and Specialized Tribunals. [§13.3241]

The federal courts have held that jury trials are incompatible with the policies that underlie the creation of administrative agencies to enforce federal regulatory programs and certain statutory rights. Accordingly, these agencies may employ their own non-jury mechanisms for finding facts and adjudicating disputes [*Atlas Roofing Co. v. OSHRC* (1977)].

Illustration. [§13.3241–1] In a proceeding before the National Labor Relations Board (an administrative agency established under the National Labor Relations Act), P, an employee, seeks reinstatement to his former job and an award of back pay for the time lost following an allegedly wrongful discharge. Even though the tribunal awards monetary relief in the form of back pay in a proceeding that is analogous to a common law tort action, the plaintiff is not entitled to a jury trial.

---

(2) Public Rights. [§13.3242]

Congress may provide for the enforcement of its laws in non-Article III courts without juries **only when the statutory cause of action involves public rights**. The Supreme Court has defined public rights to include actions in which the United States, in its sovereign authority, participates as a party and actions that are closely related to or intertwined with a valid federal regulatory program. [*Atlas Roofing Co. v. OSHRC* (1977)]. A purely private cause of action that is historically legal in character must be triable by a jury; Congress may not deprive parties of a jury trial by limiting enforcement to special forums.

Illustration. [§13.3242–1] P, a bankruptcy trustee, files suit under a federal bankruptcy statute against a corporation, D, to recover what P alleges were fraudulent transfers. The action is referred to a bankruptcy court, and D requests a jury trial under the Seventh Amendment. Even though the bankruptcy court is a specialized tribunal, the action is wholly private in nature and analogous to a suit at common law. Because public rights are not involved, D's request for a jury trial must be granted [*Granfinanciera v. Nordberg* (1989)].

---

3. Actions Brought Against the United States. [§13.3300]

The Seventh Amendment applies only to suits at common law, and at common law there is no right to sue the sovereign. **Thus, there is no constitutional right to a jury trial in an action brought against the United States**. Since the sovereign can dictate the terms under which it will be sued and deny or grant jury trial as it sees fit, the right to a jury trial in an action against the United States exists only when a statute expressly or impliedly so provides. This is not true, however, in actions brought by the United States against a private party.

359

a. Statutory Provision. [§13.3310]

Section 2402 of Title 28 of the United States Code provides that any action brought against the United States shall be tried without a jury. There is an exception for actions brought under Section 1346(a)(1), which provides a right to jury trial in suits for the recovery of taxes allegedly erroneously or illegally assessed or collected under the internal revenue laws.

4. Advisory Jury. [§13.3400]

Historically, suits in equity were not tried to a jury. However, the chancellor had discretion to empanel and submit issues to a jury for an advisory verdict, which he then was free to follow or disregard. **Federal Rule 39(c) preserves this power of the trial court to summon an advisory jury; its exercise is discretionary and essentially is non-reviewable.** Counterparts of this provision exist in most state procedural codes.

a. Role of the Advisory Jury. [§13.3410]

An advisory jury may assist the court on any matter that it is required to decide. Although an occasional opinion has suggested that an advisory jury's findings should be accepted if they are not clearly erroneous, the prevalent view is that the trial judge is free to accept or reject the work of an advisory jury.

Illustration. [§13.3411] P, in a diversity action, alleges that she is a citizen of Ohio and that defendant is a citizen of New York. Defendant objects to the subject matter jurisdiction of the court, alleging that plaintiff temporarily moved her residence from New York to Ohio specifically to invoke federal diversity jurisdiction. The court may empanel an advisory jury to help resolve the disputed jurisdictional facts.

---

b. When an Advisory Jury Should Be Summoned. [§13.3420]

Courts disagree as to when an advisory jury should be used. Some limit it to cases not triable to a jury as a matter of right; others hold that the judge may summon an advisory jury at his or her discretion in any type of action. The latter view empowers the court to summon an advisory jury even though the parties have waived their right to a jury trial that was otherwise available.

> **Illustration. [§13.3421]** In an automobile negligence action, P and D waive their right to a jury trial by failing to make a timely demand. The trial judge, considering the action appropriate for jury guidance, asks the consent of the parties to empanel an advisory jury. D consents to a trial of all issues by an advisory jury but P only consents to jury trial of the damage issues. At the discretion of the trial judge, an advisory jury may be empanelled for the trial of any or all the issues in the case.

6. **Jury Competence and the Complexity Exception. [§13.3500]**

An unresolved issue is whether the right to a jury trial can be denied because the litigation is so complex as to be beyond the competence of a jury. In a footnote in one case, the Supreme Court suggested that courts should consider the ability of juries in assessing the applicability of the Seventh Amendment [*Ross v. Bernhard* (1970)]. Lower courts generally refused to engage in such an inquiry, and **the Supreme Court never has clarified whether a complexity exception to the Seventh Amendment actually exists.** However, the Court did consider the relative abilities of judges and juries in ruling that the Seventh Amendment did not require the jury to decide the particular issue of the scope of the patent grant. Because the historical inquiry did not reveal whether patent documents were construed by a judge or a jury, the Court looked to functional considerations, concluding that the highly technical task of construing the patent documents was best left in the hands of the trial judge. It is unclear whether the Supreme Court's decision permits lower courts to apply the same reasoning in other contexts [*Markman v. Westview Instruments, Inc.* (1996)].

7. **Constitutional Right to Jury Trial in State Courts. [§13.3600]**

The Seventh Amendment has not been applied to the states through the Fourteenth Amendment, and thus there is no federal constitutional mandate compelling the states to provide a right to a jury trial in civil cases. However, most state constitutions guarantee a right to a jury trial, although the scope of that right varies from jurisdiction to jurisdiction, often depending upon when a particular state joined the Union or last revised its constitution.

E. DETERMINING WHEN THE JURY TRIAL RIGHT IS AVAILABLE: PROBLEMS OF LAW AND EQUITY. [§13.4000]

Some of the most difficult jury trial problems relate to determining when the right is available, particularly when legal and equitable matters are involved in the same action.

1. Effect of the Separation Between Law and Equity. [§13.4100]

Traditionally, equity took jurisdiction over a cause of action only when the law courts would not provide an adequate remedy. Initially, this meant that **jurisdiction existed only in those limited classes of cases for which no effective legal relief was available.** However, these restrictions imposed on equity jurisdiction frequently resulted in two lawsuits.

a. The "Clean–Up" Doctrine. [§13.4110]

Policy considerations favoring the avoidance of two lawsuits when a case had both legal and equitable aspects led to the development by the equity courts of the so-called "clean-up" doctrine. **Once equity determined that it had jurisdiction over an action, the chancellor would decide all aspects of the controversy, both legal and equitable, thereby obviating the need for two proceedings**. But the doctrine would be applied only when the legal aspects of the case were subordinate to the equitable issues.

Illustration. [§13.4111] Plaintiff, a lower riparian landowner, sought to enjoin defendant, an upper riparian landowner, from unreasonably diverting water from the stream that flowed through their respective properties. At the same time plaintiff sought damages for destruction of her crops, which had resulted from defendant's alleged unreasonable use of the water. The chancellor first would determine whether to grant injunctive relief and then, invoking the clean-up doctrine, would decide whether to award damages.

---

b. Equitable Defenses. [§13.4120]

Just as the equity courts took cognizance of some matters ordinarily restricted to the law courts, the law courts broadened their jurisdictional base by hearing defenses traditionally limited to the equity courts. Accordingly, by the eighteenth century, defenses such as duress, fraud, and illegality were being heard by the law courts, despite their equitable origins.

> **Illustration: Defense of Fraud. [§13.4121]** A, who owes money to B on a contract for the sale of goods, believes the agreement was procured fraudulently. Until equitable defenses became cognizable in the law courts, A could not interpose fraud as a defense to B's action in assumpsit at law. A was required to ask an equity court to cancel the contract and to obtain a temporary injunction against the assumpsit action until the chancellor had determined the issue of fraud. On a finding of fraud, the law action was permanently enjoined. If the chancellor found no fraud, he or she would dismiss the equity suit, dissolve the injunction, and the legal action would proceed.

2. **Modern Application of Jury Trial Provisions. [§13.4200]**

   Because of this ongoing exchange of business between the law and equity systems, it became increasingly difficult to determine which issues remained exclusively within the jurisdiction of each of the two systems. Newly created statutory causes of action and modifications of the existing causes further clouded the question of when a party was entitled to a trial by jury. As indicated in **§13.3200–§13.3222,** more recent cases suggest that the right to a jury trial in the federal courts no longer is to be determined solely in terms of whether the action was so triable in 1791. Rather, the jury trial mandate embraces both what was, and what is analogous to, a common law right.

3. **Procedural Reforms. [§13.4300]**

   Two procedural reforms added to the difficulty of determining when a party was entitled to a jury trial: (a) the merger of law and equity, and (b) the liberalized joinder of claims. Prior to these changes, equity, despite its expanding jurisdiction, continued to dismiss suitors whenever an adequate remedy existed at law. Conversely, plaintiffs were barred from raising equitable claims in the law courts even though they were related to the very occurrence upon which their legal cause of action was based. Thus, the dual system continued to produce multiple litigation, which in turn frequently produced injustice.

   a. **Merger of Law and Equity. [§13.4310]**

      The merger of law and equity came to the state courts with the enactment of the Field Code in New York in 1848, which served as a model for many other states. The Code made all appropriate remedies—legal and equitable—available in a single action so that the plaintiff's choice of court no longer was constrained by the choice of relief. Additionally, the Code liberalized joinder, which enabled a party to join multiple claims in the same action. The merger of law and equity did not take place in the federal courts until 1938, with the adoption of the Federal Rules. However, the same federal judges sat on both the law and equity sides of the court even prior to merger and certain statutes reduced the negative effects of the bifurcated system. The Rules introduced sweeping reforms, including the unification of law and equity and liberalized joinder provisions that were even broader in scope than those found in the codes.

b. Problems Created in Determining the Availability of Jury Trial. [§13.4320]

These procedural reforms raised new questions about the availability of jury trial. If the plaintiff had a claim for both legal and equitable relief, did he or she forfeit the right to jury trial by joining them in a single action? Was the plaintiff's right to a jury trial defeated if the defendant raised an equitable defense? Even if the court attempted to determine the jury trial right issue by issue, rather than by looking at the character of the entire controversy, problems remained. Although some issues clearly were legal, and thus triable to a jury, and others clearly were equitable, and not so triable, some issues were relevant to both legal and equitable claims. The problem was complicated by the fact that a prior judicial ruling on the common issue for purposes of the equitable claim would estop relitigation of the issue as it related to the legal claim [see **§16.2320**]. The effect was to destroy the right to have a jury decide the issue as part of the adjudication of the legal claim. As a result, the sequence in which the claims were decided could control the right to a jury trial.

Illustration. [§13.4321] P, the beneficiary of an insurance policy, sues D, the insurance company, to recover the face amount of the policy. D counterclaims for cancellation or rescission of the instrument (equitable remedies) on the ground that the policy was procured fraudulently. Since the facts bearing on the validity of the policy are common to both claims, a prior disposition of the counterclaim would estop plaintiff from relitigating the issue of fraud before a jury on her breach of contract claim.

---

4. New Tests to Determine The Right to Jury Trial. [§13.4400]

Courts have developed a variety of tests to determine when a right to a jury exists in a case in which both legal and equitable elements are present. Some judges have looked to the essence of the action, or the nature of the relief (i.e., legal or equitable) sought; other courts simply have decided the legal claims first; still others have taken the position that since plaintiff had an option at common law as to which remedy to pursue first, plaintiff's choice regarding the remedy must control.

a.   **Resolution of the Problem in the Federal Courts. [§13.4410]**

Uncertainty as to the right to a jury trial in complex cases in the federal courts was ended by *Beacon Theatres, Inc. v. Westover* (1959). *Beacon* established a three-part inquiry rooted in the federal policy favoring jury trials. Each case must be evaluated issue by issue: those issues that are purely equitable are determined by the trial judge; those issues that are purely legal are tried by a jury; and those issues that are common to both the legal and equitable claims must be tried first before a jury. In a subsequent case, the Supreme Court went further and held that even if a legal issue is raised in a predominantly equitable proceeding, the legal issue must be tried to a jury, thereby cutting the heart out of the clean-up doctrine [*Dairy Queen, Inc. v. Wood* (1962)] [see **§13.4110**].

Illustration. [§13.4411] P, a buyer, claims that D has failed to perform a contract to sell Blackacre, and P alternatively seeks specific performance and damages—both legal and equitable relief. P has the right to have a jury determine the breach of contract issue and, if the jury finds for P, assess damages. The court, without a jury, thereafter may determine whether to grant the equitable remedy of specific performance.

Illustration. [§13.4412] Insurer, while processing the insured's claim for reimbursement for hospital expenses, discovers that the latter failed to disclose vital medical information in the insurance application. Insurer sues to rescind the contract on the ground of misrepresentation—an equitable claim—and the insured counterclaims for recovery under the policy—a legal claim. The insured is entitled to a jury trial on the issues of fraud and damages. If the jury determines that there was fraud in the procurement of the policy, then the court can decide whether or not to rescind the contract.

Illustration. [§13.4413] Every day D trespasses on P's land. Although no tangible damage is done, the trespass interferes with P's peaceful enjoyment of the property. P sues to enjoin this continuing trespass—an equitable remedy—and for token money damages—a legal remedy. Despite the centrality of the equity claim and the triviality of the legal claim, a jury must ascertain the facts relating to the trespasses.

b. **Division of Issues and Order of Trial. [§13.4420]**

The federal jury decides the purely legal issues and any issues common to the legal and equitable claims; the court decides any purely equitable issues. **The court must submit a legal issue to the jury even if it is purely "incidental" to the equitable ones**. The sequence of the trial must be so arranged that any issues common to both the legal and equitable claims are tried to the jury before the court attempts to pass on the equitable aspects without the jury. In ruling on the equitable issues, the court is bound by the jury's findings.

Illustration. [§13.4421] A manufacturer sues to restrain a patent holder from interfering with his business relations and from harassing him by threat of suit, as well as for a declaratory judgment that the patents are invalid and thus not infringed. The patent holder counterclaims for patent infringement, fraud, and antitrust violations; he demands a jury trial on the issues of fact raised by the counterclaim. The issues of validity and infringement are common to the plaintiff's claim for equitable relief and the defendant's counterclaim for damages; consequently, they must be tried first to a jury. The jury will assess the amount of damages if it finds for the defendant. If it finds against the defendant, the court will decide whether to award the plaintiff equitable relief.

c. **Legal Claim Raised by Equitable Procedure. [§13.4430]**

Historically, certain types of suits could only be maintained in equity, despite the type of relief sought. The most important of these procedures are class actions, suits in interpleader, shareholder derivative suits, and declaratory judgment actions. Under the modern federal decisions, the judge decides all of the factual issues relating to the procedural elements of the equitable proceeding, such as whether to certify a class. All legal claims raised in the action, however, must be tried to a jury [*Ross v. Bernard* (1970)].

Illustration. [§13.4431] A widow, suing to collect on an insurance policy, demands a jury trial. The insurer denies its liability on the policy and asserts that other persons who are potential claimants to the monies due under the policy must be interpleaded. If the court allows the interpleader device to be used, a question that the court will decide without the jury's assistance, the widow is entitled to a jury trial on the legal issues that are in controversy.

---

d. Application of Federal Jury Decisions by State Courts. [§13.4440]

Because the Seventh Amendment has not been extended to the state courts [see **§13.3600**], they are not bound by federal jury trial decisions such as *Beacon Theatres* and the cases following it. Few states have chosen to follow the federal precedents; rather, they continue to apply their own tests, such as the clean-up doctrine [see **§13.4110**].

F. FEDERAL–STATE COURT RELATIONSHIP. [§13.5000]

Questions as to the availability of a jury trial arise when a federally created right is litigated in a state court and, conversely, when a state created right is asserted in a federal court [see generally Chapter Four].

1. Adjudication of Federal Rights in State Courts. [§13.5100]

The state courts must grant a jury trial in proceedings involving federally created causes of action whenever there is a strong federal policy in favor of a jury trial in the particular case.

Illustration. [§13.5110] P, a railroad worker, brings an action under the Federal Employers' Liability Act in a state court for damages for personal injuries and the railroad defends on the ground that P released it from liability. P contends the release was obtained fraudulently. Even though issues of fraud ordinarily are

---

> decided by the judge in the courts of the state in which the action was brought, the strong federal policy in favor of jury trial in FELA actions must be honored by the state court and the issue will be submitted to the jury.

2. Adjudication of State Rights in a Federal Court. [§13.5200]

Questions as to the right to a jury trial in a federal diversity action arise in three situations: (a) state law denies a jury trial but the Seventh Amendment requires it; (b) state law denies a jury trial but federal law customarily grants a jury trial; and (c) state law grants a jury trial but federal law denies that right. **In each of these situations, federal jury trial notions control**. Even though the underlying claim derives from state law, its characterization as legal or equitable is determined by federal law.

> **Illustration. [§13.5210]** P, in an action based on diversity, seeks a declaratory judgment of his non-liability to D, a lawyer, under an allegedly fraudulently procured contingent-fee contract. Although state law declares that the issue of fraud in the procurement is an equitable matter and thus is triable to a judge, the federal court's characterization of fraud as a legal issue compels its submission to the jury.

> **Illustration. [§13.5220]** In a federal diversity action to recover damages for personal injuries, it appears as a matter of law that the plaintiff is guilty of contributory negligence. Even though the state constitution provides that issues of contributory negligence must be tried to the jury no matter how clear the evidence appears to be, the federal court may direct a verdict for the defendant and thus withdraw the issue from the jury. Similarly, federal law controls the quantum of evidence that must be produced before the issue will be submitted to the jury.

G. PROCEDURE FOR OBTAINING A JURY TRIAL. [§13.6000]

The sections that follow describe the procedure for securing a jury trial in the federal courts. The practice is similar in most states.

1. Right Determined From Pleadings. [§13.6100]

In determining whether the right to a jury trial exists, the court looks at all of the pleadings—claims, defenses, counterclaims, and third-party pleadings; neither a party's characterization of the claim in the prayer for relief nor the form of the complaint is determinative of the jury trial right. However, a party is master of his or her claim to the extent of seeking only equitable or legal relief, even though alternative forms of relief may be available.

Illustration. [§13.6110] P, who cast her complaint in ambiguous, but apparently equitable, terms, seeks injunctive relief against future infringements of her patent as well as an accounting of D's profits arising from past infringements. Because P's allegations of injury suggest a legal cause of action for some money damages, D's request for a jury trial should be granted.

---

2. Requirement of Demand. [§13.6200]

Under Federal Rule 38(b) and various state provisions, if a right to jury trial exists, **the party wishing to exercise that right must formally demand a jury trial.** If no party requests a jury trial, the court, on its own motion, may convene an advisory jury [see **§13.3400**]. An action can be tried to a jury even though no right exists if the parties consent thereto. Furthermore, if no right to a jury trial exists but a demand has been made and a jury empanelled without objection, the jury's verdict is binding.

a. Demand Must Be Timely and in Writing. [§13.6210]

A party waives the right to a jury trial if a timely, written demand is not submitted as prescribed in Federal Rule 38(b). There is no prescribed form for the demand, however, which can be made in the pleadings or by a separate motion.

b. Service of Demand. [§13.6220]

The demand must be served on all parties to the proceeding. Once a demand has been served, the other parties are entitled to rely on it and need not independently ask for a jury trial. However, the plaintiff cannot rely on a demand made by the defendant or a third-party defendant for a jury trial on the third-party claim; the plaintiff must assert a timely demand that some or all of the issues in the main action be tried to a jury.

c. Specification of Issues for Jury Trial. [§13.6230]

In the demand for jury trial, the party must specify the issues it wishes to try to a jury [see Federal Rule 38(c)]. A party is entitled to request a jury trial on some or all of the issues to which the jury trial right attaches. A general demand for a jury trial that does not specify issues for submission to the jury will result in a jury trial of all issues to which the right applies. If the demanding party specifies particular issues, however, the non-demanding party may request, or the judge may order, trial by jury of those issues not specifically requested by the party who made the initial demand.

d. Withdrawal of Demand. [§13.6240]

Pursuant to Federal Rule 38(d), a proper demand cannot be withdrawn without the consent of all parties.

e. Demand in Removed Cases. [§13.6250]

A proper jury trial demand in an action commenced in a state court survives removal and a party who has complied with state law need not demand a jury trial again after removal. However, the federal court may order, and, if the non-demanding party requests, should order, that a request be made specifying the jury triable issues.

f. Time for Demand. [§13.6260]

In the federal courts, a demand must be made within 10 days of the last pleading directed to the issue on which jury trial is sought [see Federal Rule 38(b)].

Illustration. [§13.6261] P, a seller, brings an action against D, a buyer-retailer, for breach of a contractual agreement to pay for goods on shipment. D answers and counterclaims that P did not honor his agreement to ship the goods on a predetermined day. P replies that the tardy shipment was excusable. D serves a demand for a jury trial less than ten days after P's reply, but more than ten days after D's original answer. The jury trial demand extends only to the issues raised by the counterclaim and reply that were not earlier raised by P's original complaint and D's original answer. Jury trial on those earlier issues has been waived by the failure to make a timely demand.

---

g. Issues Raised in Amended and Supplemental Pleadings. [§13.6270]

Whenever a new issue is raised by an amended or supplemental pleading, a timely demand for a jury trial may be made within 10

days thereafter. When, however, an amendment occurs after a general jury trial demand has been made, no new demand is required. Moreover, whenever a new party is joined in the action, he or she is entitled to make a timely demand. But simply interposing an amended pleading that does not raise a new jury triable issue will not revive a jury trial right if that right has been waived by a failure to make a timely demand.

3. Waiver of Jury Trial Right. [§13.6300]

The right to a jury trial may be waived by failing to serve a timely and proper demand, by conduct suggesting an intent to waive, or by agreement of the parties [see Federal Rule 38(d)].

Illustration. [§13.6310] The parties to a contract agree that should any issue arise under the agreement that leads to litigation, they will waive their right to a trial by jury. This waiver usually will be honored by the courts.

H. COMPOSITION OF THE JURY. [§13.7000]

In order to assure that the jury consists of impartial members of the community, the procedural system of all jurisdictions pays considerable attention to the process of selecting its members. Jury selection in Federal courts is governed by Federal Rule 47, with reference to statutory requirements.

1. Requirements for Jury Duty. [§13.7100]

In the federal courts, a juror must be a United States citizen, eighteen years of age or older, literate and fluent in English, mentally and physically capable of service, and must not be under criminal charges or have a record of a criminal conviction. In the state courts, the factors vary but often include citizenship and residence within the state, property ownership, payment of taxes, and good health.

2. Procedure for Selecting a Panel of Jurors. [§13.7200]

The jury is supposed to represent a randomly selected cross-section of the community. To achieve this objective, courts have developed various procedures for assembling lists of potential jurors from various registers such as voting lists, property tax records, telephone directories or by compiling names referred by individuals known for their sense of civic responsibility (although the legitimacy of this procedure is doubtful).

Certain groups are sometimes exempted from jury duty such as lawyers, members of the armed forces, police and fire department personnel, public officers, and those who live outside the geographic area of the court. An exemption will not apply unless it is claimed by the individual when called to serve.

3. Systematic Exclusion and Discrimination Prohibited. [§13.7300]

It is unconstitutional to exclude automatically any group of citizens, such as women or wage earners, from the list of people eligible for jury service. On the other hand, the selection of a special or "blue ribbon" jury composed of people of higher than average intelligence or with special expertise has been upheld in the federal courts.

a. Challenge to the Jury Panel. [§13.7310]

A party may challenge the composition of the entire panel—a challenge to the array—if it does not meet constitutional or statutory requirements. For example, the systematic exclusion from the jury list of low income people or members of a certain ethnic group would be grounds for a challenge to the array.

4. Selection of Jurors for a Particular Case. [§13.7400]

In order to choose qualified jurors, a series of questions are asked of each prospective juror in a process known as the voir dire examination. In some jurisdictions the trial judge will conduct the examination, permitting the parties to ask supplementary questions; alternatively, the court may permit the parties' attorneys to conduct the examination, reserving the right to disallow or ask additional questions. The voir dire is designed to expose a juror's lack of qualification or his or her bias. The responses to the questions, therefore, furnish the attorneys with information enabling them to decide intelligently whether to challenge a particular juror.

a. Typical Voir Dire Questions. [§13.7410]

Examples of questions typically asked on a voir dire examination are: Do you have any personal knowledge of the facts of the case? Have you formed any opinion about the controversy? Do you have an affiliation with any insurance company? Have you ever been involved in a similar accident? Do you know or are you related to any of the litigants?

5. Challenges to Individual Jurors. [§13.7500]

There are two types of challenges to individual jurors, sometimes labeled challenges to the polls. They are (1) challenges for cause, and (2) peremptory challenges.

a. **Challenges for Cause. [§13.7510]**

Failure to meet the statutory qualifications for jury duty and evidence of bias or relationship to one of the litigants are grounds for challenging a potential juror for cause. The number of challenges for cause is **unlimited**, and challenges may be exercised by the parties by a timely objection or by the court on its own motion.

b. **Peremptory Challenges. [§13.7520]**

In addition to challenges for cause, each party is entitled to a certain number of peremptory challenges, which permit an attorney to reject a particular juror **without stating a reason**. In federal courts the number of peremptory challenges is provided by statute, 28 U.S.C. §1870. Attorneys will use the peremptory challenge to exclude jurors whom they believe possess attitudes, beliefs, or other characteristics unfavorable to their clients. In the federal courts, the number of peremptory challenges is three for each party, and in the state courts the number ranges between two and six. In multiple party actions, the trial judge generally has discretion to divide the challenges among co-parties or to allow each co-party a full number of peremptory challenges. In the latter situation the court may grant additional peremptory challenges to the opposing party to even the number for both sides of the lawsuit.

(1) **Improper Use of Peremptory Challenges. [§13.7521]**

The Supreme Court has held that it is a violation of the Equal Protection provisions of the Constitution to use peremptory challenges to exclude potential jurors solely on the basis of race or gender. Such action, in state as well as federal courts, is held to be a violation of the potential juror's rights to serve. If a complaining party establishes an inference of discrimination based on race or gender, the court then will require the challenging party to explain what legitimate basis, if any, he or she had for the exclusion and will determine if the challenges are shown to have been justifiable on some basis other than race or gender. [*J.E.B. v. Alabama ex rel. T.B.* (1994)]

6. **Alternate Jurors. [§13.7600]**

The court has discretion to empanel additional jurors. The reason for doing so is to guard against the risk that a prolonged case will end in a mistrial because one or more jurors become unable to continue or are disqualified. The alternate jurors must meet the same qualifications as the regular jurors, and a limited number of additional peremptory challenges are available in connection with the selection of the alternates.

7. Size of Juries. [§13.7700]

Historically, indeed until 1970, the Seventh Amendment guarantee of trial by jury was thought to mean a jury of twelve. In that year, however, the Supreme Court held that a six-person jury in a state criminal proceeding satisfied the Sixth Amendment requirement of trial by jury, which is applied to the states through the Fourteenth Amendment. In the later case of *Colgrove v. Battin* (1973), the Supreme Court upheld a local federal district court rule providing for a six-person jury in civil proceedings. Local rules to this effect have become popular; many states have authorized juries of less than twelve [see **§14.3100**]. Federal Rule 48 permits juries of less than twelve but not less than six. It further provides that a verdict from less than 6 jurors will not be accepted.

8. Requirement of Unanimity. [§13.7800]

A unanimous verdict, like a twelve-person jury, was considered an essential element of the common law trial by jury, and this principle continues to apply in federal civil cases. Thus, under the Federal Rule 48, a verdict must be unanimous unless the parties otherwise agree. In a number of states, however, something less than a unanimous verdict is binding in civil proceedings, typically two-thirds or three-fourths of the jurors. [The advantages of not requiring unanimity are discussed in **§14.3200**.] When less than unanimity is required, the same individual jurors must agree on all the issues in the case.

CHAPTER XIV

INSTRUCTIONS, VERDICTS, AND POST–TRIAL MOTIONS

A. INSTRUCTIONS, VERDICTS, AND POST–TRIAL MOTIONS: SCOPE NOTE. [§14.0000]

This chapter describes that portion of the trial devoted to submitting the case to a judge or jury, the rendition of a verdict or decision, and the various trial court procedures for challenging the sufficiency of a party's case or the trier's verdict or decision.

B. INSTRUCTIONS TO THE JURY. [§14.1000]

The instructions are the means by which the court informs the jury of the substantive law that it must apply in deciding the case and of the procedural rules and regulations governing how the jury is to conduct its deliberations to arrive at a verdict. For example, the jury is instructed on such matters as the burden of persuasion [see **§12.3520**], its obligation to consider evidence only for the purpose for which it was admitted, and the fact that the lawyers' arguments are only arguments and should not be treated as testimony.

1. Timing of Instructions. [§14.1100]

Instructions usually are given at the end of the trial, after the attorneys' closing arguments. It is generally believed that the court, not the lawyers, should have the last word prior to jury deliberations. In a few courts, however, the instructions precede the lawyers' arguments. This procedure is justified on the ground that an argument is far less meaningful if it is made in the abstract, without the jurors having first learned of the law that is to be applied. Federal Rule 51(b)(3) allows the court to instruct the jury any time after trial begins and before the jury is discharged.

2. Source of Instructions. [§14.1200]

The ultimate source of the instructions is the trial judge, who has the duty properly to guide the jury. In nearly every jurisdiction, however, each of

375

the parties is required to prepare a proposed set of instructions, which is submitted to the judge prior to the termination of trial. Often the court and counsel will meet in conference during a break in the trial to discuss the proposed instructions and hopefully to iron out differences among the lawyers and the court as to what instructions are appropriate.

a. Standard Instructions. [§14.1210]

In many jurisdictions certain standard instructions are available covering procedural matters of which every jury is informed. Use of these instructions saves time and energy otherwise needed to draft them. More controversial are standard instructions on matters of substantive law that are often available for use in simple or common tort or contract actions. In a few jurisdictions these instructions are formally approved by the courts and must be utilized if they fit the case. Because standard instructions have been accepted as correct and thus will not result in reversal, and because it requires no time or thought to draft them, courts and lawyers tend to try to use them regardless of the facts of the particular case. This practice deters development of the law, just as did the rigid writ system long ago [see **§1.2110**].

3. Failure to Request or Object to Instructions. [§14.1300]

In many jurisdictions, a party cannot successfully appeal errors in giving or failing to give instructions unless the objections were lodged immediately. This practice allows the trial judge to correct the errors, thus avoiding the cost and delay of an appeal and a subsequent retrial.

a. Exception for Fundamental Errors of Law. [§14.1310]

Fundamental errors of law will be corrected by most appellate courts, even though they were not objected to at trial. Errors of this magnitude must be corrected to preserve public confidence in the judicial system.

Illustration. [§14.1311] P sues for defamation. The issue at trial is whether D's statements about P were true. The court fails to instruct that truth is a defense to the action. Even though D's lawyer did not object to this fundamental error of omission at trial, D's appeal probably will be successful.

---

b. Exception for Erroneous Instruction Actually Given. [§14.1320]

Some states allow an aggrieved party to challenge for the first time on appeal an **erroneous instruction actually given,** although they follow the general rule and bar an appeal for the failure to give an instruction that was not requested. The rationale is that a jury cannot be presumed to have come to an improper conclusion in the absence of an instruction that should have been given; on the other hand, if an improper instruction is given, either the jury followed it and came to the wrong result, or the jury did not follow it and the verdict is tainted by jury misconduct.

4. Manner of Giving Instructions. [§14.1400]

Invariably the trial judge reads the instructions to the jury aloud. The way in which he or she does so often is as important as is the substance itself. The more care a judge takes in presenting the instructions in a meaningful way, the more likely they are to be understood and followed by the jury.

a. Taking Instructions to the Jury Room. [§14.1410]

Most courts do not provide jurors with written copies of the instructions for use during deliberations. The rationale is that jurors should apply all the instructions and not concentrate on only one or two specific matters. However, courts that do permit written instructions to be taken into the jury room argue that it is unrealistic to expect jurors to recall very much of importance about the instructions that have been read to them; without written instructions, the process can become a farce, particularly in complex cases.

b. Requests for Further Instructions. [§14.1420]

During the course of deliberations, the jurors may desire to rehear an instruction or to ask for additional instructions on matters they do not understand. When the jurors seek such additional help, the judge and the attorneys for all the parties are summoned. The trial judge cannot reinstruct the jury out of the presence of the lawyers, who must have an opportunity to object to instructions given or to propose additional instructions in response to the jury's request.

5. Harmless Versus Prejudicial Errors. [§14.1500]

An erroneous or misleading instruction will not lead to a reversal if the mistake is trivial or if all the instructions, taken together, are not misleading. Under Federal Rule 61 and its state counterparts, harmless errors are never grounds for granting a new trial, setting aside a verdict, or disturbing a judgment. But if an erroneous instruction is likely to have led to an improper result, the case will be reversed for prejudicial error.

377

Illustration 1: Harmless Error. [§14.1510] In a slander case, the court improperly refused to instruct that truth is an absolute defense. Nevertheless, the jury found for the defendant. The error was harmless and the plaintiff cannot successfully invoke it on appeal.

Illustration 2: Prejudicial Error. [§14.1520] P sued D, alleging a breach of contract. D denied the existence of a contract or, in the alternative, that there was any breach, and produced evidence to support both denials. The court instructed: "The only issue in this case is whether or not D faithfully carried out the obligations of her contract." D can successfully appeal a verdict for P since the instruction assumed a fact at issue—the existence of the contract—and implied that the court did not believe D's evidence on the issue.

C. JUDGE'S COMMENTING ON EVIDENCE. [§14.2000]

In many jurisdictions, the judge may not comment on the evidence or in any way indicate to the jury his or her opinion of the case.

1. Exceptions. [§14.2100]

In federal and in some state courts, the trial judge is permitted to give an impartial summary of the evidence. Only in a very few courts may the judge state his or her opinion.

Illustration. [§14.2110] After completing her instructions on the law, the trial judge states: "On the crucial point in this case, that of D's negligence, you have only the testimony of two witnesses: one who favors P and the other D. You must decide which is giving the more accurate version of what occurred. In my mind, P's witness is highly credible. He gave a straightforward account, whereas D's witness was hesitant and uncertain and therefore not believable." The first part of the statement is a valid summary; the second portion, however, records the court's own opinion and would be held improper in most jurisdictions.

D. JURY VERDICTS. [§14.3000]

After being instructed, the jury retires to deliberate and render its verdict. In theory, this entails rational, collegial discussion and evaluation of the evidence and the application of the judge's instructions to it.

1. Number of Jurors. [§14.3100]

Jurisdictions vary as to the number of jurors who sit on civil juries. Traditionally, the number has been twelve, but there is a strong trend toward reducing the number, usually to six. **Those who favor smaller juries argue that it reduces costs** without interfering seriously with the ability to obtain a jury that represents a cross-section of the community. By reducing the number of jurors, fewer potential jurors need be summoned. Costs are thereby reduced since every such potential juror, whether or not he or she actually serves, is paid a daily juror's fee plus an allowance for travel to and from court.

2. Majority Versus Unanimity. [§14.3200]

Jurisdictions vary widely as to the number of jurors required to agree on a verdict. Traditionally, courts required unanimity, but an increasing number now require the concurrence of only three-quarters or two-thirds of the jurors. Elimination of unanimity has the obvious advantage of substantially **reducing the number of "hung juries"**—juries that cannot reach a verdict. A hung jury results in an order for a new trial, which is costly to the courts as well as to the parties. The requirement of unanimity also affects **trial tactics,** particularly those of a defendant whose case is weak but whose financial position is much stronger than that of the plaintiff. Such a defendant may direct much of the case toward one apparently sympathetic juror, hoping that the one juror will hold out for defendant during deliberations, causing a hung jury. In such a situation, the plaintiff may be forced into a settlement rather than go forward with a costly new trial. Even if the new trial takes place, the defendant will have an advantage in cases involving large awards, because the longer defendant can avoid payment, the longer the defendant has the use of any money it ultimately is ordered to pay.

3. Types of Verdicts. [§14.3300]

There are **three different types** of verdicts: a general verdict, a general verdict with interrogatories, and a special verdict. In a general verdict, the jury is only asked to announce which party wins, and if it is the plaintiff, the extent of the relief to be awarded. In a general verdict with interrogatories, the jury renders a general verdict but, in addition, must answer specific questions regarding important aspects of the case. In a special verdict, the jury answers specific factual inquiries but renders no general verdict; the court renders the ultimate verdict on the basis of the jury's answers.

a. General Verdicts: Advantages and Disadvantages. [§14.3310]

The chief advantage of a general verdict is **simplicity:** a trial judge need not be concerned with the very difficult task of drafting specific questions for the jury to answer. Moreover, it puts great trust in the overall common sense of jurors. The trial judge, and subsequently the appellate judges, can only assume that the jury considered every aspect of the case as required by the instructions. The jury thus is free to decide the case from its overall impression of the evidence, apart from legal technicalities or even outmoded legal doctrines, which, if strictly adhered to, could result in injustice. This power of the jury to **"do justice in spite of the law"** is reinforced by rules that prohibit jurors from impeaching their own verdicts on the basis of what occurred during their deliberations [see **§14.4100**]. Because of its advantages, the general verdict is utilized in the vast majority of cases.

The perceived disadvantage of a general verdict is the jury's ability to decide the case on its overall impression of the evidence. Thus what many see as the value of the general verdict is viewed as its chief drawback to others. The general verdict opens the way for arbitrary decisions based solely on emotion. Jurors are free to ignore carefully considered legal doctrines, which, if they become outmoded or are otherwise unsatisfactory, should be changed by rational processes. General verdicts tend to encourage lawsuits by persons whose cases are weak from a legal standpoint but have a strong emotional appeal. Furthermore, these verdicts have an additional disadvantage, unlike verdicts that involve no interrogatories, in that they provide no means for ascertaining how a jury decided specific issues, which might be helpful in avoiding an unnecessary retrial.

Illustration. [§14.3311] D raised two defenses to P's claim and at trial the parties submitted conflicting evidence on both. The court instructed the jury properly on all matters except as to one of the defenses, regarding which the judge erred substantially in favor of D. The jury brought in a general verdict for D, and P appealed on the basis of the erroneous instruction. P's appeal will be successful

---

even if, in fact, the jury relied solely on the defense upon which the instructions were proper. Had the court asked the jury to answer interrogatories regarding each defense, it would have been clear that the tainted instruction did not affect the result, and the decision would have been upheld.

b. **General Verdicts With Interrogatories: Advantages and Disadvantages. [§14.3320]**

The general verdict with interrogatories preserves much of the value of the general verdict, yet at the same time it ensures that the jury properly considered vital aspects of the evidence by requiring the jury to **articulate specific factual findings** as well as its overall impression. This is particularly useful in cases in which the facts are relatively simple but strong emotional factors are present.

One disadvantage of the use of interrogatories to supplement a general verdict is the **difficulty in drafting unambiguous questions.** When the questions are very general, such as those that ask only whether a party was negligent, the job is fairly simple. But when the questions relate to detailed facts, courts have encountered a surprising amount of trouble. Because ambiguous questions can result in successful appeals, many courts have been discouraged from using them. A second disadvantage is the **erosion of confidence in the judicial process** engendered when the answers to specific interrogatories are inconsistent with each other or with the general verdict. Although there are rules for handling these situations [see **§14.3322–§14.3330**], they cannot assuage the feelings of losing parties whose faith in the jury system often is eroded.

Illustration. [§14.3321] P is involved in an automobile accident, rendering him a hopeless cripple. D is a wealthy corporation that could easily afford a large verdict. However, substantial evidence supports D's argument that P's injuries resulted primarily from P's own negligence. To avoid a result based solely on the jury's pity for P, the court could require the jury to supplement a general verdict by answering specific questions regarding P's own negligence.

(1) **Answers Inconsistent with General Verdict. [§14.3322]**

If a jury renders a general verdict inconsistent with answers to interrogatories, the answers, not the verdict, control. The court can accept the answers or, in its discretion, request the jury to reconsider the verdict and answers, or grant a new trial.

Illustration. [§14.3322–1] In an auto accident case, the jury renders a general verdict for P, but an answer to an interrogatory states that the accident was due solely to P's negligence. The court's options include entering a verdict for D based on the answers to the interrogatories, sending the jury back for further deliberation, or ordering a new trial.

---

(2) Answers Inconsistent with One Another. [§14.3323]

If an answer to an interrogatory is not only inconsistent with a general verdict but also is inconsistent with the answer to another interrogatory, the court has no choice but to order a new trial.

(3) Attempts to Harmonize Answers. [§14.3324]

Courts make every effort to harmonize the answers to interrogatories with each other and with the general verdict. Technical or trivial inconsistencies are therefore disregarded.

c. Special Verdicts: Advantages and Disadvantages. [§14.3330]

One of the chief advantages of the special verdict is that it guides the jury as to what must be decided. This is particularly important in complex cases in which jurors otherwise simply might not understand what they are supposed to do. Furthermore, the special verdict **virtually eliminates determinations** based on emotion, because the jurors never give an overall verdict stating which of the parties they believe should prevail.

The special verdict challenges the court, with the aid of the parties, to draft **unambiguous questions** covering every aspect of the case issue by issue. This has proved to be very difficult in practice. Often a question will contain a latent ambiguity or assume the existence of a fact in dispute. The difficulty may not be discovered until the verdict has been rendered. Sometimes the jury will see the problem and request further instructions. This puts the court in the difficult position of trying to correct a question in a way that will not prejudice future deliberations by implying which of the parties should prevail. In a number of cases, improperly drafted questions have necessitated a new trial. Furthermore, the same **problem of**

inconsistent findings that may arise in the case of a general verdict with interrogatories [see **§14.3320**] also may arise when a special verdict is utilized.

(1) Failure to Submit a Vital Interrogatory. [§14.3331]

Sometimes the court and the parties become so enmeshed in drafting specific questions that they fail to request or submit any question at all on one of the issues in the case. Courts have adopted a practical rule to cover this situation: the **right to a jury trial** on the omitted issue is **held to be waived** and the trial judge decides it. Of course, a trial judge commits reversible error if he or she refuses a request by one of the parties to submit a question to the jury when a decision on that issue could have affected the result in the case.

4. Jury Confinement. [§14.3400]

During the early history of the jury in England, the jurors, once selected, were sequestered and kept in the custody of the bailiff until their verdict was rendered and they were discharged by the judge. This practice has been abandoned except for highly publicized criminal proceedings. Indeed, the more common practice of keeping the jurors sequestered once they have retired to deliberate also has been discontinued in most instances, although the trial judge retains the power to order their confinement in appropriate cases. Normally jurors are permitted to return to their homes in the evening and during long breaks in the proceedings, but are ordered not to discuss the case with anyone or to read or listen to media reports of the case.

5. Manner of Returning Verdicts. [§14.3500]

When the jury arrives at a verdict, it so informs the bailiff who in turn notifies the judge and the attorneys to appear in court. When all are assembled, the foreman of the jury either announces the verdict orally or hands it in writing to the judge who reads it aloud or asks the clerk to do so.

a. Sealed Verdicts. [§14.3510]

If the jurors arrive at a verdict at a time inconvenient for assembling the judge and the attorneys—for example, late in the evening—many courts permit the jury to place its written verdict in a sealed envelope and hand it to the clerk or other designated official. The jurors are then free to leave but they must reappear at a time designated for opening the envelope. The formal rendering of the verdict takes place

383

when the envelope is opened and the verdict is announced in the presence of the judge, the jurors, and the attorneys.

b. Polling the Jury. [§14.3520]

In most jurisdictions, a party has the right to poll the jury after the verdict by asking each juror, one by one, if he or she agrees with the verdict as announced. This assures the losing party that the announced verdict reflects the consensus of the required number of jurors.

c. Handling Inconsistent or Deficient Verdicts. [§14.3530]

A verdict may be **internally inconsistent** [see §14.4350], or it may be **externally inconsistent** in that a poll shows that a requisite number of jurors do not support it. The court, in its discretion, may either declare a mistrial and order a new trial or may attempt to rectify the problem by asking the jurors to engage in further deliberations. The choice often is not easy. A new trial is costly to the court and the parties. On the other hand, further deliberations may result in coercion of dissenting jurors by the majority. The danger of coercion is greatest when the dissenters initially agreed to the announced verdict but gave a different view when polled in open court.

E. JURY MISCONDUCT. [§14.4000]

Unfortunately, the complexity of a case or the judge's instructions and natural human emotions occasionally prevent a jury from acting in the dispassionate and rational way envisioned by the system.

1. Juror Affidavits as Proof of Misconduct. [§14.4100]

In many jurisdictions, affidavits or testimony of jurors may not be used to upset a verdict. The standard cliche is that **a juror may not impeach his or her own verdict.** This policy stems from the belief that jury secrecy is essential to reasoned deliberation, and necessary to protect jurors from being pressured by losing parties after the verdict is announced.

a. Exception: Iowa Rule. [§14.4110]

An increasing number of courts now apply the so-called Iowa rule, which distinguishes between extrinsic and intrinsic misconduct by a jury, allowing juror or third-party affidavits or testimony to reexamine verdicts allegedly arrived at as a result of extrinsic misconduct. **Extrinsic misconduct** involves overt activity not directly related to a juror's thought processes in deciding an issue. **Intrinsic misconduct** involves a juror's thought processes and, unlike extrinsic misconduct, can be known for certain only by each individual juror. The reasons for an individual's decision on a factual point always are subjective, and no verdict could stand if any jury room statement could be used as evidence that individual jurors did not fairly evaluate the evidence.

Illustration 1: Extrinsic Misconduct. [§14.4111] During a trial in an auto accident case several jurors make an unauthorized visit to the scene of the accident to check distances, roadbed conditions, driver visibility, and other physical facts. The visit amounts to extrinsic misconduct, which can be the subject of juror affidavits under the Iowa rule.

Illustration 2: Intrinsic Misconduct. [§14.4112] Testimony of one of D's major witnesses, a member of a racial minority, is discounted by the jurors as untrue, and a verdict is rendered in favor of P on a vote of eleven to one. The one juror who voted for D submits an affidavit stating that the failure to believe D's witness resulted from bias and prejudice as evidenced by racial slurs during the course of deliberations. The misconduct is intrinsic and the juror's affidavit will not be considered under the Iowa rule.

---

b. Exception: Local Rules. [§14.4120]

Individual jurisdictions vary with respect to the use of juror affidavits. In a few courts juror affidavits are accepted regardless of the nature of the misconduct. In some courts jurors' affidavits are proper to show that the verdict was arrived at by chance methods [see §14.4350].

2. Non–Juror Affidavits as Proof of Misconduct. [§14.4200]

In any jurisdiction, a non-juror may testify to alleged jury misconduct that he or she witnessed, such as out-of-court conversations with parties or counsel.

a. Exception. [§14.4210]

A non-juror's testimony is **inadmissible** if it is based solely on statements made to him or her by a juror. This is true whether the juror's statements related to intrinsic or extrinsic matters.

3. **Forms of Jury Misconduct. [§14.4300]**

The jury may misbehave in a variety of ways. There often is a difference of views as to whether particular conduct constitutes misconduct and what the consequences should be.

a. **Deliberate Concealment of Facts on Voir Dire. [§14.4310]**

If a juror, when questioned as to his or her fitness to serve on a jury, deliberately conceals or misrepresents a material fact that could have affected the verdict, the verdict must be set aside.

b. **Inadvertent Concealment. [§14.4320]**

Courts have split on whether a verdict should be set aside because a juror mistakenly concealed or misrepresented a relevant fact; some courts say it is the duty of the judge and the attorneys to ask questions that will not be misunderstood.

Illustration. [§14.4321] In an auto accident case, the prospective jurors are asked: "Have you ever been involved in litigation involving an auto accident?" Three jurors, who were involved in cases that were settled before trial, answer "No," believing that "litigation" refers only to an actual trial. Courts divide on whether this constitutes misconduct.

---

c. **Holding Conversations with Litigants, Attorneys, or Witnesses. [§14.4330]**

A juror must not converse with any participants in the case during the trial. Some courts will set aside a verdict even when the conversation does not involve the case, although the judge generally has discretion in such situations.

d. **Receipt of Unauthorized Evidence. [§14.4340]**

A verdict is subject to challenge if the jurors consider matters not introduced into evidence at trial. During the trial, attorneys have no way of addressing such unauthorized information, which may be very misleading, prejudicial, or entirely inaccurate.

Illustration 1. [§14.4341] During the trial of an auto accident case, several jurors make an unauthorized visit to the scene of the collision and later, during the deliberations, report their findings. Unknown to the jurors, substantial construction work has significantly altered the roadway since the accident occurred. Under these circumstances, the court is likely to set the verdict aside.

Illustration 2. [§14.4342] P sued D for personal injuries allegedly incurred through D's negligent operation of a wrecking crane. D's lengthy uncontradicted testimony as to how the crane operated tended to show that D had not been negligent. During deliberations, X, one of the jurors, stated that he had once been a crane operator and the crane did not work the way D had testified. X went on to give a detailed explanation of what he knew about the operation of such machinery. Later on, Y another juror, analyzed D's testimony in detail, pointing out that if the cab was outfitted as other witnesses had described, D's analysis of how the crane operated was logically implausible, since it would have been difficult for D to have made the movements he said were routine. After a verdict in favor of P, D moves to set aside the verdict on the basis of the misconduct of jurors X and Y. The court will be likely to set aside the verdict because of X's statements. Such **"testimony" by a juror** is highly improper because he or she is not subject to cross-examination by counsel. However, Y's conduct is not improper. A line, albeit a somewhat imperfect one, must be drawn between jurors' "testimony" as to facts, and jurors' evaluation of testimony in light of their general knowledge and experience.

e. Chance and Quotient Verdicts. [§14.4350]

Obviously, it is improper for a jury to arrive at its verdict by the flip of a coin or other arbitrary methods. It also is improper to compute the amount of a verdict by adding each juror's damage figures and dividing by the number of jurors. This process may be appropriate to obtain a starting amount for purposes of deliberation, but not as a final compromise when the jury cannot otherwise agree. A quotient may not reflect the position of any juror; it may not even be a fair average, since some jurors may artificially inflate or deflate their own figures based upon their assumptions as to what other jurors may do. Furthermore, a quotient verdict may mask the fact that many of the jurors favor a verdict for the defendant and hence voted no award at all.

f.   Inconsistent Verdicts. [§14.4360]

If a jury renders verdicts that are internally inconsistent, they may be set aside. A verdict that itself is proper may contain additional statements from the jury indicating that the jury did not understand its functions, and the court must exercise its discretion to determine whether the verdict should stand, or be set aside, or whether the jurors should be sent back for further deliberations [see §14.3530].

Illustration 1: Internally Inconsistent Verdicts. [§14.4361] P's action is based on D's negligence. D counterclaims, alleging that P was negligent. Both P and D allege contributory negligence as a defense to the actions against them. The jury finds for P on the claim and for D on the counterclaim. The verdict must be set aside, for if both P and D are negligent, neither can recover (assuming that they are not in a comparative negligence jurisdiction).

Illustration 2: Additional Statements. [§14.4362] The jury finds for P and assesses damages at $5,000, but recommends that the award "be given to the Red Cross." The court must determine whether this gratuitous recommendation indicates that the jury did not properly decide the case.

F.   FINDINGS AND CONCLUSIONS IN NON–JURY CASES. [§14.5000]

Federal Rule 52 is typical of the law in almost every jurisdiction in requiring the trial judge to accompany the decision with formal findings of fact and conclusions of law in non-jury cases. Since no instructions are given in non-jury cases, such findings and conclusions are necessary to ensure that the trial judge **applied the appropriate law** and also **to clarify what issues were decided** for purposes of review on appeal and the application of res judicata and collateral estoppel. [For the standard of appellant review of facts found by the trial judge, see **§15.3320–§15.3330**.]

G. ATTACKS ON VERDICTS AND JUDGMENTS. [§14.6000]

Even though a consistent verdict is rendered, the case is not necessarily concluded at the trial court level. The verdict may be attacked by motions for a new trial, for judgment notwithstanding the verdict (now called the renewed motion for a judgment as a matter of law in federal practice), for relief from judgment, or by an independent suit. These strategies, except for judgment notwithstanding the verdict, are considered in the sections that follow. Motions for a judgment notwithstanding the verdict, like nonsuits and motions for directed verdict, basically are attacks on the sufficiency of the evidence. [These attacks are considered in **§14.7000**.]

1. Trial Judge's Discretion to Grant New Trial. [§14.6100]

Within a specified number of days after the entry of judgment, and upon the motion of one of the parties or upon his or her own initiative, the trial judge may grant a new trial. [See Federal Rule 59 giving a party 10 days to make the motion]. The new trial may be as to all or any of the parties, or on all or part of the issues of fact or law. If the case was tried without a jury, the court simply may open the judgment, receive additional evidence, amend the findings and conclusions, and enter a new judgment.

a. Partial New Trial. [§14.6110]

If it is clear that the error or misconduct relates solely to one claim or defense, or to one issue, such as the amount of damages, the court may order a partial new trial in order to save time and expense. If the effect of the error cannot be pinpointed, however, a new trial on all the issues may be granted.

Illustration. [§14.6111] In a case involving a bizarre accident, the jury reluctantly finds D liable. The amount of damages awarded P is unjustly low. Since the verdict involves an apparent jury compromise, it would be unsound for the trial judge to order a new trial on damages alone.

---

b. Partial New Trial and the Right to Jury Trial. [§14.6120]

Some commentators and a few judges have disapproved of partial new trials on the ground that they intrude on the right to trial by jury. This view is held particularly by persons who believe that jurors should be permitted to decide each case based on their impression of

389

all the evidence and that jury compromises among claims or between damages and liability are appropriate and inevitable. Thus, any error taints the entire case and can be cured only by a new trial on all issues.

2. Limitations on Discretion. [§14.6200]

Errors or misconduct that do not significantly affect the outcome, or errors considered waived because the aggrieved party failed to make timely objection, are not a sufficient basis for a new trial. To grant a new trial for harmless error is an **abuse of discretion.** On the other hand, errors that would result in reversal on appeal seem to demand a new trial. To deny the new trial would be to force a litigant needlessly to pay the costs of an appeal.

3. Grounds for New Trial. [§14.6300]

Many jurisdictions have enacted statutes listing the acceptable grounds for a motion for a new trial, usually covering those discussed below. Other jurisdictions and the Federal Rules do not enumerate specific grounds. When the statutes are specific, the question arises whether the trial judge nonetheless may grant a new trial **"in the interests of justice."** Some argue that this gives the trial judge an absolute and unassailable veto over any jury verdict with which he or she disagrees. Others maintain that a catch-all interpretation is important because only the trial judge can evaluate all the nuances of the actual litigation.

a. Irregularity in the Proceedings of Court, Jury, or Adverse Party. [§14.6310]

A new trial may be granted due to misconduct by the judge in coercing counsel, witnesses, or the jury, or in ruling incorrectly on evidence or other motions. Counsel may provide grounds for a new trial by improper argument to the jury or other improper conduct during trial.

Illustration. [§14.6311] A drunken jury and a sleepy judge listen to an abrasive attorney's argument berating the integrity of the opposition's key witness, although no evidence has been introduced in support of the defamation. This demonstrates three forms of irregularity, each justifying a new trial.

---

b. Excusable Lack of Preparation for Trial. [§14.6320]

In the ordinary case a losing party cannot obtain a new trial merely because his or her attorney was not properly prepared. Lack of preparation is a ground for a new trial, however, when it is due directly to deception by the opposing party or lawyer or when it involves newly discovered evidence that due diligence would not have uncovered in time for trial. Even then, a new trial is appropriate only if the new evidence is likely to change the outcome.

Illustration 1: Opponent's Deception. [§14.6321] In a contest over a will, the wife of the deceased at the time of his death seeks to recover the part of the estate left "to my wife." The opposing party conceals until trial the fact that the deceased previously was married in another state under another name, and that it is this "wife" who was intended to inherit. The second wife's counsel, misled and unprepared, is unable to undertake research and prepare a defense. If a continuance is not granted, a new trial should be.

Illustration 2: Undiscovered Evidence. [§14.6322] A case involves an accident to which there appears to be only one witness, who is favorable to D. The day after the verdict for D, P learns that there is another witness who has been in hiding and whose account will strongly support P's case. A new trial should be granted.

---

c.   **Errors of Law at Trial. [§14.6330]**

The trial judge, by granting a new trial, may **correct his or her own errors,** thus avoiding a reversal on appeal. Errors of law occur most frequently **in rulings on evidence** and in **instructions to the jury.** The moving party usually may seek relief only on the basis of errors to which timely objections were made. The allows the trial judge to consider and correct his or her errors. If no objection was made, an error of law must be fundamental and serious or it will be deemed to have been waived.

Illustration. [§14.6331] P sues D for injuries received in an auto accident. During trial P introduces, without objection, evidence that D is insured for any amount that P might recover up to $20,000. A verdict for P is rendered in the amount of $20,000. D moves for a new trial, citing the introduction of the irrelevant, highly prejudicial

---

evidence regarding insurance. In many courts the motion would be denied due to D's failure to object at the time the evidence was introduced. On the other hand, some judges have been swayed by the fact that even if a timely objection had been made, a new trial would have been required, since corrective action in the form of an admonition to the jury to disregard such highly prejudicial evidence could not have been effective as a practical matter.

d. Jury Decision against Weight of Evidence. [§14.6340]

A trial judge has the power to grant a new trial when a jury verdict is manifestly against the weight of the evidence. It is not sufficient that the judge merely disagrees with the jury's decision; the verdict generally must result from a **serious error in judgment.** It is important to recognize that the court has considerable discretion in making this decision; the judge must consider the expense of a new trial and the fact that an order for a new trial may result in a forced settlement.

Illustration. [§14.6341] P sues D for serious injuries received when P was struck by D's truck. At trial, P produces but one witness, X, an alcoholic, whose testimony, though often incoherent and self-contradictory, could support P's theory that the accident was due to D's negligence. D produces five coherent, independent witnesses who testify that P's injuries were the sole result of P's own inadvertence. The jury enters a verdict for P for a large amount. The trial judge, in her discretion, may properly set the verdict aside as against the weight of the evidence and order a new trial. At a new trial, P produces X and three additional independent witnesses who support P's version of the facts. D puts on the same witnesses who testified at the first trial. The new jury also finds for P. Even though the trial judge, on balance, believes the version put forth by D's witnesses, the judge cannot properly order a new trial; it is the right of the jury to decide between conflicting testimony that could logically support a verdict for either party.

4. Conditional New Trial. [§14.6400]

The judge may grant one party's motion for a new trial, subject to the other party's compliance with a condition. If the other party complies, the new trial becomes unnecessary.

a. Additur and Remittitur. [§14.6410]

The most common condition involves **an increase or decrease in the damages awarded** by the jury when the amount is manifestly against the weight of the evidence. An increase of an insufficient award is called **additur;** a decrease in excessive damages is called **remittitur.** Both additur and remittitur are valuable methods of adjusting the amount of a verdict that otherwise is untainted by error; they are superior, in a practical sense, to a costly new trial that tends to favor wealthy as opposed to worthy litigants.

(1) Remittitur. [§14.6411]

In remittitur the plaintiff must elect either to accept a lesser amount of damages than that awarded by the jury or to allow defendant's motion for a new trial to be granted. The smaller amount is one adjudged by the court to be reasonable damages for the case, based on the evidence.

(2) Additur. [§14.6412]

In additur the defendant has the option of permitting an increase in the amount of damages awarded to plaintiff by the jury or of allowing plaintiff's motion for a new trial to be granted. The increased amount is determined by the court to be reasonable in light of the evidence.

(3) Additur, Remittitur, and the Right to Trial by Jury. [§14.6413]

In 1935, the United States Supreme Court, in a five to four decision, determined that in the federal courts additur is unconstitutional under the Seventh Amendment right to trial by jury [*Dimick v. Schiedt* (1935)]. The rationale is that additur eliminates the plaintiff's right to a jury trial because the court and not the jury has set the amount of damages. The defendant, of course, has no similar complaint, since he or she may refuse the increase and obtain a new trial. One would think that remittitur would be subject to a similar objection, since the defendant loses the right to a jury award of damages if the plaintiff accepts the reduced amount set by the court. The Supreme Court distinguished the remittitur situation, however, on the ground that there were common law precedents establishing remittitur as a part of the jury trial process in England at the time that the Seventh Amendment was adopted. No similar precedents for additur existed. This highly technical distinction has been severely criticized and there is considerable doubt whether the Supreme Court would hold additur invalid were the question to arise today. State courts are not bound by the Seventh Amendment and many have approved the use of additur, especially in recent years.

5. Attacks on Judgment. [§14.6500]

Every jurisdiction designates certain limited grounds upon which a trial court can grant relief to a losing party after a judgment has been rendered. Even when such grounds are present, courts have broad discretion in deciding whether or not relief is proper; judges generally are more reluctant to set aside a judgment than they are to grant a new trial before judgment has been entered.

a. Time Limits. [§14.6510]

Rules allowing attacks on a judgment, of which Federal Rule 60(b) is typical, often provide rigid time limits within which a motion must be made. **Usually a year** is allowed on most grounds, but some states allow only **six months.** Furthermore, even if the motion falls within the time limit, it will be denied if it was not presented at the earliest opportunity.

b. Mistake or Inadvertence As Ground for Relief. [§14.6520]

If a party was precluded from an effective trial without substantial fault on its part, the court may set aside a judgment; however, mere negligence of a party or attorney will not suffice. Thus, if a party or a key witness misses a court appearance due to sudden illness or a breakdown in transportation, relief may be available. But if a key witness fails to appear because the attorney negligently failed to subpoena her, relief will be denied.

(1) Exception: Relief from Default. [§14.6521]

When a judgment has been entered by default against a party, courts are far more lenient in granting relief than when a trial has been held, since the opposing party will not suffer as great an inconvenience. Thus, when a default results because a party mislays and forgets about a summons and complaint, or when an attorney's secretary fails to file a response, relief often will be granted.

c. Newly Discovered Evidence. [§14.6530]

Under Federal Rule 60(b) and its state counterparts, to constitute a ground for relief, the evidence **must not have been discoverable** prior to or during trial or in time for a motion for a new trial [see **§14.6320**]. The evidence **must be so vital** that its introduction is **likely to have affected the outcome** of the trial; mere cumulative or impeaching evidence is insufficient. And in most courts, the new evidence must relate to facts that were in existence at the time of trial.

Illustration. [§14.6531] P receives a large sum for permanent paralysis of his legs. Six months after trial, a new surgical technique is developed that will enable P to walk normally. Most courts will not permit a motion by D to set aside the judgment and allow a new trial on damages.

---

d. Fraud. [§14.6540]

All courts permit relief from a judgment that is the result of the extrinsic fraud of the opposing party. Courts split on whether relief is proper to redress so-called intrinsic fraud. Federal Rule 60(b)(3) provides relief in both instances.

(1) Extrinsic Fraud. [§14.6541]

Extrinsic fraud occurs when one party reasonably relies on false promises or other misrepresentations by the opposing party, and thereby loses the ability properly to prosecute or defend the case, or, in other words, fails to get a fair day in court.

Illustration 1. [§14.6541–1] P files suit against D. D's attorney does not want to file an answer within the normal time limit and therefore requests P to grant an extension for six months. P agrees. Within two months, however, and without notice to D, P obtains a default judgment. [See **§11.2430** for a discussion of the ability of a party to obtain a default judgment without notice to the defaulting party.] This judgment has been obtained through extrinsic fraud and will be set aside.

Illustration 2. [§14.6541–2] P, a doctor, tells D that a key witness for D died and that P signed the death certificate. As a result, D does not search for the witness, and P wins the case. Subsequently,

---

D learns that the witness is alive and willing to testify. This is extrinsic fraud and relief will be granted by most courts, provided that D's reliance on P's statements was reasonable under the circumstances.

(2) Intrinsic Fraud. [§14.6542]

Intrinsic fraud involves perjury at trial by a party or the party's agent. Some courts refuse relief on the ground that the very purpose of the trial is to determine who is telling the truth; other courts, including the federal courts under an express provision in Rule 60(b), grant relief for intrinsic fraud.

Illustration. [§14.6542–1] P sues D, a collection agency, for an accounting of moneys collected on behalf of P. W, the employee of D who is in charge of P's account, testifies that only $1,000 has been collected. Accordingly, the court enters judgment for P for $1,000. Subsequently, P learns that W lied, that he had collected $10,000 and has since absconded with the additional $9,000. P moves to set aside the judgment. The case involves intrinsic fraud and courts are divided on whether it constitutes a basis for relief.

e. Other Grounds for Relief from Judgment. [§14.6550]

In addition to excusable mistake, newly discovered evidence, and fraud, certain other special circumstances warrant relief from judgment. Thus, relief is available when a judgment is void for lack of jurisdiction; or when a judgment was satisfied prior to the time it was rendered; or when the judgment is based on another judgment and the latter is reversed or modified (although an overturned precedent is not grounds for relief from a judgment based on that precedent); or when the judgment contains a clerical error so that it does not reflect the decision of the court. Federal Rule 60(b)(6) also allows relief for any other reason justifying relief as determined in the discretion of the court. Normally, rigid time limits do not apply to these latter grounds, but relief will be denied if the aggrieved party fails to act promptly after learning that one of these grounds exists.

> **Illustration. [§14.6551]** The court's decision gives T the use of certain property for ten years, and then requires T to turn the property over to X. By mistake the written judgment says "twenty years" rather than "ten years." At the end of ten years, T's successor refuses to give X the property. On the basis of testimony by the original trial judge as to his actual decision, the written judgment can be amended and the property transferred.

6. Independent Equity Suit to Set Aside Judgment. [§14.6600]

Federal Rule 60 and the rules of many state courts specifically preserve the traditional suit in equity for relief from a judgment. This may permit an aggrieved party to **avoid rigid time limits.** Equitable relief usually is available only when a judgment has been obtained through **extrinsic fraud** or is **void.**

> **Illustration. [§14.6610]** P promises D that P will not pursue his action until D returns from her eighteen-month tour of Africa. P in fact obtains a default judgment as soon as D departs. D learns of the judgment upon her return, but finds that ordinary relief on the basis of fraud must be requested within one year. A timely suit by D in equity often will be available to provide relief.

H. ATTACKS ON THE LEGAL SUFFICIENCY OF EVIDENCE. [§14.7000]

The law recognizes that in some cases the weight of the evidence presented is so one-sided as to require one party to prevail as a matter of law. In those cases, the decision will be taken from the jury by means of a non-suit, directed verdict, or judgment notwithstanding the verdict (known as a judgment n.o.v. for the Latin, non obstante veredicto or j.n.o.v. for short). The nomenclature of the latter two motions has been changed in the federal system. Federal Rule 50 now refers to a directed verdict as a motion for judgment as a matter of law and to a j.n.o.v. as a renewed motion for judgment as a matter of law. Essentially, these motions mean that the court has decided that no reasonable juror could find for the party against whom the motion for judgment has been made.

1. Ending the Action Prior to Trial. [§14.7100]

It is useful to note the similarity between the motions discussed in this chapter and devices discussed in previous chapters, such as motions to dismiss and for judgment on the pleadings [see **§5.8100**] as well as summary judgment motions [see **§11.1000**]. Although the standard for granting the motion is formulated differently for each of these devices, they all serve as screening mechanisms, filtering out cases that do not deserve a full adjudication on the merits.

2. **Nature and Timing of Challenges During Trial. [§14.7200]**

The first opportunity at trial for a party to seek an immediate judgment is just after an opposing party has made its opening statement showing that the other party cannot prevail. Such a challenge is termed a **non-suit**. It ends the case without the moving party's need to present evidence, but it will not necessarily result in an adjudication on the merits, thus permitting a losing plaintiff to bring the matter up in a new action. The next opportunity occurs when the party who first presents evidence, almost always the plaintiff, has not produced sufficient evidence possibly to prevail. That challenge normally is termed a motion for a **directed verdict** (which is called a motion for a judgment as a matter of law in federal courts under Rule 50(b)). If successful it ends the case, saving the moving party the cost and time of presenting evidence. The next opportunity for such a motion is at the end of all of the evidence, when either party may move for a directed verdict (or motion for judgment as a matter of law). If successful, it saves the time necessary to instruct the jury and for it to reach a verdict. Whenever granted, a directed verdict ends the case on the merits. Rarely will a trial court render a decision on a motion for a directed verdict at the end of all the evidence. Instead, the court will allow the case to go to the jury for a decision and thus reserve its ability to enter a judgment notwithstanding the verdict if the party who sought the directed verdict loses the jury decision and renews the motion for judgment in his or her favor. If the jury renders a verdict according to the evidence, nothing else need be done. But if the jury should enter a verdict that cannot be supported by the evidence, then the court may rule on the losing party's motion for a **judgment notwithstanding the verdict** (known as a judgment n.o.v., or, in federal courts, as a renewed motion for judgment as a matter of law). The reason for awaiting a jury verdict is to save considerable time and cost if the trial judge's decision to grant such a motion is overturned. If the court erroneously grants a directed verdict without waiting for a jury decision, the only remedy is a new trial. But if the court waits, then, if the court's decision to grant a judgment n.o.v. is held to be in error, the remedy is simply to reinstate the jury verdict.

3. **Standard for Relief. [§14.7300]**

The traditional standard used to decide these motions is to consider all the evidence in the light most favorable to the party against whom the motion is directed to determine whether the moving party must prevail as a matter of law. All issues of credibility and all conflicts in the evidence are resolved in favor of the nonmoving party. The showing on a motion for non-suit, directed verdict, or judgment n.o.v. must be **far more persuasive** than on a motion for new trial on the ground that the verdict is against the weight of the evidence [see **§14.6340**]. This is understandable since the granting of a motion for a new trial simply results in a retrial before another jury, whereas granting any one of the three motions under discussion results in the entry of a final judgment.

Illustration. [§14.7310] P sues D, alleging a trespass. P presents ten disinterested witnesses, all of excellent reputation, who testify that at the time in question they saw D trespass on P's land. D does not testify and presents as his only witness a derelict who testifies that at the crucial time he was in a bar drinking with D. Because of the conflict in the evidence, the trial judge, even though she does not believe D's witness, cannot hold as a matter of law that P must prevail. Note that the judge could grant a new trial in the event of a verdict for D [see **§14.6340**].

---

4. Relation to Burden of Proof. [§14.7400]

Applying the traditional standard appears to preclude a directed verdict or judgment n.o.v. in favor of the party with the burden of proof, since all testimonial evidence favoring that party would have to be discounted. However, on occasion, courts have **altered the standard** to allow the party with the burden of proof to obtain a directed verdict or judgment n.o.v. upon **evidence that is clear and unchallenged,** and when there is no reason to disbelieve the existing testimony.

Illustration 1: Unchallenged Evidence. [§14.7410] P sues D for breach of contract. D pleads that the parties signed a final settlement agreement. During trial, D, who has the burden of proof on the defense, presents the signed agreement and testimony of independent witnesses that P's signature is genuine. P offers no contradictory evidence. A directed verdict for D is proper.

Illustration 2: Suspect Evidence. [§14.7420] P sues for a tax refund claiming that his trip to Europe was for business purposes. The case turns on P's motive for the trip, and P has the burden of proof. At trial P testifies that the trip was solely for business, not a vacation. Even though no contradictory evidence is offered, a directed verdict is inappropriate. The only direct evidence available is P's statement as to motive, and P is biased. The trier of fact should have the opportunity to decide whether P is telling the truth.

---

5. **Technical Requirements for a Judgment N.O.V. [§14.7500]**

Since a judgment n.o.v. is rendered subsequent to a jury verdict, technically it may seem improper in federal and some state courts in which constitutional jury trial provisions prohibit **"re-examination"** of a jury decision. However, common law precedents provided that a legal question raised prior to a jury decision could be reserved and then resolved after the verdict without violation of the "re-examination prohibition." It therefore is proper to grant a judgment n.o.v. in these jurisdictions. This conception explains the change in nomenclature in the federal system [see **§14.7000**]. The judgment n.o.v. is thought of not so much as a different motion from the directed verdict, but rather as a fresh consideration of that motion; thus, a **renewed** motion for judgment as a matter of law is an apt description of the procedure. In some jurisdictions in order to be subject to renewal, the initial motion must be made after both sides have presented all of their evidence. However, in federal courts, under Federal Rule 50, a motion is renewable so long as it has been made after the opposing party has been fully heard, that is after he or she has rested the case and without any need for the moving party to present his or his evidence. If a directed verdict is not made or not made properly at the right time, then a judgment n.o.v. will be reversed on appeal, even if the verdict is not supported by the evidence. The only option available for the trial judge to correct the error is to order a new trial. If a motion for directed verdict is made at the conclusion of all evidence, but is denied or otherwise not granted, it is automatically treated as reserved for n.o.v. purposes.

a. **Rulings on Dual Motions for New Trial and Judgment N.O.V. [§14.7510]**

A losing party may move for a judgment n.o.v. and, in the alternative, for a new trial. In such a case, the trial judge is required to make a conditional ruling on the motion for a new trial when the judgment n.o.v. is granted, in order to save time in the event that the judgment n.o.v. be reversed on appeal. If the decision on the judgment n.o.v. is appealed, the appellate court also may review the question whether the trial court abused its discretion in conditionally granting or denying the new trial.

*

UNIT FOUR

APPEAL, FORMER ADJUDICATION, AND ENFORCEMENT

*

CHAPTER XV

APPELLATE REVIEW

A. APPELLATE REVIEW: INTRODUCTION. [§15.0000]

Every state has at least one appellate court to review the records of trial court proceedings. The function of an appellate court is to determine whether reversible error has been committed—appellate courts do not retry cases. This chapter will discuss when appeal may be sought, the scope of review, the basic elements of appellate procedure, and the structure of appellate systems.

B. THE PRINCIPLE OF FINALITY. [§15.1000]

At common law and in a large majority of jurisdictions today, an appeal generally is permitted only from a final judgment [see, e.g., 28 USC 1291]. As noted below, however, there are a substantial number of specific limitations and exceptions to the **final judgment rule.**

1. Rationale of the Final Judgment Rule. [§15.1100]

The reasons for the final judgment rule are, first, to prohibit wealthy litigants from destroying their less affluent adversaries before a judgment can be reached by appealing every unfavorable judicial decision during the course of litigation; second, to avoid unnecessary, intermediate appeals on the basis of errors that are rendered moot by the judgment on the merits.

Illustration. [§15.1110] In an action for personal injuries in an auto accident case, P is erroneously permitted to introduce evidence that D carries substantial auto liability insurance. D's immediate appeal of the evidentiary ruling will be rejected, since there has been no final decision in the case. If the jury finds for P and judgment is entered for him, D may then appeal; if D wins in spite of the erroneous ruling, an appeal will not be necessary.

---

2. Interlocutory Appeals—The Minority Rule. [§15.1200]

In a few jurisdictions, notably New York, appeals can be taken from most **interlocutory** (non-final) rulings of the court. Those who support this rule argue that it is justified, first, by the fact that **early resolution** of major errors can avoid a wasteful trial and, second, by the need for definitive decisions on various interlocutory procedural matters to assure uniformity of application throughout a jurisdiction.

Illustration 1: Avoiding Unnecessary Trial. [§15.1210] P sues D, alleging that P suffered injury when D "gave P a vicious, dirty look." D's motion to dismiss for failure to state a claim is erroneously overruled and D appeals. In a jurisdiction that follows the final judgment rule, the appeal would be premature and a trial would ensue, which, if P won, would be set aside. Under the minority rule, the appeal would be allowed and the case thrown out without the cost of a trial.

Illustration 2: Obtaining Procedural Uniformity. [§15.1220] In an action by X against Y Corporation for breach of contract, X successfully seeks a trial court order requiring Y's president to submit to a mental examination for the purpose of ascertaining his capacity to enter into a contract. Y's attorney believes the order to be improper, but Y's president does not want to risk a contempt citation for failing to obey it. Therefore, unless an interlocutory appeal is permitted, the president will submit to the examination, and, whatever the outcome of the case on the merits, the issue normally will not be subject to review since neither of the parties is aggrieved. It thus is possible for different trial courts in a jurisdiction that follows the final judgment rule to take inconsistent positions on a procedural issue for a substantial period of time before the issue will arise in a posture to allow appellate review.

---

3. Defining "Final Judgment." [§15.1300]

The harsh consequences that could result from a rigid application of the final judgment rule are largely ameliorated by defining the term "final judgment" to include orders disposing of distinct parts of a case even though other portions of the case remain to be decided.

a. Cases Involving Multiple Claims or Parties. [§15.1310]

Although a final decision may not be rendered on all of the claims in an entire case, a court order may be final as to one or more of the claims or parties involved. Many jurisdictions follow Federal Rule

54(b) and permit appeal from such an order if the trial judge, upon a determination that there is no reason to delay an appeal, directs the entry of a final judgment as to that order.

Illustration. [§15.1311] Several plaintiffs join to sue D for fraud in connection with a land sale contract. M, who is in the same position as the other plaintiffs, moves unsuccessfully to intervene as an additional plaintiff in the action. Because this decision finally terminates M's relation to the action, and because there is no reason to make M wait until the action is completed as to the other parties, final judgment will be entered against M, who then can immediately appeal the intervention decision.

---

b. **Collateral Orders. [§15.1320]**

Sometimes a case may involve technical or procedural matters not directly related to the substance of the dispute between the parties. An order on a collateral matter may constitute a final decision and, if so, is **generally held to be appealable,** but only if review of the order does not require the appellate court to determine ongoing aspects of the litigation.

Illustration. [§15.1321] In an action by P against D, W, a witness, refuses to obey a court subpoena, is held in contempt of court, and is sentenced to jail. W may appeal; the decision constitutes a final judgment even though the case between P and D is not concluded.

---

c. **Orders Having Irremediable Consequences. [§15.1330]**

Some courts have defined "final judgment" to include decisions that, although not collateral, will have immediate, irremediable consequences unless overturned on an immediate appeal. Because this construction tends to undermine the general finality principle by giving an aggrieved party an argument for an appeal whenever the challenged order is "important," many courts have refused to follow it.

Illustration. [§15.1331] P brings a class action on behalf of more than a million people, each of whom, like P, has only a $5 claim against D. The trial court determines that a class suit is improper

---

and that P can sue only on her own behalf. The nature of the case is such that P cannot possibly afford to continue the suit to recover only $5. In this situation, the order is said to sound the "death knell" of the class action and some courts will find it to be "final" and hence appealable by P. Others, however, will reject this deviation from the finality principle and permit appeal only after P's individual case has been resolved. The "death knell" doctrine has been rejected for the federal courts by the Supreme Court in *Coopers & Lybrand v. Livesay* (1978). The specific holding of *Coopers* was partially superceded by the 1998 amendment to Rule 23 that added subdivision (f) to the rule. This amendment gives the court of appeals discretion in deciding whether to entertain an interlocutory appeal of an order granting or denying class certification. [For further discussion on Rule 23(f), see **§8.1450**.]

4. **Statutory Exceptions to the Finality Rule. [§15.1400]**

Because some non-final orders do have important consequences in situations in which an appeal would be appropriate, legislatures have eroded the final judgment rule by creating specific exceptions to it. Exceptions are of two types: automatic and discretionary.

a. **Automatic Exception When Order Involved Injunctive Relief. [§15.1410]**

Most jurisdictions follow federal law [28 USC 1292(a)], in permitting an **immediate** appeal of any order granting, denying, or modifying an injunction. Such orders are presumed to involve claims of irreparable harm for which a speedy method of appeal is considered very important. It is not entirely clear whether the exception applies to **temporary restraining orders** sought at the outset of the case as well as to requests for injunctions ruled on after the presentation of evidence, although the logic of the exception should encompass all such relief. Indeed, an order involving a restraining order could well be considered appealable as an order having irremediable consequences. [See the discussion under **§15.1330**.] Nevertheless, the courts have evinced a **tendency to construe the statutory categories strictly,** sometimes finding that temporary restraining orders are not considered injunctions, and thus do not fall within the scope of the statute, unless they are in effect for more than 20 days.

(1) **Minority Rule for New Trial Grant. [§15.1411]**

In a few jurisdictions special statutes provide that the trial judge's decision to grant a new trial may be appealed, although it does not constitute a final judgment. The legislators in these jurisdictions argue that the cost of a new trial normally outweighs the cost of an appeal and that a substantial number of new trials are erroneously granted; therefore, interlocutory appeals will save time and expense overall.

b.   Discretionary Exceptions. [§15.1420]

Section 1292(b) of Title 28 of the United States Code was added in 1958 to allow appeals in cases in which a long, costly, and unnecessary trial might be avoided by permitting a relatively inexpensive interlocutory appeal. An appeal is permitted only if the trial court certifies that the issue involves a controlling question of law that should be resolved at once, and the appellate court, in its discretion, accepts the case.

Illustration. [§15.1421] P sues D, alleging violations of the antitrust laws. D asserts that P's allegations, even if true, do not state a legally cognizable claim for relief. The court finds that P's case raises novel theories of relief under the antitrust laws but holds, on balance, that the claim is a valid one. D wants an immediate appeal on the legal issue. D notes that a trial will take six months and cost over $200,000, whereas an appeal will cost $5,000 at most. Given the closeness of the legal question and the possibility that a costly and perhaps useless trial would be required if the theory of relief is rejected by the higher courts, the courts probably will allow D to appeal.

---

5.   The Use of Extraordinary Writs. [§15.1500]

Historically, appellate courts have had the discretionary power to question the propriety of actions of trial judges and have been permitted to issue orders to such judges requiring or prohibiting specific actions. These orders are known as **writs of mandamus and prohibition.** Obviously, if any aggrieved litigant could apply for a writ and automatically obtain a hearing, the principle of finality would be meaningless. Accordingly, there are restrictions on the granting of these writs which have strictly limited their use. Most courts permit recourse to the writs only to **redress an abuse of power or jurisdiction,** as opposed to a mere legal error. Furthermore, writs, which are **discretionary,** are not normally permitted if an ordinary appeal will suffice. Despite these restrictions, however, courts have been rather unpredictable as to when a matter is held to be so serious as to justify extraordinary relief and on occasion have granted a writ even though an appeal would have seemed appropriate under one of the limitations or exceptions to the final judgment rule, discussed in the preceding sections.

Illustration. [§15.1510] P sues D for personal injuries suffered in a motor vehicle collision. The trial court grants P's motion requiring D to submit to a psychiatric examination, designed to show that D has a "negligent driving mentality." D believes the order is improper but wishes to avoid being held in contempt for failing to comply. In some jurisdictions appellate courts will entertain a writ of mandamus to enable D to obtain an immediate decision. Otherwise, such a decision may never be reviewable, since the judgment on the merits of the case, no matter which side prevails, is not tainted by the discovery order.

C. TIMELINESS OF APPEAL. [§15.2000]

Every jurisdiction provides certain time limits within which appeals must be filed. Normally the period runs from the time that the order or judgment was rendered.

1. When a Judgment Is Rendered. [§15.2100]

A major source of difficulty has been in determining when a judgment is rendered. Is it the date the judge's decision is announced in court, or the entry of the decision on the court's docket or minute book, or the filing of a separate document entitled "Judgment"? An error as to which is "the" date of judgment has led many attorneys to file an appeal too late. In the federal courts, Rule 58(b) now provides that, for purposes of appeal, a judgment is effective only when it is **set forth in a separate document and filed in the civil docket of the court.**

2. When Filing Is Timely; Premature Appeals. [§15.2200]

If the first appeal papers are filed after the proper time limit has run, the appeal will be dismissed. But suppose an appeal is prematurely filed after the court announces its judgment in court but before the judgment actually is rendered, and then the time for filing a proper appeal elapses before appellant realizes his or her mistake. Although some courts have dismissed such an appeal, the modern trend is to hold that the premature appeal suffices to satisfy the time requirements of the appeal rule.

D. REVIEWABILITY OF DECISIONS. [§15.3000]

Not every decision made by a lower court during trial is subject to review by an appellate court during the course of an appeal. Various policy reasons dictate that appellate courts not consider certain types of determinations made below. It is important to note that decisions on issues not subject to review in the action in which they are rendered are not given binding effect in subsequent litigation under the principles of collateral estoppel [see **§16.7330**].

1. **Matters Not Appearing on the Record. [§15.3100]**

An appellate court will review only those decisions upon which there is a **lower court record,** properly preserved and presented as the basis for appeal. This means that the attorney who handled the case in the lower court had to have been on guard at the time the challenged ruling was made to ensure that it and the objection to it were properly recorded. Furthermore, the appellant must present the court of appeals with that portion of the record below containing the ruling and the challenge, plus any other parts of the record below necessary for reversal. The appellee can supply additional parts of the record, if necessary, to support an affirmance of the trial court's decision. As an alternative to submitting portions of the trial record itself, appellant and appellee can agree to submit the appeal on a **joint (or "settled") statement** setting forth all the details necessary for appellate court adjudication. The latter is usually a far cheaper method of appeal; it is costly to pay for the transcription and typing of the trial court record itself.

   a. **Reasons for Requiring a Record. [§15.3110]**

If a losing party could appeal on the basis of an alleged ruling of the trial judge that does not appear in the trial court record, the appellate court, before deciding on the merits, frequently would have to conduct its own trial merely to determine what the trial judge did or did not do. This would increase the costs of appeal enormously and would tie up the appellate process to the point of strangulation. Moreover, even if it were clear what the trial judge did or said off the record, the appellate court could not be certain how the judge would have decided had the matter been put to him or her for a formal ruling.

Illustration. [§15.3111] During the course of trial, P intends to offer an important document into evidence. D knows of the document and has indicated that she will object to its admission. At a recess P and D meet informally with the judge to discuss the general progress of the trial, and P raises the question of the admissibility of his document. According to P, the judge clearly indicated that

---

she was disposed not to admit it but she made no final ruling on the issue and no court reporter was present to record the conversation. According to D, the court gave no indication whatsoever as to how she would rule if the issue were to arise. P decides, on the basis of the discussion, not to offer the document into evidence. Subsequently, P loses the case and appeals, arguing as one ground the court's decision as to the admissibility of the document. The appellate court will not review the admissibility issue; it has no way of deciding which version of the facts is correct or how the trial court would have ruled had the issue been squarely placed before it.

b. Introduction of New Evidence on Appeal. [§15.3120]

Except in very few jurisdictions, parties cannot introduce evidence on appeal or rely on evidence that was not introduced during the trial. Frequently, however, courts do permit litigants to make legal arguments to support a judgment, even though the arguments were not presented to the trial court.

Illustration. [§15.3121] P sues D for punitive damages under a special statute dealing with consumer fraud, and a large judgment is returned. On appeal D claims, successfully, that the statute does not apply to P's case. Even if this proves to be true, P may avoid reversal by showing that the court's findings justify punitive damages under a common law rule in force in the jurisdiction.

c. Exception: Remedy for Party Whose Judgment Is Reversed. [§15.3130]

When an appellate court reverses a judgment for a party who was granted relief at the trial level, the court may have a choice to enter judgment for the opposing party or to order a new trial. Many courts permit the appellee to present information demonstrating that a **new trial** rather than the entry of judgment should be ordered.

Illustration. [§15.3131] P brings suit for injuries received when D gave P a vicious, dirty look. D's demurrer is overruled and P prevails on the evidence at trial. D successfully appeals on the ground that the law provides no redress for this claim. P may successfully argue that a new trial should be granted upon a showing that he can establish a prima facie case of assault against D and would have done so had the trial court properly upheld D's demurrer.

2. Issues Decided Against the Winning Party. [§15.3200]

An appellate court will not review unfavorable findings or trial court rulings against the party who prevailed in the action, unless the rulings could have affected the decision, such as limiting the amount of recoverable damages.

Illustration. [§15.3210] P seeks damages from defendant doctor as a result of an unsuccessful operation designed to enable P to use a paralyzed arm. P's claim is in two counts, one for negligence and one for breach of an express contract. The court finds for P on the negligence count but holds that no contract ever was formed. The latter issue is not reviewable, unless P can show that the measure of damages for breach of contract possibly could have allowed a greater award of damages then he received under the tort theory.

3. Review of Facts. [§15.3300]

An appellate court may review a lower court's decision on a motion for judgment as a matter of law (directed verdict or judgment n.o.v.), since the taking of the case from the jury is a question of law. A more difficult question is whether the court should review the grant or denial of a new trial based upon the weight of the evidence. Appellate courts are most reluctant to overturn trial court decisions on this basis. Most jurisdictions avoid the problem when a new trial is granted, because there is no final decision at that point [but see **§15.1411**]. Even when review is permitted, its scope necessarily is restricted by the fact that only the trial judge has seen and heard the witnesses and observed the impact of various aspects of the case on the trier of fact. Only when there is a clear showing that the trial court has **abused its discretion** will its decision be reversed.

a. Review of Conditional New Trial Decisions. [§15.3310]

Appellate courts have been more willing to review trial court decisions granting additur and remittitur than other new trial decisions. Because additur and remittitur can result in the taking of an important segment of a case from the jury, these procedures must carefully be monitored to ensure that they are not misused to subvert the constitutionally based jury trial system.

b. Review of Non–Jury Verdicts. [§15.3320]

Appellate courts have exercised considerable freedom in reviewing non-jury decisions, overturning them when the outcome is **"clearly erroneous"** on the evidence. Unlike cases in which a right to jury trial exists, there is no psychological barrier to review in cases decided by a judge. The "clearly erroneous" rule often has been criticized by legal scholars who believe that the appellate court is in the same position with regard to a trial judge's decision as it is with regard to a jury's decision. The principal argument in support of this position is that the trier of fact, whether judge or jury, must evaluate the credibility of witnesses, a task that an appellate court cannot perform.

c. Review of Decisions Based Solely on Uncontested or Documentary Evidence. [§15.3330]

On occasion, the plaintiff and the defendant will submit their case for decision solely on the basis of documents or uncontested evidence. In such a situation an appellate court is in as good a position to decide the case as is the trial court. As a result, in some jurisdictions the appellate court will not hesitate to overturn a lower court decision when the appellate judges disagree with the trial judge's assessment of the evidence. In federal courts, however, Federal Rule 52(a) was amended specifically to state that findings of fact by the trial judge, "whether based on oral or documentary evidence, shall not be set aside unless clearly erroneous," thus eliminating the power of the appellate courts to overturn the trial judges' findings merely because they would come to a different conclusion when reasonable people could differ.

E. STRUCTURE OF APPELLATE SYSTEMS. [§15.4000]

In some states there is but one appellate court to which all cases must be directed. In many jurisdictions today, however, there are two appellate levels, intermediate appellate courts, to which there is a right to appeal and a higher court that has considerable power to select what cases it will decide. Constitutional and legislative provisions vary. The highest court in a three-tiered system may have discretion about most cases but still may be required to accept certain types of appeals directly from trial court decisions and other appeals from decisions of lower appellate courts.

1. Structure of Federal Court System. [§15.4100]

In the ordinary case, appeals from federal district court decisions are taken to the appropriate federal appeals court, which has no discretion to reject any appropriate appeal [28 USC 1291]. Decisions of the federal appeals court are appealed to the Supreme Court of the United States. However, the Supreme Court now has virtually unlimited power to accept or to reject the appeal [28 USC 1254(1)]. The principal exceptions to this power require the Supreme Court to accept appeals from a judgment by a three-judge district court panel granting or denying injunctive relief [28 USC 1253] and to hear questions certified to it by the federal courts of appeals [28 USC 1254(2)].

2. Standards of Discretion. [§15.4200]

Provisions for discretionary review by the highest court in a jurisdiction do not set forth any standards by which this discretion is to be exercised. Courts, however, have articulated a number of factors that are important in deciding whether or not an appeal should be permitted. They are as follows: (a) will the decision resolve legal conflicts among trial or lower appellate courts? (b) will a decision definitively resolve matters that have great impact on society or a segment thereof? and (c) will a decision overturn an erroneous ruling that otherwise will result in substantial unfairness to an individual litigant?

*

CHAPTER XVI

THE DOCTRINES OF FORMER ADJUDICATION

A. FORMER ADJUDICATION: DEFINITION. [§16.0000]

When a party attempts to relitigate a cause of action or an issue that already has been determined in a previous lawsuit, the opposing party may be entitled to prevent the matter from being raised again. The rules governing the question as to whether the matter is precluded constitute the doctrines of former adjudication.

B. POLICY BEHIND FORMER ADJUDICATION. [§16.1000]

The principles of former adjudication are based on the desire (a) to foster judicial efficiency by avoiding the relitigation of matters that a court already has determined, (b) to prevent the unnecessary vexation of litigants by assuring that they will not be called upon to relitigate the same controversy or issue, and (c) to allow the parties to rely on judgments once they are entered by ensuring that they are final and stable with respect to the parties and issues previously before the court.

C. ASPECTS OF FORMER ADJUDICATION. [§16.2000]

Former adjudication generally may be divided into parts. The first is claim preclusion (or the older term res judicata) that prevents the relitigation of the same cause of action between the same parties. The application of this doctrine when the plaintiff prevails in the first action is called "merger," its effect when the plaintiff loses the first suit is referred to as "bar." The second type of former adjudication is issue preclusion (or the older term collateral estoppel) that precludes the relitigation of an issue that actually was litigated and necessarily determined in a previous lawsuit involving a different cause of action. A closely related doctrine, called **direct estoppel**, arises when an issue that has finally been decided in a case arises again in the same case or, if the first case has not been decided on the merits, in a subsequent case involving the identical cause of action. "Historically, courts used only the terms "res judicata" and "collateral estoppel" and it is only in recent years that many have switched to the more modern terms of "claim and issue preclusion." Even today a number of courts have not made the switch; some even use the term "res judicata" to refer to all types of former adjudication. In this book, however, any reference to "res judicata" will encompass only claim preclusion, that is merger and bar.

Illustration 1: Claim Preclusion (Res Judicata). [§16.2100] P sues for injuries to his chest resulting from an automobile accident. P is successful and receives $10,000 in damages. P then brings a second action for injury to his neck caused by the same accident. A defense of res judicata will succeed. P's cause of action has been merged in the judgment in the first action.

Illustration 2: Issue Preclusion (Collateral Estoppel). [§16.2200] P sues D for the latter's alleged infringement of P's patent. D unsuccessfully defends on the ground that P's patent is invalid. After D has paid the judgment, D procures a license to use P's patent and agrees to pay a royalty. Later P sues D for nonpayment of the royalty and D again asserts the defense of patent invalidity. The issue will not be relitigated since the question of the patent's validity was determined in the first action and D is collaterally estopped from retrying it.

Illustration 3: Direct Estoppel. [§16.2300] P sues his neighbor, D, alleging that D, when backing his car out of his driveway, repeatedly ran over P's prize roses. P seeks damages for the destruction of the roses and an injunction prohibiting D from causing further damage. D denies that he ran over the roses claiming that P himself did the damage. P demands a jury trial. The jury renders a damage verdict for P, thus deciding that D did in fact run over P's flowers. Because actions for injunctions do not go to the jury, it is then up to the judge to decide if an injunction should be granted. In making that determination the judge is directly estopped from finding that P has failed to prove that D did indeed run over P's roses.

1. Related Doctrines. [§16.2400]

Several legal doctrines have effects that are similar to those of former adjudication in that they prevent or affect the relitigation of some portion of a dispute. Care should be taken not to confuse them with issue and claim preclusion principles.

a. Stare Decisis. [§16.2410]

The doctrine of stare decisis provides that, in the absence of special circumstances, a prior determination of a point of law by a court must be followed by that court and by the lower courts within the jurisdiction in subsequent actions. This principle applies even though there is no relationship between the original and subsequent cases or the parties involved in them. However, stare decisis is given a significantly more flexible application than are the rules of former adjudication and prior decisions will be overruled when they are thought erroneous or when societal circumstances have changed.

b. Law of the Case. [§16.2420]

When a legal issue that has been ruled on at some point in a case arises again in the same action, the principle of law of the case provides that unless changed circumstances or clear error is shown, the prior determination will be followed. This rule reflects policies relating to the efficient judicial administration of a single lawsuit (e.g., discouraging lawyers from running to different judges in the same court with the same issue) and therefore does not involve the effect of one lawsuit on subsequent litigation.

c. Election of Remedies. [§16.2430]

In some circumstances a party may have a choice between two or more inconsistent remedies. For example, after the breach of some aspect of a contract the aggrieved party may either treat the contract as nullified and sue for rescission or continue the contract in force and sue for damages. Once the aggrieved party selects a remedy, he or she is bound by that choice; a subsequent change could lead to economic waste and unfairness to the other party. However, courts have not agreed on what constitutes a binding election. In some cases the mere commencement of an action for a particular remedy has been deemed an election of remedies precluding a subsequent suit on the same cause of action for a different remedy, even if the first suit did not result in a judgment on the merits. Under modern practice, which attempts to have disputes determined on their merits, a party may seek inconsistent remedies and is not required to elect between them at the pleading stage [see **§5.3340**]. In addition, restrictions on bringing a second action seeking a different remedy from that requested in an earlier action that was dismissed on the pleadings have been significantly ameliorated.

d. Affirmance. [§16.2440]

Another doctrine that prevents a party from taking inconsistent positions and that is very similar to election of remedies is "affirmance," which is applied primarily in contract disputes. Certain contracts are voidable if they have been procured by fraud. This option is lost, however, if the injured party chooses to affirm the contract by, for example, bringing a lawsuit to enforce it.

e. Estoppel. [§16.2450]

When a person makes a statement of fact that is relied upon by another to the latter's detriment, the speaker often is estopped to deny its truth in subsequent litigation. This rule, often called estoppel in pais, applies both to out-of-court statements and to factual positions taken in a prior lawsuit.

f. Waiver by Failing to Counterclaim. [§16.2460]

In actions brought in the federal courts and in a number of states, if a defendant fails to raise a counterclaim that arises out of the same transaction or occurrence as the main action, the claim is waived and may not be asserted subsequently. [See **§7.1400** for a discussion of compulsory counterclaims.] Although waiver has effects similar to former adjudication, and courts frequently speak of waived claims as being barred by res judicata, the waiver occurs because of the application of a procedural rule of the court, rather than as a result of the specific application of res judicata or collateral estoppel [see **§16.3500**].

g. Former Recovery. [§16.2470]

When two independent tortfeasors contribute separately to a single injury and the injured party sues each tortfeasor separately, the recovery in the second action is limited to the difference between the plaintiff's total damages and the amount recovered in the earlier action. This rule is based on a policy of avoiding double recoveries rather than the considerations underlying former adjudication—judicial economy and finality of judgments.

2. When Former Adjudication Takes Effect. [§16.2500]

The preclusive effect of a decision, for purposes of both claim and issue preclusion, dates from the time the trial court's decision becomes final.

This applies regardless of when, where, or by whom the action was begun. This rule sometimes leads to a "race to judgment" when litigation involving a dispute has been commenced in two courts that might tend toward different views of how to resolve the controversy. This problem is minimized by many courts, which follow the informal practice of staying an action pending the conclusion of a prior lawsuit involving the same subject matter.

Illustration. [§16.2510] A theater sues in Texas for a declaratory judgment that it is not in violation of a contract with a distributor. Subsequently, the distributor persuades a California court to hear its action for breach of the same contract. If the California action is not stayed and the distributor wins a money judgment, that decision will be binding on the Texas courts that will have to enforce it.

D. CLAIM PRECLUSION IN GENERAL. [§16.3000]

When a valid and final judgment on the merits has been rendered, the principle of claim preclusion precludes a subsequent action between the same parties or their privies on the same cause of action, even as to matters that might have been, but were not, raised or litigated in the former case.

1. Policy Behind Claim Preclusion. [§16.3100]

It is in the interests of both the litigants and the judicial system that there be an end to litigation. Once the plaintiff has been provided an opportunity to establish a cause of action and the defendant has had the chance to oppose it, considerations of judicial economy require that the matter be considered closed, even if the parties failed to present favorable facts or legal positions exhaustively or with full vigor.

a. Relationship to Compulsory Joinder. [§16.3110]

The practical effect of the claim preclusion doctrine is to compel the plaintiff to join in the first action all of the claims he or she has against the defendant that are sufficiently related to be considered part of a single cause of action. Thus, although almost all jurisdictions view joinder of claims as permissive only [see **§6.8300**], the threat of claim preclusion acts to create an incentive to join related claims.

b. Relationship to Liberality of Pleading. [§16.3120]

In the federal system and many state systems, strict claim preclusion goes hand in hand with the liberality permitted at the pleading phase of the action. The flexibility offered in stating a claim for relief, in amending pleadings, and in joinder of claims justifies and ameliorates the harsh effects of the claim preclusion doctrine.

c. Reopening the Judgment. [§16.3130]

The safety valve that prevents most of the serious hardships that claim preclusion otherwise might cause is the possibility of reopening the original judgment on the ground of excusable neglect, newly discovered evidence, fraud, or any other appropriate reason. Federal Rule 60(b) and similar state provisions give the rendering court fairly broad power to relieve a party from a prior judgment. Moreover, this power usually is exercised liberally with regard to default judgments and dismissals with prejudice for procedural errors, such as a failure to prosecute, thereby partially mitigating the rule that they are judgments on the merits for prior adjudication doctrine purposes. But there are strict time limits after which relief will not be available.

2. Res Judicata: Basic Principles. [§16.3200]

When a plaintiff prevails in an action, **the doctrine of merger precludes** him or her from **bringing a second suit on the same cause of action.** Thus, the plaintiff cannot split a single cause of action by suing for some damages in one action and other damages in a subsequent suit or by seeking different remedies in separate actions. Conversely, **if the plaintiff loses the first action, he is barred from reasserting the same cause of action in a subsequent proceeding.** Moreover, a defendant may assert a cause of action of her own as a counterclaim or defense, and thereby become precluded from raising it again as a plaintiff. [The meaning of "cause of action" is explored in **§16.4100**.]

Illustration 1: Merger. [§16.3210] D purchases a car from P under an installment agreement with a proviso that all payments are to become due automatically upon the buyer's default. When D fails to make the first payment, P sues and recovers the amount due. D then defaults on subsequent payments and P sues to collect them. Since all the payments became due under the contract when the first suit was brought, P had a single cause of action for the entire amount covered by the installment agreement when D failed to make the first payment. The defense of merger will be upheld and D, in effect, will receive a car for the cost of one installment! Note that if there were no contract provision automatically making all the payments due at the time of the first suit,

---

merger would not apply inasmuch as each payment would constitute a separate cause of action.

Illustration 2: Merger. [§16.3220] A bank contracts to make three loans to P at one-year intervals. If the contract is considered "divisible," P's recovery of damages for a breach of the promise to make the first loan will not operate as a merger to preclude a second suit should the bank fail to make the second loan.

Illustration 3: Bar. [§16.3230] Plaintiff begins a tort action but then abandons it and allows a final judgment on the merits to be rendered in favor of defendant. The doctrine of bar makes this a final adjudication, precluding any subsequent suit, regardless of the fact that no issues actually were litigated or determined [see **§16.4320**].

Illustration 4: Bar. [§16.3240] A is involved in a two-car collision in which his car is totally demolished, and he suffers two broken legs and a punctured lung. A sues B, the driver of the other automobile, for $19,000 for personal injuries and A loses. A then attempts to bring an action for $4,600 for property damage. In most jurisdictions the second suit is barred by the judgment in the first action and will be dismissed because there is only a single cause of action for personal injuries and property damages arising out of the accident [see **§16.4163**]. A fortiori, if A had only sought damages for the broken legs in the first action, A would not be allowed to maintain a second action for the injury to his lung.

3. Res Judicata: Effect on Defendant. [§16.3300]

A defendant is required to raise all of the defenses that are available at the time the cause of action is asserted against her or be barred from asserting them in a later action.

Illustration 1. [§16.3310] In a breach of contract suit brought on a loan agreement, D alleges that there has been no breach and seeks to establish this defense by introducing a supplementary document in which P purportedly agreed to accept a substituted form of performance by D. D loses the action, however, because the second agreement was not signed by P and therefore ran afoul of the Statute of Frauds. Subsequently, D sues for reformation of the loan agreement to add P's signature. The reformation suit will be precluded because reformation was an "equitable defense" that could have been raised in the initial action.

Illustration 2. [§16.3320] A is the owner of a bus that is involved in a collision with a car owned and driven by B. At the time of the accident, A's bus was being driven by C, an employee of A. B sues A for personal injuries alleged to be the result of C's negligence. A defends on the ground that C was not negligent and that B was contributorily negligent. A loses. Subsequently, A learns that C was acting outside the scope of his duties and was on a private errand at the time of the accident. In a suit by B seeking to enforce his judgment against A's property, A is precluded by merger from raising this new defense.

---

a. **Claim Preclusion Effect of a Second Case Denying Effect of or Ignoring a Prior Decision. [§16.3330]**

Suppose that the defendant in a second case fails to raise a defense of claim preclusion based on the first suit or, having raised it, fails to appeal an erroneous decision rejecting it. In a third suit on the same cause, the court is bound by the decision in the second suit. The defense of claim preclusion arising from the first action is treated as barred, just as any other defense that defendant failed to pursue in the earlier action [see **§16.3300**].

4. **Merger or Bar Applied to Counterclaims or Other Claims. [§16.3400]**

When a counterclaim, cross-claim, or third-party claim is asserted, it is treated for claim preclusion purposes in exactly the same fashion as is an original claim. Merger or bar is applied if the counterclaimant, cross-claimant, or third-party claimant prevails or fails on the merits.

> **Illustration 1. [§16.3410]** An auto dealer who has been sued in replevin for wrongfully repossessing the plaintiff's car counterclaims for payment of a note given to pay for the car. Regardless of the outcome on the replevin claim, if the defendant is unsuccessful on the counterclaim, the dealer will be barred from prosecuting any subsequent action to collect on the note.

> **Illustration 2. [§16.3420]** In an action brought by a lender to recover the amount of an unpaid debt, the defendant borrower successfully counterclaimed for the amount of usurious interest charged by plaintiff. Subsequently, the borrower brought an independent suit for twice the amount of the interest under a statute providing for treble damages in such cases. The second suit will be precluded by the doctrine of merger because it is based on the same cause of action as the one asserted in the first counterclaim. The borrower has split that cause of action between the counterclaim in the first action and the claim in the subsequent action.

5. **Failure to Join Counterclaim, Cross–Claim, or Third–Party Claim. [§16.3500]**

As was discussed earlier [see **§16.2460**], Federal Rule 13(a) and similar rules in many states provide that a defendant must assert any counterclaims arising out of the same transaction or occurrence as the plaintiff's claim. The failure to do so results in the waiver of the unasserted claim, preventing the defendant from raising it in a subsequent action. However, a cross-claim or third-party claim is never compulsory and therefore the defendant does not waive it by failing to assert the claim in the first action.

E. PREREQUISITES TO THE APPLICATION OF CLAIM PRECLUSION. [§16.4000]

To establish claim preclusion, it must be found that the prior judgment (1) was **based on the same cause of action** as the one asserted in the second action, (2) **was final,** (3) **was on the merits,** and (4) **involved the same parties or their privies.** It is not a prerequisite to res judicata, however, that the particular claim or defense at issue in the second action actually have been litigated. Merger and bar apply to all claims and defenses that might have been raised with respect to the cause of action involved in the original action. **It is important to remember that claim preclusion is an affirmative defense and**

defendants must assert it or it will be waived.

1. Requirement of Same Cause of Action. [§16.4100]

What constitutes a cause of action is one of the most pervasive and difficult questions in the law. The only certain propositions are (a) claims arising from different transactions or occurrences are distinct causes of action for claim preclusion purposes; and (b) identical complaints raise the same cause of action. But under what circumstances a single event or agreement can give rise to two or more separate causes of action for claim preclusion purposes is unclear. The different tests discussed below have been proposed by various courts and commentators. They represent two schools of thought. One uses a transactional approach; the other focuses on the question whether the primary right or type of injury is the same in both actions. But it must be remembered that no precise formulation commands anything approximating universal acceptance.

a. Same-Transaction Test [§16.4110]

The test that may be most in accord with contemporary procedural notions declares that there is a single cause of action when the rights asserted in both lawsuits arise out of the same transaction or a series of closely connected transactions. A "transaction" is defined pragmatically in terms of whether the facts relating to the two claims are closely connected in time, space, and origin, whether the two claims make a convenient litigation unit, and whether characterizing them as part of the same transaction is consistent with the parties' expectations. The transaction test extends the claim preclusion effect of a judgment more than any of the other tests. Its use is possible only in jurisdictions having procedural systems that permit the assertion of all transactionally related claims in a single action.

b. Destruction-of-Prior–Judgment. [§16.4120]

One test, proposed by New York Court of Appeals Judge (later Justice) Cardozo, is that a claim is precluded by res judicata when "the substance of the rights or interests established in the first action will be destroyed or impaired by the prosecution of the second" [*Schuylkill Fuel Corp. v. B & C Nieberg Realty Corp.* (NY 1929)]. This test can be criticized as begging the question, since the very problem in applying claim preclusion is determining whether a later action would undo a prior judgment or whether it merely would allow the award of relief on a separate cause of action. However, the Cardozo formulation does focus attention on whether the claim preclusion policy favoring stability of judgments is offended by allowing a second suit.

c.   Same-Right-or-Wrong Test. [§16.4130]

Some courts ask whether the two actions involve the infringement of a single right or of separate rights in determining whether res judicata precludes the maintenance of the second suit. This involves an inquiry into whether the type of injury at the root of the two actions is the same—injury to realty, to personal property, to character, or to person are considered separate and thus separate suits can be maintained for each different type of injury. A closely related standard states that the causes of action are the same whenever they proceed from a single wrong or invasion of the plaintiff's rights.

d.   Same–Evidence Test. [§16.4140]

The judicial economy objective underlying claim preclusion would be impaired if a second suit would involve a duplication of the fact-finding effort undertaken in the original action. Consequently, one test frequently employed for determining whether two claims are embraced by the same cause of action asks if they both involve the presentation of substantially the same evidence. Although there is no precise formula for determining how similar the evidentiary presentation in the two actions must be, the evidence certainly need not be absolutely identical. Thus, for example, the same-evidence test would apply to personal injury and property damage claims arising out of a single tort, even though the evidence relating to damages would be different.

e.   Same–Law Test. [§16.4150]

When identical procedural and substantive law is applicable to two claims, arising from a related set of facts, most courts agree that both fall within the same cause of action and claim preclusion may be applied if the two are asserted in separate suits. This test clearly does not cover all situations in which claim preclusion might apply, however, because claims can be part of a single cause of action even though they do not involve the same legal principles.

f.   Tests Applied. [§16.4160]

The meaning of "cause of action" for purposes of claim preclusion can best be understood by considering how the tests just described are applied in particular contexts.

Illustration 1. [§16.4161] A seaman successfully sues his master for failing to take him to the nearest port for treatment of an injury. He then brings a second suit against the master to recover wages for the voyage. Although the two claims could have been joined in one action, they involve different rights and substantially different evidence would be required to prove them. Moreover, only an extremely broad reading of the term transaction would classify the claims as stemming from a single transaction. Thus, they are different causes of action and res judicata should not prevent the second suit.

Illustration 2. [§16.4162] P is injured by a machine when he falls against it after slipping on a greasy spot in D's factory. After losing an action for damages based on the theory that D was negligent in failing to place a safety guard around the machine, P brings suit for the same damages on the ground that D was negligent in allowing the grease spot to remain on the walkway. Because of the identity of evidence pertaining to damages, the fact that both claims arise from the one wrongful infringement of P's right of personal security, and the transactional unity of the slip and fall, only one cause of action exists. Note, however, that the evidence relating to the machine is different from the evidence pertaining to the grease.

Illustration 3. [§16.4163] P is run down by D's car while riding her bicycle. She sues for damages to the bicycle caused by D's negligent operation of his automobile and collects $100. Subsequently, she institutes a second action to recover $100,000 for personal injury damages based on D's negligent driving. Some courts, applying the "primary right" test, conclude that the right to personal integrity is distinct from the right to collect for property damage and therefore they are different causes of action. This approach has its roots in the fact that a trespass to property involved a different form of action at common law than a trespass to the person. Most jurisdictions, however, noting the overlap in evidence relating to the circumstances of the accident and the fact that both injuries resulted from a single transaction event or wrong, would preclude the second action.

Illustration 4. [§16.4164] Although stemming from a single wrong, a husband's claim for personal injury and a wife's claim for loss of consortium are different rights constituting distinct causes of action. This point is made particularly graphic by the fact that the rights are held by different people.

Illustration 5. [§16.4165] A suit for breach of an oral contract that is barred by the Statute of Frauds does not necessarily preclude a subsequent action in quantum meruit. Even though they arise from the same transaction and much of the evidence is the same, the two legal theories can be considered to be separate causes of action on the theory that they involve different rights [*Smith v. Kirkpatrick* (NY 1953)].

Illustration 6. [§16.4166] A successfully brings an action against a street railway alleging that she broke her arm while getting off the car because the motorman prematurely started the vehicle. A then brings a second action against the company claiming damages for a broken leg caused by her falling into a trench left open by the street railway as she was getting off the car. Because of the extremely close relationship between the transactions producing the two injuries, the second action would be precluded if a transaction test were applied.

2. Requirement of Finality. [§16.4200]

Claim preclusion applies only when the prior judgment was based on a final determination of the cause of action asserted in the first action, so that no further issues remained to be decided with respect to that claim.

a. Interlocutory Orders. [§16.4210]

Claim preclusion never attaches to an interlocutory order (e.g., the denial of a summary judgment motion) because such orders are never final. In a similar vein, the grant or denial of a preliminary injunction or a temporary restraining order is not final and will not be given claim preclusive effects as no ruling has been made on the merits of the plaintiff's claim for relief, which typically is a request for a permanent injunction. Finally, claim preclusion does not apply to a conditional judgment until the condition is satisfied and the judgment is final.

Illustration 1. [§16.4211] A trial on defendant's alleged liability for a tort leads to a decision in plaintiff's favor, but the question of damages is deferred for separate trial. Although the first trial concludes the issue of liability, it is not a sufficiently final judgment for claim preclusion purposes as long as the issue of damages, which is part of the cause of action, remains unadjudicated.

Illustration 2. [§16.4212] N joins tort and contract claims in the same lawsuit against O. If a final judgment is rendered on the contract claim, it will be given claim preclusion effect even though the tort claim is still pending. If no final judgment is rendered while a decision on the tort claim is pending, however, there will be no claim preclusion effect.

---

(1) Application to Judgments on Appeal. [§16.4213]

Although courts differ, a judgment generally is final if it conclusively disposes of the lawsuit in the court that rendered it, notwithstanding the fact that an appeal is possible or actually has been taken. Only when a case is reversed is its claim preclusive effect vitiated.

3. Requirement That a Decision Be on the Merits. [§16.4300]

Broadly speaking, a judgment is on the merits if it relates to the validity of the plaintiff's cause of action rather than to technical procedural questions. A summary judgment and a judgment after a trial ending in a verdict are the most common examples of determinations on the merits. A judgment on the merits is a prerequisite to applying claim preclusion because every party has the right to a day in court before a cause of action is deemed finally decided and further litigation proscribed. However, considerations of judicial efficiency have led to an expanded conception of what constitutes a judgment on the merits.

a. Default Judgments. [§16.4310]

A default judgment against a defendant typically is considered to be on the merits, despite the lack of an adversary trial or a detailed examination of the facts. Otherwise there would be no finality whenever the defendant failed to defend a lawsuit and no way for the plaintiff to obtain a final judgment without the defendant's cooperation. Since there is no adversary litigation to define the issues actually before the court, the claim preclusive effect of a default judgment is determined on the basis of the cause of action set forth in the plaintiff's complaint.

Illustration. [§16.4311] P airline sues D, a billionaire, for $125,000,000 for antitrust violations. D defaults and P recovers a judgment for the $125,000,000. P subsequently realizes that its damages really were far more than $125,000,000 and brings another suit on the same cause of action to recover the excess. The second lawsuit is precluded by the doctrine of merger, since the default judgment was on the merits and the same antitrust violations are being asserted in the second action. Note, however, that in some courts the second suit may be allowed if the court decides that the damages were unascertainable at the time of the first suit.

---

b. Dismissal Prior to an Adjudication on the Merits. [§16.4320]

The most difficult question in determining when a judgment is on the merits arises when the action is dismissed before the validity of the plaintiff's claim has been fully determined. A pretrial dismissal usually has claim preclusive effect when it is entered with prejudice but does not when it is entered without prejudice. As a general rule, the decision whether to dismiss with prejudice is a matter of the trial judge's discretion.

(1) Dismissal Based on Lack of Venue or Jurisdiction—Not on the Merits. [§16.4321]

A dismissal because of improper venue or a lack of personal or subject matter jurisdiction is never on the merits; it only decides that the court either is an inconvenient forum or is without power to adjudicate the dispute. The dismissal will have direct estoppel effect as to the particular venue or jurisdiction question involved, however.

(2) Dismissal Based on the Statute of Limitations—Not on the Merits. [§16.4322]

The dismissal of an action because it is barred by the statute of limitations is not an adjudication of the merits of the underlying claim. Claim preclusion will not prevent the plaintiff from reasserting the claim in a different state having a longer limitations period.

(3) Dismissal for Failure to Join a Party—Not on the Merits. [§16.4323]

A dismissal based on the failure to join a necessary or indispensable party generally is not considered to be on the merits. Accordingly, if plaintiff can bring the action in another forum where the absent party may be joined, a defense of claim preclusion will not prevail.

(4) Dismissal for Failure to Prosecute or to Give Security—Differing Opinions. [§16.4324]

State courts differ about whether a dismissal for failure to give security for costs or to prosecute an action constitutes a judgment on the merits. Although the merits of the claim have not been adjudicated, some courts feel that the plaintiff's improper conduct justifies preventing a second suit. In actions brought in the federal courts, Federal Rule 41(b) provides that all such dismissals are "on the merits," unless the court specifies otherwise. However, the Supreme Court made clear in *Semtek International, Inc. v. Lockheed Martin Corp.* (2001) that the term "on the merits" in Rule 41(b) does not necessarily mean that such a dismissal will invariably have claim preclusive effect in a different court, although usually that will be true. In some special situations Rule 41(b) dismissals only serve to bar the plaintiff from bringing the same action in the same federal court, not in another court. For further discussion of the *Semtek* case, see **§16.B310**.

(5) Dismissal for Failure to State a Cause of Action—Not on the Merits in Many State Courts. [§16.4325]

Except in states following the federal practice [see **§16.4326**], a dismissal for failure to state a cause of action generally is not on the merits because it only decides the insufficiency of a particular complaint and does not determine the merits of the underlying cause of action. However, if the plaintiff is given leave to amend, the failure to take advantage of that opportunity may result in the dismissal being entered with prejudice.

(6) Dismissal with Prejudice for Failure to State a Claim for Relief—On the Merits in Federal Court. [§16.4326]

A dismissal under Federal Rule 12(b)(6) for failure to state a claim upon which relief may be granted probably constitutes a judgment on the merits unless the court specified that it is without prejudice. That certainly seems to be indicated by the text of Federal Rule 41(b). However, the general practice is to enter the dismissal with leave to amend within a certain period of time. If the plaintiff does not comply with that condition, a judgment will be entered with prejudice. But a judgment on the merits based on a pleading dismissal may not preclude anything more than a second action based on the same complaint.

(7) Voluntary Dismissal—Generally Not on the Merits. [§16.4327]

Typically, a voluntary dismissal does not constitute a judgment on the merits. The one exception to this rule occurs under Federal Rule 41(a) and its state counterparts when a plaintiff attempts to secure a voluntary dismissal more than once in the same action. These rules specifically provide that the second dismissal is with prejudice.

(8) Consent Judgment—On the Merits. [§16.4328]

A judgment entered by the consent of all the parties is given full claim preclusive effect.

(9) Settlement—Akin to Judgment on the Merits. [§16.4329]

An out-of-court settlement technically is only a contract between the parties without any adjudicatory effect. However, to avoid possible multiple actions in the event of a default—the first on the original claim and the second for breach of the settlement contract—a settlement is given essentially the same effect as a judgment on the merits. The principal difference is that a settlement contract, unlike a judgment, may be collaterally attacked under general contract principles for fraud or lack of consideration.

4. Requirement That the Parties Be the Same or in Privity. [§16.4400]

Only the parties to the original action and their privies will be subject to claim preclusion. [This aspect of the former adjudication doctrine is discussed fully in **§16.9000**.]

F. EXCEPTIONS TO THE APPLICATION OF CLAIM PRECLUSION. [§16.5000]

In several types of cases, countervailing policies override the policies favoring the application of claim preclusion. Most of the exceptions that the courts have recognized are based on a concern that the prior action did not provide an effective opportunity for a full consideration of the claim being presented in the second suit.

1. **Effect of a Change in the Law. [§16.5100]**

    When the state of the law at the time of the first action was such that the plaintiff could not have known that the claims asserted in the subsequent action were maintainable, the doctrine of merger may not be strictly applied. However, the mere fact that the law on which a judgment is based has been changed does not make that judgment erroneous and the plaintiff may not relitigate the same claim in a second action.

Illustration. [§16.5110] The defendant transferred 325 of her 326 shares in a bank just before its insolvency, but the transfer was not registered until later. The State Superintendent of Banks sued successfully for a shareholder's contribution due from the defendant on the one remaining share. A state court subsequently decided that transfers of this type made by the defendant had to be registered to be effective. The Superintendent then sued for a contribution on the other 325 shares. The second suit may be allowed because the plaintiff has not behaved inequitably, the plaintiff may not have been able to predict the judicial development, and there is a policy favoring the equal distribution of the burden of shareholder contributions for the protection of a bank's creditors.

---

2. **Judgments in Quasi in Rem Actions. [§16.5200]**

    As discussed earlier [see **§3.4600–§3.4610**], a judgment in a quasi in rem action will be satisfied only to the extent of the value of the property that has been attached in order to give the court jurisdiction. In any subsequent suit brought by the plaintiff to collect the remainder of his or her claim, the plaintiff cannot rely on the quasi in rem judgment as claim preclusion. This exception to former adjudication principles reflects the fact that the court did not have personal jurisdiction over the defendant in the first suit. Because the court lacked plenary power and the defendant was not afforded a full day in court, the parties should not be bound by the judgment. Considerations of due process require this conclusion even when the defendant has been permitted to make a limited appearance [see **§3.4610**] and defend without submitting to the court's jurisdiction.

3. **In Rem Judgments Distinguished. [§16.5300]**

    Since a judgment in an in rem action purports to determine the rights of all claimants to the property that is before the court, it is given full claim preclusive effect in subsequent actions involving claims to the same property. The only limitation on the judgment's binding effect is that anyone interested in the first action who was not properly notified of it will not be bound [see **§3.4600**].

4. **Void Judgments. [§16.5400]**

A judgment that is void because the court lacked personal or subject matter jurisdiction need not be appealed. Nor need the defendant make a formal motion to set it aside. Rather, the judgment may be collaterally attacked when the plaintiff attempts to enforce it. However, if the rendering court adjudicated the question of whether it had jurisdiction, that decision cannot be collaterally attacked [see **§16.8200**]. A judgment that merely is erroneous in law or fact has claim preclusive effect and is not subject to collateral attack.

a. **Class Actions. [§16.5410]**

In a class action suit, the judgment is void with respect to absentee class members if there was no adequacy of representation or, in a common question of law or fact class action, there was no opportunity to opt-out of the class. [See the discussion of class actions in **§8.1000–§8.1920**.]

G. ISSUE PRECLUSION: IN GENERAL. [§16.6000]

When an issue of fact or law actually is litigated and necessarily determined, the parties to the action, as well as certain non-parties, are barred from relitigating the same issue in any subsequent lawsuit, even if the second proceeding is based on an entirely different cause of action. This principle is known as issue preclusion (collateral estoppel).

1. **Policy Behind Issue Preclusion. [§16.6100]**

Issue preclusion is designed to simplify and speed litigation, not necessarily to end it. When an issue has been fully litigated between the parties, nothing would be gained by spending more time and money to duplicate the process. Thus issue preclusion considers the first court's determination on that issue to be binding so that the subsequent litigation is limited to the issues between the parties that are being presented for the first time. However, issue preclusive effect is given only to those issues in the first action that the parties gave serious attention to and fully litigated.

2. **Comparison of Issue Preclusion and Claim Preclusion. [§16.6200]**

Claim preclusion precludes the relitigation of issues germane to a cause of action without regard to whether they actually were raised or determined in the original suit; however, both actions must involve the same cause of action. Issue preclusion operates only to preclude the reassertion of specific issues that actually were litigated and necessarily determined in the previous action; unlike claim preclusion, the cause of action will be different in the two actions.

H. PREREQUISITES OF THE APPLICATION OF ISSUE PRECLUSION. [§16.7000]

As previously noted, issue preclusion is applied **only when an issue that was actually litigated and necessarily determined in a prior lawsuit is raised in a subsequent action.** Generally speaking, the two actions will be between the same parties or their privies. But courts are increasingly willing to apply the doctrine in favor of litigants who were not parties to the first action when the opposing litigant was a party in the first action and lost on an issue that was fully and necessarily tried. [See **§16.A000–§16.A600** for a discussion of the extent to which the principle of mutuality of estoppel may limit this latter application of collateral estoppel.]

1. Same Issue. [§16.7100]

Issue preclusion applies only when the **identical factual issue** is involved in both cases. Stated generally, an issue may be defined as any single, legally relevant point in the case, but some limitations have been placed on the meaning of the term.

> **Illustration 1. [§16.7110]** In an action by a car driver and a passenger in the vehicle against a bus company, the question whether the bus driver was negligent in causing the accident that injured the two occupants of the car is considered a single issue, even though as a technical matter separate duties were owed to each injured party.

> **Illustration 2. [§16.7120]** A recovers an installment payment due on a contract, despite B's defense that the contract was unenforceable under the Statute of Frauds. In an action for a subsequently accruing installment on the same contract, B is collaterally estopped on the legal issue of the contract's enforceability under the Statute, but B may assert any other defense.

a. Mediate and Ultimate Facts. [§16.7130]

Some courts have said that issue preclusion should apply only to the ultimate facts in the case—those facts upon whose combined occurrence the law raises the right or duty in question—and not to the mediate or evidentiary facts that comprise the determinations of ultimate fact. According to this approach, only the ultimate factual issues in the first suit would be given preclusive effect, and then only with regard to the ultimate facts in the second action. Theoretically, this rule is justifiable in that the ultimate facts, by their very nature, were central to the resolution of the first controversy, and it can be assumed that they were litigated fully so that it is fair to bind the parties to the prior result. Unfortunately, it is nearly impossible to distinguish mediate from ultimate facts in any consistent fashion, so that the distinction is of little practical utility.

b. **Issue Preclusion Inapplicable to Issues Arising from Different Situations. [§16.7140]**

Issue preclusion may not be applied to issues of fact arising from different fact situations than those presented in the first action, however similar the two contexts may appear. Thus, analogous issues pertaining to different contracts, different parcels of land, or different tax years do not fall within the issue preclusion principle and must be separately determined in the second action. The logic of this practice is that differences in context make it potentially unfair to extend collateral estoppel to situations the parties may not have anticipated when they litigated the first action. Moreover, it often will be as time-consuming to litigate whether the facts are identical to those in the earlier case as to establish them de novo in the second action.

Illustration 1. [§16.7141] In a tax proceeding, it is adjudicated that certain expenditures made by the taxpayer in 1993 and 1994 were not deductible as necessary business expenses. In a later proceeding plaintiff is entitled to litigate whether similar payments made in 1995 are deductible as business expenses on that year's return.

Illustration 2. [§16.7142] An insured recovers benefits on an insurance policy on the ground that she had been "permanently and totally disabled" for the period preceding the suit. Issue preclusion is not available to her in a suit for benefits covering a subsequent period, because whether she continues to be permanently and totally disabled is a different issue than the one litigated in the first action.

---

2. **Actually Litigated. [§16.7200]**

It is necessary that **an issue actually have been litigated by the parties before issue preclusion will be extended to it.** This prerequisite seems particularly sound in light of the fact that issue preclusion may be applied in litigation involving an entirely different cause of action than the one in which it originally was raised; due process considerations require that the parties actually have a full opportunity to litigate all the issues between them. Moreover, the actual litigation requirement enables a party to concede a particular issue or to allow a default judgment to be entered against him without that decision having effects beyond the context of the suit in which the concession or default is made. Without this limitation litigants would be encouraged to dispute all conceivable issues, no matter how trivial the lawsuit, rather than suffer the potentially severe penalty of having all the issues in the action resolved against the losing side for purposes of subsequent litigation between the parties.

Illustration. [§16.7210] An employer sues an employee for damages caused by the employee's negligent operation of the employer's truck. The employee is found liable after a trial that is solely concerned with the employee's fault. In a subsequent FELA action against the employer for contributing to the employee's injuries by defective maintenance of the truck, the issue of the employer's negligence is not issue precluded because even though it might have been a defense to the first action, it was not actually litigated at that time.

---

a. **Default Judgment—No Issue Preclusive Effect. [§16.7220]**

A default judgment, by definition, does not involve any adversarial litigation. Consequently, a default judgment has no issue preclusive effect. [See **§16.4310,** which points out that claim preclusion does apply to a default judgment.]

b. **Admissions—Not Generally Considered Litigated. [§16.7230]**

An admission in the pleadings or during discovery or in response to a specific request generally is not considered to be a "litigated" issue for issue preclusive purposes. This is appropriate because the contrary rule would deter parties from entering into simplifying stipulations because of possible unanticipated effects on the admitting litigant's position in future litigation. Federal Rule 36 specifically provides that admissions made pursuant to its terms are "for purposes of the pending action only." [Admissions are discussed in **§9.5400–§9.5463–1.**]

c. Consent Judgments. [§16.7240]

Consent judgments arguably should be treated in the same way as admissions. Nonetheless, some courts have given them the same issue preclusive effect as ordinary judgments. The better practice probably is for the court to attempt to effectuate the intent of the parties as to the judgment's issue preclusive implications.

d. The Use of Extrinsic Evidence. [§16.7250]

The issues set forth in the pleadings do not necessarily determine what actually was litigated in an action, particularly in a notice pleading system. Accordingly, extrinsic evidence—typically the record of the trial of the first action or the testimony of people who were present at the trial—is admissible to show what issues actually were litigated in the earlier action.

Illustration. [§16.7251] A sues B for breach of contract and B's answer alleges that the contract was procured through fraud and was entered into for an illegal purpose. Judgment is rendered for A. In a subsequent suit for a declaration that the contract was illegal and voidable, B may overcome an issue preclusion defense if she can prove that the illegality issue was abandoned in the prior action and therefore only the fraud issue actually was litigated.

---

3. Necessarily Determined. [§16.7300]

The determination of an issue can have issue preclusive effect only **if the finding was necessary to the outcome of the lawsuit.** Issue preclusion does not apply to incidental or irrelevant issues, even if they were actually litigated and decided. The purpose of this rule is to assure that the issue was sufficiently important to the prior action to have received the full attention of the litigants and the court. Accordingly, when a lawsuit ends before reaching the merits, only those issues necessary to the particular basis for the termination of the action are directly estopped [see **§16.8000**].

Illustration 1. [§16.7310] A sues B for trespassing on tract number 4 of a small housing development. The court renders judgment for B and finds specially that B had title not only to tract number 4 but to tracts 1, 2, and 3 as well. In a subsequent action to quiet title by A against B only the issue of ownership of tract number 4 is collaterally estopped. The findings regarding the other tracts were unnecessary to the result.

> **Illustration 2. [§16.7320]** P sues D for breach of an oral contract. D defends on three grounds: (a) that no contract in fact was made; (b) that the contract, if made, would be barred by the Statute of Frauds; and (c) that even had the contract been made there has been no breach of it. A general verdict and judgment for P collaterally estops all three issues, since each necessarily must have been decided in P's favor for him to prevail.

a. Protection of the Prevailing Party. [§16.7330]

One of the principles underlying the requirement that the determination of an issue be necessary to the result is the idea that a party should not be permanently estopped on an issue without an opportunity to have appellate review of the trial court's decision on it. A party who has prevailed at the trial typically cannot seek review of an issue that was decided against him. For this reason, the necessary determination rule denies issue preclusive effect to issues decided against the successful party in the first action.

> **Illustration. [§16.7331]** A sues B for damages resulting from an accident allegedly caused by B's negligence and B defends on a theory of contributory negligence. Judgment is for B on the basis of a special verdict finding both parties negligent. Naturally, B does not appeal. The decision that A was contributorily negligent was essential to the result, but the finding that B was also at fault was not. Consequently, in a subsequent suit by B against A for his own damages, A is issue precluded from arguing that he was not negligent, but if A raises the issue of B's own negligence as a defense, that issue must be relitigated. Conversely, a special verdict finding neither party negligent would preclude only the relitigation of B's non-negligence.

b. Issue Preclusion When Judgment Is Based on Alternative Issues. [§16.7340]

Sometimes two or more issues are presented to the trier and any one of them would support the result ultimately reached. Examples are cases resulting in a judgment for the defendant when several barring defenses have been raised or a judgment for plaintiff when several theories of liability have been presented. In some cases the multiple or alternative issues are explicitly decided, as would be true in a judge-tried case in which the court writes an opinion articulating the precise bases for the result or of a jury verdict based on special interrogatories. When this occurs, all of the issues typically will be given issue preclusive effect, even though the judgment could have been based on any one of the issues alone. **However, if a general verdict is rendered, there is no way of knowing which of the issues the jury relied on to reach its decision, which means that none of the issues should be given issue preclusive effect.**

Illustration 1. [§16.7341] A sues B for negligence, and B defends on the ground that A was contributorily negligent. If A had the burden of pleading and proving his own freedom from fault, a general verdict for A would establish both that A was not negligent and that B was negligent for issue preclusion purposes. However, a general verdict for B would establish nothing for issue preclusion purposes, since it might have rested solely on A's contributory negligence or B's lack of negligence and there is no way of determining which is the case.

Illustration 2. [§16.7342] P sues D for battery, and D answers that she is not liable, first because plaintiff consented to the contact and second because D was privileged to detain P as a suspected shoplifter. A general verdict for D would not have issue preclusive effect as to either issue, since it cannot be determined which defense persuaded the trier of fact.

---

4. **Exceptions to the Application of Issue Preclusion. [§16.7400]**

In addition to the exceptions to the application of claim preclusion [see **§16.5000–§16.5410**], which generally are applicable to issue preclusion as well, a few additional exceptions to issue preclusion deserve mention.

a. **Effect of a Change in the Law. [§16.7410]**

When a legal principle is changed by statute after judgment has been rendered in an action in which it has been applied, the issue preclusion doctrine generally does not preclude the new statute's application to the same issue in a subsequent suit between the parties. This is not true, however, when the law is changed by judicial decision in an unrelated case, the theory being that such a change provides an insufficient reason to reconsider an issue that was settled between the parties to the first action. This approach can be criticized because it results in certain parties being governed by different legal principles from others who are in a similar position simply because they were sued before the new rule was established. Thus it has been held that if applying issue preclusion following a change in doctrine will place a party at a competitive or significant disadvantage, the court may relieve that party of the preclusive effect of the first action's judgment.

Illustration 1. [§16.7411] In a proceeding between a taxpayer and the Internal Revenue Service it is determined that the taxpayer was not taxable for royalties paid in a particular tax year on a contract that had been assigned to his wife without consideration. After the "legal climate" has been greatly changed by intervening decisions, the Service seeks to tax the taxpayer for royalties received under the contract in a later tax year. The doctrine of issue preclusion may be held inapplicable to the tax status of royalties paid during the later year under the same contract despite the identity of the issues involved in the two cases [*Comm'r of Internal Revenue v. Sunnen* (1948)].

Illustration 2. [§16.7412] In a first action, importer A unsuccessfully sought to establish a favorable import duty for a particular grade of jute. In a later case involving importer B, the court upheld importer A's earlier contention that a lower tariff was applicable. In a second action between importer A and the government, the importer may be relieved of the issue preclusive effect of the former judgment because to do otherwise would put it at a competitive disadvantage vis-a-vis other importers.

b. Effect of a Change in the Facts. [§16.7420]

Issue preclusion does not preclude the relitigation of an issue if the facts or the circumstances relating to it have changed significantly since the prior judgment.

Illustration. [§16.7421] P's action is dismissed for lack of personal jurisdiction because D does not have minimum contacts with the forum. Subsequently, P sues again in the same court on the same claim and serves D personally within the state. Since the former judgment was not on the merits it has no claim preclusive effect, and because the facts underlying the jurisdiction issue have changed—minimum contacts now being irrelevant—issue preclusion does not apply.

c. Judgments in Quasi in Rem Actions. [§16.7430]

When a limited appearance is made in a quasi in rem action, the issues relating to the merits of the dispute often are actually litigated and necessarily determined. Nonetheless, **they traditionally have not been given issue preclusive effect**. To do so would negate the purpose of the limited appearance procedure, which is to permit the defendant to enter the jurisdiction to protect his or her interests in the res that was attached without actually submitting to the court's general personal jurisdiction. [See **§3.7400** for a discussion of the limited appearance.] There has been some erosion in this limitation on the application of issue preclusion in recent years.

d. Issues Decided in Criminal Cases. [§16.7440]

Because of the different burdens of proof applicable to criminal and civil proceedings, there are special rules governing the issue preclusion effect of issues decided in a criminal suit that also are involved in civil litigation. **Issue preclusion effect is not given to issues decided in a criminal case that ends in an acquittal** since the failure to prove defendant's guilt beyond a reasonable doubt does not preclude the possibility that civil liability can be established when the standard is only a preponderance of the evidence. **Issues actually litigated and necessary to the decision in a criminal proceeding that results in conviction, however, are given issue preclusive effect** because they have been determined under a more rigorous standard of proof than is required in a civil action.

Illustration. [§16.7441] X is indicted for having a cache of marijuana in her apartment, but is acquitted after succeeding on a motion to exclude the contraband from evidence because it was obtained by an illegal search and seizure. The issue of the legality of the search is not thereby estopped in a later action by X against the police for trespass because the exclusion in the criminal case

> only adjudicated that the search was not legal beyond a reason-
> able doubt.

(1) Guilty Plea. [§16.7442]

Despite the usual requirement that an issue actually be litigated,
a guilty plea occasionally is given issue preclusive effect as to
all of the issues necessary to support a conviction for the crime
that is the subject of the plea. Under the usual rules of evidence,
a plea would be admissible and could be considered along with
the other evidence in the case in deciding any of the issues
common to the criminal and civil cases. Thus it seems unnecessary and unduly harsh to give issue preclusive effect to the
issues embraced by the plea. A plea of nolo contendere is not
given issue preclusive effect.

e. Effect of a Different Burden of Proof. [§16.7450]

For reasons similar to those described in **§16.7440,** issue preclusion
will not apply when there is a significant difference in the burden of
proof on the issue in the two actions. This is true when (a) the party
against whom the preclusive effect is sought had a much heavier
burden in the first action than in the second action, or (b) the burden
has shifted from that party to the party invoking issue preclusion in
the second action, or (c) the party asserting issue preclusion has a
much heavier burden in the second action than he had in the first
action.

f. Effect of Decisions in Minor Cases. [§16.7460]

A judgment in a minor case involving a small sum often will not be
accorded issue preclusive effect, particularly if the subsequent action
involves far more significant issues and amounts.

(1) Cases in Small Claims Courts. [§16.7461]

Decisions in small claims courts usually will not be given issue
preclusive effect for a number of reasons. For one thing, the
decision may not be appealable [see **§16.7330**]. Moreover, in
some jurisdictions, the parties will not be permitted to have
legal representation, or the formal rules of evidence will not
apply, or the decision may be made by volunteer lawyers rather
than by judges.

(2) Limited Motive to Litigate Fully. [§16.7462]

In any action, the intensity with which a party litigates an issue
depends on the amount at stake. Thus, in a suit for $2,000 for

personal injury allegedly due to a defectively designed piece of machinery, the defendant manufacturer is not likely to employ an expert who, for $25,000 in fees and expenses, would refute the plaintiff's claims. The manufacturer will take its chances by relying solely on the testimony of the foreman. If a decision is rendered against the manufacturer, it would be grossly unfair to apply issue preclusion as to the design issue in a subsequent case in which $500,000 in damages are at stake and in which the expert would be used. Thus, courts are wary of employing collateral estoppel whenever the impetus to litigate in the initial case was vastly inferior to that in the subsequent suit.

g. Effect of Jury Trial Availability. [§16.7470]

Generally the availability of a jury trial in a second action will have no effect on the application of issue preclusion to issues decided by the judge in a previous equitable action. If a party was denied a jury trial wrongfully in the first action, however, issue preclusion will not apply in a subsequent action, since the jury trial right would be further undermined by the application of former adjudication [*Lytle v. Household Mfg.* (1990)].

I. DIRECT ESTOPPEL. [§16.8000]

When an action ends in a judgment that is not on the merits, the doctrine of direct estoppel provides that the issues actually litigated and necessarily determined cannot be relitigated in any later suit on the same cause of action. Except for the fact that it pertains to a suit on the same cause of action, direct estoppel is governed by the same principles as issue preclusion.

> **Illustration. [§16.8100]** If an action is dismissed by a Texas state court on the ground that it is barred by the applicable Texas statute of limitations, the judgment is not on the merits and has no res judicata effect. However, it does have a direct estoppel effect as to the applicability of the Texas statute of limitations should the plaintiff bring another suit in Texas on the same cause of action.

1. Jurisdiction to Determine Jurisdiction. [§16.8200]

When a court's jurisdiction to adjudicate an action is litigated and determined, direct estoppel precludes that issue from being reconsidered in a subsequent action. As long as the opposing party appears and litigates the question, the principle that a court has jurisdiction to determine jurisdiction permits a court to make a binding determination of its own jurisdiction and that decision cannot be collaterally attacked [see **§16.5400**]. A party can preserve his or her right to attack a judgment collaterally on the ground that it was rendered without jurisdiction by not appearing at all.

J. PERSONS BOUND AND BENEFITED BY A FORMER ADJUDICATION. [§16.9000]

A lawsuit is primarily a contest between the parties to it. Generally speaking, the winner is benefited by the result and the loser is bound by it. However, a number of questions arise when people who are not actual parties nevertheless are so intimately associated with a party to or the subject matter of a dispute that it seems fair to bind and benefit them by the outcome. Moreover, in certain circumstances a person who had no connection whatsoever to an action may be accorded the benefit of issue preclusion.

1. Right to Be Heard. [§16.9100]

Due process requirements indicate that a party be given a day in court before being adversely affected by a judgment. Consequently, it never is possible to bind someone who was not a party or who did not at least have notice and an opportunity to appear in a case, either in person or through a privy or adequate representative. [The requirements of notice and an opportunity to be heard are discussed at **§3.5000–§3.5620**.]

2. Parties to the Action. [§16.9200]

The actual litigants to an action necessarily are bound to whatever extent a judgment has any former adjudication effect.

a. Suit in Different Capacities. [§16.9210]

It is possible for a person to sue or be sued in different capacities— for example, as an executor of an estate, as an individual on his or her own behalf, as an infant's next friend, or as a trustee in bankruptcy. For former adjudication purposes, when the initial suit involves a person acting in a different capacity than in the second suit, the person is treated as two individuals and will be bound in the second suit only to the extent that a stranger to the first action would be bound.

446

Illustration [§16.9211] A sues as a trustee to recover for B's trespass to trust property. B's defense that he was privileged to enter the property as a police officer with a warrant is rejected and A prevails. In a subsequent action by A for personal injuries sustained in repelling B from the property, it traditionally has been held that A is not entitled to rely on the issue preclusive effect of the prior judgment as if it had been obtained by A acting in the same capacity in both suits. This does not necessarily mean that A is precluded from using issue preclusion since under the modern doctrine of many jurisdictions, strangers to the first action nevertheless may utilize its determinations for issue preclusive purposes in appropriate circumstances [see **§16.A200–§16.A700**].

3. Only Adverse Parties Bound. [§16.9300]

Claim preclusion is applicable only with respect to causes of action litigated between adverse parties to the prior action, and issue preclusion may be invoked only with regard to issues determined in connection with a claim for relief between adverse parties.

Illustration [§16.9310] An employer sues A for property damage sustained in a collision between the plaintiff's truck, driven by an employee, and A's car. A defends on the ground that the employee was guilty of contributory negligence and asserts a counterclaim against the employer for damage to his car, joining the employee as an additional party to the counterclaim. The jury concludes that both A and the employee were negligent, and finds for A on the employer's claim and for the employer and the employee on A's counterclaim. Although the determination of the employee's negligence was essential to the disposition of the employer's claim, and perhaps even to the decision on the counterclaim, the employer and the employee were not adverse parties in the suit so that collateral estoppel does not apply to the issue of contributory negligence in a subsequent suit by the employee against the employer for personal injuries.

4. Persons Controlling the Litigation. [§16.9400]

In many circumstances the actual prosecution or defense of the lawsuit is controlled by someone other than the named plaintiff or defendant. The most common situation in which this occurs is when an insurance

447

company defends a suit against its insured pursuant to the terms of the insurance policy. The person controlling the litigation is bound and, if notice of its participation is given to the opposing parties, is benefited by the outcome as if he were an actual party. This conclusion is sound since the person in control is able to assert his interests in the action; there is no reason to allow or require him to do so again in a subsequent suit involving the same issues.

5. Privies. [§16.9500]

Judgments bind not only parties but persons who are in privity with parties. In this context "privy" has been defined as someone who has a "mutual or successive relationship to the same property." A person is considered a privy when he or she succeeds to a party's property interest, has a concurrent interest with a party in the same property, or was represented by a party in the earlier action.

a. Succession to Property. [§16.9510]

Whenever a person obtains an interest in property, he or she will be bound by any prior judgments concerning the property, or by any future judgments in actions against the predecessor in title that were begun before the transfer. The successor also will be benefited by the favorable result of any lawsuit in favor of the predecessor, whether begun before or after the transfer.

Illustration [§16.9511] X owns three parcels of land that the state condemns for public use without complying with the applicable condemnation statute. X sells one of the parcels to Z and subsequently successfully sues to void the condemnation of all three parcels. Even though the lawsuit was begun after the transfer, Z is entitled to assert the judgment as res judicata in a subsequent suit by the state to quiet title to Z's parcel.

---

b. Mutual Interests in Property. [§16.9520]

A person not involved in an action nonetheless may be bound by the judgment in the case if the non-party and a party to the action both have interests in the property that is the subject matter of the suit. Thus, a recovery by either a bailee or a bailor with regard to a trespass to the bailed item bars a similar action by the other against the trespasser. In a community property state, a spouse is bound by the result of an action by the other spouse when the recovery would benefit the marital community.

c.   **Persons Who Are Represented. [§16.9530]**

When a person's interests are represented adequately in an action, he or she will be bound or benefited by the judgment. Subsequent representatives of the same non-party's rights are affected in the same way. For the purpose of applying this rule, a trustee represents the beneficiaries of a trust, an executor represents the beneficiaries of a will, and a guardian ad litem represents the person who lacks capacity to sue.

Illustration. [§16.9531] T sues successfully for a tax refund as the trustee for the X trust on the ground that the interest on particular municipal development bonds held by the trust is tax exempt. T subsequently is replaced as trustee by V. In subsequent actions involving other shares of the same stock, V will be able to invoke collateral estoppel on the exemption issue when litigating in a representative capacity. However, both T and V will be treated as strangers to the prior suits if they should later sue to establish tax exemptions on bonds owned by them personally.

---

d.   **Class Actions. [§16.9540]**

Class actions constitute a significant exception to the general rule that a judgment binds only the parties actually before the court. The theory, of course, is that all the members of the class have been represented adequately [see **§8.1260**]. All class members who do not request exclusion from a class action based on the existence of common questions of law or fact are bound by the judgment, whether it is favorable or unfavorable. This binding effect from failing to opt-out stems in federal practice from Rule 23(c)(2), and many states have comparable provisions. [See the discussion of class actions in **§8.1000–§8.1930**.]

(1) **No Collateral Estoppel for Opt–Outs. [§16.9541]**

On the other hand, it generally is held that potential class members who do opt-out may not claim collateral estoppel benefits from a favorable judgment.

e.   **Acceptors of Benefits. [§16.9550]**

A person who accepts the benefits of a judgment may be precluded from attacking its validity in subsequent litigation, even though that person was not formally a party to the action. This is technically a form of estoppel rather than part of the privity principle, but in practice it has much the same effect.

6. Persons Vouched in. [§16.9600]

In some jurisdictions when a person is sued on a claim that another person contractually is obligated to defend, the defendant may vouch in the absentee. A person who has been vouched in properly is bound by the issues determined and by the judgment, even if he or she does not actually appear to defend. In a subsequent suit by either the plaintiff or the defendant in the first action to collect a judgment against the vouchee, the latter can defend only on the ground that he was not under an obligation to defend or that he was not given an adequate opportunity to enter the action and do so; the vouchee cannot relitigate the merits of the underlying claim.

Illustration. [§16.9610] Insured, upon being sued by Victim for damages sustained in an auto accident, vouches in the Insurer on the latter's obligation under a liability policy. If Insurer refuses to defend on the ground that the accident was not covered by the policy, it will be bound by all the issues concerning Insured's liability to Victim that were necessarily determined in the prior action. In a subsequent action brought by Victim against Insurer to collect the amount of Victim's judgment against Insured, Insurer can defend only on the ground that the policy did not apply.

---

7. Persons Who Fail to Intervene. [§16.9700]

In general, a person who has the opportunity to intervene in an action, but who fails to exercise that opportunity, will be treated like any other non-party and will not be bound by the judgment. Outside of the class action or representative suit context and a number of specific remedial schemes that do foreclose successive litigation by non-parties, such as bankruptcy and probate, a party seeking to bind a stranger to an action must formally join that person [*Martin v. Wilks* (1989)].

a. Special Exception: Employment Consent Decrees. [§16.9710]

The specific holding of *Martin,* which involved Title VII discrimination claims, was legislatively overruled by Section 108 of the Civil Rights Act of 1991, which prohibits challenges to employment consent decrees by persons who had notice and an opportunity to intervene.

K. MUTUALITY OF COLLATERAL ESTOPPEL. [§16.A000]

A rule of long historical standing, but one that has been substantially eroded in a number of jurisdictions in recent years, requires that the application of issue preclusion be mutual, which means that A is permitted to assert issue preclusion against B only if B could have asserted the doctrine against A had it been in B's interest to do so. This rule restricts the effect of issue preclusion to parties and privies. Since a cause of action only exists between two particular parties and their privies, claim preclusion always is mutual; it never can be asserted by one who is not a party or privy to a prior action.

1. Policies Underlying Mutuality. [§16.A100]

The mutuality rule has been supported by two related policies. The first is the idea that a party should not be permitted to benefit from the resolution of an issue without earning that reward by participating and expending energy in the litigation process. Since this reason would tolerate repetitive litigation solely to vindicate a rather dubious moralistic ideal, it generally is rejected by modern commentators. The second is the fear that the absence of a mutuality rule would give the party who seeks to benefit from the prior action an unfair advantage. If the prior action decided the issue in the non-party's favor, she could invoke issue preclusion in the second action; but if the issue were decided against the nonparty's position in the first action, she could not constitutionally be bound by it since she had not been a party and could proceed to litigate the issue again. The appeal of this argument is largely emotional.

Illustration 1. [§16.A110] A sues B alleging that B and C converted papers from A's office safe; A loses. In a subsequent suit by A against C for the same tort, the doctrine of mutuality would preclude C from using issue preclusion with regard to the issues determined in the first suit, since C did not earn the right to do so by participating in the first action and by being subject to the risk of an adverse judgment.

Illustration 2. [§16.A120] F sues T in the latter's capacity as a trustee, asserting T's breach of a fiduciary obligation to a trust of which S is a beneficiary. Since S, as a represented person, would

---

be bound by an adverse judgment in the first action [see **§16.8530**], S can invoke issue preclusion in a later action against T on a different cause of action.

2. **Decline of Mutuality Doctrine. [§16.A200]**

    The doctrine of mutuality of collateral estoppel has experienced a steady decline in the past four decades. Many courts and commentators feel that the need to prevent unnecessarily repetitious litigation outweighs the policies that support the rule. Although mutuality has been completely abandoned in some contexts, this area of the law is in flux and the limits on a non-party's ability to take advantage of the issue preclusion effect of an adjudication are uncertain.

    a. **Derivative Liability Exception: Shield Rule. [§16.A210]**

        A well recognized exception to mutuality applies in the situation in which one person's liability derives from that of another, as is true of the master-servant, principal-agent, and indemnitor-indemnitee relationships. The person who is derivatively liable is allowed to use the collateral estoppel effect of a prior judgment in favor of the person from whom his or her liability derives. Mutuality is not satisfied because due process precludes prior judgment against a defendant from binding the person derivatively liable who was neither a party nor in privity with the defendant and who cannot be bound by defendant's choice of attorney or methods of defense. The derivative liability exception is desirable because otherwise if a judgment subsequently was obtained by the injured party against the person derivatively liable, the latter's only recourse would be to bring suit against the person primarily liable. Should that action be successful, the person primarily liable would be deprived of the effect of the favorable judgment in the first action. In addition, three lawsuits would have resulted.

Illustration. [§16.A211] A brings an action against a truck driver for injuries received in an accident involving a truck driven by the defendant. Judgment is rendered in favor of the truck driver on the ground that A was contributorily negligent. In a subsequent action by A against the truck owner, the latter is entitled to invoke collateral estoppel on the issue of A's contributory negligence.

b. Derivative Liability Exception: Expanded Application. [§16.A220]

Some courts have extended the derivative liability exception to permit either the person derivatively liable or the person primarily liable to assert issue preclusion as to issues actually and necessarily decided in an action by or against the other, despite the fact that the person invoking issue preclusion would not have been bound by an adverse result in the first action.

Illustration. [§16.A221] Victim unsuccessfully sues Master for a tort allegedly committed by Servant. If the issue of Servant's negligence actually has been litigated and necessarily determined, the derivative liability principle will preclude relitigation of the issue in a subsequent action by Victim against Servant. But if the prior action turned on another issue, such as the Master's successful showing that the Servant was not acting within the scope of employment at the time of the accident, then Servant could derive no benefit from the judgment in favor of the Master.

---

3. Effect of the Decline of Mutuality. [§16.A300]

With the debilitation of the mutuality doctrine a widespread feeling has developed that some alternative limitation on the use of issue preclusion is necessary. Both courts and commentators have advocated that the court in the second action investigate a number of circumstances relating to the first action to determine whether it is proper to allow a non-participant in that action to take advantage of it in subsequent litigation. Many of these factors are involved in the federal court's requirements for non-mutual issue preclusion. [see Parklane Hosiery Co. v. Shore, 439 U.S. 322 (1979)].

a. Full and Fair Opportunity to Litigate. [§16.A310]

Courts seem to be converging on the principle that someone who was not a party to the first action may assert issue preclusion against a party to that action with regard to any issue that that party had a full and fair opportunity to litigate in the prior action.

(1) Incentive to Exercise Opportunity to Litigate. [§16.A311]

By far the most important factor in determining whether there was a full opportunity to litigate an issue is whether the party against whom collateral estoppel is to be applied had an incentive to exert his or her best efforts in the previous suit. It would be unfair to give unlimited collateral estoppel effect to the determination of an issue that was only half-heartedly disputed in the first suit but which proves vitally important in a subsequent case. The fact that the party put forth his or her best effort may be shown as an evidentiary fact or it may be inferred from the circumstances that a large amount of money or important rights were at stake in the prior action, especially if further litigation was foreseeable at that time. Conversely, the mutuality requirement usually will be imposed when the earlier case involved a small amount or when it is shown that in fact it was not vigorously contested. Whether the prior judgment was appealed is another significant factor in deciding whether full efforts were exerted.

(2) Foreseeability of Subsequent Litigation. [§16.A312]

If the subsequent use of the issue could have been anticipated by the party sought to be estopped, it is likely that full efforts were exerted in the first action. Conversely, if an issue's later importance was not foreseeable at the time of the first suit, the parties may not have contested it as vigorously as they otherwise might have.

b. Party with the Initiative. [§16.A320]

Some commentators have suggested that the plaintiff has such a substantial tactical advantage by virtue of being able to choose the time and place of suit that, in the absence of mutuality, issue preclusion should not be permitted to be used against a party who did not have the initiative in the prior action, especially if he also does not have it in the subsequent litigation. Recently, a number of courts have been unwilling to use this rule mechanically, however, and have considered whether an actual hardship will be imposed on the party against whom the issue preclusion will operate by not having been able to choose the time and forum for the first litigation. Accordingly, unless special inconvenience is shown by the party against whom issue preclusion will operate, this factor is likely to be given relatively slight weight.

Illustration. [§16.A321] Twenty-four of 31 pending actions brought on behalf of passengers who had been killed in an airplane crash

---

culminate in judgments of over $2,000,000 against the airline. Collateral estoppel on the issue of the airline's negligence may be allowed in subsequent actions brought by the remaining passengers against the airline on the ground that defendant must have used its best efforts in defending the previous actions since so much was at stake.

4. Two Types of Non-Mutual Issue Preclusion Generally Allowed. [§16.A400]

Many courts, including the federal courts, expressly allow two types of non-mutual issue preclusion in specific circumstances: defensive non-mutual issue preclusion and offensive non-mutual issue preclusion. It is important to keep in mind that under no circumstances in a second action can issue preclusion be utilized **against** a party who was not a party to the first action. However, if the requirements for non-mutual issue preclusion are met, a person who was not a party to the first action may seek the benefit of issue preclusion.

a. Defensive Non-mutual Issue Preclusion. [§16.A410]

The most common situation in which mutuality has been abandoned by the courts is one in which an unsuccessful plaintiff sues, in a second action, a defendant who was not a party in the first suit. In this situation, the defendant in the second suit can assert issue preclusion, as a defense, against the plaintiff. As long as the plaintiff had a full and fair opportunity to litigate in the former action, he will be subject to an issue preclusion defense in the second action.

Those that support the use of defensive non-mutual issue preclusion cite its benefits as promoting judicial economy, providing plaintiffs with the proper incentives to sue all potential defendants (at least all known potential defendants) at the same time, and alleviating the new defendant's burden to litigate when plaintiff has already lost elsewhere.

Illustration 1. [§16.A411] P sues the executor of an estate for misappropriation of funds but loses when the transfer is held to be a gift to the executor. P subsequently sues the bank that permitted the withdrawal. The bank is allowed to invoke collateral estoppel against the relitigation of the legality of the transfer to the executor [*Bernhard v. Bank of America Nat'l Trust & Sav. Ass'n* (Cal. 1942)].

Illustration 2. [§16.A412] P sues D1 for patent infringement but loses when the patent is declared invalid. In a later action against D2, another alleged infringer, P, will be estopped from relitigating the validity of the patent [*Blonder-Tongue Labs., Inc. v. University of Illinois Foundation* (1971)].

---

b. Offensive Non-mutual Collateral Estoppel. [§16.A420]

Offensive non-mutual issue preclusion exists when a person who was not a plaintiff in an initial action that was won by the person who brought the suit is permitted to take advantage of that victorious decision in a new action against the same defendant. The requirements for offensive non-mutual issue preclusion are that the stranger wishing to assert issue preclusion could not have easily joined the original action, that the defendant had a full and fair opportunity to litigate in the original action, that the defendant did fully litigate the issue in the original action, and that the subsequent action was foreseeable [*Parklane Hosiery Co. v. Shore* (1979)].

(1) *Parklane* Facts. [§16.A421]

In the original action the Securities and Exchange Commission won a verdict against Parklane for violation of the federal securities statute. In a second action Shore, a Parklane shareholder, who could not join the SEC action, was permitted to employ issue preclusion to avoid the relitigation of the proxy violation in his shareholders' class action suit even though the second action, unlike the first, was tried before a jury. Obviously, at the time of the SEC proceeding, Parklane could foresee the shareholders' action.

5. Multiple Claimant Anomaly. [§16.A500]

One argument against the abolition of mutuality stems from the fear of anomalous results in cases involving a large number of claimants pursuing an identical liability theory for damages arising out of a single event, such as the victims of airplane crashes. Let us assume that the individual claimants bring suit against the airline one by one and the first 25 lose. The carrier has received no issue preclusion benefit from the adjudication of non-liability in each of these suits. Then, in the 26th suit, the plaintiff wins. If mutuality is abandoned, all of the remaining passengers can win by invoking issue preclusion with respect to the issues determined against the carrier in the 26th suit. Despite the apparent unfairness of this scenario, courts undoubtedly are able to deal with this problem by examining each case to see if the judgment in favor of the 26th passenger is justifiable or aberrational, and applying issue preclusion if it seems appropriate to do so in the particular case.

Illustration 1. [§16.A510] Accident victim V–1 sued defendant airline, but the jury verdict goes against her. In a new trial, granted because of improper exclusion of evidence, however, she recovered $35,000, although her original claim had been for $500,000. The judgment was not appealed. In a later action by V–2 for more than seven million dollars, plaintiff's attempt to invoke issue preclusion probably will be rejected on the ground that had the second, much larger, action been foreseen by defendant, it might have exerted greater efforts to obtain a favorable result in the earlier case. The questionable character of the prior judgment and the lack of an appeal from it also are factors that might influence the court not to apply collateral estoppel.

Illustration 2. [§16.A520] An HIV infected hemophiliac in State A successfully sues a nationwide supplier of blood solids. The jury's special verdict contains factual findings which are not specific to the law of State A, e.g., that the manufacturer was aware of the HIV danger on a certain date, and findings that are dependent on the law of State A, e.g., that the manufacturer was negligent. Assuming State B sanctions the use of offensive non-mutual issue preclusion, at least one important court has concluded that a similar plaintiff in State B should be able to invoke issue preclusion as to the factual findings of the previous suit, but not to the finding of negligence unless there are no relevant differences between the law of negligence of State A and State B [*Matter of Rhone–Poulenc Rorer, Inc.* (1995)].

---

6. **Synthesis and Comment. [§16.A600]**

As the preceding sections suggest, the mechanical rule of mutuality has been replaced by a process of balancing the factors presented by each case in order to achieve a just result. One consideration that often is omitted from the scale, however, is the additional cost—both to the court and the litigants—of analyzing each case rather than simply applying a clear rule on the subject. In big cases, of course, the enormous cost of relitigation justifies the significant time and energy that may have to be devoted to the subject. But in a small lawsuit it may be more efficient to duplicate the former trial than to spend time weighing all the factors bearing on whether the first adjudication was sufficiently fair and definitive to apply issue preclusion.

L. INTERSYSTEM PRECLUSION. [§16.B000]

The preceding discussion of preclusion assumed that both the original and subsequent actions were raised in the same judicial system—either the federal or a state system. When a subsequent action is brought in a different system, however, special problems arise that are governed by the constitutional and statutory principles of full faith and credit.

1. Full Faith and Credit. [§16.B100]

The general idea of intersystem preclusion is based on the full faith and credit requirement embodied in the Full Faith and Credit clause of the United States Constitution [Article IV, §1] and the Full Faith and Credit Statute [28 U.S.C. §1738]. The Full Faith and Credit Clause and Statute require that the courts of each state enforce a judgment of a court in any other state to the extent that the judgment would have been enforced in the rendering state. After much uncertainty on the question, the Supreme Court has now indicated that full faith and credit applies not only to the enforcement of judgments but also to other aspects of former adjudication, such as issue preclusion. Thus, the second court (the recognizing court) dealing with potential preclusive judgments must look to the preclusion rules of the state in which the rendering (first) court sits–the state in which the first suit was tried. The recognizing court must apply the rules of the rendering court. It makes no difference that the case would have been decided differently had it originally been brought in the second state's court. The effect of this provision is to give the doctrine of former adjudication constitutional significance when the subsequent action is brought in a state other than the one in which the original action was litigated.

Illustration. [§B110]. A plane crash in Kentucky leads to the death of all of the passengers. A group of passengers' families sues the airline in state court in Texas. Judgment is rendered against the

---

> airline and it is found to have been negligent in its plane maintenance, thereby leading to the crash. A second group of families sues in state court in New York, asserting non-mutual offensive issue preclusion prevents defendant from seeking to argue lack of negligence. The New York state court applies Texas law on non-mutual offensive issue preclusion to determine if the issue is precluded in New York, regardless of what New York law may say.

a. Limitations on Interstate Preclusion. [§16.B120]

There are a number of important limitations on the constitutional requirements of full faith and credit. First, the court of the rendering state must have had proper jurisdiction over the defendant or full faith and credit will not apply, since the judgment would be invalid in the rendering state. The court of the enforcing state must, at the behest of the defendant, determine whether the rendering state had jurisdiction over him or her and refuse to exercise full faith and credit if it did not. Second, the Full Faith and Credit Clause is not to be taken to require a court in the enforcing state to give more force to a judgment than it would have received in the courts of the rendering state. Thus, if a judgment, such as an award for child support, is modifiable in the court that rendered it, it can be similarly modified in the court in which enforcement is sought.

2. State to Federal Preclusion. [§16.B200]

Although the Full Faith and Credit Clause of the Constitution applies only to state courts, the statute that codifies the doctrine, 28 USC 1738, imposes the same general principles on the federal courts, requiring them to accord full faith and credit to the judgments of state courts. The Supreme Court has held that the statute requires that federal courts apply no more and no less preclusive effect to a judgment than would a court of the rendering state [*Marrese v. American Academy of Orthopaedic Surgeons* (1985)].

3. Federal to State Preclusion. [§16.B300]

Although the Full Faith and Credit Clause and 28 USC 1738 are both inapplicable, the general requirement that federal judgments be given full faith and credit in state courts is supported by the Supremacy Clause and never has been challenged seriously.

a. Determining the Governing Law for Res Judicata Purposes. [§16.B310]

The Supreme Court in *Semtek International, Inc. v. Lockheed Martin Corp.* (2001), held that federal common law governs the claim-preclusive effect of a dismissal by a federal court sitting in diversity jurisdiction. In determining what the federal common law should be, the Court stated that since state, rather than federal, substantive law is at issue there was no need to create a uniform federal rule. Furthermore, the best way to achieve nationwide uniformity would not be to create a uniform federal rule but rather to have the same claim-preclusive rule (the state rule) apply whether the dismissal was ordered by a state or federal court in the same state. Therefore, the Court held that federal common law requires federal diversity judgments to be accorded the same preclusive effect that would be applied by the state courts in the state in which the federal court sits.

4.   Focus on the Rendering Jurisdiction's Preclusion Rules. [§16.B400]

In addressing the preclusive effect of judgments in the intersystem context, it is important to remember that the preclusion rules of the system in which the original action was litigated govern the effect of the judgment in a subsequent action in a different judicial system.

a.   Hypotheticals. [§16.B410]

A and B are involved in an auto collision. A sues B in Ohio for property damage to his car; A wins and brings a second action for bodily injury in Indiana.

> **Q1.**   Assume (only for this hypothetical) that Ohio employs a transaction standard to define a cause of action and that Indiana employs a same right-wrong test. Is the second action precluded in Indiana?
>
> > **A1.**   Yes, since the auto collision yielding both claims is a single transaction, the second action would be precluded in Ohio, and this outcome must be given full faith and credit by the courts of Indiana.
>
> **Q2.**   Now assume that Ohio employs the right-wrong standard for defining a cause of action, while Indiana employs the transaction based standard. Is the second action precluded?
>
> > **A2.**   No, since the second action could be heard in Ohio it may be heard in Indiana. Moreover, the Supreme Court's *Marrese* opinion [see **§16.B200**] suggests that 28 USC 1738 would prohibit the Indiana court from exercising preclusion in this example.

CHAPTER XVII

SECURING AND ENFORCING JUDGMENTS AND ORDERS

A. SECURING AND ENFORCING JUDGMENTS AND ORDERS: INTRODUCTION. [§17.0000]

A favorable judgment does not necessarily mean that the plaintiff actually will obtain redress for his or her grievance. The collection of a damages award or the enforcement of an injunction remains, and this often proves as difficult as securing the judgment. In every state there is a network of statutes providing for the sequestration of the defendant's assets during litigation and for the discovery, liquidation, and collection of those assets after judgment. This chapter will provide an overview of the basic instruments for securing and enforcing judgments or orders.

B. PROVISIONAL REMEDIES. [§17.1000]

In some cases, if a plaintiff were required to wait until after judgment before anything could be done to insure the enforceability of the award or order, the defendant might either intentionally become judgment proof or engage in activities that would irreparably injure the plaintiff. Accordingly, the plaintiff may be afforded some security during the action by obtaining one or more of these provisional remedies.

1. Attachment. [§17.1100]

The attachment of real or personal property may be used at the outset of the action (a) to obtain in rem or quasi in rem jurisdiction when the defendant is not amenable to process [see §3.4000], or (b) to prevent the defendant from disposing or otherwise impairing the value of property that might be used to satisfy the ultimate judgment in the lawsuit.

a. Availability of Attachment. [§17.1110]

Under the typical attachment provision, the remedy is available when the defendant has departed from the jurisdiction or has concealed him

461

or herself, or when the defendant's conduct indicates that he or she may attempt to avoid process or to defraud creditors. Some states, however, go further and permit attachment in certain classes of action—for example, fraud and intentional tort cases—or in any action against a non-resident.

b. Procedure for Attachment. [§17.1120]

Attachment procedures must comply with the due process requirements of notice and an opportunity to be heard [see **§3.5000**]. Usually, the plaintiff is required to show that a ground for attachment exists. Then, a writ of attachment is issued by the court to an appropriate officer, usually a sheriff, who will take the property into custody pending the determination of the merits. An application is addressed to the court's discretion and the court may refuse to grant it even though the statutory criteria are met.

2. Preliminary Injunctions. [§17.1200]

If the defendant is acting in a way that would irreparably injure the plaintiff or would render the final judgment in the action ineffectual, the plaintiff may obtain a preliminary injunction. Since a preliminary injunction may cause serious injury to the defendant, and since it is granted prior to an adjudication on the merits, the remedy is available only in extraordinary circumstances. Moreover, the court typically will require the plaintiff to show that he or she cannot be protected by less drastic measures. The decision whether to grant a preliminary injunction, therefore, reflects a balancing of the potential harm to the plaintiff of denying the request against the possible detrimental effect on the defendant of granting the motion.

a. Temporary Restraining Order. [§17.1210]

Some jurisdictions permit the granting of a temporary restraining order on a showing that, without it, immediate irreparable harm will occur. The distinguishing characteristics of the temporary restraining order are that it is sought by ex parte application, it is granted with great speed, and it has an extremely brief duration. The fear of potential unfairness to the defendant has led most rulemakers to impose conditions on the granting of temporary restraining orders, particularly when notice has not been given to all parties [see, e.g., Federal Rule 65(b)].

b. Nature of Orders. [§17.1220]

The hallmark of preliminary injunctions and temporary restraining orders is that they are designed to preserve the status quo. They are flexible remedies and may be molded to fit the circumstances of the particular case. The orders may require the continuation of a given course of action, the observance of certain standards of conduct, or the cessation of particular acts.

c. Discretion of the Court. [§17.1230]

Requests for preliminary injunctions and temporary restraining orders are addressed to the trial court's discretion. In determining whether to grant the request, the court may consider the following factors: the availability of an adequate legal remedy, the difficulties of administering and enforcing the order, the likelihood that the injunction will be effective, the possibility of irreparable harm, and whether the applicant has "unclean hands" or is guilty of laches.

d. Who Is Bound? [§17.1240]

Ordinarily, the court's order will bind the defendant, the defendant's agents and servants, and those acting in concert with or for the benefit of the defendant. The order, however, cannot bind persons who have not had an opportunity to be heard on the propriety of the injunction.

3. Receivership. [§17.1300]

When there is a substantial danger that disputed property will be removed from the jurisdiction, lost, materially damaged, or destroyed, the court may appoint a receiver to act as a custodian for the duration of the law suit. The primary circumstance in which the appointment of a receiver is thought desirable is when the defendant is actually or likely to become insolvent.

a. Characteristics of Receiver. [§17.1310]

A receiver's duties are to preserve or improve the property until the resolution of the controversy. The receiver's primary allegiance is to the appointing court and not to the person who sought the appointment. In fact, the receiver's acts usually must be ratified by the court. Consequently, a person who deals with a receiver assumes the risk that the court will not approve the receiver's actions. Before beginning to execute any official duties, the receiver is required to file and execute a bond as security. Because a receivership may prevent people from using their property before there has been a full hearing on the merits, a number of courts have refused to authorize the remedy when an adequate alternative exists.

b. Who Can Request a Receiver. [§17.1320]

In most states only a plaintiff can secure the appointment of a receiver; however, some jurisdictions permit anyone having an interest in the disputed property to do so. In either case, the receivership typically is restricted to the property that is the subject of the litigation.

4. Civil Arrest. [§17.1400]

Historically, civil arrest involved taking a defendant who was likely to leave the jurisdiction into custody and keeping him physically restrained until either bail was posted or judgment was rendered. The abuses that accompanied this practice led many legislatures either to prohibit or to restrict the availability of this provisional remedy. For example, New York first limited civil arrest to actions based on fraud, deceit, or conversion. Even in those cases the remedy could be used only when the person to be arrested was not a parent or guardian or a dependent child or incompetent. Subsequently, New York eliminated the remedy completely.

a. Discretion of the Court. [§17.1410]

In most jurisdictions a motion for civil arrest is addressed to the court's discretion. In view of the consequences that may result, judges use the greatest restraint in considering an application for the remedy.

b. Procedure for Civil Arrest. [§17.1420]

The party seeking a civil arrest order usually is required to file a bond sufficient to cover any damages and costs to the defendant in the event the arrest should prove to have been wrongful. The arrested defendant may secure release by posting bail, which will then provide security for any judgment the plaintiff recovers.

5. Notice of Pendency. [§17.1500]

In a number of jurisdictions the plaintiff can file a notice of the pendency of litigation with the registry of deeds respecting certain types of property to give others constructive notice of the dispute and thereby prevent them from becoming bona fide purchasers or encumbrancers. This procedure also relieves prospective vendees of the burdensome task of examining numerous courthouse records to determine whether the vendor's title to the property is threatened by litigation. A plaintiff who fails to file and index the notice of pendency will not be protected against a purchaser or encumbrancer who does not have actual notice of the litigation.

C. COLLECTION OF A JUDGMENT. [§17.2000]

A judgment will be of little use if the judgment debtor can avoid its collection by concealing or carrying away his or her assets. Thus, state statutes often provide a number of devices for the location and collection of the judgment debtor's property. Certain types of property (for example, homesteads, personal effects, and part of the debtor's earnings) are exempt from this process.

1. Discovery of Assets. [§17.2100]

A judgment creditor may discover the assets of the judgment debtor by serving a subpoena on anyone, including the judgment debtor, requiring him or her to testify as to the whereabouts of any of the latter's property. Testimony is given under oath and non-compliance with the subpoena is punishable as a contempt.

a. Disclosure Procedures. [§17.2110]

Some states provide that a subpoena may require a person to be deposed upon oral or written questions, require the production of documents, or require a response to written questions within a prescribed time. If a subpoena is of the last type, the answers must be written and under oath. The procedures and limitations followed in these post-judgment disclosure proceedings usually are similar to those employed in pretrial discovery.

Illustration. [§17.2111] A judgment creditor causes a testimonial subpoena to be issued against a utility company claiming, in the accompanying affidavit, that it has knowledge concerning the judgment debtor's property. The utility company objects to the subpoena on the ground that its records are being used by the judgment creditor to locate the judgment debtor and that frequent subpoenas of this type have subjected it to harassment and expense. If this is true, the subpoena should be quashed; disclosure should be limited to locating resources and not as a way to track down debtors.

---

2. Orders Directing Payment. [§17.2200]

After judgment has been entered, the court may order the judgment debtor to deliver money or property to the sheriff. If the money or property is in the hands of a third person, the judgment creditor may commence a special proceeding to secure an order directing that it be turned over to satisfy the judgment.

3. Executions. [§17.2300]

Instead of obtaining a payment order [see **§17.2200**], a judgment creditor may have an execution issued under which the property of (or debts due) a judgment debtor may be levied upon or sold by an appropriate official. The execution is effective against all of the judgment debtor's property within the jurisdiction of the sheriff to whom the execution is delivered. If, however, jurisdiction in the original action was based on the attachment of property, the execution usually is effective only against the attached property [see **§3.4600**].

4. Income Executions. [§17.2400]

An execution may be issued against income to be received by the judgment debtor. Normally, a certain percentage or a fixed dollar amount of the debtor's income is exempted from the execution to permit the debtor to subsist (federal law requires at least 75 percent to be exempt from execution). Some states provide that if the judgment debtor fails to pay the installments specified in the execution, the sheriff may serve an endorsed copy of the execution on the person obligated to pay income to the judgment debtor—the garnishee. The garnishee must then withhold the amount specified in the income execution from the debtor or risk being personally liable for the amount not withheld.

5. Proceedings Against Assets Other Than Real Property. [§17.2500]

After an execution is issued, a levy is secured either by service of the execution upon the person holding the asset or by seizure of the property if that is feasible. If the property is incapable of delivery, the execution is simply served in the same manner as a summons. Garnishees and persons possessing the debtor's property are required to transfer it to the sheriff.

a. Judicial Sale of Chattels. [§17.2510]

Chattels obtained pursuant to an execution or a court order may be sold at a judicial sale, the proceeds being applied to the judgment. The sale usually is a public auction conducted by the sheriff or someone employed by him or her. The sheriff often has discretion to postpone the sale if the bids are grossly inadequate or there is an insufficient number of bidders. If the proceeds of the sale exceed the judgment, the excess is paid to the judgment debtor.

6. Proceedings Against Real Property. [§17.2600]

In many jurisdictions a judgment creditor can levy on real property in much the same way as he or she can levy against chattels. In other states a judgment creditor does not levy on realty; instead, the creditor acquires a lien on the real property of a judgment debtor merely by docketing the judgment with the clerk of the county in which the real property is located. The lien usually remains in force for a specified number of years; the judgment creditor may levy on the real property only after the expiration of the lien. A levy on real property is effective only when notice is filed with the clerk of the court in the county in which the property is situated.

a.   Judicial Sale of Real Property. [§17.2610]

A judicial sale of real property typically follows the execution and levy. The purchaser at the sale acquires all the rights and interests in the property possessed by the judgment debtor.

7.   Enforcement of a Specific Performance Order. [§17.2700]

Statutes governing the enforcement of judgments awarding specific property to the successful litigant require the execution to describe the property and to designate the person to whom it is to be transferred by the sheriff. In the event that the item to be transferred cannot be found within the sheriff's jurisdiction, the judgment creditor often can levy upon the debtor's real and personal property as if the execution were for the enforcement of a money judgment [see **§17.2300**].

8.   Proceedings to Determine Adverse Claims. [§17.2800]

A person who claims an interest in property in the custody of the sheriff or receiver may seek to establish an interest superior to that of the judgment debtor. If issues of fact are disputed, a separate trial may be ordered. During the course of the proceeding, custody of the property will remain with the sheriff or the receiver, if doing so will not impair its value.

D.   CONTEMPT. [§17.3000]

Non-compliance with a judicial order not involving an award of money may result in the court's exercise of its inherent power to declare the miscreant to be in contempt of court—the historic mode of enforcing equity decrees. Contempt proceedings are usually summary, involving a brief trial and no jury.

1.   Distinction Between Civil and Criminal Contempt. [§17.3100]

If the primary purpose of punishing the contemnor is to vindicate the authority of the judicial system, the contempt is criminal. On the other hand, if the ultimate objective of the sanction is to give the successful litigant the benefits of the order that is being disobeyed, the contempt is civil. In either case, the penalty may be a fine or imprisonment or both. However, a person may terminate incarceration for civil contempt simply by complying with the court's order. In that sense the contemnor is said to have the keys to the jailhouse door. But since the objective of criminal contempt is primarily punitive, a criminal contemnor usually is incarcerated for a fixed period. As long as the contemnor is not prejudiced, civil and criminal proceedings may proceed simultaneously.

Illustration. [§17.3110] A voluntary auxiliary sheriff is held in contempt for intimidating people and interfering with their right to enjoy desegregated facilities in violation of an injunction. As a result, she is prohibited from acting as a peace officer. Since the punishment is primarily to protect the rights of those seeking to use the facilities, the contempt should be characterized as civil.

---

2. Procedure in Contempt Proceedings. [§17.3200]

A criminal contempt proceeding is instituted by the government or court and has many of the trappings of a criminal case. It is treated as a completely separate action. By way of contrast, a civil contempt proceeding is initiated by the aggrieved party and is deemed part of the original action. An accusation, pleading, or affidavit setting forth the facts constituting the contempt usually is filed with the court.

3. Personal Jurisdiction and Venue. [§17.3300]

Since a civil contempt proceeding is a continuation of the original action, service of process is not required for persons who were properly subject to the court's jurisdiction in the original suit, but a new notice is necessary. If the alleged contemnor was not a party in the original action, service of process must be made. Because a court should be able to sanction a violation of its order regardless of where that violation takes place, there should be no venue objections. A criminal contempt proceeding requires the court to establish independent jurisdiction and venue.

4. Appellate Review. [§17.3400]

A civil contempt citation against a party to the original action is interlocutory; thus, in a final judgment rule jurisdiction [see **§15.1000**], an appeal must await the rendition of a final judgment. If, however, the civil contemnor is a non-party, the appeal may be taken immediately. When the contempt order is criminal, or both civil and criminal, the order is final and appeal is available at once.

5. Defenses to the Contempt Sanction. [§17.3500]

Ordinarily, the validity of the underlying decree may not be challenged in a criminal contempt proceeding. If, however, there were no effective opportunity for securing judicial review of the order before its effect became oppressive, the order's validity may be challenged collaterally in the contempt proceeding. But the policy against self-help requires this exception to be construed restrictively. Error or even probable unconstitutionality of the order does not justify non-compliance. Only a transparently invalid court order, when speedy appellate review is unavailable, may be disobeyed and later challenged in the contempt proceeding [*Walker v. City of Birmingham* (1967)]. In many states, the validity of the underlying decree may be attacked in a civil contempt proceeding on the theory that if the order is invalid, the party who was successful in the original action is not entitled to damages for the alleged contemnor's noncompliance.

Illustration. [§17.3510] P sued D, a newspaper, for wrongful invasion of privacy. The court entered a temporary restraining order against publication of the article in question. The newspaper printed the story in defiance of the order. In criminal contempt proceedings, the newspaper challenged the order as an unconstitutional prior restraint on speech. Because prior restraint on pure speech is transparently invalid and journalistic deadlines did not allow for timely appellate review, the newspaper prevailed in its collateral challenge to the court's decree [*In Matter of Providence Journal* (1986)].

---

*

TABLE OF CASES

Tellabs, Inc. v. Makor Issues and Rights, Ltd., 127 S.Ct. 853 (2007)—§ **5.3411**

Tull v. United States, 481 U.S. 412 (1987)—§§ **13.3230, 13.3232–1**

United Mine Workers v. Gibbs, 383 U.S. 715 (1966)—§§ **2.5321, 2.5400, 2.5430**

Vons Companies v. Seabest Foods, Inc., 926 P.2d 1085 (Cal., 1996)—§ **3.3430**

Walker v. Armco Steel Corp., 446 U.S. 740 (1980)—§ **4.3331–2**

Walker v. City of Birmingham, 388 U.S. 307 (1967)—§ **17.3500**

Waste Management Holdings, Inc. v. Mowbray, 208 F.3d 288 (2000)—§ **8.1451**

Western Union Telegraph Co. v. Pennsylvania, 368 U.S. 71 (1961)—§ **3.3550**

World–Wide Volkswagen Corp. v. Woodson, 444 U.S. 286 (1980)—§ **3.3410**

York v. Texas, 127 U.S. 15 (1890)—§ **3.7110**

Zahn v. International Paper Co., 414 U.S. 291 (1973)—§§ **2.4350, 2.5330, 2.5331, 2.5423, 8.1832**

*

TABLE OF STATUTES AND REGULATIONS

TABLE OF STATUTES AND REGULATIONS

TABLE OF STATUTES AND REGULATIONS

INDEX

References are to section numbers

ABATEMENT
Pleading matters in, 5.8300 et seq., 5.9234

ADDITUR
Motion for, 14.6410 et seq.

ADJUDICATION WITHOUT TRIAL
Generally, 11.0000 et seq.
See also Former Adjudication Doctrines, this index
Default Judgment, this index
Dismissal, this index
Summary Judgment, this index

ADMINISTRATIVE PROCEEDINGS
Jury trial rights, 13.3241

ADMISSIONS
Binding effect of, 9.5460
Deemed admissions, 9.8200
Discovery, this index
Issue preclusion, 16.7230

AFFIDAVITS
Jury misconduct issues, 14.4100
Summary judgment practice, 11.1700

AFFIRMANCE DOCTRINE
Generally, 16.2440

AFFIRMATIVE DEFENSES
Generally, 5.5300 et seq.
Counterclaims distinguished, 5.5350

AGENCY LAW
Process, agency to receive, 3.2131

ALIENS
See also Citizenship, this index
Jurisdiction as to, 2.3000, 2.3420 et seq.
Venue, 2.7450

ALLEGATIONS
See Complaints, this index

AMOUNT IN CONTROVERSY JURISDICTIONAL REQUIREMENT
Generally, 2.4000 et seq.
Aggregation of separate claims, 2.4300
Class Action Fairness Act, 2.4340, 8.1832
Counterclaims, effect of, 2.4400
Diversity of citizenship jurisdiction, 2.3120
Equitable remedies, 2.4220
Federal courts, 2.4100 et seq.
Federal question cases, 2.2600, 2.4110
Interpleader, 8.4730
Judicial Improvement and Access to Justice Act, 2.3111
Non damage claims, 2.4220
Pleading, 2.4200
Removal jurisdiction, 2.4500, 2.6210
Supplemental jurisdiction, 2.4331

ANCILLARY JURISDICTION
See Supplemental Federal Jurisdiction, this index

491

When judgment rendered and
timeliness of appeal, 15.2100

ARREST, CIVIL
See Provisional Remedies, this index

ASSIGNMENTS
Diversity jurisdiction, assignments to
create, 2.3800
Real parties in interest, 6.2400

ATTACHMENT
See Provisional Remedies, this index

**ATTACKS ON SUFFICIENCY OF
EVIDENCE**
Generally, 14.7000, 14.7000 et seq.
See also Attacks on Verdicts and
Judgments, this index
Burden of proof, relation to, 14.7400
Challenges to pleadings, 14.7100
Directed verdict motions, 14.7000
Dismissal motions, 14.7100
Judgment nov motions, 14.7000,
14.7500
Non-suit motions, 14.7000
Pleadings, challenges to, 14.7100
Standard for relief, 14.7200
Summary judgment, 14.7100
Timing of challenges, 14.7200
Trial, challenges during, 14.7200

**ATTACKS ON VERDICTS AND
JUDGMENTS**
Generally, 14.6000 et seq.
See also Attacks on Sufficiency of
Evidence, this index
Additur, 14.6410 et seq.
Claim preclusion, reopening judgment
and, 16.3130
Clerical errors, 14.6550
Conditional new trials
Generally, 14.6400
Appellate review, 15.3310
Default, relief from, 14.6521
Discretion of court, 14.6550

Equitable relief, 14.6600
Fraud
Extrinsic, 14.6541
Intrinsic, 14.6542
Grounds for new trial, 14.6300 et seq.
Inadvertence as ground for relief,
14.6520
Independent suit in equity to set aside
judgment, 14.6600
Intrinsic fraud, 14.6542
Judgment attacks, 14.6500 et seq.
Jurisdictional defects, 14.6550
Mistake as ground for relief, 14.6520
New trial motions, 14.6100 et seq.
Newly discovered evidence, 14.6530
Partial new trial motions, 14.6110,
14.6120
Remittitur, 14.6410 et seq.
Reopening judgment and claim
preclusion, 16.3130
Verdict against weight of evidence,
14.6340

ATTORNEY-CLIENT PRIVILEGE
Discovery, 9.3140

BAR
See Former Adjudication Doctrines,
this index

BIFURCATION
Liability and damages trials, 6.9330

BREACH OF WARRANTY
Third-party claims, 7.5200

BUSINESS RECORDS
See Discovery, this index

**CAPACITY TO SUE AND BE
SUED**
Generally, 6.3000 et seq.

CASE MANAGEMENT
Pretrial conferences, 10.1100
Scheduling orders, 10.2100

Incompatible standards of defendant conduct, avoidance of, 8.1311

Inconsistent adjudications, avoidance of, 8.1310

Injunctive relief, 8.1320 et seq.

Intervention by absent members, 8.1730

Judgments, 8.1600

Judicial management, 8.1700

Limited fund cases, 8.1313

Mass torts, 8.1335

Notice and opportunity to be heard, 3.5400

Notice requirements to absent class members, 8.1500 et seq., 8.1720

Numerosity requirements, 8.1200, 8.1230

Opt out rights
  Generally, 8.1334
  Former adjudication doctrines, 16.9541

Partial class action orders, 8.1420

Policy considerations, 8.1000

Representative requirements, 8.1200, 8.1220, 8.1260

Settlement and compromise, 8.1710

Settlement classes, 8.1336

Size requirements, 8.1200, 8.1230

Spurious class actions, 8.1610

State statutes, 8.1110, 8.1610, 8.1900

Subclasses, 8.1430

Subject matter jurisdiction, 8.1800

Typicality requirements, 8.1200, 8.1250

Void judgments, claim preclusion, 16.5410

COGNOVIT NOTES
Generally, 3.2140

Due process requirements, 3.5620

COLLATERAL ESTOPPEL
See Former Adjudication Doctrines, this index

COLLECTION OF JUDGMENTS
Generally, 17.2000 et seq.

Adverse claimants, 17.2800

Discovery of assets, 17.2100

Execution, issuance of, 17.2300

Fraud in procuring process, 3.6700

Garnishment, 17.2400

Income executions, 17.2400

Interests of adverse claimants, 17.2800

Judicial sales, 17.2510

Liens on real property, 17.2600

Payment orders, 17.2200

Personal property levies, 17.2500

Process, fraud in procuring, 3.6700

Real property, proceedings against, 17.2600

Sales of real property, 17.2610

Specific performance orders, enforcement of, 17.2700

COMMON LAW
English Common Law, this index

Federal Common Law, this index

COMPLAINTS
Generally, 5.4000

See also Pleading, this index

Alternative, joinder in, 6.8210

Alternative claims and permissive joinder, 6.4400

Amendments to. See Pleading, this index

Answers to verified complaints, 5.5212

Challenges to pleadings. See Pleading, this index

Counterclaims and cross-claims compared, 5.7100

Cross-complaints, 7.0000, 7.3500

Default judgments, pleading insufficiencies, 11.2600

Defenses, pleading nonexistence of, 5.4211

Improper allegations, 5.3231

Information and belief, allegations based on, 5.3330, 5.5230 et seq.

FEDERAL COURTS

Supplemental claims, 4.4600
Supplemental jurisdiction, 4.1000
Transferred cases, 4.4500
Unsettled issues in applicable state
law, 4.5200

IMMUNITY
Process, immunity from, 3.6600

IMPEACHMENT
Discovery of impeachment matter,
9.2230

IMPLEADER
See Third-Party Claims, this index

IN PERSONAM JURISDICTION
See Personal Jurisdiction, this index

IN REM JURISDICTION
See Property, Jurisdiction as to, this
index

INCONSISTENT REMEDIES
Generally, 16.2430

INDEMNITY
Third-party claims, 7.5200

INJUNCTIONS
See also Provisional Remedies, this
index
Final judgment rule, application to
injunctive relief, 15.1410
Interpleader, 8.4900

INSTRUCTIONS TO JURY
Generally, 13.2220, 14.1000 et seq.
Further instructions, requests for,
14.1420
Judicial comments on evidence,
14.2000
Manner of giving, 14.1400
Objections to, 14.1300
Requests for further instructions,
14.1420
Requests for instructions, 14.1300
Standard instructions, 14.1210

Written copies, 14.1410

INSURANCE
Discovery as to coverage, 9.2322,
9.2414
Diversity of citizenship jurisdiction,
2.3520

INTERLOCUTORY APPEALS
Generally, 15.1200
See also Final Judgment Rule, this
index

INTERNET
Jurisdiction in actions involving,
3.3350

INTERPLEADER
Generally, 8.0000, 8.4000 et seq.
Amount in controversy jurisdiction,
8.4730
Bonds, 8.4420
Choice of law, 4.4300
Citizenship determinations, 8.4711
Defensive interpleader, 8.4600
Deposits in court, 8.4420
Diversity of citizenship jurisdiction,
8.4711
Federal courts
Generally, 8.4700 et seq.
Nationwide service statutes, 3.3610
Federal Interpleader Act, 2.3220
Governing law, 8.4820
Injunctions against parallel state court
actions, 8.4900
Interestedness, 8.4310, 8.4510
Modern practice, 8.4310
Nationwide service statutes, 3.3610
Perquisites, 8.4000 et seq.
Process, 8.4750
Prospective claims, 8.4430
Rule interpleader, 2.3230
Stages of, 8.4400
Statutory interpleader, 2.3230
Subject matter jurisdiction, 8.4710,
8.4720

PLEADING

Generally, 5.0000 et seq.

Abatement, matters in, 5.8300 et seq.

Affirmative defenses, 5.5300 et seq.

Allegations based on information and belief, 5.3330, 5.5230 et seq.

Alternative, joinder in, 6.8210

Alternative, pleading in, 5.3340

Alternative claims and permissive joinder, 6.4400

Amendments
 Generally, 5.9000
 Appeal eliminating, 5.8531
 Challenges, amendments to remedy, 5.9000
 Effect of, 5.9400
 Evidence, amendment to conform to, 5.9300 et seq.
 John Doe defendants, 5.9424
 Leave of court not required, 5.9100 et seq.
 Misnomer corrections, 5.9425
 New causes of action or defenses, adding, 5.9235
 Number of, 5.9232
 Parties added by, 5.9420
 Prejudice and, 5.9210
 Statutes of limitations and, 5.9410 et seq.
 Successor to party, substitution of, 5.9426
 Sufficiency of, 5.9233
 Superseding effect of, 5.9400
 Supplemental pleadings, 5.9500
 Time for, 5.9200, 5.9231

Amount in controversy jurisdictional requirement, 2.4200

Answers, this index

Antitrust pleading standards, 5.3421

Appeals from challenges to pleadings, 5.8500 et seq.

Causes of action, 5.3220

Challenges to pleadings
 Generally, 5.8000 et seq.

Abatement, matters in, 5.8300 et seq.
 Amendments to remedy, 5.9000
 Appeals, 5.8500 et seq.
 Attacks on sufficiency of evidence, 14.7100
 Demurrers, 5.8100
 Form, waiver of challenges to, 5.8420
 General challenges, 5.8120
 Joinder defects, 5.8422
 Judicial notice, 5.8132
 Jurisdictional challenges, 5.8131, 5.8421
 More definite statement motions, 5.3130, 5.8210
 Partial challenges, 5.8120
 Strike motions, 5.8220
 Substantive challenges, 5.8100
 Sufficiency of evidence, attacks on, 14.7100
 Summary judgment motions, 11.1100
 Summary judgments distinguished, 5.8130
 Waivers of challenges, 5.8400 et seq.

Claim preclusion, liberality of pleading and, 16.3120

Code pleading, 5.3000, 5.3200 et seq.

Complaints, this index

Conclusions of law, 5.3212

Consistency requirements, 5.3300

Counterclaims, this index

Cross-Claims, this index

Default judgments, pleading insufficiencies, 11.2600

Defective fact pleading, 5.3230

Defenses
 Generally, 5.3220
 Affirmative defenses, 5.5300 et seq.
 Pleading nonexistence of, 5.4211
 Waivers, 5.5340

Demurrers, this index

INDEX

Special appearances to challenge jurisdiction, 3.7100

Stocks, situs determinations, 3.4520

Substantive limitations on exercise, 3.3540

Tangible and intangible, 3.4000, 3.4300 et seq.

Traditional bases of jurisdiction, 3.1100

Uniform Stock Transfer Act, 3.4520

Waiver of defective jurisdiction, 3.7100

PROVISIONAL REMEDIES
Generally, 17.1000 et seq.
Attachment
    Generally, 17.1100
    Notice and opportunity to be heard, 3.5610
    Property, jurisdiction as to, 3.4400
Availability of attachment, 17.1110
Civil arrest, 17.1400
Contempt, this index
Notice of pendency, 17.1500
Policy considerations, 17.1000
Preliminary injunctions
    Generally, 17.1200 et seq.
    Discretion of court, 17.1230
    Parties bound by, 17.1240
Receiverships, 17.1300, 17.1310
Sanctions, this index
Temporary restraining orders
    Generally, 17.1210 et seq.
    Discretion of court, 17.1230
    Parties bound by, 17.1240

REAL PARTIES IN INTEREST
Generally, 6.2000 et seq.

RECEIVERSHIPS
See Provisional Remedies, this index

RELITIGATION
See Former Adjudication Doctrines, this index

REMEDIES
Provisional Remedies, this index

REMITTITUR
Motion for, 14.6410 et seq.

REMOVAL JURISDICTION
Generally, 2.6000, 2.6000 et seq.
Amount in controversy jurisdictional requirement, 2.4500
Amount in controversy requirements, 2.6210
Bond requirements, 2.6700
Civil rights claims, 2.6600
Class Action Fairness Act, 2.6200, 2.6630 et seq.
Consent of all defendants to, 2.6621, 2.6631
Costs, 2.6700
Countering removal, 2.6240
Delayed removal, 2.6710
Discretion of federal court, 2.6310
Federal Employers' Liability Act, 2.6611
Federal officer parties, 2.6600
Federal question requirements, 2.6210
Fraudulent joinder, 2.3830
Independent federal question claim, 2.6300
Jurisdictional questions in the state court, 2.6400
Jury trials, 13.6250
Multidistrict litigation, 2.7700
Multiparty, Multiforum Trial Jurisdiction Act, 2.6620
Nonconsenting defendants, 2.6621, 2.6631
Non-removable claims, 2.6610
Notice of removal, timing of, 2.6333, 2.6622
Plaintiff's options, 2.6240
Pleading requirements, 2.6230
Policy considerations, 2.6100, 2.6320
Procedural requirements, 2.6700 et seq.
Remand, 2.6310, 2.6800

525

†